D1277649

A HISTORY OF
LIFE IN THE UNITED STATES

THE BEGINNERS OF A NATION
A HISTORY OF THE SOURCE AND RISE OF THE EARLIEST ENGLISH SETTLEMENTS IN AMERICA WITH SPECIAL REFERENCE TO THE LIFE AND CHARACTER OF THE PEOPLE

BY

EDWARD EGGLESTON

NEW YORK
D. APPLETON AND COMPANY
1899

FOURTH EDITION

TO

THE RIGHT HONORABLE JAMES BRYCE, M.P.

My dear Mr. Bryce:

In giving an account of the origins of the United States, I have told a story of English achievement. It is fitting that I should inscribe it to you, who of all the Englishmen of this generation have rendered the most eminent service to the American Commonwealth. You have shown with admirable clearness and candor, and with marvelous breadth of thought and sympathy, what are the results in the present time of the English beginnings in America, and to you, therefore, I offer this volume. I need not assure you that it gives me great pleasure to write your name here as godfather to my book, and to subscribe myself, my dear Mr. Bryce,

Yours very sincerely,

Edward Eggleston.

PREFACE.

IN this work, brought to completion after many years of patient research, I have sought to trace from their source the various and often complex movements that resulted in the early English settlements in America, and in the evolution of a great nation with English speech and traditions. It has been my aim to make these pages reflect the character of the age in which the English colonies were begun, and the traits of the colonists, and to bring into relief the social, political, intellectual, and religious forces that promoted emigration. This does not pretend to be the usual account of all the events attending early colonization; it is rather a history in which the succession of cause and effect is the main topic—a history of the dynamics of colony-planting in the first half of the seventeenth century. Who were the beginners of English life in America? What propulsions sent them for refuge to a wilderness? What visions beckoned them to undertake the founding of new states? What manner of men were their leaders? And what is the story of their hopes, their experiments, and their disappointments? These are the questions I have tried to answer.

The founders of the little settlements that had the unexpected fortune to expand into an empire I have not been able to treat otherwise than unreverently. Here are no forefathers or foremothers, but simply English men and women of the seventeenth century, with the faults and fanaticisms as well as the virtues of their age. I have disregarded that convention which

vii

makes it obligatory for a writer of American history to explain that intolerance in the first settlers was not just like other intolerance, and that their cruelty and injustice were justifiable under the circumstances. This walking backward to throw a mantle over the nakedness of ancestors may be admirable as an example of diluvian piety, but it is none the less reprehensible in the writing of history.

While the present work is complete in itself, it is also part of a larger enterprise, as the half-title indicates. In January, 1880, I began to make studies for a History of Life in the United States. For the last sixteen or seventeen years by far the greater part of my time has been given to researches on the culture history of the United States in the period of English domination, that " good old colony time " about which we have had more sentiment than information. As year after year was consumed in this toilsome preparation, the magnitude of the task became apparent, and I began to feel the fear for my work so felicitously expressed by Ralegh, " that the darkness of age and death would have covered over both it and me before the performance." It seemed better, therefore, to redeem from the chance of such mishap a portion of my work, by completing this most difficult part of the task, in order that when, early or late, the inevitable night shall fall, the results of my labor, such as they are, may not be wholly covered over by the darkness.

There is always difference of opinion in regard to the comparative fullness with which the several portions of a historical narrative should be treated, and I can not hope to escape criticism on this point. I have related some events with what will be considered disproportionate amplitude of detail. But the distinctive purpose of this work is to give an insight into the life and character of the people, and there are details that make the reader feel the very spirit and manner of the time. It is better to let the age disclose itself in action ; it is only by ingenious eavesdropping and peeps through keyholes that we can win this kind of knowledge from the past. Literary considerations should have some weight in deciding how fully an episode shall be treated, unless the historian is content to perform the homely service of a purveyor of the crude ore of knowledge. I have sought to make this "a work of art as well as of historical science," to borrow a phrase from Augustin Thierry. Some omissions in this volume will be explained when its successors appear.

I find it an embarrassing task to make acknowledgment to those who have assisted me; the debts that have accumulated since I began are too many to be recorded. I must not neglect to express my grateful remembrance of the hospitality shown to my researches during my various sojourns in England. At the British Museum and at the Public Record Office every facility has been extended to me, and a similar attention was shown to my wants at other less public repositories of books, such as the Society for the Propagation of the Gospel. To Dr. Richard Garnett, the head of the printed book department of the Museum, I owe thanks for many personal attentions. I am also indebted to Mr. E. M. Thompson, keeper of the manuscripts in the museum. The late Mr. W. Noel Sainsbury, of the Public Record Office, was very obliging. I owe most of all to the unfailing kindness of the Right Honorable James Bryce, M. P., who found time, in the midst of his preoccupations as a member of Parliament and his duties in high office, to secure for me access to private stores of historical material. Lord Edmund Fitzmaurice with generous kindness put himself to much trouble to facilitate my examination of the manuscripts at Landsdowne House. I am indebted to Lord Leconsfield for permission to visit Petworth House and read there Percy's Trewe Relacion in the original manuscript. I must ask others in England who befriended my researches to accept a general acknowledgment, but I can not forget their courtesy to a stranger. In common with other students I received polite attentions during my researches in Paris at the Bibliothèque Nationale.

In this country I owe much to the librarians of public libraries and their assistants—too much to allow me to specify my obligations to individuals. At the Astor, and at the Lenox, under its more recent management, my debt has been continual for many years. Acknowledgments are due to the officers of the Boston Public Library, the Library of Congress, the Peabody Institute in Baltimore, and the libraries of the New York, the Massachusetts, the Pennsylvania, the Maryland, and the Virginia Historical Societies. To Harvard College Library and to the New York State Library I am specially indebted; from them I have been able to supplement my own collection by borrowing. The Brooklyn Mercantile Library has granted me similar privileges. The New York Mercantile Library, on the other hand, I have not found hospitable to research.

To my generous friend Mr. Justin Winsor I owe thanks for many favors. Dr. Thomas Addis Emmet opened his valuable collection to me, and the late Mr. S. L. M. Barlow showed me similar kindness. My friend, Mr. Oscar S. Straus, permitted me to use at my own desk valuable works from his collection. There are others whose friendly attentions can be more fitly recognized in later volumes of this series, and yet others whom I must beg to accept this general but grateful acknowledgment.

Mr. W. W. Duffield, the Superintendent of the Coast and Geodetic Survey, supplied the artist with the coast charts from which the maps in this volume were drawn.

To avoid misapprehension, it is needful to say that this is not a re-issue of anything I have heretofore produced. The lectures on the culture history of the United States given at Columbia College and other institutions were never written or reported. The papers on colonial life contributed to the Century Magazine in

1882, and the years following, were on a different plan and scale ; they have merely served the purpose of preliminary studies of the general subject. To the editor and publishers of the Century Magazine I am obliged for their courtesy in all affairs relating to my contract with them, and for an arrangement which enables me to have free use of my material.

JOSHUA'S ROCK, LAKE GEORGE, *October, 1896.*

CONTENTS.

BOOK I.

RISE OF THE FIRST ENGLISH COLONY.

CHAPTER THE FIRST.

PAGE

ENGLISH KNOWLEDGE AND NOTION OF AMERICA AT
THE PERIOD OF SETTLEMENT 1

CHAPTER THE SECOND.

JAMES RIVER EXPERIMENTS 25

CHAPTER THE THIRD.

THE PROCESSION OF MOTIVES. 73

BOOK II.

THE PURITAN MIGRATION.

CHAPTER THE FIRST.

RISE AND DEVELOPMENT OF PURITANISM . . . 98

CHAPTER THE SECOND.

SEPARATISM AND THE SCROOBY CHURCH . . . 141

CHAPTER THE THIRD.

THE PILGRIM MIGRATIONS 159

CHAPTER THE FOURTH.

THE GREAT PURITAN EXODUS 188

CONTENTS.

BOOK III.

CENTRIFUGAL FORCES IN COLONY-PLANTING.

CHAPTER THE FIRST.
                                                              PAGE
THE CATHOLIC MIGRATION 220

CHAPTER THE SECOND.
THE PROPHET OF RELIGIOUS FREEDOM   .   .   . 266

CHAPTER THE THIRD.
NEW ENGLAND DISPERSIONS 315

Maps.

LIST OF MAPS.

(IN the coast line the American maps follow the charts of the United States Coast and Geodetic Survey ; the third map conforms to the British Ordnance Survey.)

                                                        FACING
                                                          PAGE
   I.—Chesapeake Bay I

   II.—James River   28

   III.—The cradle of the Pilgrims.   149

   IV.—Coast explored by the Pilgrims 177

   V.—The colony at St. Mary's 245

   VI.—Massachusetts Bay and Plymouth   .   .   . 275

   VII.—The early settlements on Narragansett Bay   . 296

VIII.—New England after the dispersions .   .   . 343

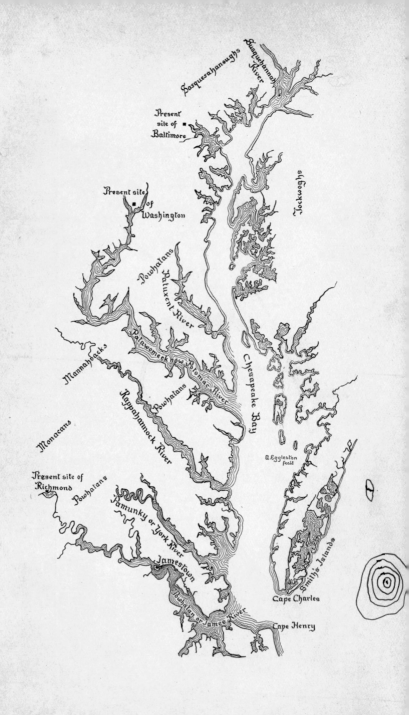

BOOK I.

RISE OF THE FIRST ENGLISH COLONY.

CHAPTER THE FIRST.

ENGLISH KNOWLEDGE AND NOTIONS OF AMERICA AT THE PERIOD OF SETTLEMENT.

I.

THE age of Elizabeth and James—the age of Spenser, of Shakespeare, and of Bacon—was a new point of departure in the history of the English race. All the conditions excited men to unwonted intellectual activity. The art of printing was yet a modern invention; the New World with its novelties and unexplained mysteries was a modern discovery; and there were endless discussions and agitations of spirit growing out of the recent reformation in religion. Imagination was powerfully stimulated by the progress of American exploration, by the romantic adventures of the Spaniards in the West Indies, and their dazzling conquest of new-found empires in Mexico and Peru. It was an age of creation in poetry, in science, and in religion, and men of action were everywhere set on deeds of daring. The world had regained something of the vigor and spontaneity of youth, but

The Elizabethan age.

2   I

the credulity and curiosity of youth were not wanting. The mind of the time accepted and reveled in
marvelous stories. The stage plays of that drama-
loving age reflected the interest in the supernatural and the eager curiosity about far-away countries. Books of travel fitted the prevailing taste.
He who could afford to buy them regaled himself
with the great folios of Hakluyt's Voyages and
Purchas his Pilgrimes. General readers delighted
in little tracts and pamphlets relating incidents of
far-away travels, or describing remote countries
and the peoples inhabiting them, or the "monstrous strange beasts" found in lands beyond the
bounds of Christendom.

America excited the most lively curiosity as a
world by itself and the least known of all the
"four parts" into which the globe was then divided. There were those, indeed, who made six
parts of the world by adding an arctic continent,

George
Beste,
First Voy-
age of Sir
Martin
Frobisher.

which included Greenland and a vast southern land
supposed to stretch from Magellan's Strait southward to the pole. It was easy to believe in these
two superfluous continents; they were mirages of
the New World. Every great discovery excites expectation of others like it. And in a time when
vague report or well-worn tradition counted for
more than observation or experimental knowledge,
it was inevitable that current information about
America should be distorted and mixed with fable.
In that age, still pre-Baconian, men had few standards by which to measure probabilities, and to

those shut in by the narrow limits of mediæval knowledge the mere uncovering of a new conti- nent whose existence contravened the fixed beliefs of the ages was so marvelous that nothing told about it afterward seemed incredible.

The history of American exploration is a story of delusion and mistake. The New World was discovered because it lay between Europe and the East Indian Spice Islands by the westward route. Columbus, seeking the less, found the greater by stumbling on it in the dark. Zuan Caboto—in English, John Cabot—who is described by a con- temporary as " a Venetian fellow with a fine mind, greatly skilled in navigation," discovered North America in 1497. But he did not exult that he was the finder of a vast and fertile continent in which great nations might germinate, for he be- lieved that his landfall at Cape Breton was within the dominions of the Grand Cham of China, and he sailed down the coast again the next year, " ever with the intent to find said passage to India." It was announced on his return from his first voyage that Henry VII had " won a part of Asia without a stroke of the sword."

√ The discovery of the Pacific by Balboa in 1513, and the voyage of Magellan's ship across that ocean in 1520, were not sufficient to remove the illusion that America was connected with Asia. The no- tion that the New World was an Asiatic peninsula died lingeringly about the middle of the sixteenth century ; but to reach Asia was still the main pur-

Illusions of discov- erers.

Note 1.

pose of western exploration, and America was for a long time regarded mainly as an obstruction. The belief in a passage to the Pacific by means of some yet-to-be-discovered strait severing the continent of America, survived far into the seventeenth century, and the hope of coming by some short cut into a rich commerce with the Orient led to a prying exploration of all the inlets, bays, and estuaries on the American coast and so promoted discovery, but it retarded settlement by blinding

Note 2.

men to the value of the New World.

II.

Frobisher.

Adventure by sea became a favorite road to renown for ambitious Englishmen in the time of Elizabeth, and the belief in a passage through or round North America grew into a superstition. The discovery of this strait seemed, in the phrase of George Beste, a writer of the time, "the onely thing of the world that was left undone whereby a notable mind might be made famous and fortunate." Sir Martin Frobisher, who is reckoned by Camden "among the famousest men of our age for counsell and glory gotten at sea," made three voyages in 1576 and the following years to that part of the American coast almost under the arctic circle. He desisted from the attempt to get to

Frobisher's Voyages, Hakl. Soc., *passim*.

China by an arctic channel only when he had involved the "venturers" or stockholders associated with him in heavy debts, and spent the fortune of his wife and stepchildren, to whom "glory gotten

at sea" must have been insufficient compensation.
"Sir Martin Frobisher whome God forgive" is the
phrase in which he is spoken of by his wife.

In the year of Frobisher's first voyage, Sir
Humphrey Gilbert issued a treatise to prove that
there was a way to the East Indies round North
America. This he demonstrated by a hydra-
headed argument constructed after the elaborate
fashion of that unscientific age, proving the existence of a northwest passage, first by authority,
secondly by reason, thirdly by experience of sun-
dry men's travels, and fourthly by circumstance.
Not content with getting to China by logic, and
nothing daunted by Frobisher's brilliant failure,
Gilbert mortgaged his estate that he might engage
in attempts yet more disastrous than Frobisher's,
and lost his life during his second voyage, in 1584.

About this time there appeared on the scene
the famous geographer, Richard Hakluyt, one of
those men that exert a marked influence in favor of
a new movement mainly by ardor and industry.
Hakluyt's fervor was akin to enthusiasm, his belief of every story favorable to projects for colonization, and his unwavering faith in the projects
themselves bordered on flat credulity. To men of
his own time his tireless advocacy of American exploration and colony-planting must have seemed
irksome hobby-riding. But he was the indispen-
sable forerunner of colonization. "Your Mr. Hakluyt hath served for a very good trumpet," says
Sidney. Believing in everything American as un-

Book I.

waveringly as if his soul's salvation depended on his faith, he believed in nothing more sublimely than in a passage to the "South Sea" or Pacific Ocean. He seized on every vague intimation of ignorant map-makers, on every suspicion of an explorer, on every fond tale of an Indian that tended to lend support to the theory in hand. All evidence was of equal weight in his scales, provided it lay on the affirmative side of the balance. It mattered little to him where his witnesses placed this elusive passage. In Hakluyt's mind it was ubiquitous. The Pacific is now "on the backside" of Montreal Island, and the great Laurentian lakes suffer a sea change; now it is reached by a river flowing three months to the southward—that is, the Mississippi. Then the much-sought strait is carried northward on the authority of an old map —"a great old round carde"—shown him "by the King of Portingall." But he had also seen "a mightie large old mappe in parchment" which showed, as far south as latitude 40°, a little neck of land "much like the streyte neck or Isthmus of Darienna." He had seen the same isthmus on another old map "with the sea joynninge hard on both sides as it doth on Panama." In a paper meant for private use, he expresses solicitude that the nearness of the Pacific to Florida shall not become known too commonly. Many years later an injunction was granted in Holland forbidding a publisher to insert in a map the newly discovered channel into the South Sea.

Hakl. Disc. on Western Planting.

N. Y. Col. Docs. I, 16.

III.

Both Frobisher and Gilbert made ineffectual attempts to plant colonies in the new lands, but colony-planting held a place in their minds quite secondary to the search for the South Sea in the north and the finding of gold. It was only when the large and lucid mind of Sir Walter Ralegh took up the subject seriously that the settlement of an agricultural colony became for a while the real object of American voyages. Ralegh sent no men to the arctic or to the wintry shores of Newfoundland, as Frobisher and Gilbert had done. He turned to milder latitudes, and dispatched his explorers in 1584, and his colonists in 1585, to the coast of what is now North Carolina.

But the ever-mischievous South Sea delusion did not vanish when the period of colonization was reached. Ralph Lane, the governor of Ralegh's first colony on Roanoke Island, having inquired perhaps for that western sea which Hakluyt had seen "on the mightie old mappe in parchment," understood the inventive savages to say that the Roanoke River sprang from a rock so near to a sea that the waves in storm often dashed into this fountain, making the river brackish for some distance below. That the story might be more interesting, they added that there was gold there, and that the walls of a town in that land were made of pearls. This is what the white men fancied the Indians said; but whatever they said was spoken in

Book I.

Note 3.

Lane's Ac-
count in
Hakl. III.

Note 4.

Seeking
the Pacific
on James
River.

a tongue of which Lane's men had but the most scanty knowledge, if indeed it were not given mainly by signs. Nothing dispirited by the extravagance of these tales, Lane and some of his men set out to immortalize and enrich themselves— like a company of children running after the pot of gold at the end of the rainbow. While the crafty Indians were plotting the destruction of the colonists left behind, the governor and his followers pursued their quest until they were obliged to eat their dogs, made palatable by seething with a dressing of sassafras leaves. They returned, half famished and wholly disappointed, just in time to rescue the colony from destruction. But faith is faith, and despite his severe experience Lane went back to England believing that the Roanoke rose near to the Bay of Mexico " that openeth out into the South Sea." The map which the colonists brought with them when they abandoned the country in 1586 handed down the delusion, in another form, by showing a strait leading from the neighborhood of Port Royal into a body of water to the westward.

IV.

Twenty years after the return of Ralegh's first colonists the Jamestown company was sent to plant the germ of an English-speaking nation in North America. Beginning with the first voyage of Columbus, the search for a route through America had lasted a hundred and fourteen years. No

passage north of Magellan's Strait had been found, CHAP. I.
yet a belief in the existence of such a water-way
remained a part of the geographical creed of the
time.   The Jamestown emigrants were officially instructed to explore that branch of any river
that lay toward the northwest, perhaps because
the charmed latitude of 40° might thus be reached.
It was in carrying out this instruction that Captain John Smith came to grief at the hands of
the Indians while looking for the Pacific in the
swamps of the Chickahominy.   Smith rarely mixed
his abounding romance with his geography; he is
as sober and trustworthy in topographical description and in map-making as he is imaginative in
narration.   But Smith was at this time under the
influence of the prevailing delusion, and he hoped
that his second voyage up the Chesapeake would
lead him into the Pacific.   His belief in a passage to the westward in latitude 40°, just beyond the northward limit of his own explorations, he communicated to his friend Henry Hud- Hudson.
son, who was so moved by it that he sailed to
America in 1609 in violation of his orders, and in
seeking the strait to the South Sea penetrated the
solitudes of the picturesque river that bears his
name.   The explorer Dermer was intent on win- Dermer.
ning immortality by finding a passage to the Pacific when, in 1619, he was storm-driven into Long
Island Sound.   At Manhattan Island, or thereabout,
he got information from the obliging Indians that
made plain his way to the Orient.   He was very

BOOK I.

secretive about this route, which, however, seems to have lain through Delaware Bay.

A false notion once generally accepted is able to live in some ghostly shape after the breath is out of its body. The hope of a passage to the Pacific by means of a strait and the belief in a narrow isthmus in latitude 40° could not long survive the increase of knowledge that followed the settlement Note 5. of Virginia and Captain Smith's explorations. But sixteen years after the landing at Jamestown, when these two geographical jack-o'-lanterns had ceased Sandys's plan. to flicker, the poet George Sandys, who was secretary of the colony, wrote that he was ready to venture his life in finding a way to the South Sea, but this way was now to be by an overland route. About the same time Henry Briggs, the famous Savile lecturer at Oxford, proved to the satisfaction of many that the rivers running westward from the Virginia mountains must reach the Pacific Note 6. in about one hundred and fifty miles. One Marmaduke Parkinson, an explorer sailing in the Potomac, confirmed the theory of the learned mathematician by discovering in the house of a chief a " China Boxe," whatever that may have been. In 1631 Luke Fox. Luke Fox set sail by the northwest, carrying a letter from Charles I addressed " to the Emperor of Northwest. Fox, p. 172. Japan," which he probably was not able to deliver. In 1634 Captain Thomas Yong got as far as the falls of the Delaware in the endeavor to go through the continent in latitude 40°. The strait and isthmus and northwest passage having failed, Yong was content to go by fresh water till he should reach a Mediterranean Sea in the heart of America, which he believed to open into both the "North Ocean" and the South Sea. As the century advanced the fresh-water route had in turn to be finally abandoned, and seekers after the Pacific were fain to betake themselves to dry-shod travel, and even to mountain-climbing, as George Sandys had proposed. A Colonel Catlet is mentioned who reached the Alleghanies in the endeavor to find a river flowing westward, but he was daunted by what seemed to him almost impassable ranges of mountains that barred his way. Over these "rocky hills and sandy desarts" scarce a bird was seen to fly. In 1669, Lederer, a German surveyor, set out from Virginia on a similar futile exploration. As late as 1700 the well-informed Lawson speaks hopefully of the proximity of the Pacific to North Carolina. This fallacy had prompted many desperate adventures, and had been the cause of many important discoveries, in the two centuries that it held possession of men's minds. It reached its last attenuation in 1765, when the public prints announced that large boats were fitting out at Quebec to try the whale-fishing in Lake Ontario, and that "they have hopes of finding a communication by water with the western ocean, founded on the favorable reports of some Indians, who inform that a river runs westward many hundreds of miles as large as the Mississippi."

CHAP. I.

Weston Documents 45 and 47 and ff.

Catlet and Lederer.

Glover, in Phil. Trans., xi, 626. Comp. Perfect Descr. of Va., 1649, and Lederer's Voyage.

Lawson's Carolina, 47.

Scot's Magazine, 1765, page 161.

V.

As the mistake made by Columbus had left for
heritage an almost ineradicable passion for the discovery of a westward sea way to Japan and China,
so the vast treasure of gold and silver drawn by
the Spaniards from Mexico and Peru produced a
belief in the English mind that a colony planted at
any place on the American coast might find gold.
Here, again, the undoubting Hakluyt and other
writers after him were ready with learned conclusions balancing on the tight rope of very slender
premises. If an Indian had been seen wearing a
piece of copper that "bowed easily," this flexibility
proved it to be tarnished gold. If a savage seemed
to say in his idiom, or by gestures and other signs,
something which the puzzled newcomers took to
signify that in a country farther on the copper was

Hakluyt.
Pref. to
Va., mag-
nified.

too soft for use, or that it was yellow, or that it
had a good luster, what further evidence could an
ingenious writer desire of the existence of the precious metal in that country ? Purchas, the successor of Hakluyt in geographical research, explains the divine purpose in thus endowing a
heathen land with gold, which is that the Indian
race "as a rich bride, though withered and deformed, . . . might find many suitors for love of

Pilgrim-
age, 795.

her portion," and thus the pagans be converted.
But Purchas filches both the simile and the pious
thought from Herrera, who in turn probably pil-
fered it with many better things from the good

Las Casas. Purchas also speaks with more opti-
mism than elegance of the "silver bowels and
golden entrails of the hills," as though one had but
to dig into the first mountain to be enriched.

Frobisher brought home from sub-arctic islands
what his clumsy assayers avouched to be "gold
eure." Refining works were erected for this stuff
at Deptford to no profit. And the worthless
stones brought from arctic America with so much
pains served at last to repair English highways.
The main causes of the suffering at Jamestown
during the first winter were the waste of time
and the consumption of supplies while lading the
ships with the glittering "dust mica" which is so
abundant in the Virginia sands. The worthless-
ness of this cargo could not weaken the hopes of
those alchemists who were able to produce gold
merely by the use of arguments. The mines in
Virginia moved farther west. It wanted only
that explorers should reach the mountains. In
spite of the sickness that wasted the colony in 1610,
Lord De la Warr sent an expedition to dig gold
on the upper James, but the warlike up-river tribes
soon drove the prospectors back. In 1634, Sir John
Harvey sent another body of men on the same
fool's errand, though there had not been found in
all the years preceding a particle of tangible evidence that gold existed in Virginia. But on the
James, as on the Hudson, the glistering pigment
with which the Indians besmeared their faces on
occasions of display was believed to contain gold,

Book I.
Note 7.

Fact and
fable
about
America.

and the places of its procurement were sought with ludicrous secrecy.

The unfaltering faith in the existence of abundant gold on the eastern coast of North America could not have subsisted on thin air so long if it had not been stimulated by the almost fabulous wealth drawn from South America by Spain. It had received encouragement also from the tales told by adventurers returned from America, who seem to have thought it necessary to bring back stories that would match in some degree the prevalent beliefs about the New World. The earliest but one of all the documents relating to America preserved among the British state papers is the statement of one David or Davy Ingram. With a hundred other luckless seamen he was put ashore in Mexico by Sir John Hawkins, because the ship lacked provisions. Ingram, traveling from tribe to tribe, achieved the notable feat of crossing the continent in a year. In 1569 he embarked on a French ship that he found near the mouth of the St. John River in what is now the province of New Brunswick. It was eleven years later that Davy Ingram, at home in England, made his statement, and the sailor's story had by that time gained much, perhaps, by frequent telling to wonder-loving listeners.

Sometimes he relates facts with sobriety, speaking the truth by relapse, it may be; again, he seems to be repeating tales told him by the savages, who were habitual marvel-mongers, or weaving into the account of what he had seen legends common in the folklore about America that had grown up in Europe ; or perchance he only falls into an old forecastle habit of incontinent lying without provocation. The American women are described as " wearing great plates of gold covering their whole bodies like armor. . . . In every cottage pearls are to be found, and in some houses a peck " —an assertion that had a grain of truth in it, since the sailor no doubt mistook wampum beads for pearls. Fireflies, in this old tar's exalted memory, are " fire dragons, which make the air very red as they fly," while the buffalo appears as an animal "as big as two of our oxen." The streets in one " city " are broader than London streets, which we may readily believe. The banqueting houses are built of crystal, " with pillars of massie silver, some of gold." This is a fine example of the manner of a mind afflicted with the vice of exaggeration ; crystal becomes silver in the next breath, and silver is as instantly transmuted to gold. All that optimistic projectors sought in America—gold, silver, pearls by the peck, and great abundance of silkworms—are obligingly supplied in Ingram's narrative. Such tales impressed the imagination in a romantic and uncritical age.

Note 8.

VI.

The interest in America was heightened by popular curiosity regarding the Indians. The American savages were sometimes treated as sun-worshipers, but they were more commonly thought

Indian devil-worship.

to be worshipers of devils. The prevailing belief in witchcraft, divination, and abounding evil spirits rendered it easy for Europeans to accept the Indian deities as supernatural beings, and to credit the pretensions of the powwows, or Indian priests, to give knowledge of distant or future events, to heal the sick, and even to bring rain in time of drought. But it was observed at Plymouth that when the Pilgrims prayed for rain it fell gently, and that the rain procured by the Indian conjurers was violent and destructive—a rain with something devilish about it. According to writers of the time, the demons worshiped by the savages were able to materialize themselves on great occasions, appearing to their votaries in some beastly form. This belief in Indian devil-worship fitted well with the religious faith of the period, which can hardly be described as anything but a sort of Manichæism dividing the government of the universe almost equally between good and evil powers. Religionists of all schools desired to convert these subjects of Satan, not from those philanthropic motives that are main considerations in modern propagandism, but because their conversion would glorify God, and yet more because it would despite the devil. Sometimes the religious motive was incongruously supported by hopes of commercial advantage. The navigator Davis wrote to Secretary Walsingham that if the Indians " were once brought over to the Christian faith they might soon be brought to relish a more civilized kind of life and be thereby induced to take off great quantities of our coarser woolen manufactures."

The early explorers made a practice of kidnaping Indians and transporting them to England, where the sight of barbarians without doublet or hose quickened the interest in projects for colonization and adventure. In our age of commercial activity and extended geographical knowledge one can form but a weak conception of the excitement produced by the sight of "the Indian man and woman," no doubt Esquimaux, brought by Frobisher. Portraits of these rarities were made for the king and queen and others. In 1605 Weymouth brought from the coast of Maine five kidnapped Indians, "with all their bows and arrows" and two beautiful birch-bark canoes. "This accident," exclaimed Sir Ferdinando Gorges, "hath been the means of putting life into all our plantations." Some of the savages captured at various times were exhibited for money, and one perhaps was shown after he was dead; at least we may venture to conjecture so much from Shakespeare's jeer in The Tempest at the idle curiosity of the crowd. In England, says Trinculo, "any strange beast makes a man. When they will not give a doit to relieve a lame beggar, they will lay out ten to see a dead Indian." This interest in outlandish savages no doubt suggested to the poet the creation of the monster Caliban, who probably seemed a realistic figure to the imagination of that age.

Chap. I.

Indians exhibited.

Rosier's True Relation.

Tempest, ii, 2.

VII.

The animals of the new continent excited the wonder of the people of Europe and increased the interest in America. Regarding them, also, the most extravagant stories were easily credited. It was recorded in the sober Latin of Peter Martyr that the advance of Cabot's ships was retarded by the multitude of codfish on the Newfoundland coast, and that the bears were accustomed to catch

these fish in their claws. It is hard to recognize the familiar opossum in the description by Purchas : " A monstrous deformed beast, whose fore part resembleth a fox, the hinder part an ape, excepting the feet, which are like a man's; beneath her belly she hath a receptacle like a purse, where she bestows her young until they can shift for themselves." The humming bird was believed to be a cross between a fly and a bird. The Hudson River Dutch settlers went further, and named it simply " the West Indian bee." These dainty creatures were prepared for exportation to Europe in New Amsterdam by drying them, in Barbadoes by filling them with sand. They were accounted " pretty delicacies for ladies, who wore them at

their breasts and girdles." Evelyn saw two preserved as great rarities at Oxford, in 1654. A New England versifier extols

> The humbird for some queen's rich cage more fit
> Than in the vacant wilderness to sit.

Flying squirrels, when brought into English

parks in 1608, were the occasion of much wondering excitement. King James begged for one of them, like a spoiled child. The skins of muskrats were esteemed for their odor and were brought to England "as rich presents." It was thought that musk might be extracted from this animal. Hariot, the learned man of Ralegh's first colony, fancied that the civet cat would prove profitable to settlers in America, but his words indicate that he had been misled by traces of the skunk, whose perfume has never yet come into request. Speaking of the "civet catte," he says, "in our travails there was found one to have been killed by a salvage or inhabitant; and in many places the smell where one had lately beene before."

De Bry's Hariot, p. 10.

The raccoon, the "aroughcun" of the Virginia Indians, being a plantigrade, was esteemed a monkey; the peccaries were called the wild hogs of America, and were thought to have "their navels on the ridge of their backs." Somewhere in the region of the Hudson River a beast is described as having a horn in the middle of his forehead, from which it would appear that the unicorn on the royal coat of arms may have been found running at large. It is not easy to account for the "camel mare," reported to have been seen about three hundred miles west from the coast of New Jersey, unless it belonged to the genus *Incubus*. The bewildering number of new creatures found in America troubled the European scholars of that day, who were ever theological. They were puzzled

Note 10.

to get so many four-footed beasts and creeping things into the compass of Noah's ark. Mercator, the Flemish geographer, avoided this difficult embarkation by concluding that America had been excepted from the Deluge.

VIII.

Thus grotesque and misleading were many of the glimpses that Europe got of the New World as the mists of ignorance slowly lifted from it. These erratic notions regarding America give one an insight into the character of the English people at the period of discovery and colony-planting. Credulity and the romantic spirit dwell together. The imagination in such an age usurped the place of discrimination, and the wonderful became the probable. The appetite for the marvelous fostered exaggeration; every man who had sailed in foreign seas thought it shame not to tell of wonders. The seventeenth century indeed betrayed a consciousness of its own weakness in a current proverb, "Travelers lie by license." History and fiction had not yet been separated. Like every other romantic age, the period of Elizabeth and James was prodigal of daring adventure; every notable man aspired to be the hero of a tale. English beginnings in America were thus made in a time abounding in bold enterprises—enterprises brilliant in conception, but in the execution of which there was often a lack of foresight and practical wisdom.

An age of romance and adventure.

ELUCIDATIONS.

See the careful and learned discussion of the Voyages of Cabot by the late Charles Deane, in Winsor's Narrative and Critical History of America, vol. iii. Mr. Deane effectually destroys the delusion which so long gave the credit of this discovery, or a part of it, to Sebastian Cabot, the son of the real discoverer. Mr. Henry Harrisse, in John Cabot, the Discoverer of America, and in an earlier work, Jean et Sebastien Cabot, etc., reaches the same conclusion. He even doubts Sebastian's presence in the expeditions of his father, John Cabot, etc., p. 48.

Note 1, page 3.

Yet George Beste, who sailed with Frobisher, says : " Now men neede no more contentiously strive for roume to build an house on, or for a little turffe of ground, . . . when great countreys and whole worldes offer and reache out themselves to them that will first voutsafe to possesse, inhabite, and till them." These countries, he says, " are fertile to bring forth all manner of corne and grayne, infinite sortes of land cattell, as horse, elephantes, kine, sheepe, great varietie of flying fowles of the ayre, as phesants, partridge, quayle, popingeys, ostridges, etc., infinite kinds of fruits, as almonds, dates, quinces, pomegranats, oringes, etc., holesome, medicinable, and delectable " (Frobisher's Voyages, Hakluyt Society, p. 38).

Note 2, page 4.

Ralegh, in his History of the World, book i, chap. viii, sec. xv, has an interesting digression on the danger of trusting such communications, and he relates an anecdote of misapprehension by this very party sent under Grenville and Lane : " The same happened among the English, which I sent under Sir Richard Greeneville to inhabit Virginia. For when some of my people asked the name of that country, one of the savages answered, ' *Wingandacon,*' which is as much as to say, as, ' *You wear good cloaths,*' or gay cloaths." From this answer it came that the coast of North Carolina was called " Wingandacon," or, in its Latinized form, Wingindacoa, while the chief, or " king," of the country appears in the narratives of the time as Wingina. Ralegh says that Yucatan means merely " What say you ? " and that Peru got its name from a similar mistake.

Note 3, page 8.

I found the original of this map among the drawings made by John White in the Grenville Collection in the British Museum.

Note 4, page 8.

It was reproduced to accompany a paper of mine on the Virginia Colony in the Century Magazine of November, 1882. It excited interest among scholars, as it was supposed to have been previously unknown. A copy was afterward found, however, in the collection made by Dr. Kohl for the State Department at Washington. The drawings in the Sloane MSS., British Museum, attributed to John White by Dr. E. E. Hale, in the Transactions of the American Antiquarian Society, iv, 21, are not White's originals. The latter are in the Grenville Collection. See my comparison of the two in The Nation of April 23, 1891.

Note 5, page 10.

As late as December 5, 1621, in a letter from the Virginia Company to Governor Wyatt, these words occur: "The Conjectures of the Southwest Passage and the piece of copper which you sent us gladly saw and heard." This long-surviving desire for a short passage to the East Indies is traceable to the passion that existed in Europe in the fifteenth and sixteenth centuries for spices, and this no doubt came from the gross forms of cookery in that time. Anderson's Commerce, sub anno 1504, cites Guicciardini on the great quantities of spices used, and adds: "For in those days the people of Europe were much fonder of spices in their cookery, etc., than they have been in later times." The rise in the price of commodities in Elizabeth's time may have been only apparent, but it promoted voyages looking to the extension of commerce. Compare Holinshed, i, 274.

Note 6, page 10.

Waterhouse's Declaration of Virginia, 1622, a rare tract. Also Purchas, iii, 892, 893, where these words are quoted from Briggs: "The Indian Ocean, which we commonly call the South Sea, which lyeth on the West and Northwest Side of Virginia, on the other side of the mountains beyond our Falls [of James River] and openeth a free and faire passage, not only to China, Japan, and the Moluccas, but also to New Spaine, Peru, and Chili, and those rich countries of Terra Australis not as yet discovered." It is one of many marks of practical sagacity in Captain John Smith that after his experience on the American coast he was able to form views of the geography of the continent almost a century in advance of the opinions held in his time. He speaks of "those large Dominions which doe stretch themselves into the main God knoweth how many thousand miles" (Generall Historie, book vi).

Note 7, page 14.

So late as 1626, Fleet, the only survivor of the massacre of Spelman's party, after spending five years in captivity among the

Virginia Indians, persuaded a London merchant to intrust him with a vessel for the Indian trade by his stories of the "powder of gold" with which the savages made a paint for their faces. To this story he added a statement that he had often been in sight of the South Sea or Pacific Ocean. Fleet's Journal may be found in Scharf's History of Maryland, i, 13, etc. Van der Donck relates, in his description of New Netherland, that Kieft, the director of New Netherland, and Van der Donck, found an Indian painting himself and bought the pigment, which being burned in a crucible yielded two pieces of gold. (See the translation in New York Historical Society Collection, ii, 161, 162.) A bag of specimens of the precious ores of the Hudson River region was sent to Holland by the ill-fated ship that sailed out of New Haven in 1645. The ship was seen no more except by the New Haven people, who beheld its specter in the sky. Of the Hudson River gold mines no specter has ever been seen in earth or sky.

Note 8, page 15.

I have quoted from Mr. Sainsbury's abstract of the fragment in the British Public Record Office, but a similar statement by Ingram was inserted in Hakluyt's Divers Voyages in 1589. It was omitted in the later edition as too incredible even for Hakluyt. See also a paper by Dr. De Costa, in the Magazine of American History, March, 1883, on the copy of Ingram's Statement preserved in the Bodleian Library. Ingram's story, and others like it, seem to be satirized in the play of Eastward, Ho! by Chapman, Jonson, and Marston. The assertion of Seagull, in the play, that "they have in their houses scowpes, buckets, and diverse other vessels of massie silver," would seem at first sight to be an unmistakable allusion to the extravagance of Ingram's narrative. But in the second edition of Bullein's A Dialogue against the Fever Pestilence, which was published in 1573, one Mendax, describing an unknown land, declares that "their pottes, panns, and all vessells are cleane gold garnished with diamondes." This shows that Ingram's story had probably absorbed certain traits from what I have ventured to call European folklore tales about America—folk tales originally applied to the Orient, no doubt; echoes of Sir John Mandeville and Marco Polo, perhaps. Of course it is just possible, but not probable, that Bullein had heard the tales of Ingram, who had returned three years or more before he printed his second edition. The authors of Eastward, Ho! probably enlarged on Bullein.

BOOK I.
Note 9,
page 18.

"Unguibusque inter squamas immissis," Decade III, book vi. These details are probably given on the authority of Sebastian Cabot, whose veracity is not above suspicion.

Note 10,
page 19.

Some of the early writers speak of "apes." Strachey calls what appears to be a raccoon a monkey, and Brickell, as late as 1743, uses the same word. The peccaries are recorded as in the text by the marvel-loving Purchas, p. 805. One finds unicorns in Speed's Prospect, Description of New York. Speed also lets us know that the buffalo was accustomed to defend himself by vomiting "a hot scalding liquor" on the dogs that chased it. Argall was the first Englishman to see the bison, in 1613. Citing his letter, Purchas says, p. 943, "In one voyage . . . they found a slow kind of cattell as bigge as kine, which were good meate."

CHAPTER THE SECOND.

JAMES RIVER EXPERIMENTS.

I.

In December, 1606, there lay at Blackwall, below London, the Susan Constant, of one hundred tons, the Godspeed, of forty tons, and the little pinnace Discovery, of but twenty tons—three puny ships to bear across the wintry Atlantic the beginners of a new nation. The setting forth of these argonauts produced much excitement in London. Patriotic feeling was deeply stirred, public prayers were offered for the success of the expedition, sermons appropriate to the occasion were preached, and the popular feeling was expressed in a poem by Michael Drayton. Even those who were too sober to indulge the vain expectations of gold mines and spice islands that filled the imaginations of most Englishmen on this occasion could say, as Lord Bacon did later: " It is with the kingdoms on earth as it is with the kingdom of heaven: sometimes a grain of mustard seed proves a great tree. Who can tell?" On the 19th of that most tempestuous December the little fleet weighed anchor and ran down on an ebb tide, no doubt, as one may nowadays see ships rush past Blackwall toward the sea. Never were men engaged in a great enter-

Departure of the emigrants.

Ld. Chancellor's Speech in reply to the Speaker.

prise doomed to greater sorrows. From the time they left the Thames the ships were tossed and delayed by tempests, while the company aboard was rent by factious dissensions.

II.

Those who shaped the destinies of the colony had left little undone that inventive stupidity could suggest to assure the failure of the enterprise. King James, who was frivolously fond of puttering in novel projects, had personally framed a code of unwise laws and orders. The supremacy of the sovereign and the interests of the Church were pedantically guarded, but the colony was left without any ruler with authority enough to maintain order. The private interest of the individual, the most available of all motives to industry, was merged in that of the commercial company to which Virginia had been granted. All the produce of the colony was to go into a common stock for five years, and the emigrants, men without families, were thrown into a semi-monastic trading community like the Hanseatic agencies of the time, with the saving element of a strong authority left out. Better devices for promoting indolence and aggravating the natural proneness to dissension of men in hard circumstances could scarcely have been hit upon. Anarchy and despotism are the inevitable alternatives under such a communistic arrangement, and each of these ensued in turn.

III.

The people sent over in the first years were for the most part utterly unfit. Of the first hundred, four were carpenters, there was a blacksmith, a tailor, a barber, a bricklayer, a mason, a drummer. There were fifty-five who ranked as gentlemen, and four were boys, while there were but twelve so-called laborers, including footmen, " that never did know what a day's work was." The company is described by one of its members as composed of poor gentlemen, tradesmen, serving men, libertines, and such like. " A hundred good workmen were better than a thousand such gallants," says Captain Smith. Of the moral character of the first emigrants no better account is given. It was perhaps with these men in view that Bacon declared it " a shameful and unblessed thing " to settle a colony with " the scum of the people."

Character
of the emi-
grants.

Smith's
Gen. Hist.,
iii, c. i and
c. xii.

Advertise-
ments for
Planters of
New Eng.,
p. 5.

Comp.
Briefe De-
claration in
Pub. Rec.
Off., Sains-
bury i, 66 ;
and New
Life of Va.

Essay on
Planta-
tions.

IV.

The ships sailed round by the Canaries, after the fashion of that time, doubling the distance to Virginia. They loitered in the West Indies to " refresh themselves " and quarrel, and they did not reach their destination until seedtime had well-nigh passed. They arrived on the 6th of May, according to our style. Driven into Hampton Roads by a storm, they sailed up the wide mouth of a river which they called the James, in honor of the king. At that season of the year the

The arri-
val.

Book I.

A. D. 1607.

Percy, in
Purchas,
p. 1689.

The first
meetings
with In-
dians.

Percy, in
Purchas iv,
pp. 1685,
1686.

banks must have shown masses of the white flowers of the dogwood, mingled with the pink-purple
blossoms of the redbud against the dark primeval
forest.   Wherever they went ashore the newcomers found " all the ground bespread with many
sweet and delicate flowers of divers colors and
kinds."   The sea-weary voyagers concluded that
" heaven and earth had never agreed better to
frame a place for man's habitation."

They were like people in an enchanted land—
all was so new and strange.   On the first landing
of a small party they had a taste of savage war-
fare.   "At night, when wee were going aboard,
there came the savages creeping from the Hills
like Beares, with their Bowes in their Mouthes,
charged us very desperately, hurt Captain Gabrill
Archer in both hands, and a Sayler in two places
of the body very dangerous.   After they had spent
their arrowes, and felt the sharpness of our shot,
they retired into the Woods with a great noise and
so left us."

But the newly arrived did not find all the Indians hostile.   The chief of the Rappahannocks came
to welcome them, marching at the head of his
train, piping on a reed flute, and clad in the fantastic dress of an Indian dandy.   He wore a plate of
copper on the shorn side of his head.   The hair on
the other side was wrapped about with deer's hair
dyed red, " in the fashion of a rose."   Two long
feathers " like a pair of horns " were stuck in this
rosy crown.   His body was stained crimson, his

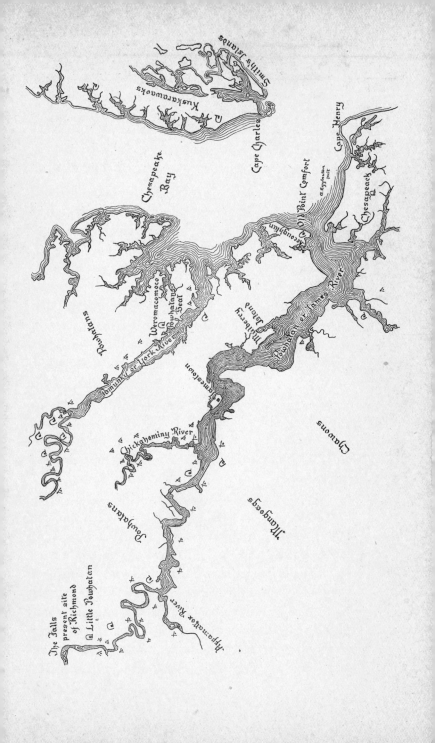

face painted blue and besmeared with some glistering pigment which to the greedy eyes of the English seemed to be silver ore. He wore a chain of beads, or wampum, about his neck, and his ears were "all behung with bracelets of pearls." There also depended from each ear a bird's claw set with copper—or "gold," adds the narrator, indulging a delightful dubiety.

CHAP. II.

A. D. 1607.

During the period of preliminary exploration every trait of savage life was eagerly observed by the English. The costume, the wigwams, and most of all the ingenious weapons of wood and stone, gave delight to the curiosity of the newcomers.

Purchas i, 686 and following.

V.

The colonists chose for the site of their town what was then a malarial peninsula; it has since become an island. The place was naturally defended by the river on all sides, except where a narrow stretch of sand made a bridge to the main. Its chief advantage in the eyes of the newcomers was that the deep water near the shore made it possible to moor the ships by merely tying them up to trees on the river bank. Here the settlers planted cotton and orange trees at once, and experimental potatoes, melons, and pumpkins, but they postponed sowing grain until about the first of June in our reckoning.

Founding of Jamestown.

Note 1.

Relatyon of the Discovery of our River, Am. Antiq. Soc., iv, 61.

They took up their abode in hastily built cabins roofed with sedge or bark, and in ragged tents. The poorer sort were even fain to shelter them-

The winter of misery.

selves in mere burrows in the ground. Ill provided at the start, the greater part of their food was consumed by the seamen, who lingered to gather comminuted mica for gold. In this hard environment, rent by faction, destitute of a competent leader and of any leader with competent authority, the wonder is that of this little company a single man survived the winter. "There never were Englishmen left in any foreign country in such misery as we were in this new-discovered Virginia," says George Percy, brother to the Earl of Northumberland. A pint of worm-eaten barley or wheat was allowed for a day's ration. This was made into pottage and served out at the rate of one small ladleful at each meal. "Our drink was water, our lodgings castles in the air," says Smith. The misery was aggravated by a constant fear of attack from the Indians, who had been repulsed in an energetic assault made soon after the landing of the English. It was necessary for each man to watch every third night "lying on the cold, bare ground," and this exposure in a fever swamp, with the slender allowance of food of bad quality and the brackish river water, brought on swellings, dysenteries, and fevers. Sometimes there were not five men able to bear arms. "If there were any conscience in men," says Percy, "it would make their hearts bleed to hear the pitiful murmurings and outcries of our sick men without relief every day and night for the space of about six weeks." The living were hardly able to bury the dead, whose bodies were "trailed out like dogs." Half of the hundred colonists died, and the survivors were saved by the Indians, who, having got a taste of muskets and cannon in their early attack on Jamestown, now brought in supplies of game, corn, persimmons, and other food, to trade for the novel trinkets of the white men.

VI.

Peril and adversity bring the capable man to the front. The colony proceeded, by means of the technicalities habitually used in those days, to rid itself of its president, Wingfield, a man of good intentions but with no talents suitable to a place of such difficulty. Slowly, by one change and then another, the leadership fell into the hands of Captain John Smith. During the voyage he had drawn upon himself the jealousy of the others, probably by his boastful and self-asserting habit of speech. When the list of councilors, till then kept secret, was opened at Jamestown and his name was found in it, he was promptly excluded by his associates. It was only on the intercession of the clergyman, Hunt, that he was at length admitted to the Council.

His paradoxical character has been much misunderstood. Those who discredit the historical accuracy of Captain Smith's narratives consider his deeds of no value. It is the natural result and retribution of boasting that the real merit of the boaster is cast into the rubbish heap of contempt along with his false pretensions. On the other hand, those who appreciate Smith's services to the colony in its dire extremities believe that the historical authority of such a man must be valid.

His romantic tendencies.

His character, double and paradoxical as it is, presents no insoluble enigma if we consider the forces of nature and of habit underlying its manifestations. According to his own highly colored narrative, he had fed his fervid imagination on romances of chivalry. The first natural result in a youth so energetic as he, was that he should set out to emulate the imaginary heroes of whom he had read. It was equally a matter of course that a man of his vanity should exaggerate his own adventures to the size of those that had excited his admiration. The same romantic turn of the imagination that sent him a-wandering after exploits in Flanders and in the wars with the Turks, in Barbary, and in Ireland, made his every adventure seem an exploit of heroic size. Such a man is valuable when boldness and aggressive action are in request; to relate facts where autobiography is involved he is little fitted.

His story of his own life.

According to Smith's own narrative, he was robbed and shipwrecked at sea; he slew three infidel champions in single combat and cut off their heads, just for the amusement of the ladies; he was made captive by the Turks and escaped by slaying his master with a flail; he encountered pirates; in the plunder of a ship he secured by the grace of God a box of jewels; and, to round off his story, he was beloved in romance fashion by a fair Turkish lady, one Tragabigzanda; befriended by a Russian lady, the good Calamata; and, later, was snatched from the open jaws of death by the devotion of the lovely Princess Pocahontas, daughter of King Powhatan, of Virginia. What more could one ask? Here are the elements of all the romances. But, to crown all, he emulated the misadventure of the prophet Jonah, and he even out-Jonahed Jonah. He got ashore by mere swimming without the aid of a whale, when cast overboard by Catholic pilgrims to appease a tempest. Never any other wanderer since the safe return of Ulysses passed through such a succession of marvelous escapes as this young John Smith. His accidents and achievements, even without exaggeration, were fairly notable, doubtless, but they are forever obscured by his vices of narration.

By the time he was twenty-eight years old this knight-errant had pretty well exhausted Europe as a field for adventure. Soon after his return to his own land he found the navigator Gosnold agitating for a new colony in Virginia, the scene of Ralegh's failures. That being the most difficult and dangerous enterprise then in sight, nothing was more natural than that Smith should embark in it. From this time to the end of his life this really able man gave his best endeavors to the advancement of American colonization. Make what reductions we may, the results of his journeys and the testimony of his contemporaries show him to have been

Interest in colonization.

His character.

4

brave, vigilant, conciliatory, and successful. In labor he was indefatigable, in emergencies he proved himself ready-witted and resourceful. His recorded geographical observations are remarkably accurate considering his circumstances, and his understanding of Indian life shows his intelligence. His writings on practical questions are terse, epigrammatic, and wise beyond the wisdom of his time. But where his own adventures or credit are involved he is hardly more trustworthy than Falstaff. His boasting is one of the many difficulties a historian has to encounter in seeking to discover the truth regarding the events of an age much given to lying.

VII.

Smith's exploration and trading.

On Smith principally devolved the explorations for a passage to the Pacific and the conduct of the Indian trade. He was captured by the Indians in the swamps of the Chickahominy and carried from village to village in triumph. Contriving to secure his release from the head chief, Powhatan, he returned to Jamestown. Nothing could have suited better his bold genius and roving disposition than

A. D. 1607, 1608.

the life he thereafter led in Virginia. He sailed up and down the bays and estuaries, discovering and naming unknown islands, ascending great unknown rivers, cajoling or bullying the Indians, and re-

Oxford Tract, *passim.*

turning to his hungry countrymen at Jamestown laden with maize from the granaries of the savages.

Gen. Hist. *passim.*

Smith and his companions coasted in all seasons

and all weather in an open boat, exercising themselves in morning psalm-singing and praying, in
manœuvring strange Indians by blustering or point-
blank lying, and in trying to propagate the Christian religion among the heathen—all in turn as
occasion offered, like true Englishmen of the Jaco-
bean time.

Captain Smith's earlier accounts of these achievements in Virginia seem to be nearer the truth than
his later Generall Historie.   As years rolled on his
exploits gained in number and magnitude in his
memory.   The apocryphal story of his expound-
ing the solar system by means of a pocket compass
to savages whose idiom he had had no opportunity
to learn is to be found only in his later writings.
He is a prisoner but a month in the narrative of
the Oxford Tract of 1612, which was written by
his associates and published with his authority, but
his captivity had grown to six or seven weeks in
the Generall Historie of 1624.   His prosaic release
by Powhatan had developed into a romantic rescue
by Pocahontas.   Two or three hundred savages in
the earlier account become four or five hundred
in the later.   Certain Poles assist him in the capture of an Indian chief in the authorized narrative
of Pots and Phettiplace.   In the later story our
hero performs this feat single-handed.   A mere
cipher attaches itself sometimes to the figure representing the number of his enemies, who by this
simple feat of memory become ten times more re-
doubtable than before.

His narra-
tive.

BOOK I.

His serv-
ice to the
colony.

Oxf. Tract,
p. 32.
Gen. Hist.,
bk. iii,
ch. v.

Historie of
Travaile
into Vir-
ginia, p.
41.

Smith
over-
thrown.

But it does not matter greatly whether the "strangely grimmed and disguised" Indians seen by Smith at one place on the Potomac, who, according to the story, were shouting and yelling horribly, though in ambuscade, numbered three or four hundred as in one account, or three or four thousand as in his later story. To Captain Smith remains the credit of having been the one energetic and capable man in those first years—the man who wasted no time in a search for gold, but won from the Indians what was of infinitely greater value—the corn needed to preserve the lives of the colonists. In an open boat, with no instrument but a compass, he explored and mapped Chesapeake Bay so well that his map was not wholly superseded for a hundred and forty years. Even Wingfield, who had reason to dislike Smith, recognizes the value of his services ; and Strachey, who had every means of knowing, says that "there will not return from" Virginia "in hast any one who hath bene more industrious or who hath had (Captain Geo. Percie excepted) greater experience amongst them, however misconstruction maye traduce here at home."

During the autumn of 1608 and the winter following Captain Smith was sole ruler of Jamestown, all the other councilors having gone ; but the next spring there arrived five hundred new colonists inadequately provisioned, and under two of the old faction leaders who were Smith's mortal enemies. These were the visionary and turbulent Archer and his follower Ratcliffe. Smith got some of the newcomers to settle at Nansemond, and others took up their abode near the falls of the James River. After much turmoil Smith was disabled by an accident, and his enemies contrived to have him sent home charged, among other things, with having " incensed" the Indians to assault the insubordinate settlers under West near the falls, and with having designed to wed Pocahontas in order to secure royal rights in Virginia as son-in-law to Powhatan.

He afterward explored the New England coast with characteristic thoroughness and intelligence. What he published in his later years by way of advice on the subject of colony-planting is full of admirable good sense. With rare foresight he predicted the coming importance of the colonial trade and the part to be played by the American fisheries in promoting the greatness of England by " breeding mariners." He only of the men of his time suspected the imperial size and future greatness of North America. He urged that the colonies should not annoy " with large pilotage and such like dues " those who came to trade in their ports. Low customs, he says, enrich a people. This is a strange doctrine in an age when foreign trade seemed almost an evil, and false conceptions of economic principles were nearly universal. Captain Smith's words are often pregnant with a wit whose pungency is delightful. In mental and physical hardihood, and in what may be called

Chap. II.

A. D. 1609.

Note 2.

His later years.

BOOK I.

Note 3.

The fam-
ine of
1609-'10.

Note 4.

A. D. 1609,
1610.

shiftiness, as well as in proneness to exaggeration and in boastfulness, he was in some sense a typical American pioneer—a forerunner of the daring and ready-witted men who have subdued a savage continent.

VIII.

Disaster of some sort could hardly have been avoided had Captain Smith been allowed to stay, but after his departure ruin came swiftly, and there was no hand strong enough to stay it. The unchecked hostility of the savages drove the outsettlers from Nansemond and the falls of the James. The Indians found exercise for their devilish ingenuity in torturing those who fell into their hands alive, and outraging the dead. The brave but unwise Percy added fuel to their consuming fury by visiting their shrine and desecrating the tombs of their chiefs. There was now no one who could carry on the difficult Indian trade. Ratcliffe, who had conspired to send Smith back to England, fell into an ambuscade while emulating Captain Smith's example in trading with Powhatan. He was tortured to death by the Indian women, and only fifteen of his fifty men got back to Jamestown. The brood hogs of the colony were all eaten, the dogs came next, and then the horses, which were to have stocked Virginia, were consumed to their very hides. Rats, mice, and adders were relished when they were to be had, and fungi of various sorts were eaten with whatever else " would fill either mouth or belly." An Indian slain in an assault on the stockade was dug up after he had been three days buried, and eaten "by the poorer sort," their consuming hunger not being embarrassed by the restraints of gentility. From this horrible expedient it was but one step to the digging up of their own dead for food. Famine-crazed men even dogged the steps of those of their comrades who were not quite wasted, threatening to kill and devour them. Among these despairing and shiftless men there was but one man of resources. Daniel Tucker—let his later sins as tyrant of Bermuda be forgiven—bethought himself to build a boat to catch fish in the river, and this small relief " did keep us from killing one another to eat," says Percy. He seems to have been the only man who bethought himself to do anything. One man, in the ferocity engendered by famine, slew his own wife and salted what he did not eat at once of her flesh, but he was put to death at the stake for this crime. Some, braving the savages, sought food in the woods and died while seeking it, and were eaten by those who found them dead. Others, in sheer desperation, threw themselves on the tender mercies of the Indians and were slain. To physical were added spiritual torments. One despairing wretch threw his Bible into the fire, crying out in the market place that there was no God in heaven. Percy adds, with grim theological satisfaction characteristic of the time, that he was killed by the Indians in the very

Note 5.

Book I.

Tragicall Relation, 1623. Briefe Declaration, 1624, both in British Pub. Record Office. Percy's Trewe Relacyon, MS., Petworth House.

market place where he had blasphemed in his agony. The depopulated houses, and even the palisades so necessary for protection, were burned for firewood by the enfeebled people, and Jamestown came presently to look like the slumbering ruins of some ancient fortification. Fortunately, the Indians did not think it worth while to lose any more of their men in attacking the desperate remainder. It seemed inevitable that all who were shut up in the Jamestown peninsula should perish of hunger in a very few days. Of the nearly five hundred colonists in Virginia in the autumn of 1609, there were but sixty famine-smitten wretches alive in the following June, and hardly one of these could have survived had help been delayed a few days longer.

IX.

The arrival of Gates and Somers, 1610.

Relief came to the little remnant from a quarter whence it was least expected. The emigrants of the preceding year had been sent out under the authority of Sir Thomas Gates and Sir George Somers. The two leaders were jealous of each other, and for fear either should gain advantage by prior arrival they embarked in the same ship. This ship became separated from the rest of the fleet and went ashore on the Bermudas, then uninhabited, and "accounted as an inchaunted pile of rockes and a desert inhabitation for Divels," in the words of a writer of the time; "but all the fairies of the rocks were but flocks of birds, and all the

A True Declaration of the Estate of the Colony of Virginia, 1610, p. 23.

Divels that haunted the woods were but herds of swine." Here old Sir George Somers, a veteran seaman, constructed two little cedar vessels, and provisioning them for the voyage with what the islands afforded—live turtles, and the flesh of wild hogs and waterfowl salted—the company set sail for Virginia in the spring of 1610, arriving barely in time to save the colony from extinction. Finding that their provisions would not last more than two or three weeks, they abandoned the wreck of Jamestown, crowding all the people into four pinnaces, including the two improvised cedar boats built on the Bermudas. They sailed down the river in the desperate hope of surviving until they could reach Newfoundland and get supplies from fishing vessels. The four little craft were turned back on encountering Lord De la Warr, the new governor, ascending the James to take charge of the colony. The meeting with De la Warr was bitterly regretted by the old settlers, who preferred the desperate chance of a voyage in pinnaces on a shipless sea with but a fortnight's provision to facing again the horrors of life at Jamestown.

With all the formalities thought necessary at that time, De la Warr took possession of Jamestown, now become a forlorn ruin full of dead men's bones. Gates was sent to England for a new stock of cattle, while the brave old Sir George Somers once more embarked for the Bermudas in the Patience, the little cedar pinnace which he had built

Chap. II.

Note 6.

De la Warr's arrival, 1610.

wholly of the wood of that island without a particle of iron except one bolt in the keel. In this boat
he sailed up and down until he found again "the
still vexed Bermoothes," where he hoped to secure
provisions. He died in the islands. Argall was
also sent to the Bermudas, but missed them, and
went north to the fishing banks in search of food.

Jamestown was cleansed, and with a piety characteristic of that age the deserted little church was
enlarged and reoccupied and daily decorated with

Virginia wild flowers. All the bitter experience of
the first three years had not taught the true method of settling a new country. The colony was still

but a camp of men without families, and the old
common stock system was retained. To escape
from the anarchy which resulted from a system
that sank the interest of the individual in that of
the community, it had been needful to arm De la

British Mu-
seum, MS.
21,993,
ff. 174, 178.
Instr. to
Gates and
De la
Warr.

Warr with the sharp sword of martial law. Some
of the instructions given him were unwise, some
impossible of execution. To convert the Indians
out of hand, as he was told to do, by shutting up
their medicine men or sending them to England to
be Christianized by the methods then in use, did
not seem a task easy of accomplishment, for Indian priests are not to be caught in time of war.
But De la Warr undertook another part of his in-

structions. A hundred men under two captains
were sent on a wild-goose chase up the James
River to find gold or silver in the mountains,
whither the phantom of mines had now betaken

itself. This plan originated with the London managers of Virginia affairs, and men had been sent
with De la Warr who were supposed to be skillful in "finding out mines." But being especially
unskillful in dealing with the Indians, they were
tempted ashore by savages, who offered them food
and slew them "while the meate was in theire
mouthes." The expedition thereupon turned back
at a point about forty miles above the present site
of Richmond.

Briefe Dec-
laration,
MS., Pub.
Rec. Off.

A new town was begun at the falls, in the fond
belief that two mines were near, and De la Warr
took up his residence there. Jamestown, drawing
its water from a shallow and probably polluted
well, became the seat of a fresh epidemic. In the
month of March following his arrival the governor
fled from the colony to save his own life, leaving
Virginia more than ever discredited.

Flight of
De la
Warr.

X.

As the hope of immediate profit from Virginia
died away, the colony would have been abandoned
if there had not arisen in its favor a patriotic enthusiasm which gave it a second lease of life.
Many of the great noblemen were deeply engaged
in this new agitation in favor of the unlucky colony, and none more deeply, perhaps, than Prince
Henry, the heir apparent. At Henry's request,
Sir Thomas Dale, an officer who had been employed about the prince's person, and who with
other English officers was now in the service of

Sir
Thomas
Dale, 1611.

Docs. Rel.
to Col.
Hist. N.Y.,
i, pp. 1, 2,
3, 9, 10,
16–21.

the Netherlands, was granted leave of absence to go to Virginia. Since the colony was a check to Spain, the Netherlands were supposed to have an indirect interest in the enterprise and were persuaded to continue Captain Dale's pay. De la Warr, who remained in England, was nominally governor; Gates, when present in Virginia, was the ranking officer; but for five years Dale appears to have been the ruling spirit in the colony.

The heavy hand of Dale, 1611–1616.

To induce him to go, Dale had been deceived regarding the condition of the plantation, as had been everybody else that had gone to Jamestown after the first ships sailed. The vice-admiral, Newport, was the principal reporter of Virginia affairs in England and the principal agent of the company in this deception. Dale's rough temper was already well known. It was for this, no doubt, that he had been chosen to do a rude piece of work.

A Briefe Declaration of the Plantation of Virginia, 1624, MS., Pub. Rec. Off.

On his arrival he saw the desperate state of the undertaking. He pulled Vice-Admiral Newport's beard and threatened him with the gallows, demanding "whether it weare meant that people heere in Virginia shoulde feed uppon trees."

Under the inefficient government of George Percy, who had again been placed in charge, the seedtime of 1611 was allowed to pass without the planting of corn. The Jamestown people were found by Dale "at their daily and usual work

Brit. Museum, MS., 21,993, f. 174.

bowling in the streets." But the days of unthrifty idleness were at an end. "The libertyes, ffranchises, and immunityes of free denizens and natural-born subjects of any our other dominions" promised to the colonists, were also at an end from the moment of the arrival of this sharp-set soldier and disciplinarian. Dale's pitiless use of martial law turned Virginia not exactly into a military camp, but rather into a penal settlement where men suffered for the crime of emigration. The men taken to Virginia in Dale's own company were hardly fit for anything else, and were so "diseased and crazed in their bodies" that at one time not more than sixty out of three hundred were capable of labor. The food sent with Sir Thomas Dale by the corrupt contractors was "of such qualitie as hoggs refused to eat." Sir Thomas Gates afterward made oath to its badness before the Chief Justice in London.

Briefe Declaration.

XI.

Dale regarded himself as an agent of the company. His aim was by hook or crook to make the hitherto unprofitable colony pay dividends to the shareholders, who were his employers. His relation to the emigrants was that of a taskmaster; one might, perhaps, more fitly call him a slave-driver. Instead of seeking to render the colony self-supporting by clearing corn ground, he gave his first attention to lading vessels with sassafras root, then much prized as a medicine, and cedar timber, valued especially for its odor.

The years of slavery.

During a part of Dale's time eight or nine ounces of meal and half a pint of peas was the

BOOK I.

Briefe Dec-
laration.
Percy to
Northum-
berland,
Hist. MS.,
Commis-
sion,
Rept., iii,
53, 54.

daily ration. In their declaration, made some years afterward, the surviving colonists aver that both the meal and the peas were "moldy, rotten, full of cobwebs and maggots, loathsome to man and unfit for beasts." Better men than these might have been driven to mutiny by the enforced toil and bad food. And mutiny and desertion were usually but other names for suicide under the rule of the pitiless high marshal. Some fled to the woods, hoping to reach a mythical Spanish settlement believed to be not very far away. Dale set the Indians on them, and they were brought back to be burned at the stake. Others, who in desperation or deadly homesickness resolved to venture their lives in a barge and a shallop "for their native country," suffered in various ways for their temerity. Death by shooting or hanging was clemency. One offender was put to death by the awful torture of breaking on the wheel, a penalty that Dale may have learned during his stay on the Continent.

Observa-
tions and
Travel
from Lon-
don to
Hamburgh,
p. 13.

Taylor, the water poet, has left us the sickening details of such an execution in Germany in 1616. One need not waste any sympathy on those who were hanged for stealing to satisfy hunger; death is more merciful than life to men in such a case. But one poor rogue, who thought to better his rations by filching two or three pints of oatmeal, had a bodkin run through his tongue and was chained to a tree until he perished of hunger. Though these things were twice attested by the best men in the colony, one prefers to make some allowance for their passionate resentment, and to hope that some of the horrors related are exaggerated. It is hard to believe, for example, that men unable to work were denied food, and left to creep away into the wretched burrows in the ground used for shelter, there to die unregarded in the general misery.

In 1612 a company of ten men sent out to catch fish braved the perils of the ocean in a little bark and got back to England. It was the only escape from Dale's tyranny, pitiless and infernal. "Abandon every hope who enter here" was almost as appropriate to the mouth of the James River as to the gate of Dante's hell. All letters of complaint sent to England were intercepted, and all efforts of friends of the colonists in England to succor or rescue them were thwarted by the company in London. The king's pass to one of the colonists authorizing him to leave Virginia was sent to him by his friends closely made up in a garter, to avoid the vigilance of Sir Thomas Dale.

Briefe Declaration.

Dale's administration was strongest on its military side. There was no danger that the Indians would reduce the colony to any straits while he was in charge. He gave his first attention to fortification, and he even begged for two thousand convicts out of English jails to form a line of posts from Hampton to a point a hundred miles above Jamestown. He sent Argall all the way to Mount Desert to plunder a Jesuit settlement and make prize of a French ship—an undertaking congenial

Dale's services.

to Dale's military temper and the Viking tastes of Argall. As his experience increased, Dale came to understand that other than military measures were needed to found a colony, though he never more than half comprehended the elements of the problem. In his later time he cleared more corn ground, and he could boast at his departure that Virginia contained six horses, a hundred and forty-nine neat cattle, two hundred and sixteen goats, and hogs without number. Dale set off a private garden of three acres of land to each of the old planters, on the condition that they should provide food for themselves while still giving nearly all of their time to the service of the common stock. Even this slave's-patch of private interest given to only a fraction of the colonists put some life into Virginia; but two thirds of the people were retained in the old intolerable bondage, and not even the most favored secured personal ownership of land. Dale's administration was remembered as "the five years of slavery."

Note 9.

XII.

Dale's
return.

The rough-handed soldier from the Low Countries had indeed brought the Virginia chaos into order, but it was an order almost as deadly as the preceding anarchy. Dale confessed that the government of Virginia was "the hardest task he had ever undertaken," and he got himself out of it after five years by making a theatrical return to England in 1616 with a train of Indians, including the " Princess " Pocahontas, converted, baptized with a Christian name as Rebecca, and wedded to an Englishman. He added glowing reports of the country, and proved all by exhibiting " at least sixteen several sorts of staple commodities to be raised in this plantation." For greater effect, samples of twelve of these products of the colony were sold by public auction in the open court of the company. Though Dale could show many commodities, some of which have never flourished in Virginia since his time, he left behind him not an established community, but a mere camp of unhappy men retained in the country by the sheer impossibility of getting away. After nine years of suffering, Virginia consisted of some three hundred and twenty-six men, twenty-five women and children, and graves outnumbering many times over all the living souls.

Three things had been discovered in Dale's time that were of importance to the colony. Dale had by personal experiment learned the two fishing seasons in the James River. The colonists had begun the profitable cultivation of tobacco, and the economic success of the colony was thereby assured. Lastly, even Dale's small experiment with private interest rendered the apportionment of the land and the establishment of private ownership certain to come in time. As early as 1614 it was estimated that three men working for themselves raised more corn than ten times as many when the labor was for the public stock.

XIII.

Captain Argall, who succeeded Sir Thomas Dale, was a bold and notable mariner. He had built the first Virginia vessel; he had traded with the Indians for corn with as much enterprise and address as Captain Smith had shown; he had in a small ship called the Dainty made the first experimental voyage to James River by the westward route, avoiding the long circuit by the Canaries and West Indies. It had been his fortune to be the first Englishman to see the American bison, which he found near the Potomac. He it was who by a shrewd trick had captured Pocahontas and held her as hostage; and he drove the French out of Maine, despoiling their settlement at Mount Desert. To a mastery of all the arts that make the skillful navigator he added the courteous politeness of a man of the city and the unfaltering rapacity of a pirate. As governor, he robbed the company with one hand and the hapless colonists with the other. While using the ships and men of the colony to carry on the Indian trade, he turned all the profits of it into his own wallet. The breeding animals of the colony accumulated by Dale he sold, and made no account of the proceeds. There was hardly anything portable or salable in Virginia that he did not purloin. He even plundered the property of Lady De la Warr, the widow of his predecessor. He boldly fitted out a ship belonging to Lord Rich, and sent an expedition of sheer piracy to the West Indies under an old letter of marque from the Duke of Savoy. When advices from England warned Argall that his downfall was imminent, he forthwith redoubled his felonious diligence. His chief partner in England was Lord Rich, who became the second Earl of Warwick in 1619, about the time of Argall's return, and who is known to history in his later character as a great Puritan nobleman, who served God while he contrived to better his estate with both hands by such means as troublous times put within his reach. He was not content with small pickings. Rich appears to have aimed at nothing less than wrecking the company and securing the land and government of Virginia. The first step toward this was to get a charter for a private or proprietary plantation within Virginia which should be exempt from all authority of the company and the colony. This independent government was to serve as a refuge from prosecutions for Argall and other piratical agents, and at last to possess itself of the wreck and remainder of Virginia. The second step in this intrigue was one that could have availed nothing in any time less respectful to shadowy technicalities and less prone to legal chicanery than that of James I. As we have seen, jealousy was excited in Virginia by the possibility of Captain Smith's wedding Pocahontas and setting up a claim to authority based on her inheritance from Powhatan. A tradition lingered in Virginia a hundred years later that King James questioned

Rolfe's right to intermarry with a foreign princess without the consent of his sovereign. If this had any foundation, it grew out of the value of a pretext in a time of technicality and intrigue. There may have been already a scheme to trade upon the hereditary right of Powhatan's daughter. Pocahontas died in England, leaving an infant son. Argall, on his arrival, hastened to notify the company that Opechankano, the brother and successor of Powhatan, had resolved not to sell any more land, but to reserve it for the son of Pocahontas when he should be grown. The company charged that this was a ruse to serve the ends which Argall, Rich, and others had in view. The larger plan miscarried, but Argall found his prey so tempting that he lingered longer than was safe, and got away in the nick of time by the aid of Lord Rich, who had stood guard like a burglar's pal, and who contrived to delay the ship carrying out the new governor until a small swift-sailing vessel could be sent to fetch away Argall and his varied booty of public and private plunder. In that day justice often went by favor, and Argall consigned his spoils to hands so powerful that the Virginia Company, stripped bare by his treacherous villainy, could never recover any of its lost property. The embittered colonists had the bootless satisfaction of sending over after the runaway governor twenty-four bundles of accusatory depositions.

The Companie's root of difference. MS. Rec. Va. Co., May 7, 1623.

MS. Rec. Va. Co., *passim.*

XIV.

From the first nobody reaped any profit from investments made in the new colony except the clique of merchants who had been allowed to sell wretched supplies for the distant settlers at ruinous rates. Rich and those interested with him had abundantly reimbursed themselves for all outlays on their part. The Virginia Company, swindled by commercial peculators at home, robbed by a pirate governor in America, and embarrassed by Spanish intrigues at the English court, had also been deprived of the lotteries, large and small, which had supplied money for sending eight hundred emigrants to Virginia. The lottery, which had fallen into great disrepute and had suffered "many foul aspersions," was abolished in compliance with a public sentiment. The company was tottering swiftly to a fall; vultures like Warwick were waiting longingly for its death.

But there set in once more a widespread patriotic movement in its behalf. Such movements were characteristic of that vital age when love of country was fast coming to count for more as a motive to action than loyalty to the person of a prince. "Divers lords, knights, gentlemen, and citizens, grieved to see this great action fall to nothing," came to its rescue with one final effort which resulted after some years in putting the enterprise well beyond the danger of failure. They formed auxiliary societies within the Virginia Com-

BOOK I.

pany, after the custom of corporations in that day. Each of these undertook to plant a settlement or "hundred." In one year the population rose from less than four hundred to about a thousand. The newly active element infused a more liberal spirit into the company, and set about correcting the abuses in its management.

XV.

The Great Charter, 1618.

The movement of 1618 was retarded by the disgrace into which the colony had fallen. An unbroken series of misfortunes and disappointments, the bad conduct of the company's affairs, the ill fame of Dale's remorseless tyranny, and the fresh Argall scandal, had made Virginia odious. One convict to whom the alternative was proposed, chose hanging in preference to transportation to Virginia. It was needful that something should be done to restore credit. The men who took the lead in the patriotic movement of 1618 on behalf of Virginia were mainly liberal statesmen—that Earl of Southampton who is known as the friend of Shakespeare; Sir Edwin Sandys, one of the greatest men of a great age, whose brave support of popular liberty had lost him the favor of the king; Sir John Danvers, and others. The records before the election of Sandys in 1619 were probably destroyed to conceal the guilt of the managers. We can only conjecture that the rising influence of the men who were able a few months later to over-

Pub. Rec. Off. Col. Papers, iii, 40. Disc. of the Old Va. Co.

throw the ruling party had much to do with the most notable change that took place in the conduct of affairs in the Virginia Company at this time. On the 18th of November, 1618—memorable but neglected and forgotten date—the Virginia Company, acting within the powers conferred on it by its charter, granted to the residents in Virginia a document styled a " Great Charter or Commissions of Priviledges, Orders, and Lawes." No copy of this instrument now exists, but some of its provisions have been preserved. It established a legislative body, to consist of councilors of estate and of representatives or burgesses chosen by the several "plantations" or hundreds, and it limited the power of the governor. This charter was the starting point of constitutional government in the New World. It contained in embryo the American system of an executive power lodged mainly in one person, and a Legislature of two houses. One might without much exaggeration call this paper a sort of Magna Charta of America, and it was a long and probably a deliberate step toward popular government. If the results that have followed it be considered, it can hardly be accounted second in importance to any other state paper of the seventeenth century.

Note 15.

XVI.

Not only did this admirable charter establish a representative form of government and do away

Division of land.

BOOK I.
Note 16.
with martial law, but it fairly launched the Virginians on the current of freedom and advancement
by authorizing a liberal division of land to all
those who had arrived before the departure of Sir

Aspinwall
Papers, p.
14, note.
Thomas Dale. The oldest land titles in Virginia
are deduced from the authority of the Great Charter of 1618. Communism, pernicious everywhere,

True Dec-
laration, p.
25.
is at its worst in an infant settlement. " Every
man sharked for his own bootie," says a writer
on Virginia in 1609, " but was altogether careless
of the succeeding penurie." The distribution of
land abolished the common stock system of labor,
and opened a pathway to the ambition of the
diligent.

The good
news in
Virginia.
Tidings of the great change wrought in their
condition and prospects by the new charter reached
the dwellers on the James River in the spring of
1619, and the colonists were " ravished with so
much joy " that they felt themselves " now fully
satisfied for their long labors and as happy men as

Note 17.
there were in the world." They valued their liberties as no man can who has not known the bitterness of bondage, and in 1623, when they had reason
to fear the re-establishment of the old tyranny, the
Virginia Assembly petitioned the king in these
strong words: " Rather than be reduced to live
under the like government, we desire his Majesty

Tragicall
Relation,
1623.
that commissioners may be sent over to hang us."
We have here, perhaps, the very first of the many
protests of colonial Legislatures against oppression from England.

XVII.

In 1618, before the adoption of the charter, it was concluded, in the quaint phrase of the time, "that a plantation can never flourish till families be planted and the respects of Wives and Children fix the people on the soyle," or, in simpler words, that a colony of bachelors can hardly found a state. The first ship laden with home-makers carried over ninety maids, and the company thought it necessary to promise special rewards to the men who should marry these young women. If the maids were as certified, "young, handsome, and well recommended," they needed no such dowry in a land that had hardly a woman in it. Young or old, handsome or homely, the maids did not prove a drug. Shipload after shipload of them were eagerly bought by the planters, who had to pay a round sum in the high-priced tobacco of that early time to defray the cost of transporting these wives. Besides having to pay for his wife, the planter could have her only on the condition of winning her consent; and the eager courtship that ensued on the arrival of a shipload of maids must have been one of the most amusing scenes in the settlement of America. Suitors far outnumbered the women, and the latter had things pretty much their own way. The first cargo of this interesting merchandise was landed in 1619, but as late as 1624 the women were probably in danger of setting the colonists by the ears, for the governor felt obliged to issue a proclamation threatening fine or whipping for the offense of betrothal to more than one person at a time. In 1632, thirteen years after the first shipment, we find the colony still being replenished with women sent in the same fashion. In that year, two, whose behavior during the voyage had been disgraceful, were sent back as unfit to be mothers of Virginians. The precaution could not have been of much practical use, but it indicates the early growth of a wholesome local pride. When there were house mothers in the cabins, and children born in the country, the settlers no longer dreamed of returning to England; and there was soon a young generation that knew no other skies than those that spanned the rivers, fields, and vast primeval forests of their native Virginia, which now for the first time became a home.

XVIII.

It is not the Virginia colony alone that we have seen in the crucible. The fate of English colonization was no doubt settled by the experiments made during the first years on the James River, and the story told in this chapter is but the overture to the whole history of life in the United States. In our colonizing age a settlement might be made in the heart of Africa with a far smaller loss of life than was incurred in the first sixteen years in Virginia. From 1607 to 1623 there were landed in Virginia more than six thousand people. The number that returned to England was inconsiderable, but in the year 1624, when the colony passed under a royal government, there remained alive in the colony only twelve hundred and seventy-five. Of those who came in these early years four fifths perished. A part of this loss was due to radically wrong conceptions of the nature, end, and proper methods of colonization, a part to corrupt and incompetent management in the London Company. The bad character of many of the earliest emigrants was one cause of difficulty. The writers of the time probably exaggerated this evil in order to excuse the severity of the government and the miseries into which the settlers fell. But the loss of many of the early comers must be accounted a distinct gain to Virginia. Unfitted for their environment, they were doomed to extinction by that pitiless law which works ever to abolish from the earth the improvident, the idle, and the vicious.

ELUCIDATIONS.

Note 1, page 29.

In 1889, when I visited Jamestown, there was no apparent trace of Sandy Beach which had connected the island with the mainland. This bit of sand, in the antique phrase of one of the early colonists, was "no broader than a man may well quaite a tileshard." Strachey, in Purchas, p. 1752. Jamestown is now a farm; the ruins of the church and many of the tombs in the eighteenth-century churchyard remain; but the upper end of the island is wearing away, and I picked out of the crumbling sand, far from the later burying place, human bones of earlier burials, possibly of the victims of the famines and epidemics. The walls of the magazine had been exposed by erosion. I brought away wrought nails, bits of glass grown iridescent from long burial, and an exploded bombshell of so small a caliber as to mark its antiquity. By the aid of a negro youth living on the farm I found the hearth bricks turned up in various places by the plow, and the arrangement, or rather lack of arrangement, of the town could thus be made out. My guide volunteered the information that Jamestown was "the first place discovered after the Flood." Some drawings made at the time were reproduced with an article on Nathaniel Bacon in the Century Magazine for July, 1890.

Whether Smith was injured by gunpowder and required treatment, as he asserts, or was sent home under charges, has been matter of dispute. Both accounts are correct, as is shown by the testimony of an important manuscript at Petworth House, in Surrey, which I was allowed to examine by the courtesy of Lord Leconsfield. It is from the pen of George Percy, a brother of the Earl of Northumberland, who was chosen to succeed Smith on his departure from the colony. It is not the narrative from which Purchas makes extracts, but a sequel to it. The title is " A Trewe Relacyon of the pceedinge and Ocvrrentes of momente wch have hapned in Virginia from the Tyme Sr Thomas Gates was shipwrackde vpon the Bermudes Ano. 1609 vntill my depture ovtt of the country wch was in Ano Dni 1612." It is a quarto of forty-one pages. Percy was a man of courage, but his own narrative in this little book shows that he had no qualification for the office ot governor except the rank of his family. His ill health is made an excuse for his inefficiency, but Dale's letter of May 25, 1611, shows that even the horrible events of Percy's first government had not taught him to plant corn when again left in charge. Percy naturally resents Smith's boastfulness, and bluntly accuses him of laying claim to credit that was not his. The charge that Smith, unable to control the unruly settlers at the Falls under West, advised the Indians to attack them, is supported by Percy; and a very different charge, that he stirred up the Indians to assassinate West himself, appears at a later time in Spelman's Relation, a tract that bears abundant internal evidence of the writer's mental inability to speak the truth. Percy himself relates that the Indians were already hostile to West's party, and that they had wounded and killed some of West's men in resentment of their wanton outrages. See also the account in the Oxford Tract, with the signatures of Pots and Phettiplace, for Smith's version of the affair. "Bloody-mindedness" seems not to have been a trait of Smith. But the exigency was a terrible one, for death by starvation was already impending, and only the restoration of discipline at any cost could have saved the colony from the horrible fate it met. Such a course would not have done much violence to the notions of the time, and would have found precedents in the various plots against the lives of Smith, Wingfield, and others in the colony. It is quite probable, however, that there is no truth in the story. The violent hatred of the factions will account for the suspicion.

Note 3, page 38.

Captain Smith's True Relation was sent from Virginia and was printed in London in 1608. In 1612 he published what is commonly referred to as the Oxford Tract. Its proper title is very long. The first part of it is as follows : " Map of Virginia, with a description of the Covntry, the Commodities, People, Government, and Religion. Written by Captain Smyth, sometime Governor of the Covntry. And wherevnto is annexed the proceedings of those colonies since their first departure from England," etc. The second part of the book professes to be taken from the writings of eight of the colonists, whose names are given, and to have been edited by W. S.—that is, the Reverend Dr. Symonds. A history of Virginia was first proposed in a well-considered speech by " Mr. Smith " at a meeting of the Virginia Company, April 12, 1621. This seems to have been not Captain Smith, but John Smith of Nibley. He suggested the writing of a history to preserve the memory of the worthies of Virginia, dead and living, and gave it as his opinion that no Spanish settlement of the same age afforded matter more interesting. " Which worthy speech," says the record, " had of the whole court a very great applause as spoken freely to a speciall purpose, and therefore thought fitt to be considered and put in practice in his due time. And for which also Mr. Smyth as preferring allwaies mocions of speciall consequence was exceedingly commended." MS. Records of the Virginia Company, i, 197–200. We have no means of knowing whether or not this suggestion had any relation to the production of Captain John Smith's Generall Historie, the first edition of which appeared in 1624, the last two editions in 1632. The book is a compilation of Smith's earlier works, somewhat expanded, not to say inflated. The later portions are mostly made up from the official and *quasi*-official pamphlets. Just what was Dr. Symonds's part in the preparation of the Oxford Tract and the Generall Historie it would be interesting to know. Its descriptive portions are of high value, and we are now able to control its historical errors to a certain extent. Besides these three works on Virginia, Smith published a Description of New England, 1616, New England's Trials, 1620, and Advertisements for the Unexperienced Planters of New England or Elsewhere, in 1631, the year of his death. These all contain valuable matter relating to Virginia. He also published in 1627 two works on seamanship, a Sea Grammar, and the Accidence or Pathway to Experience necessary for a Young Seaman. In 1630 he published his True Travels, a book which contains an account of his own adventures previous to his going to Virginia. More than a quarter of a century had elapsed between the occurrence of these adventures and their publication. Smith's vivid imagination had meantime no doubt greatly magnified his own exploits. It is quite impossible at this day to sift what truth there is in the True Travels from the exaggerations. Travelers in that time were not held to a very rigid account, and their first obligation seems to have been to amuse their readers. No distinct line had yet been drawn in literature between fact and fiction.

Many years ago, before I had had an opportunity to examine and compare all his writings, I rashly printed a brief argument in favor of the trustworthiness of Captain John Smith and the credibility of the Pocahontas story. I believe no person of critical judgment can make a thorough comparison of Smith's successive books without being convinced of the ineradicable tendency of his mind to romance in narrating adventure, especially his own adventure. Even his style where his vanity speaks loses something of its native directness and force. His practical writings on navigation and on the proper conduct of colonization, and his descriptions of the country and the savages, are plain, direct, and lucid. His personal morals were probably unexceptionable. One of his associates certifies to his freedom from tobacco, wines, dice, debts, and oaths. But a comparison between the statements made in the Oxford Tract and those in the Generall Historie leaves upon the mind of the critic a distinct impression of the very processes by which his adventures were exaggerated in his own memory as time elapsed. The three or four hundred savages on the Potomac (Oxford Tract, p. 32, a sufficiently marvelous story) rise to three or four thousand in the Generall Historie. Pocahontas becomes the central figure in incidents as told in 1624 in which she had no place in 1612. There is but one allusion to Pocahontas in the entire Oxford Tract p. 103), and that has to do with the charge that Smith intended to marry her. A just and witty judgment of Captain Smith was made almost in his own time by Thomas Fuller. He says: " Such his perils, preservations, dangers, deliverances, they seem to most men beyond belief, to some beyond truth. Yet we have two witnesses to attest them, the prose and the pictures, both in his own book ; and it soundeth much to the diminution of his deeds that he alone is the herald to publish and proclaim them. . . . However, moderate men must allow Captain Smith to have been very instrumental in settling the plantation in Virginia, whereof he was Governor, as also admiral of New England." Fuller's Worthies, edition of 1840, i, 276. Those who desire to see an ingenious and learned defense of Captain Smith, particularly in the matter of the Pocahontas story, will find it in an address by Mr. William Wirt Henry, published by the Virginia Historical Society. Prof. Arber's discussion of the subject in his edition of Smith's Works is sentimental rather than critical. Compare Deane's Wingfield for the other side. Unnecessary heat has characterized some of the debates about John Smith. History pitched in a shrill polemical key is not instructive and is something less than amusing. These debates center themselves on the Pocahontas story, which is of little historical importance except as it involves the trustworthiness of Smith's narrative.

The conduct of Captain Smith in the Virginia colony will be better understood if we appreciate the character of his principal opponent, Gabriel Archer. Archer's return to Virginia in 1609 and his agency in overthrowing Captain Smith are alluded to apparently in a passage in the New Life of Virginea, 1612, " In which distemper that envious man stept in, sowing plentifull tares in the hearts of all," etc. One of Archer's schemes seems to have been to establish a parliament and a complicated government at the beginning. Purchas and Strachey both take sides against Archer in his controversy with Smith. Purchas, iv, p. 1749, Oxford Tract, 22. Wingfield warned Newport of the danger of disturbance from Archer, who was " troubled with an ambitious spirit." Wingfield's Discourse, 77, 94, 95. Wingfield also says, " In all their disorders was Mr. Archer a ringleader." He adds that Radcliffe " did wear no other eies or eares than grew on Mr. Archer's head." For a bibliographical account of Smith's works the reader is referred to the valuable notes in Mr. Winsor's Narrative and Critical History of America, vol. iii, *passim.*

In the note above, as it appeared in the first impression of this volume, I attributed to Captain John Smith certain speeches and motions made by a Mr. John Smyth or Smith in the Virginia Company. Those who had examined the Manuscript Records before me had made the same attribution. But soon after the appearance of this volume I met by accident with Quaritch's Rough List No. 87, and from the list of papers of John Smith of Nibley therein, and from the manuscripts themselves, since examined by me, it became evident that he and not Captain Smith had made these wise speeches.

A Trewe Relacyon, etc., at Petworth House, as above. The Indians in sheer wantonness scraped out the brains of their dead victims with mussel shells. Percy seems to have retaliated in a way to exasperate without disabling the savages. He " burned their hawses, Ransacked their Temples, tooke downe the corpses off their deade Kings from off their Toambes [that is, the scaffold on which their well-dried remains were deposited], and caryed away their pearles, caps, and bracelets wherewith they doe decore their Kings fvneralls." (For this sacred house thus desecrated by Percy the Indians had such reverence that none but priests and chiefs were allowed to enter, and the Indians never ventured to pass it without casting some offering of tobacco, wampum, copper, or puccoon root into the water.— Strachey, 90.) When Percy had captured a chief's wife and children, the soldiers in revengeful wantonness, according to Percy's account, threw the children out of the boat and shot them in the water. The inefficient Percy was able to save the life of the " queen" or chief's wife with difficulty. West and Ratcliffe, who had overthrown Smith, are accused by Percy of unnecessary cruelty to the savages. West sailed away in the ship, leaving Jamestown to its fate. Ratcliffe was put to death with exquisite tortures. There is no doubt some truth, as there is certainly jealousy, in Percy's charge that Captain Smith was " an ambitious, unworthy, and vainglorious fellow, attempting to take all men's authorities from them," but he was neither weak, like Percy and Ratcliffe, nor visionary, like the gold-hunting Martin and the doctrinary and demagogical Archer, nor treacherous and cruel, like West. With all his faults he only was master of the situation in these early years. Percy admits that the lawful authority was that of Smith. The history of the government of Percy and his supporters seems to justify Smith's refusal to share his lawful power with incompetent factionaries.

So far the State Papers, but Percy, in his A Trewe Relacyon, adds that he caused the man to be tortured till he confessed, and he relates repulsive details of the crime. The effrontery of an official publication went so far as to deny (True Declaration, 1610), on the authority of Sir Thomas Gates, this fact so circumstantially and abundantly attested. In Peckard's Life of Ferrar, p. 158, a petition from the Virginia colony to the king is preserved in which occur these words: " To tell how great things many of us have suffered through hunger alone would be as incredible as horrible for us to repeat to your sacred ears."

See, among other authorities, A Plaine Declaration of Barmudas, in black letter, 1613, written by one of the party. Myriads of birds nested on the island. How the hogs came to be there is matter of conjecture. The writer of the Plaine Declaration makes old Sir George Somers the resourceful hero of their marvelous escape, and it was from him that the islands took the name of Somers or Summer Islands. For want of pitch, the seams of the vessels were paid with " a kind of hard lime " and some " wax cast up by the sea." Strachey's A True Reportory of the Wracke and Redemption of Sir Thomas Gates, Knight, etc., Purchas, iv, p. 1734, is also by one of the shipwrecked party. The Rev. Joseph Hunter has written with much learning, patient research, and fatiguing prolixity to disprove the theory that Shakespeare's Tempest was suggested by the wreck of Gates and Somers. He succeeds in showing its relation to another occurrence, but works of imagination do not usually have their origin in a single fact, and it is hard to resist the conviction that the Tempest, as we have it, contains more than one allusion to the wreck upon " the still vexed Bermoothes."

The beauty of the wood of certain American trees had already been noted. The communion table in Jamestown in De la Warr's time was made of black walnut. The pews were of cedar, and there were " fair, broad windows," with shutters of cedar, " to shut and open as the weather shall occasion," but there appears to have been no glass. Window glass was little used at that time, and there probably was not a glazed window in the colony. The pulpit was of cedar, and the font was " hewen hollow like a canoa." Strachey, in Purchas, p. 1755.

Some families appear to have gone to Virginia with De la Warr. The purpose to send families of wives and children and servants is expressed in A True Declaration, which was dated

1610, but, as Mr. Alexander Brown points out, issued in December, 1609.

The Tragicall Relation of 1623, and the Briefe Declaration of 1624, manuscripts in the British Public Record Office, are the most important authorities for the facts given in the text. The Briefe Declaration is rather the fuller, but the earlier paper supplies some particulars. These two formal documents are not from the same hand, and the slight difference between them in details tends rather to confirm than to shake the reader's confidence in their testimony. The names of Sir Francis Wyatt, George Sandys, and other prominent colonists appended to the Tragicall Relation are a guarantee of its good faith. It is curious to note that Raphe Hamor, whose relation is so favorable to Dale, and who held the post of secretary under Dale and that of vice-admiral under Argall, signs this paper, which is a severe impeachment of Sir Thomas Smythe's administration of the affairs of the company before 1619. Hamor's True Discourse has heretofore usually been taken as an authority, but after reading the documents in the Public Record Office one is compelled to believe that Hamor, or perhaps one might say Dale, under cover of his secretary, misrepresents the state of the colony, and makes promises to those who may emigrate that it was hardly possible to carry out. The Discourse of the old Virginia Company (Colonial Papers, iii, 40), and other papers in the Public Record Office relating to the strife between the company and the Court, throw light on this period. The half-apologies for Dale's cruelties in Smith's Generall Historie, book iv, prove their existence. " For amongst them, so hardened in evil," says this writer, " the fear of a cruel, painful, and unusual death more restrains them than death itself." See also Hamor, p. 27. There is a letter from Whitaker appended to Hamor's Discourse. Though apparently an incidental letter, it bears marks of having been procured for purposes of vindication. Its defensive tone goes to show that the character of Dale's tyranny had transpired in England. Whitaker praises Sir Thomas Dale mainly for being religious and valiant, and says that he had " great knowledge in Divinity and good conscience in all his doings ; both which bee rare in a martiall man." In Whitaker's Good Newes of Virginia, 1613, there is no praise of Sir Thomas Dale. That Dale was famous for his severity before he left Europe is manifest from the phrase used by the Jesuit Biard, " Le Mareschal Thomas Deel que vous auez ouy estre fort aspre en ses humeurs." Relation, chap. xxxiii.

See in this and the preceding chapter the whole account of his savage temper toward his French prisoners, etc. It has been the custom of our older writers to speak of Dale's administration only in praise, but careful weighing of the original authorities shows that Dale was utterly pitiless in the cruelty of his discipline and unjust in his detention of the old planters, and that when he left the colony he was more generally execrated than any other man that ruled in these early days, not even excepting his successor, Argall. Dale's severity was serviceable in carrying the enterprise through straits, but the reports of his harshness brought the colony into disrepute and checked immigration. The detestation of Dale was shared by the best men in Virginia, yet it is to be remembered that the savagery of Dale's government was due not wholly to the brutal temper of the man, but partly to the age and the school in which he had been bred. Legal torture was in use long after this. The Clarendon Papers, quoted by Southey, state that at Henley-on-Thames, as late as 1646, it was ordered that a woman's tongue should be nailed to a tree for complaining of the tax levied by Parliament. The cruel practices of the agents of the Virginia Company are paralleled by those of the East India Company at the same time. "Before they were intrusted with martial law they made it a rule to whip to death or starve to death those of whom they wished to get rid." Mills, British India, i, 38. Even that champion of popular liberty, Sir Edwin Sandys, found it in his heart to approve of Dale's course while admitting its harshness. He said to the court of the Virginia Company of the 17th of November, 1619, that "Sir Thomas Dale, building upon these foundations with great and constant severity, reclaymed almost miraculously those idle and disordered people, and reduced them to labor and an honest fashion of life." MS. Records of the Virginia Company. Compare also Sir Thomas Smythe's defense, note to Aspinwall Papers in IV Massachusetts Historical Collections, ix, p. 1. My citations from the Tragicall Relation and Briefe Declaration are partly from the originals in the British Public Record Office, which I carefully examined in 1885, but the first of these is printed in Neill's Virginia Company, and the Briefe Declaration was published by the State of Virginia in 1874 in a Senate document entitled Colonial Records of Virginia. Very good abstracts of both papers appear in Sainsbury's Calendar. I cite the Discourse of the Old Virginia Company from the MS. in the British Public Record Office. I do not remember to have seen it in print.

Book I.

Note 10,
page 49.

Birch's Court of James I, i, 415. Chamberlain to Carleton, June 22, 1616: "Sir Thomas Dale is arrived from Virginia, and brought with him some ten or twelve old and young of that country, among whom is Pocahuntas, daughter of Powhatan, married to one Rolfe, an Englishman. I hear not of any other riches or matter of worth, but only some quantity of sassafras, tobacco, pitch, tar, and clapboard, things of no great value unless there were plenty, and nearer hand. All I can hear of it is, that the country is good to live in, if it were stored with people, and might in time become commodious. But there is no present profit to be expected."

Note 11,
page 49.

The Discourse of the Old Virginia Company, an exceedingly interesting manuscript in the British Record Office, makes it appear that as late as 1618 the colonists had no thought of staying in Virginia, and even the directors at home were interested only in making money out of tobacco and sassafras, with little or no care to plant a permanent colony. Some allowance must be made, perhaps, for the *ex-parte* nature of this paper, but its tone and the high character of those who offered it give reason to trust it. Colonial Papers, iii, 40. Answer of the Virginia Company to Queries of the Privy Council in 1625.

Note 12,
page 49.

We may trust Hamor's True Discourse, p. 17, for some of these details, though the book generally is discredited by the account given in the Tragicall Relation, which Hamor himself signed with others in 1623. A comparison of all these authorities makes it evident that only eighty-one who were ranked as "farmers" derived any benefit from Dale's three-acre division, while about two hundred others were probably left in unmitigated bondage.

Note 13,
page 51.

"And to protect Captain Argall from being called to an account for his government under shew of a new plantation to be set up in Virginia by Captain Argall and his partners, whereof the said earl (Warwick) hath since appeared to be one (which yet to this day hath had no beginning), there was procured a patent to the said captain and his associates for the said new plantation ; whereby he and his Company, their heirs and assigns (save only in time of defence by war), were exempted from all power, authority, and jurisdiction to be from hence derived or there established, that so he might reign there as great and absolute master, without law or controulment, and without the fear of ever being called to any future reckoning. . . . Whatsoever was remaining at that time in the colony belonging to the public . . . he converted it in a manner wholly to his own private use and possession, the very public lands cultivated, the Company's tenants and servants, their rents, corn and tributes of corn, their kine and other cattle, their stores and other provisions ; whereby the company, being disabled in all appearance of ever setting up the same again or to bear the great burden of public charge both at home and abroad, being thus stripped of all revenue, the said Company must have failed and decayed and the whole colony have fallen in time into the hands of the said captain and his association to be there established, which seemeth to have been his prime and original desire. . . . This course of depredation and roving not sufficing as likely to receive encounter and check from hence, new engines were used, some to dishearten and some to disgrace the Company, that so as it seemeth they might in time obtain the plantation and leave it as a prey to the said captain, his friends and followers, etc." Burk's History of Virginia, Appendix, vol. i. The extract is from the document known as The Company's Chief Root of Differences, etc. I have compared this copy with that in the MS. Records of the Virginia Company, Library of Congress, and find only slight verbal differences. At the instance of Warwick the authors of this paper—Lord Cavendish, Sir Edwin Sandys, and John and Nicholas Ferrar—were put under arrest in their own houses for this "impertinent declaration." The Warwick party had made "threats of blood" to deter Southampton from complaining to the king.

Note 14, page 53.

Birch's Court and Times of James the First, i, 311. Chamberlain to Carleton, May 16, 1614 : "Sir Thomas Gates is come from Virginia, and brings word that plantation will fall to the ground if it be not presently supplied. He speaks of wonderful commodities that are to be had there if we could but have patience and would be at the cost to bring them to perfection." Out of this necessity for some present support came the great lottery. It was recommended by the Privy Council to the Mayor of Canterbury, February 22, 1615. There was a "running lottery" of smaller adventures in Paul's Churchyard before the "great standing lottery" was instituted, and then there were other "running lotteries" "in many other places after." Purchas, p. 1773. No doubt there were corruptions and abuses in these lotteries. The merchants prospered while Virginia languished. Its unpopularity is attributed to "malignant tongues," in the MS. Records of the

Virginia Company, i, 158, and the overthrow of the lottery may have been part of the plot of those who sought soon after to wreck the company itself.

My attention was first attracted to the date of the Great Charter by a minute in the handwriting of Secretary Williamson in the Public Record Office, as follows: "Those Adventurers & Planters by Vertue of ye sd Lettrs Patent of Incorporacōn &c. made a Great charter of Lawes and Ordrs for ye governmt of the Country. It bore date at London Nov 13th 1618." Col. Pprs. i, 11. A note to the Aspinwall Papers, 14, refers to certain land grants which cite the Great Charter of November 13th. Following these two authorities I gave the same date in the first and second edition of this work. I was aware that Yeardley's Instructions, printed in the Virginia Magazine of History, are dated the 18th, and Wyatt's Instructions refer to Yeardley's "commission" as dated the 18th. I have now examined the land grants recorded in the First Book of Patents in the office of the Register of Lands at Richmond. A large number of the earlier ones refer to the Great Charter as authority, and they uniformly give the same date, the 18th. The evidence is thus convincing in favor of the later date. I defer any fuller treatment of the character and influence of the charter to a later volume of this series.

The Code of Lawes, Divine, Morall and Martiall, by which Dale reigned was edited and published by Strachey in 1612, and reprinted in Force's Tracts, vol. iii. This code appears to have had no other sanction than the approval of Sir Thomas Smythe, the governor of the company. The beneficial effect of these laws is maintained in Hamor's Discourse, in Rolfe's Relation, and in certain letters of Dale in the Record Office. It was not, indeed, the government by martial law, but Dale's abuse of his power, that wrought the mischief. After the emancipation the old settlers lived in perpetual terror lest some turn of the wheel should put them once more in the power of Sir Thomas Smythe and his divine and martial laws. See especially the Additional Statement appended to the Discourse of the Old Virginia Company. On the long and bitter dissension that resulted in the overthrow of the company, see Arthur Woodnoth's Short Collection of the most remarkable Passages from the Original to the Dissolution of the Virginia Company, a rare work of great value to the historian of this period.

CHAP. II.

Note 17,
page 56.

Rolfe's Relation has it that the ship which brought Yeardley brought also the news of the election of Sandys and John Ferrar. But Yeardley arrived in Virginia on the 18th of April (O. S.), and Sir Thomas Smythe's resignation did not take place until ten days later. Manuscript Records of the Virginia Company. The news that Sir George Yeardley did bring was no doubt that the power of Sir Thomas Smythe and his party was broken, and that the actual control of affairs was in the hands of such men as Sandys, Southampton, Cavendish, Danvers, and the two Ferrars. The whole policy of the company indicates that the new party was really in power, and the appointment of such a man as Yeardley was probably the work of the rising party. The records before the resignation of Sir Thomas Smythe were probably destroyed for purposes of concealment.

Note 18,
page 57.

Manuscript Book of Instructions, etc., Library of Congress. Letter to the Governor and Council by the ship Marmaduke, August 12, 1621. A proposal to send women had been made seven years earlier. Commons Journal, i, 487, May 17, 1614. Extract from Martyn's Speech (for which he was reprimanded): "That they require but a few honest Labourers burthened with Children.—Moveth, a committee may consider of the means for this, for Seven Years; at which some of the Company may be present." On November 17, 1619, Sir Edwin Sandys pointed out in the court of the company that the people of Virginia "were not settled in their mindes to make it their place of rest and continuance." "For the remedying of the Mischiefe and for establishing a perpetuitie of the Plantation," he proposed the sending of "one hundred young maides to become wives." Manuscript Records of the Virginia Company, i, 44, 45. Two women, the first in the colony, had arrived in September, 1608. Oxford Tract, 47. There were women in Gates's party in 1610. It was even reported that some English women had intermingled with the natives. Calendar Colonial Papers, i. 13. An allowance of food to women in De la Warr's time is proof that women were there. In 1629 there was living Mistress Pearce, "an honest, industrious woman," who had been in Virginia "near twenty years." Rolfe (a copy of whose Relation is among the Duke of Manchester's MSS. now in the British Public Record Office) sets down a remainder of seventy-five of the three hundred and fifty-one persons in the colony at Dale's departure, as women and children. It is worth recalling here that D'Ogeron, who governed Santo Domingo in 1663 and after, supplied the buccaneers with wives brought from France; and the plan was also put into practice in Louisiana about a century later than the Virginia experiment, and the same expedient, as is well known, was resorted to in Canada. In Virginia more pains were taken to have all the women thus imported of a good character than in some of the French colonies.

The belief that these maids were " pressed " or coerced into going is probably erroneous. See the speech of Sandys, July 7, 1620, Manuscript Records of the Virginia Company. He says, " These people (including the maids) are to be provided as they have formerly beene, partlie by printed publication of the supplies indicated, together with the conditions offered to these publique tennants, partlie by help of such noble friends and others in remote parts as have formerlie given great assistance." The notion that some of the maidens were pressed seems to have had its rise in the counterfeiting of the great seal and the issuing of forged commissions to press maidens for " breeders for the King " in the Bermudas and Virginia in order to extort money. One Owen Evans was accused of such practices in October, 1618 (Sainsbury, p. 19), and one Robinson was hanged, drawn, and quartered for this or similar offences in November of the same year (Birch's Court of James I, 108). In order to encourage the adventurers or shareholders to subscribe to the sending of maids, a town was laid off in Virginia to be called Maydstown. The subscribers were to be allowed shares in this town. Manuscript Records, May 20, 1622, on the general subject; also Records under date of November 3, 1621, and the 17th of the same month, June 11, and November 21, 1621, and the manuscript book in the Library of Congress, which I refer to in these notes as Manuscript Book of Instructions, pp. 76 and 89. I may remark here that this book has not been in use in recent times for reference. Its origin is uncertain, nor can the authorities of the library tell where it came from. It was compiled in the latter part of the seventeenth century, judging from internal evidence, and was perhaps kept among the records of the colony for reference on what we should call constitutional questions. I found a loose memorandum laid in its pages in the handwriting of Thomas Jefferson, to whom the book probably once belonged.

CHAPTER THE THIRD.

THE PROCESSION OF MOTIVES.

I.

THE cause of the sorrows of Virginia will be more plainly seen if we turn again to the motives that propelled Englishmen to plant a colony. The chief mistake lay in the main purpose. If the founding of a state had been other than a secondary and remote end, the managers might have sent at first families and not bachelors, farmers and not gentlemen, laborers and not riff-raff. But more visionary motives dominated the action. A state was planted, but something else was mainly intended by the first projectors. The work seemed continuous, but the end in view shifted and the actors gradually changed. The only motive that held from first to last, and ran through all the rest, was the rivalry with Spain.

The colonies attempted by Frobisher and Gilbert were to serve as relays in the work of exploration for a sea passage to the Pacific and the search for mines, but they mark strongly the influence of the Spanish example on English projects. Ralegh was a lifelong opponent in peace and war of Spanish intrigue and aggression, and his efforts to plant colonies in the virgin land were suggested by a

73

knowledge of the almost exhaustless treasure that flowed into Spanish coffers from America. The opportune capture of a Spanish carack bound homeward from Mexico with letters describing the wealth of Mexican mines brought the support of English merchants to Ralegh's undertaking. Imbued with the same spirit, Ralegh's governor wrote from Roanoke Island in 1585 that his colony would be a means of deliverance from the domination of Spain, "whose strength doth altogether grow from the mines of her treasure." In the perilous isolation of the little company on Roanoke Island, Lane assures himself that God will feed his men by means of ravens rather than suffer their "enemies the papists" "to triumph at the overthrow of this most Christian action." The home-staying English of that age were spurred to colony-planting by three main motives—cupidity, patriotic feeling, and religious zeal—and all of these were provoked by emulation and jealousy of Spain.

Lane to Sydney. Aug. 12, 1585. Sainsbury.

Lane to Walsingham. Aug. 12, 1585. Sainsbury.

Note 1.

II.

Delusions in colony-planting.

The prolonged movement for a colonial establishment, which extended over the latter half of the reign of Elizabeth and almost the whole of the reign of James I, was kept alive by delusions. The ultimate ends for which colonies were proposed and planted in the last quarter of the sixteenth and the first quarter of the seventeenth century were none of them attained. The movable passage through North America to the Pacific was still leading explorers a merry dance when the first Jamestown emigrants sailed in 1606, and gold mines of comminuted mica, of iron pyrites, of Indian mineral paints, and of pure fable were potent attractions for some time after. The gradual increase of geographical knowledge caused the "South Sea" to take shelter in the unknown region behind the mountains, and the gold mines reported by Indians and discovered by sanguine prospectors were somehow lost in the interminable forests. In this exigency the first colony must have perished for want of support if new hopes as illusive as the old had not moved the English people to avert such a calamity.

The production of commodities which the ungenial climate of the British Islands refused to grow was thought of from the beginning, and they became after 1616 the main hope of wealth from Virginia. It seemed grievous that England should spend her money in buying wine and silk from southern Europe and naval stores from the Baltic. The only maxim of political economy generally accepted in that day was that a nation is enriched by getting money from abroad and keeping it at home. The precious metals constituted the only recognized riches. Laws were made to restrain the exportation of gold and silver, and sumptuary laws to discourage the consumption of those things that must be bought of the foreigner. Efforts to raise in Great Britain the products of the Mediterranean region would have proved successful if the

Commodities.

For example, Carlisle's treatise, Anderson's Commerce, year 1583.

climate had been half as favorable to such enterprises as the government. The arguments advanced in favor of the possibility of producing
wine in England did much, no doubt, to secure the
sunshine of royal favor for experiments made to
that end, but climatic conditions were inexorable.
King James busied himself to no profit in raising
mulberry trees and nursing a private stock of silkworms, in imitation of Henry IV, the reigning
King of France, who succeeded in producing co-
coons in the Tuileries but not in making silk
culture profitable in the north of France. Mulberries were first planted in England in 1608, two
years after the sailing of the Virginia argonauts.
James sent circulars to persons of influence among
his subjects asking them to cultivate mulberry
trees, and, in the years immediately following, the
silk fever ran its course alongside the excitement
about the great lottery in behalf of the Virginia
colony. Hakluyt, spreading sails for America in
every breeze, hastened to announce at the first
mention of silk culture that mulberry trees, "apt to
feed silke wormes to make silke," were a "chiefe
commoditie" of Virginia.

The first principles that govern colony-planting
were not yet understood. It was proposed to force
everything from a forlorn camp of men dwelling
under roofs of bark and sedge, environed by treacherous foes and in constant peril of starvation. The
raising of silkworms was begun in Virginia in 1613,
and before the colony was nine years old it was

able to send to England silk that doubtless had
cost more than a hundred times its market value.
The experiment came to nothing. It could not
have happened otherwise amid the miseries of
those early years. The rats, which opportunely
destroyed the eggs of the silk moth, were made to
bear the responsibility for the failure.

Silk was little known in England at the begin- A new silk
ning of Elizabeth's reign, but it came into great fever.
request a few years later. In 1617 Lord Carew Cal. Dom.
declares that there is "a madness for silk instead S. P.
of cloth." This rage for silk led to the establish- James I, p.
ment of silk manufacturing in England; throw- 428.
sters, dyers, and weavers were brought to England
from abroad and settled in Spitalfields, "the
cheap end of its metropolis," and in Moorfields.
It seemed more than ever important to produce
silk in the king's dominions, in order to supply
these manufacturers with material without impor-
tation from alien lands. Accordingly, a new effort
was made in 1620 to secure raw silk from Virginia.
The Earl of Southampton, ever eager to promote
the Virginia colony, "writt into Italy, France, and
Spayne" for silkworm "seed"; the king gave
some from his own stock, and the expert who had
charge of the king's worms was sent over to look
after the business. A French book on the sub-
ject was translated to instruct the colonists. The Pory's Re-
first Virginia Assembly in 1619 had passed a law Rec. Off.
to promote the raising of the mulberry. To save
expense, the colonists at this time, or later, planted

BOOK I.

Phil.
Trans. I,
201.

Hening i,
14.

Original
Records of
Colony
of Va.

Note 2.

1655.

the trees in hedgerows and mowed them with a
scythe. In 1621 orders were sent from England
that none but members of the Council and the
heads of hundreds should wear silk, unless they
had made it themselves. The prohibition shows
how general was the craze for silk clothing. The
climate of Virginia proved genial enough, but the
massacre of 1622, the bitter Indian conflicts that
ensued in 1623, and the epidemic of the same year,
following one another swiftly, were enough to an-
nihilate a hundred feeble projects. The real doom
of silk-raising, however, came from the fact that
the culture of tobacco in virgin soil was incalcu-
lably more profitable and vastly less troublesome
to pioneers than hatching silkworms' eggs in one's
pocket or bosom, or sleeping with them in a small
box under one's bolster and covering them in the
warm bed on rising. The project was blighted
in the bud by adverse economic conditions—a
killing frost more deadly to such enterprises than
an ungenial climate. But a lesson in economic
principles is one of the hardest for men to learn.
Long after the colony had become prosperous,
English projectors and Virginia experimenters
tried again and again to supplant tobacco with
silk. If we may credit the report, Virginia furnished a coronation robe of silk for Charles I,
and Charles II certainly wore silk from worms
hatched and fed in his Virginia dominions. One
Esquire Digges brought Armenians to Virginia to
attend his worms. But in the Reformed Virginia

Silkworm, by Hartlib, the friend of Milton, it is announced that a young lady had discovered that silkworms would care for themselves on the trees, " to the instant wonderful enrichment of all the planters there, requiring neither cost, labour, or hindrance in any of their other employments." It is also suggested on the eager title-page of the pamphlet that " the Indians, seeing and finding that there is neither Art, Pains, or Skill in the thing," will " incontinently fall to raising silk." Not only were the gentle savages, and especially their women and children, to devote themselves to silk, but the American caterpillar—" the natural silkworm " as it was called—was expected to spin for the market if his cocoon could be " refined."

Comp. Va. Richly Valued, 1650, and Leah and Rachel, 1656.

Note 3.

By 1666 the silk delusion had passed, and the Virginia Assembly repealed all acts for the encouragement of mulberry trees. Ten years later, Glover, the botanist, found many of these trees still standing as melancholy witnesses to the waste of energy by the earlier promoters and settlers of the colony. Almost every other American colony made the same experiment for itself, and Virginia renewed its endeavors from time to time, each generation forgetting what its fathers had learned.

Hening ii, 242.

Phil. Trans. XI, 628.

III.

Along with the silk fever went the silk-grass craze. Ralegh's people had seen the Indians wearing garments woven of the fiber of the *Yucca filamentosa*, the " Adam's needle and thread " of

Silk-grass.

1585.

BOOK I.

A Briefe
and True
Report of
the New
Found
Land of
Virginia.

our popular speech.   Hariot, in his account of it,
declares that "the like grows in Persia," and that
much of the "silk-works" coming thence to
Europe was made of this fiber.   He probably
confounded the yucca with the ramie plant of the
East, of which grass cloth is made.   Of the yucca
fiber taken to England in 1585, "a piece of silk
grogram" was made, and of course pronounced
"excellent good"; it was even presented to the
queen.   The coarse and rather brittle fiber of this
plant was exalted by enthusiasts into something
nearly equal to silk.   Ordinances for planting it
were sent from England ; at least one legislative
act in its favor was passed by the Virginia Assembly, and the most foolish hopes were entertained

Proceed-
ings of Va.
Assembly,
1619.
2d N. Y.
Hist.
Society
Coll. iii,
348.

regarding the profit to be had from it.   By 1619 it
had come to be called "silk flax," and it was then
advocated for homelier uses, such as cordage and
linen, and every householder was compelled by
law to set a hundred plants ; the governor himself
set five thousand.   In 1624 it is spoken of as "a
commoditie of speciall hope and much use."

There were by this time those who ventured to
say that the silk-grass enterprise was "full of diffi-
cultie"; but the managers in England easily got

rid of this objection by attributing the difficulty
to "negligence and want of experience."   They
were just then intent on finding some commodity
that would take the place of tobacco, which was
frowned upon by both court and Parliament.   In
spite of all discouragement, the hope of good re-

sults from the yucca fiber outlasted that generation, and was in full vigor in 1649, sixty-four years
after Hariot's mistake.

IV.

It was also proposed to produce wine in Virginia for English consumption. No more gold
and silver should go out of the realm to buy port
and canary to the profit of foreigners and the im-
poverishment of the good and loyal subjects of his
Majesty. The instructions on this point were clear,
and before the Virginia exiles had secured bread
to stay their hunger they had made wine of the
sour wild grapes of the country. French vine-
dressers were sent over a little later and were forbidden to plant tobacco, but were compelled to
employ themselves about vines, with the care of
silkworms for variety. In 1621 these Frenchmen
sent to England a cask of wine, the arrival of which
was duly celebrated. Other experimental casks of
wine were afterward sent to England from America
at long intervals, but without decreasing the profits
of wine growers in the Old World.

All the commodities sought from Virginia were
unsuited to conditions in a new country. To the
folly of making such experiments at all where living itself was an experiment, the managers added
the folly of crowding a multiplicity of problematic
enterprises on the colony at the same time. With
a virgin continent in which to produce novelties,
all things seemed possible in an age so hopeful.

Wine.

MS. Rec.
Va. Co. i,
343.

Other
products
sought.

7

Book I.

Nova Brit-
tania.

Timber
and naval
stores.

MS. Rec.
Va. Co. 31
May and 23
June, 1620.

Note 4.

Plants of every clime grew rank in the imagination of projectors. Virginia was a wonderland,
and it was readily believed without evidence that
the "soyle and clymate" were "very apt and fit
for sugar canes"; "also linseed and rapeseeds to
make oiles," as a black-letter pamphlet of 1609 expresses it. Along with "orenges, limons, and almonds," this official writer proposes to plant "an-
niseeds, rice, cummin, cottonwool, carroway seeds,
ginger, madder, olives, oris, sumacke," and, as if
this breathless list were not enough for one new
land, he adds, "and many such like that I can not
now name." If we may trust the publications of
the company, various West India plants were tried
in the very first days of the colony, while the three-
fold peril of death from famine, pestilence, and savage war was imminent.

But it was not enough to wring from an infant
colony the products of the south; those derived
from the north of Europe were straightway to
be got there also. German millwrights—"Dutch
carpenters," in the phrase of the records—were
brought from Hamburg by John Ferrar to build
Virginia sawmills; timber was still sawed by hand
in England. Pitch, tar, and potash were to be
produced by Poles sent out for the purpose in the
second year of the colony. Patriotism dictated
that England should be relieved of her dependence
on foreign countries for naval stores. Virginia
had forests: why should she not produce these
things?

It had been found that the savages eagerly received glass beads in exchange for corn and peltries. Nothing more was required to prove the profitableness of glass-making. Some Germans were sent to the colony in 1608, and glass works were established. For some reason no proper materials were available at first, and it became necessary to request that sand might be sent from England to make Virginia glass of at the glass works in the woods near Jamestown. The German glass blowers were prone to run away to the Indians, among whom work was lighter and food more abundant. The tribesmen encouraged these desertions by providing dusky wives for the men whose skill with tools and weapons they valued highly. In 1621 the glass business was revived, and this time it was intrusted to Italian workmen. About the same time iron works were established at Falling Creek, with "forty skilled workmen from Sussex to carry them forward." Twenty-five ship carpenters were sent to ply their trade on the James River, and it was also arranged that oil was to be distilled from walnuts by the "apothecaries." George Sandys was sent over in July, 1621, to have entire control of all schemes for staple commodities. There was a certain fitness in intrusting these creatures of the imagination to a poet. Pineapples, plantains, and other fruits were to be started forthwith. There was once again great hope from the "rich commodity of silk," an endowed school for Indians was founded, and the little Virginia

CHAP. III.

Glass-making.

Note 5.

Iron works.

Note 6.

pool became iridescent with many frail bubbles. The sudden and frightful massacre by the savages in March, 1622, obliterated instantly all vain and premature projects. This calamity did not cause the failure of these foredoomed schemes; it only saved them from a painful and lingering death, and provided their friends with a decent epitaph for them. The people who survived the massacre were decimated by an epidemic in the following year. What strength they could spare from frequent battles with the savages they spent in growing corn and tobacco, which last, of all the things tried, proved to be the only commodity profitable for export.

V.

Against tobacco King James had written a book. It was denounced in Parliament and regarded by all public-spirited men as an evil. Nevertheless, it turned the scale and saved the colony. In colony-planting the problem is fundamentally an economic one, and economic problems are solved by coarse and homely means. John Rolfe, the

first Englishman that ventured to wed an Indian, planted the first tobacco at Jamestown in 1612, and by 1616 the better West India variety had perhaps been substituted for the harsh kind grown by the Virginia Indians, and by them called "uppowoc" or "apooke." Tobacco prospered and was profitable, to the disgust of the pedantic king and the sorrow of all who had cherished hopes of beautiful

products from a colony upon which so much poetic sentiment had been lavished. Neither gold
nor spices came as had been expected; the strings
of pearls seen by Ralegh's men were not again to
be found, or were perhaps transformed on investi-
gation into wampum beads; the silver mine once
discovered on the upper James had vanished forever; tropical fruits refused to grow; even madder and woad failed, and, though the indigo plant
would readily mature, nobody knew how to manufacture the dye. Silk was troublesome and unprofitable, shipbuilding, and such coarse but patriotic products as naval stores had come to naught.
But the detestable "weed," as King James had
dubbed it, throve apace. As early as 1617 the
waste margins of the broad streets of Jamestown were planted with it by the eager settlers.
The English merchants grasped at the profits
of it, the farmers of the customs rejoiced in the
heavy duties imposed on it, and a powerful mercenary interest in the prosperity of Virginia was
established. By 1624, when the Virginia Company was dissolved, the danger that the colony
would be abandoned as a result of Spanish intrigues, Indian massacres, or prolonged discouragement had passed away. Public spirit, patriotism, and religious enthusiasm no longer guarded
it as a feeble house plant. It had struck root in
the outdoor soil of human self-interest and its life
was assured. From that time the colony that had
been for seventeen years a fairyland to dreamers

Note 8.

BOOK I.

Note 9.

in England and a perdition to its inhabitants, became a sober money-making enterprise, uninteresting to enthusiasts and philanthropists.

VI.

Motives of sentiment.

In the preceding sections of this chapter we have traced what may be called the series of commercial motives that, sometimes in succession, often in co-operation, propelled the Virginia movement. The agitation for a colony was primarily a commercial one. The London or Virginia Company by which it was carried forward had been organized in the form of the great trading corporations of the time, such as the Muscovy Company and the East India Company, and it was expected to yield large returns. But though commercial in form and purpose, the Virginia Company from the outset was able to appeal successfully in every emergency to motives that were far from mercenary. Into the chain-threads of commercial enterprise was woven a woof of patriotic feeling and religious sentiment.

VII.

Rise of the patriot party in the Virginia Company.

Dale's empty-handed return, and Argall's homecoming with hands full of the spoil of both colony and colonists, were severe blows to the hope of profit from Virginia, and thereafter commercial motives fell to a second place. The company began to pass more and more out of the control of traders like Sir Thomas Smyth and Alderman

Johnson, and the corrupt clique of predatory merchants, as well as out of the reach of voracious noblemen like Warwick. More and more it passed into the hands of the great liberal statesmen whose leader was the incorruptible Sir Edwin Sandys, a man of rare gifts and knowledge and of great resoluteness. These men had suffered some disappointment, no doubt, in their struggle for parliamentary freedom in England. They might have succeeded better had their antagonist been a strong king, but against the pusillanimity, the vanity, the vacillation, and the pedantic dogmatism of James little permanent headway could be made. Without relinquishing the conflict in the House of Commons, they took it up in the Quarter Courts of the Virginia Company. In this new field they found themselves afresh confronted by the obstinacy of the king, who was stirred up to oppose them by the discarded governor, Sir Thomas Smyth, and his friends, by Warwick, and by all the partisans of high prerogative and all the advocates of the Spanish match. "Bedchamber men" and others about the king's person were engaged to work upon the king to come to the rescue of Sir Thomas Smyth's "honor." The Spanish ambassador Gondomar, who had spies in the Virginia Company, took pains to feed James's discontent. He told the king that it was time for him to look into the Virginia courts, which were held in the great hall of the house of the Ferrar family. Too many of the king's nobility and gentry resorted

Woodnoth's Short Collection, p. 6.

Peckard's Ferrar, 113.

thither, in order to be in company with the popular Lord Southampton and the dangerous Sandys. They were deep politicians, and they entertained designs beyond a tobacco plantation. Their leaders, he said, were "subtle men of high courage who regarded neither his master nor their own."

Sir Edwin Sandys.

Sandys, as assistant to Sir Thomas Smyth and virtual governor, had already succeeded in establishing in Virginia a constitutional state with a representative government. He was furthering plans for the foundation of the little separatist state of New Plymouth, and his enemies set agoing tales that he had dark designs of removing with the Pilgrims to America, in order to found a democratic state there. In 1619 Sir Thomas Smyth tendered his resignation, and the company, to his surprise, it would appear, accepted it, and chose Sandys to his place. When, in 1620, his first year of government drew to a close, Sir Edwin Sandys erected an elegant ballot-box in the midst of the hall of the Ferrars, that the brilliant assemblage of noblemen, knights, gentlemen, and merchants might by a secret vote exercise the right of choice without any constraint. Just as the assemblage was about to begin voting, two clerks of the signet were announced with a message from the king forbidding the company to choose Sandys. "Choose the devil, if you will, but not Sir Edwin Sandys," was one form in which the king expressed his aversion. Southampton, braving the king's displeasure, allowed himself to

Royal Hist. MS. Comm. viii, II 45

The king's interference.

1620.

be elected, with Sandys for deputy. In June, 1621, both Southampton and Sandys were imprisoned. This attracted attention to Virginia as a "refuge from a more oppressive government in England." In three months' time twenty-five ships set sail for the colony, which gained an impetus from the king's opposition that put it beyond the danger of destruction by the calamities of the next two years. Even before the massacre and pestilence of 1622 and 1623, Southampton was assured by friends at court that it would come to "push of pike," and that the company would be overthrown. The charter of the company was vacated in 1624, but free government had so taken root in the colony that it could never afterward be quite extirpated. A new English state with a popular government had been founded of deliberate purpose by a group of English statesmen, at the head of which, and easily first, was Sir Edwin Sandys, whose great service to the people and nation that were to come has been almost forgotten.

VIII.

We shall not have taken a just account of Virginia colonization if we do not reckon religious motives among the many forces that carried that wavering enterprise to success. From the excitement about American exploration and colonization the English church caught its first missionary impulse. The Indian captives brought from America at various times gave to Englishmen

CHAP. III.

A land of freedom.

Note 10.

Religious propagandism.

the novel sight of men and women from beyond the bounds of Christendom; people who had never been baptized, and had never learned to wear English garments, "naked slaves of the devil," as one of the early Virginia clergymen described them. To the benevolent desire of Englishmen for the deliverance of the savages from devil-worship and semi-nudity, there was added the natural wish for ecclesiastical extension. The separation of England from the Roman hierarchy had been a blow to the aspiration for an unattainable catholicity cherished in one form or another by Christian ecclesiastics of almost every school. It was not possible that the great men who were leaders of the English church in the reigns of Elizabeth and James should be content with the narrow limits of "the little English paddock," while Spanish conquerors and missionary priests were winning for the Roman communion a new and vast dominion in America. English ecclesiastics felt keenly the

Note 11.

reproach made against them by the Roman Catholics that they were not "converters of infidels."

Zeal of the clergy.

Perhaps the earliest of all Anglican missionaries was Robert Hunt, the first minister in Virginia, a light shining in a dark place indeed. He bore with unfaltering courage and a sweet-hearted patience rarely equaled in the history of martyrdom the accumulating miseries of Jamestown, until he also perished in the general mortality. His nobleness of spirit softened the detestable rivalries of the early leaders. The most active and influen-

tial writers in favor of colonization were clergymen such as Hakluyt, Symonds, Purchas, and
Crashaw. Other clergymen, following in the foot-
steps of Hunt, risked life itself in the Virginia colony, while devout laymen spent their money in its
behalf. Thus did Anglican zeal further a colonization that, by a curious perversity of outcome,
resulted in founding a nation of dissenters.

IX.

In the great hall of the house of Nicholas Ferrar, a London merchant, the courts or meetings of
the Virginia Company were held for years. The
two sons of this Nicholas Ferrar, John and Nicholas, served in turn as deputy governors of the Virginia Company. This pious Ferrar family, as it
became influential, lent to the scheme of colonizing
Virginia something of the air of a project for prop-
agating the gospel. Nicholas, the father, gave
money for the education of infidels in Virginia. A
school was founded there by the gifts of the pious,
and rewards were given to those colonists who
would educate Indian children in their families.
After the younger Nicholas, who was a man of
remarkable zeal and activity, tinged with a romantic enthusiasm, became deputy in 1622, the production of silk and wine and iron and the educating of Indians in Christianity traveled on abreast.
A college was proposed, for which an endowment
of thirteen hundred pounds was collected, and to
which a valuable library was bequeathed by a set-

tler. Practical men grumbled at the prematurity of all this, and complained of those in charge that "they spent Michaelmas rent in mid-summer moone." The governor of the colony, honest Sir Francis Wyatt, wished that "little Mr. Ferrar were in Virginia, where he might add to his zeal a knowledge of the country."

The horrible massacre of March, 1622, made the Indian question something other than the Ferrars saw it. All schemes for educating the savages were obliterated in a day. The only thought after this was how to put the savages to death, old and young, men and women, more often by foul means than by fair. The settlers even emulated, if they did not surpass, the treachery of the Indians. With the dissolution of the company by *quo warranto* proceedings in 1624 the government of the colony passed to the Crown, and the Ferrars had no more to do with Virginia.

X.

The later career of Nicholas Ferrar the younger, though without direct relation to colonization, throws light on the age of colony beginnings. Rejecting the offer of a rich bride, he bought for his mother, now a widow, the manor lordship of Little Gidding, in Huntingdonshire, and took the entire Ferrar family, including his brother and his sister with eighteen children, into religious retirement. Here this half-domestic, half-monastic community gave alms to the poor, illuminated manuscripts of the Bible, and worshiped in its little chapel with genuflections and other observances that procured for it the nickname of the "Protestant Nunnery," and brought down upon it the pious fury of the Puritans. Nicholas Ferrar, who had taken deacon's orders, was the real head of the community. He prepared at Little Gidding what is perhaps the earliest English monatesseron of the four gospels. By means of relays of worshipers the Ferrars kept their devotions always in progress. The entire Psalter was chanted antiphonally during each twenty-four hours. Those whose turn it was to keep vigil were wont to leave a candle at the door of Nicholas and to wish him good-morrow at one o'clock in the morning, at which hour he was accustomed to rise and begin the exercises of the day. The strength of this belated mediæval saint gave way under a discipline so austere, and he died in 1637. Little Gidding, with its "fair grove and sweet walks letticed and gardened on both sides," was devastated a few years later by the counter-zeal of the Puritans, who showed an especial indignation against the organ, which they broke into pieces to light fires for roasting the sheep of the Ferrars. Behold an epitome of the first half of the seventeenth century—its idealism in affairs, and its war to the death of opposing ideals in religion!

Peckard's Life of N. Ferrar. Arminian Nunnery 1641. Hearne's Langtoft's Chronicle, App. to Pref., cix.

In the very years during which the Ferrars were most active on behalf of Virginia the earliest Puritan movement toward America set in. The

Advent of Puritan-ism.

attenuated mediævalism of the Ferrars did not lack a certain refined beauty, but it was hardly suited to the rough work of hewing a road along which civilization might march into a savage wilderness. The Puritans, with their robust contempt for æsthetic considerations—making firewood of organs with delight, and feasting without scruple on the sheep of those whom they esteemed idolaters—were much the fitter to be champions against the American Canaanites.

ELUCIDATIONS.

Note 1, page 74.

Two of the chapter heads to Hakluyt's Westerne Planting, printed in 2d Maine Historical Collections, ii, sufficiently indicate the views prevailing at the time :

" V. That this voyadge will be a greate bridle to the Indies of the Kinge of Spaine, and a meane that wee may arreste at our pleasure for the space of tenne weekes or three monethes every yere, one or two hundred saile of his subjectes Shippes at the fysshinge in Newfounde lande.

" VI. That the mischefe that the Indian threasure wroughte in time of Charles the late Emperor, father to the Spanishe Kinge, is to be had in consideration of the Queens moste excellent Majestie, least the contynuall comynge of the like threasure from thence to his sonne worke the unrecoverable annoye of this realme, wherof already wee have had very dangerous experience."

The heading of the first chapter should be added : " I. That this westerne discoverie will be greately for thinlargemente of the gospell of Christe whereunto the princes of the refourmed relligion are chefely bounde, amongst whome her Majestie ys principall."

It would be foreign to the purpose of the present work to tell the story of Spanish jealousy of Virginia, and of the diplomatic intrigues for the overthrow of the colony. See documents in Mr. Alexander Brown's Genesis of the United States. One can not but regret that Mr. Brown did not give also the original of his Spanish papers ; no translation is adequate to the use of the historian.

This method was recommended to the colonists as late as 1753 in Pullein's Culture of Silk for the Use of the American Colonies, and it had probably long prevailed on the continent of Europe.

The authorities on the early efforts to raise silk, in addition to those cited in the text and the margin, are too numerous to find place here. The most valuable of all is, of course, the copy of the Records of the Virginia Company after April, 1619, in the Library of Congress, *passim*. See, for example, under date of December 13, 1620, and June 11, 1621. See also A Declaration of Virginia, 1620, and Purchas, pp. 1777–1787, Hamor's True Discourse, Smith's General History, Book II, Anderson's Commerce under 1620, and various state papers abstracted by Sainsbury, with Sainsbury's preface to the first volume of his Calendar, and Hening, *passim*. The reader is also referred to Mr. Bruce's Economic History of Virginia in the Seventeenth Century, issued as these pages are passing into the hands of the printer. The wildness of some of the proposals for the production of Virginia silk in the Commonwealth period is almost surpassed by other projects of the time. In Virginia Richly Valued, 1650, perfume was to be extracted from the muskrat, and the James River sturgeon were to be domesticated. Fishes may be "unwilded," says the author. Besides feeding silkworms, the Indians were to be used in pearl fisheries in Virginia waters. Wyckoff on Silk Manufacture, Tenth Census, says that experimental silkworms had been taken to Mexico by the Spaniards in 1531, without any permanent results.

Even in Elizabeth's time efforts had been made to procure naval stores without the intervention of foreign merchants. As early as 1583, Carlisle, who was son-in-law to Secretary Walsingham, had subscribed a thousand pounds toward an American colony, which it was urged would buy English woolens, take off idle and burdensome people, and, among other things, produce naval stores. In 1601 Ralegh had protested eloquently against the act to compel Englishmen to sow hemp. "Rather let every man use his ground to that which it is most fit for," he said. Edwards, Life of Ralegh, p. 272.

Why Germans were sent it is hard to say, as glass was made in England as early as 1557. Glass was produced in Virginia, according to Strachey, who says: "Although the country wants not Salsodiack enough to make glasse of, and of which we have

made some stoore in a goodly howse sett up for the same purpose, with all offices and furnases thereto belonging, a little
without the island, where Jamestown now stands." History of
Travaile into Virginnia Brittannia, p. 71. The house appears to
have been standing and in operation in 1624. Calendar of Colonial Documents, January 30, February 16, and number 20, pp.
38, 39.

Purchas, p. 1777, says that one hundred and fifty persons
were sent over two years earlier to set up three iron works, but
the statement seems hardly credible. In the midst of the misery
following the massacre of 1622, and notwithstanding the imminent probability of the overthrow of the company, which was
already impoverished, some of the adventurers or shareholders
sent nine men to Virginia to try a different method of making
iron from the one that had previously been used. Letter of
August 6, 1623, in Manuscript Book of Instructions in Library of
Congress, fol. 120. Having "failed to effect " the making of iron
"by those great wayes which we have formerly attempted," the
undiscouraged visionaries "most gladly embraced this more
facile project " of making iron "by bloom," but with a like result,
of course.

The raising of tobacco in Virginia was one of the earliest
projects entertained. "We can send . . . tobacco after a yeare
or two, five thousand pounds a yeare." Description of the
Now-discovered river and Country of Virginia, with the Likly-
hood of ensuing Ritches by England's Ayd and Industry, May
21, 1607. Public Record Office, printed in Transactions of the
American Antiquarian Society, iv, 59, 62. The paper is supposed to be from the pen of Captain Gabriel Archer.

In 1604 the king had, by a royal commission addressed to
"our treasurer of England," arbitrarily raised the duty on tobacco
from twopence a pound to six shillings tenpence. He was probably moved to make this surprising change by his antipathy to
tobacco ; but by increasing the profits of the farmers of customs
and monopolists of tobacco, he no doubt contributed to that
abandonment of Virginia to tobacco raising which seemed to him
so lamentable. The use of Spanish tobacco in England was
general before that from Virginia began to take its place. Barnabee Rich says, in 1614 : " I have heard it tolde that now very
lately there hath bin a cathologue taken of all those new erected
houses that have set vppe that trade of selling tobacco in Lon-

don, ande neare about London, and if a man may beleeue what
is confidently reported, there are found to be vpward of 7000
houses that doth liue by that trade." He says such shops were
"almost in euery lane and in euery by-corner round about London." The Honestie of this Age, p. 30.

The MS. records of the Virginia Company, and the State Note 9,
papers relating to Virginia in the Public Record Office, London, page 86.
are the most important authorities on the subjects treated in the
text. On the commodities attempted at the outset, Manuscript
Book of Instructions, Library of Congress, the first volume of
Hening's Statutes, *passim*, and Purchas, pp. 1777–1786, *passim*.
On the inferiority of the Indian tobacco, see Strachey, p, 121.

Peckard's Life of Ferrar supplies many of the particulars in Note 10,
this section. The Records of the Virginia Company and other page 89.
original authorities do not sustain all of Peckard's statements.
The author's view is evidently distorted by biographer's myopia.
He often seems to depend on tradition, but in some passages his
touch is more sure, and he writes like a man who has documents
before him. Arthur Woodnoth's Short Collection of the Most
Remarkable Passages from the Originall to the Dissolution of the
Virginia Company is of great value. It is a scarce tract, which I
met first in the White-Kennett Library, in the rooms of the Society for the Propagation of the Gospel. It is also in the British
Museum, Harvard College, and the Library of Congress. It is
to be taken with discrimination, but the view of the inner work-
ings of court intrigue as it affected Virginia is so fresh and detailed that it would be a pity to miss its information. It was
printed in 1651. There is a brief sketch of the life of Sandys in
Brown's Genesis of the United States, ii, 993.

Hakluyt's Discourse concerneing Westerne Planting, printed Note 11,
first in the Maine Historical Collections, second series, vol. ii, page 90.
page 11. "And this enterprise the princes of religion (amonge
whome her Majestie ys principall) oughte the rather to take in
hande because papists confirme themselves and drawe other to
theire side shewinge that they are the true Catholicke churche
because they have bene the onely converters of many millions of
infidells. Yea, I myself have bene demanded of them how many
infidells have bene by us converted."

BOOK II.

THE PURITAN MIGRATION.

CHAPTER THE FIRST.

RISE AND DEVELOPMENT OF PURITANISM.

I.

NOT religious disputants only, but the world in general, exaggerated the importance of vestments and ceremonies in the reign of Elizabeth. The love of formality and display that characterized the Renascence was then at its height. It was a time of pomps and royal progresses. Great historic characters went about dressed like performers in a show. Some of the queen's gowns were adorned with jewels on every available inch of space. These bespangled robes were draped over vast farthingales, which spread out like tables on which her arms might rest, and her appearance when thus attired has been compared to that of an Oriental idol. Her courtiers and statesmen were equally fond of dazzling the spectator. Ralegh wore a pendent jewel on his hat feather, and the value of the gems on his shoes was estimated at six thousand six hundred pieces of gold. The love of pomp was not confined to the court;

every nobleman and country gentleman kept his house filled with idle serving men, the sons of neighboring gentlemen or yeomen, whose use was to "grace the halls" of their patron by their attendance and to give dignity to his hospitality. High sheriffs and other officials performed their functions with thirty or forty men in livery at their heels, even borrowing the retainers of their friends to lend state to their office. Edward VI set out upon a progress in 1551 with a train of four thousand mounted men. These were noblemen and gentlemen with their retainers. He was obliged to dismiss all but a hundred and fifty of this vast army of display lest it should "eat up the country." The gorgeous progresses of Elizabeth are too well known to need description. A painting of the time shows her to us in the act of making a friendly call on her cousin-german, Lord Hunsdon. She is sitting under a canopy, and is borne on the shoulders of men and attended by a brilliant train of lords and ladies on foot. It was truer in the days of Shakespeare than it has been since that " all the world's a stage, and all the men and women merely players."

A passionate love of the theater was inevitable in such a time. The best poetry then took a dramatic form ; even history was taught from the stage ; and satire and polemics felt the attraction and were often put into imaginary dialogues. It was Shakespeare's good fortune that he happened to live among a people fond of show and in an

Note 1.

Machyn's Diary, 324, note.

The age of the drama.

age dramatic as well as poetic to its very core. Genius is nourished by sympathy, and supremely great performance is rendered possible only by the rare coincidence of the great man and a fitting environment.

Display in dress.

Dress signified more to the men of the time of Elizabeth and James than it is easy for us moderns to imagine. Greatness declared itself by external display. The son of a rich merchant when he returned from his travels decked himself in gorgeous apparel, and formally made his appearance

Peckard's Life of Ferrar.

on the Exchange like a butterfly newly emerged. It was thus that his parents brought the young man out in the world. A sum equal in purchasing power to several thousand dollars in our time is said to have been spent on one pair of trunk hose. Men of the lowest ranks, desirous of appearing more than they were, impoverished themselves

Stubbes, Anatomie of Abuses, passim.

in buying expensive hats and hose ; and it is recorded that women suffering for the necessaries of life sometimes contrived to adorn themselves with velvet. For the very reason that so much importance was attached to dress, laws were made to repress inappropriate display in people of lower rank. Even the severe Puritan moralists did not

Note 2.

object to the pomp of the great, but to the extravagant imitation of it by those who had no right to such ostentation. It was with difficulty that men could conceive of greatness without display. To refuse a bishop his vestments was to abate something of his lofty rank.

II.

Along with a love for external show went a scrupulous observance of decorous and often pomp-ous ceremonies. Englishmen in the sixteenth and the early part of the seventeenth century never omitted to observe proper formality, no matter how dire the emergency. One may see this exem-plified by reverting to some of the earliest events in American history. When Gates arrived at Jamestown near the close of the "starving time," he found only the gaunt ghosts of men clamoring to be taken from the scene of so many horrible miseries. Instead of giving immediate attention to the sufferings of the people, he caused the little church bell to be rung. Such of the inhabitants as could drag themselves out of their huts repaired once more to the now ruined and unfrequented church with its roof of sedge and earth supported by timbers set in crotches. Here the newly ar-rived chaplain offered a sorrowful prayer, and then George Percy, the retiring governor, delivered up his authority to Sir Thomas Gates, who thus found himself in due and proper form installed governor of death, famine, and desperation. When Gates abandoned the wrecked town with his starv-ing company he fired a "peale of small shott," in order not to be wanting in respect for a royal fort; and when De la Warr arrived, a few days later, he made his landing with still greater pomp than that of Gates. There was a flourish of trumpets on

Observ-ance of ceremo-nies.

Compare *supra*, p. 41.

shipboard before he struck sail in front of James-town. A gentleman of his party bore the colors of the governor before him. The governor's first act when he set foot on American soil was to fall on his knees and offer a long, silent prayer, which was probably sincere though theatrical, after the manner of the age. He rose at length and marched up into the ruined town. As he passed into the stockade by the water gate, which was shabbily off its hinges, the color bearer dropped down before him and allowed the colors to fall at the feet of his lordship, who proceeded to the tumble-down chapel, under the earthen roof of which the authority over the colony was duly transferred to his hands with such solemnities as were thought proper. Whenever Lord De la Warr went to church at Jamestown he was attended by the councilors, captains, and gentlemen, and guarded by fifty men with halberds, wearing De la Warr's livery of showy red cloaks. The governor's seat was a chair covered with green velvet. It was in the choir of the now reconstructed little church, and a velvet cushion lay on the table before him to enable him to worship his Maker in a manner becoming the dignity of a great lord over a howling wilderness. More than a quarter of the able-bodied men in Virginia were needed to get the governor to church and back again aboard the ship where he dwelt.

Strachey, in Purchas, iv, 17-54.

De la Warr's letter, in Strachey's Virginia, p. xxix.

Formality at Plymouth.

Even at a later date in the rather hungry little Pilgrim colony at Plymouth almost as much ceremony was observed, though the people were extreme Puritans without rank. At beat of drum on Sunday morning the men came to Captain Standish's door with their cloaks on, each bearing a musket or matchlock. They proceeded to church three abreast, led by a sergeant. In the rear walked the governor, in a long robe. On his right was Elder Brewster, wearing a cloak. On the governor's left was Captain Miles Standish, who also wore a cloak and side arms, and carried a small cane as a sort of baton of authority perhaps. Thus "they march in good order, and each sets his arms down near him."

De Rasieres's letter, 2d N. Y. Hist. Coll., ii, 352.

It was only in an age such as this that resistance to the celebration of rites and the observance of forms could be made a capital article of faith by the Puritan, and later by the Quaker. The wearing of a surplice, the propriety of doffing the hat on certain occasions, was a matter for scruple and violent debate, for the grave consideration of the lawgiver and magistrate, and for severe penalties.

Puritanism an outgrowth of the time.

III.

In the brief Protestant reign of Edward VI there were those who objected to "the vestments," and one may even find what were afterward called Puritan opinions condemned among current errors in the twenty-eighth year of Henry VIII; but Puritanism—as a party protest against pomp and ceremonialism in religious worship—had its origin in the persecution of Queen Mary's

Origin of the Puritan movement.

Fuller's Ch. Hist., book v, sec. iv, 27, 28.

1536.

time. The English Protestants who fled from that fiery ordeal found refuge chiefly in Protestant cities of the Continent. Strasburg, Frankfort, Basel, Zurich, and Geneva were the places to which these English exiles mainly resorted. Zurich and Strasburg became cities of refuge for many of those who were to become leaders of the Anglican or Conservative party, while others who tended to what were afterward called Puritan views went sooner or later to Geneva, where Calvin was the dominant influence.

A. D. 1553.

The English exiles.

In the cities in which they found safety the exiles organized English churches. More remarkable religious communities were never gathered into single congregations. Five bishops and five deans of the English Church, and more than fifty eminent doctors of divinity, with younger men who were destined to play a leading part in the future, were comprised in these little churches. Such communities soon became centers of animated discussion and debate.

Outbreak of dissension.

During the preceding reign of King Edward VI, English Protestantism had been forced into many compromises within itself. No form of religious life can become national without exacting of its advocates of differing shades of opinion many sacrifices for the sake of unity ; but now that the leaders of English Protestantism were in exile they found themselves in a measure freed from motives of policy and with leisure to develop and apply their theories. A passion for the ideal thus suddenly unchained easily becomes rampant. There sprang up swiftly a dispute between the church in Strasburg and the church in Frankfort on matters of government. The reformatory spirit is rarely conciliatory, and in its excess and overflow it is wont to be pragmatic and impertinent. Some of the reformers of Strasburg felt bound to go over to Frankfort and re-reform the reformed English church there; and the little English community in Frankfort was soon torn asunder between the followers of Richard Cox and those of John Knox—the same who was afterward so famous in the Scottish reformation.

This dispute in Frankfort between the Coxans and the Knoxans, as they were called, had all the characteristics that render church quarrels odious. One finds in it the bitterness of slanderous violence—the little deceptions and unmanly treacheries that characterize such debates and disclose the sorry threadbareness of human saintship even in exiles and martyrs for conscience' sake. But, petty as were these squabbles at Frankfort, they produced results of the first magnitude. Small things change the whole course of history when they lie near the fountain head of a great current. From the conflicting factions in the church of the exiles at Frankfort were evolved the opposing parties that were to give character to English Protestantism, and to modify profoundly the history of England and as profoundly the history of the United States.

Character of the debates at Frankfort.

BOOK II.

The rise of
the two
great par-
ties.

In the contentions of the English at Frankfort,
resulting now in the exiling from the city of one
beaten minority and now in the departure of another, and in the driving away of one leading dis-
putant after another, there appeared at length the
features of the two great parties of English Protestantism face to face for the first time. One of these
parties tried to hold all of antique ritual that the
Protestant conscience could be made to bear, insisted upon the superior authority of the clergy,
and sought to disturb as little as possible the ancient
order of the English church. On the other hand,
in the rapid changes produced by the Frankfort
contentions, the tendency of the ultra wing of the
Protestants to the notion of a local and independent
church and to a democratic church government
was already apparent. Even the peculiarity of
two ministers presiding over one church, which
Note 3. was cherished later in New England, appeared
among the English at Frankfort and Geneva at this
time.

A purified
ritual. While attempting to mediate between the parties at Frankfort, Calvin expressed his preference
for a ritual of greater purity than that established
by the English Prayer Book of King Edward's time.
Extreme Protestants rallied round this ideal of a
liturgy purified of human tradition. It was some
years later, after the Frankfort church had been
dissolved and the exiles had returned to England,
that this party came to be known by the name
Note 4. of Puritan—that is, a party not so much bent on

purity of conduct as on purifying Protestant worship from mediæval forms.

After the death of Mary and the accession of Elizabeth the English Protestants returned to their own country. The two great parties that were to divide the English church had already begun to crystallize. Those who had settled at Strasburg and Zurich came back hoping to re-establish the Anglican Church on the conservative basis of the Prayer Book of Edward VI. Those who returned from Basel and Geneva had caught the spirit of the Calvinistic churches, and wished to push the reformation to a more logical extreme; while the Frankfort church, or what remained of it, had been storm-driven well-nigh to a theory of congregational independence in church government.

The petty squabbles of the English exiles, transplanted to England, grew into bitter feuds and brought forth persecutions and political struggles. The settlement of New England, the battles of Marston Moor and Naseby, the temporary overthrow of the English monarchy, the growth of nonconformity, the modification of the English Constitution and of all English life, were germinally present in the differences between the exiles at Zurich and those at Geneva, and in the squabbles of Cox and Knox, of Whithead and Horne at Frankfort-on-the-Main about gowns and litanies and the authority of the priest. It is not often that a great historical movement can be traced through a single rill to its rise at the fountain head.

IV.

The theological debates that fill so large a place in the history of the first half of the sixteenth century in Europe were mainly concerned with speculative dogmas. However futile controversies may seem that seek to reduce to formulas the relations between God and man, they have at least a topical dignity. But the debates about ceremonies and vestments which the exiles brought back to England from the Continent, and which held first place there during the reign of Elizabeth and James, were bitter without being serious. A life-and-death struggle concerning the wearing of "white surplices" or the making of the sign of the cross in baptism can not but seem frivolous to the modern mind. Learned scholars like Broughton and Ainsworth thought it not beneath them to write tractates discussing the material of which the ephod of a Jewish high priest was made. It was learnedly demonstrated that the ephod was of silk, and there were sober essays on the linsey-woolsey side of that controversy. To the fine-spun mind of that time the character of the Jewish ephod was thought to settle the propriety of the Christian surplice. To the modern reader the whole debate about vestments and liturgies would be amusing if it were not so tedious. It is necessary to steady one's judgment of that age by remembering that deeper things sometimes lay concealed under these disputes regarding the con-

Certayne
Qvestions
concerning
silk or
vvool in
the high
priest's
ephod,
1605.

temptible mint and cumin of ecclesiasticism. Puritanism at its rise was an effort to escape from formalism, the outgrowth of an aspiration for greater spirituality in worship; but it gradually passed into an opposite formalism as rigid as that from which it had escaped.

It was in vain that Elizabeth tried to compel uniformity. The difference between the radical and the conservative is constitutional, and is manifest in every period of agitation. Neither the mediation of moderate men nor the compulsion of authority can bring these two sempiternal divisions of the human race into agreement. The conservative English churchman limited his Protestantism to the rejection of the pope's authority, and to certain moderate reforms in church government and ritual. He shuddered with alarm at every proposal to reconstruct religious institutions which were moss-grown with ancient sentiment. The extreme Puritan, on the other hand, went about his work in the spirit of a Jehu. He saved all his reverence for the precepts of the Bible, now becoming common in the vulgar tongue. He applied biblical phraseology to the affairs of life in a way that would have been impossible had he possessed any sense of humor. He felt himself impelled by the call of God to carry out in England the changes that had taken place in the Calvinistic churches of the Continent, and to go even further. He would have no surplices, no sign of the cross, no liturgy, no church holy days. Away with these rags of Antichrist, was his cry. Let us get back to the simplicity of the primitive ages. The Anglican, on the other hand, felt himself an Englishman above all, and without a stately liturgy, great bishops in square caps and lawn sleeves, Christmas feasts, solemn Good Fridays, and joyous Easters, there would have remained for him no merry England.

V.

Growth of party spirit.

The party line between Anglican and Puritan was not at once sharply drawn. It was only after debates growing ever more acrimonious, after persecutions and numberless exasperations, that the parties in the Church of England fell into well-defined and hostile camps. If there had been some relaxation of the requirements of uniformity, if a conciliatory policy had been pursued by the government, the ultimate division might have been postponed until party spirit had cooled; but in that day blows took the place of words, and words had the force of blows. The queen herself could write to a bishop who scrupled to do what she desired, " By God, I will unfrock you ! " and moderation in debate was not to be expected from lesser folk.

Puritanism the party of opposition.

When the reformer has warmed to his work he looks about him for new abuses to fall upon. The dominant discontent of any age is prone to spread its wings over other grievances, and feebler movements seek shelter from the strong. Puritanism no doubt gathered momentum from the wide-spread agrarian and industrial disturbance in this and the preceding reigns. The profit from sheep-raising had induced many manor lords to inclose the wastes on which the peasants had pastured their cattle for ages. The humble copy-hold tenant, having no longer grass for his cows or mast for his pigs, was driven to distress by agricultural progress. In some cases even the common fields, cultivated in allotments from ancient times by the members of the village communities, first as serfs and later as tenants, were turned into sheepwalks, and hamlets of tenants' cottages were torn down to make room for more profitable occupants of the soil. The worst offenders were the greedy court-iers who had secured the estates of the English monasteries. Workmen ruined by the dissolution of the guilds were added to the ranks of the un-happy. All the discontent begotten of these tran-sitions from mediæval life tended to strengthen the leading opposition—and that leading opposition was Puritanism.

Note 5.

VI.

Puritanism also progressively widened its field of protest. Beliefs that Protestants rejected were symbolized by the vestments of bishop and clergy. Advanced Protestants insisted that the shadows should be banished with the substance, that the symbol should disappear with the dogma. We have seen that in Frankfort the inchoate Puritan

Widening the field of protest.

party wished to abolish the litany and purge the
service book of all the remains of the old religion.
This controversy raged in England, and the Puritan side did not at first lack support even among
the bishops. But Elizabeth, the real founder of
Anglicanism, molded the church to her will, putting down Catholics and Puritans with a hard
hand. The more advanced of the party came at
length to believe that all "stinted" prayers "read
out of a book" were contrary to the purity and
simplicity of Christian worship. The hostility of
the bishops to that which the Puritans believed to
be the cause of God no doubt helped to convince
the persecuted party that the episcopal office itself
was contrary to Scripture.

Puritan-
ism be-
comes dog-
matic.

Most of the Puritans of Elizabeth's time, under
the lead of the great Cartwright, became Presbyterian in theory and sought to assimilate the Church
of England to the Calvinistic churches of the Continent, holding that theirs was the very order pre-

Note 6.

scribed by the apostles. Another but much smaller
division of the Puritans tended toward independency, finding in the New Testament a system different from that of Cartwright. Both the Presbyterians and those who held to local church
government wished to see their own system established by law. Neither faction thought of tolerating Anglican practices if the Anglicans could be
put down. The notion of a state church with prescribed forms of worship enforced by law was too
deeply imbedded in the English mind to be easily

got rid of, and the spirit of persecution pervaded every party, Catholic or Protestant. Every one was sure that divine authority was on his side, and that human authority ought to be.

VII.

A corresponding change began to take place in the Episcopal party. The earlier defenders of Elizabeth's establishment argued, somewhat as Hooker did later, that the "practice of the apostles" was not an "invariable rule or law to succeeding ages, because they acted according to the circumstances of the church in its infant and persecuted state." Episcopal government they held to be allowable, and maintained the attitude of prudent men who justify their compromise with history and the exigency of the time, and advocate, above all, submission to civil authority. But the tendency of party division is to push both sides to more positive ground. There arose in the last years of Elizabeth a school of High-churchmen led by Bancroft, afterward primate, who turned away from Hooker's moderation and assumed a more aggressive attitude. Like the Presbyterians and the Independents and the Catholics, these in turn maintained that their favorite system of church economy was warranted by divine authority, and that all others were excluded.

When the High-church leaders had reached the dogmatic assertion of apostolic succession and a divinely appointed episcopal form of government

Anglicanism becomes dogmatic.

Failure of Elizabeth's policy.

9

as essentials of a Christian church, the fissure between the two ecclesiastical parties in England
was complete. Each had settled itself upon a supposed divine authority; each regarded the other
as teaching a theory contrary to the divine plan.
Elizabeth's policy of repression had produced a
certain organic uniformity, but the civil war of the
seventeenth century was its ultimate result.

VIII.

Bitterness
of the de-
bate.

The controversy between the two Protestant
parties naturally grew more bitter as time went on.
The silencing of ministers, the Fleet Prison, the
inquisitorial Ecclesiastical Commission, and other
such unanswerable arguments did not sweeten the
temper of the Puritans. The bitterness of the controversy reached its greatest intensity in 1588, when
there appeared a succession of anonymous tracts,
most of them signed Martin Marprelate. They
seem to have been written mainly by the same
hand, but their authorship has been a matter of
debate to this day.

The Mar-
prelate
tracts.

1588.

The sensation produced by these violent assaults
is hardly conceivable now. There were no news-
papers then, and there was but little popular literature. Here were little books printed no one
knew where, written by no one knew whom,
concerning a religious controversy of universal
interest. They were couched in the phrase of the
street, in the very slang and cant of the populace,
and were violent and abusive, sometimes descend-

ing to sheer blackguardism. Marprelate went
gunning for large game; his deadliest abuse he let
fly as from a blunderbuss at the very heads of the
English church. The Dean of Salisbury he calls
" Doctor of Diviltrie and Deane of Sarum." It
was the first time in the history of polemics that
any one had addressed a high dignitary of the
church with such irreverent titles as " You grosse
beaste !" " You block, you !" Sometimes Martin
bends his knees with mock reverence, as when he
calls the clergy " right poysond, persecuting and
terrible priests." He blurts out epithets against
" the sinful, the unlawful, the broken, the unnatural,
false, and bastardly governours of the church; to
wit, archbishops and bishops "; and addresses them
as " you enemies to the state, you traytors to God
and his worde, you Mar-prince, Mar-land, Mar-ma-
gestrate, Mar-church, and Mar-commonwealth."
The spice of the books, that which gave them their
popularity, was doubtless their rollicking impu-
dence. " Wo—ho, now, Brother London!" he cries
to the Bishop of London. " Go to, you Asse!" is a
kind of kennel eloquence relished by the populace.
Martin seems even to giggle and sneer and hiss in
type in such expressions as " tse, tse, tse."

The little books went everywhere. The Bishop
of Winchester sadly confessed that these " slanderous pamphlets, freshe from the presse," were " in
men's hands and bosoms commonly." The queen
and courtiers read them, and students had nothing
better to laugh at. Who will not stop in the street

CHAP. I.

The Mar-
prelate
tracts in
Lenox
Library.

An Ad-
monition to
the People
of Eng-
land, p. 25.

Book II.

to hear one clown rail cleverly at another? But to see the bishops collectively and the primate and others severally put into a pillory and pelted in this daring fashion by a man who knew that his life would pay the forfeit for his libel if he could by any means be discovered, was livelier sport than bull-baiting.

Dr. Cooper, Bishop of Winchester, replied to the first pamphlet somewhat ponderously, as became a bishop who feels that the proprieties forbid his being too interesting. Marprelate wanted nothing better than a bishop for an antagonist; and while the whole constabulary force of the kingdom was hunting him for his life, the nimble Martin was chuckling over the excitement made by a new tract of his, headed with the well-known street cry of a tub-mender, which played derisively on Bishop Cooper's name, " Hay any worke for Cooper?" This tract professed to be "printed in Europe not farre from some of the Bounsing priestes." In this paper Martin shows to what depth a religious debate in Elizabeth's time could descend; he stoops to make the bishop ridiculous by twitting him with the infidelity of his wife, a

Nugæ Antiquæ, ii, 89, 90.

scandal which the unfortunate prelate had treated with " Socratical and philosophical patience."

There were not wanting many imitators of Martin's grossness on the other side of the controversy,

Lenox Collection, N. Y. Pub. Library.

who were just as libelous but for the most part less clever. One of the tracts in reply was called An Almond for a Parrat. The author says he had heard that Martin was dead, or, as he expressed it, "that your grout-headed holinesse had turned uppe your heeles like a tired jade in a medow and snorted out your sorrowefull soule, like a mesled hogge on a mucke-hille." This is beastly without being vivacious. While the press and the stage were occupied with coarse retorts on Martinism, there appeared tracts in favor of peace. There are other evidences of the existence of a moderate party that lamented the excesses of both sides in this debate.

CHAP. I.

Comp. Bacon's An Adver- tisement touching Controver- sies, etc.

IX.

Puritanism was evolutionary from the begin- ning. Its earlier disputes about vestments and litanies grew by degrees to a rejection of all litur- gies as idolatrous. Even the reading of the Bible as a part of the service came at last to be repre- hended by extremists, and the repetition of the Lord's Prayer was thought dangerously liturgical. The advanced Puritans sought to exclude from Christian worship everything pleasing to the æs- thetic sense, confounding bareness with simplicity. Compromises continued to be made inside the church, but in the ultimate ideal of Puritan wor- ship there remained, besides the sermon, nothing but long extemporary prayers and the singing by the untrained voices of the congregation of literal versions of the Hebrew Psalms—doggerel verse in cobblestone meters.

X.

In its early stages Puritanism was a crusade against idolatry, and drew its inspiration in this, as in nearly everything else, from the Old Testament. To the word "idolatry" it gave an inclusiveness not found in the Jewish Scriptures, and puzzling to a mind accustomed to modern ways of thinking. There was hardly any set observance of the church in which constructive idolatry did not lie concealed. All holy days except Sunday were abhorred as things that bore the mark of the Beast. Even in the reign of Edward VI, long before the name of Puritanism was known, the May-poles round which English people made merry once a year were denounced as idols in a sermon preached at Paul's Cross by Sir Stephen—the "Sir" being a polite prefix to a clergyman's name. This Stephen, curate of St. Catherine Cree, was a forerunner of Puritanism, who sometimes defiantly preached from an elm tree in the chuchyard and read the service standing on a tomb on the north side of the church. He wanted the saintly names of churches and the heathen names of days of the week changed, so keen was his scent for idolatry. The parish of St. Andrew Undershaft had received its distinctive name from a very tall May-pole that overtopped the church steeple. This pole, no longer used, rested on hooks under the eaves of a row of houses and stalls. Sir Stephen denounced the lofty shaft as an idol that had given a name

to the parish. The people in their rage took
it from the hooks and sawed it in pieces, and
its sections were appropriated by the several
householders who had given it shelter and who
presently heaped its parts upon one great bon-
fire. Puritanism kept up its Don Quixote battle
against May-poles until there was hardly one
standing to seduce the people to idolatry. When
the Puritan party came into power, nearly a hundred years after the days of Sir Stephen of St.
Catherine Cree, one of its earliest laws ordered
that all May-poles—"an heathenish vanity generally abused to superstition and wickedness"—
be taken down.

CHAP. I.

1549.

Rush-
worth, Pt.
III, vol. ii,
749. A. D.
1644.

XI.

From denouncing constructive idolatry in organ music, litanies, and May-poles, the transition
to attack on the more real and substantial evils in
ordinary conduct was inevitable. History has
many examples of this pervasiveness of scrupulosity. The Puritan conscience had been let loose
to tear in pieces the remnants of old superstitions.
It was certain to break over into the field of conduct. Having set out to reform the church, it took
the world by the way.

As early as 1583 Philip Stubbes, a Puritan
lawyer, issued his hot little book, The Anatomie of
Abuses. It deals with the immoralities and extravagances of the time. Stubbes repeats the early
Puritan objection to the May-pole: it is a "stinck-

yng idòl," he declares, which the people bring from the woods, "followyng it with greate devotion." And when they have set it up they "leape and daunce aboute it, as the heathen people did at the dedication of their idolles." But Stubbes takes a step forward and objects to the all-night May frolics on account of their immorality. He says, "I have heard it credibly reported by men of great gravitie, credite and reputation, that of fourtie, three score, or a hundred maides goyng to the woods

Pickering's ed., p. 172.

over night, there have scarcely the third parte of them returned home againe undefiled." As men of " great gravitie, credite and reputation " were not likely to know the facts in this case, some of the immorality with which Stubbes charges the young people may have been as fanciful as the heathenism attributed to them. Imputed unrighteousness was a part of the Puritan system. He denounces the wild excesses in dress and the other follies of the time with a lack of a sense of proportion which already foreshadows later Puritanism.

This secondary development of Puritanism by which its energies were turned toward the regulation of conduct, as the disputes of the Reformation period lost their violence, gave to the name Puritan a new and higher sense. It is a phase of its history more important than all its primary contentions over gowns and liturgies and hierarchies, or its later debates about the five points of Calvinism and a sabbatical Sunday. One may easily forget its austerity and extravagance, for by the reform of manners this movement made the English race its debtor. In no succeeding reaction have English morals reverted to the ante-Puritan level. It is only by the religious ferments infused successively by new sects and movements, of preaching friars, Lollards, Puritans, Quakers, Methodists, Salvationists, that the great unleavened mass of men is rendered gradually less sodden.

XII.

The last years of Elizabeth's long reign were years of apparent Puritan decline. The old bugbear of popery was receding into the past, and a new generation had come on the stage that had no memory of the struggles of the reigns of Henry and Edward and Mary. The danger from the Armada had brought English patriotism to the point of fusion. Even the persecuted Catholics rallied to the support of the queen against Philip. The government of Elizabeth rose to the zenith of its popularity on the overthrow of the Armada. It was just at this inopportune moment, when the nation had come to feel that the England of Elizabeth was the greatest England the ages had known, that there came forth from a small coterie of the oppressed ultra-Puritans the Martin Marprelate tracts. However effective these may have been at first in making the bishops ridiculous, there followed a swift reaction. The Puritans were dubbed Martinists, and henceforth had to bear the odium of the boisterous vulgarity and

Puritan decline.

Supra, page 115.

libelous exaggeration of the Marprelate lampoons. The queen's government, stronger now than ever in the affection of the people, put in force severe ecclesiastical measures against nonconformists in the church, and sent Brownists, or Separatists, to die by the score in loathsome prisons. Half a dozen of their leaders were dispatched by the shorter road of the gallows. The long reign of the queen had by this time discouraged those who hoped for a change of policy at her death. Hooker's masterful and delightful prose, informed by a spirit of winning moderation, was arrayed on the side of the Anglicans by the publication of parts of his Ecclesiastical Polity in 1594 and 1597. But Puritanism suffered most from the persistence of Archbishop Whitgift and others in efforts to suppress all nonconformity in the church. These champions of Anglicanism, in the swaggering words of one of them, "defended the prelacy,

Rogers's Pref. to the 39 Articles.

stood for the power of the state, put the new doctors to the foil, profligated the elders, set upon the presbytery, and so battered the new discipline as hitherto they could never nor hereafter shall ever fortify and repair the decay thereof." The presbyteries which Cartwright and his friends had formed within the Church of England were swept out utterly by the archbishop's broom. The Puritan movement which had begun almost simultaneously with Elizabeth's reign seemed to be doomed to languish and die with the old queen who had been its resolute and lifelong antagonist.

XIII.

For the first thirty years or more of its existence Puritanism was mainly a bundle of negations, and no bundle of mere negations is a sufficient reason for maintaining a party. No vestments, no ceremonies, no bishops, were effective cries in the hot Reformation period. But the new generation had ceased to abhor these left-overs of Romanism. Bishops, gowns, prayer books, had become Protestant to most of the people by association. To find additional reasons for differing from Anglican opponents was a party necessity. The new debates which sprang up in the last years of the sixteenth century were not deliberately planned by the Puritans, as some of their opponents asserted. They came by a process of evolution. But a period of temporary decline in a movement of this sort hastens its natural unfolding. The leaders are forced to seek the advantage of such new issues as offer when the old ones fail. In the last years of Elizabeth, Puritanism was molting, not dying.

Seeking a positive ground.

Note 7.

XIV.

The great reformers of the sixteenth century had sought to strip from the Christianity of their time what they deemed the second-hand garments of Judaism. Along with the theory of a priesthood they declared also against a doctrine known in the church at least from the fifth century, that the fourth commandment enforced on Christians

The Puritan Sabbath.

the keeping sacred in some sense of Sundays and other church holy days. Luther maintained that a commandment to keep the Sabbath "literally understood does not apply to Christians, for it is entirely outward, like other ordinances of the Old Testament." He thought a festival day important for rest and for attending religious worship; but with characteristic oppugnancy he says: "If anywhere the day is made holy for the mere day's sake, . . . then I order you to dance on it, and feast on it, to do anything that shall remove this encroachment on Christian liberty." The Augsburg Confession makes a similar statement of the Protestant position. Calvin considered the fourth commandment binding on Christians only in a sense mystical and highly Calvinistic. It signified that "we should rest from our own works" under the Christian dispensation. He even suggested that some other day of the week might be chosen as a day of rest and worship at Geneva for an exhibition of Christian liberty in this regard. His practice was conformed to his theory. It is incidentally related that when John Knox once visited the Genevan reformer on Sunday, he found him playing at bowls. Knox was not more a sabbatarian than Calvin.

XV.

Writers on this subject have generally agreed in dating the rise of the Puritan Sabbath from the appearance, in 1595, of Dr. Bownd's book on The

Sabbath of the Old and of the New Testament. But the doctrine of the strict keeping of Sunday may be traced farther back. In truth, the difference between the English and the Continental Sunday dates from the Reformation. The protests of Luther and Calvin go to show that Sunday had in the church before the Reformation, theoretically if not in practice, the sanctity of a church feast. The English Reformation was conservative, like all other English revolutions. English reformers retained the Catholic Sunday, as they did the vestments and national hierarchy of the old church. Thomas Hancock has been styled "the Luther of the southwest of England." He was the great preacher of Poole in the days of Edward VI. That he, like other English reformers, did not agree with Luther in rejecting the obligation to rest on Sunday is shown by the record, for the voice of Poole was the voice of Hancock. About 1550 the juries in the Admiralty Court of Poole were charged to inquire into Sunday fishing; and so advanced was the premature Puritanism of Edward's time that even the leaving of nets in the sea over Sunday was to be investigated. Here was a strictness unknown in Catholic times.

Note 8.

Cranmer's Catechism, 40 ff., edition 1829, and Beacon's Catechism, Works, 82 ff.

Robert's Social Hist. of the Southern Counties, p. 239.

Note 9.

XVI.

The word Sabbath does not occur in these early entries, though it is applied to Sunday argumentatively in some of the catechisms of the Reformation period which couple it with other holy days, as in the phrase, " Sabbaths and feastful days." Sabbath as applied to Sunday occurs in literature as early as 1573, and then it is considered necessary to explain it. Bullein's Dialogue against the Fever Pestilence, a work of considerable popularity, first appeared as early as 1564. In the edition of 1573 there was inserted a new passage not found in the earlier issue. Mendax is relating incredible tales of travel in lands unknown, after the manner of David Ingram and other returned adventurers. Up to this point all is pure lying merely for the fun of the thing, or perhaps to ridicule the exaggerations of travelers. But the interpolated passage is not of a piece with the old garment into which it is patched. It is less grotesque and humorous, and it smacks of incipient Puritanism in several flavors. It treats first of all of the " Kepyng of the Saboth Daie," " whiche is the seventh daie, that is sondaie," in the imaginary city of " Nodnol," an anagram of London. The gates are shut, and nobody is allowed to "goe, neither ride forth of the Citie duryng that daie, except it be after the euenyng praier; then to walke honestlie into the sweete fieldes, and at every gate in the time of service there are warders." " What so ever hee be he muste kepe hollie the Sabboth daie, and come to the churche both man, woman, young and olde." " There were no people walking abroad in the service tyme; no, not a Dogge or catte in the streate, neither any Taverne doore open that daie, nor wine bibbyng

Supra,
page 16.

Early English Text Society Reprint, 106, 107, 108.

in them, but onely almose, fasting and praier."
This is perhaps the oldest extant statement of an
early Puritan ideal of enforced Sabbath-keeping.

XVII.

Scruples regarding recreations on Sunday
come distinctly into view in the title of a sermon
preached at Paul's Cross in 1576. In 1580 the
magistrates of London secured from the queen a
prohibition of the performance of plays within the
limits of the city on Sundays. In other municipali-
ties—Brighton, Yarmouth, and Lyme—ordinances
were made about this time against such offenses as
the prosecution on Sunday of the herring fisheries,
cloth working, and other labors, and even against
the Sunday practice of archery, formerly thought
a patriotic exercise. There are other evidences of
a movement, especially in the south of England, in
favor of a stricter Sabbath in these and the following years. Stubbes does not fail to denounce
"heathnicall exercises upon the Sabbaoth day,
which the Lorde would have consecrated to holy
uses." The Puritan mode of Sabbath-keeping already existed among the chosen few. "The Sabboth daie of some is well observed," says Stubbes,
"namely, in hearing the blessed worde of God
read, preached, and interpreted; in private and
publique praiers; in reading of godly psalmes; in
celebrating the sacraments; and in collecting for
the poore and indigent, which are the true uses
and endes whereto the Sabbaoth was ordained."

Cox's Lit-
erature of
the Sab-
bath Ques-
tion, *sub
anno.*

Robert's
Southern
Counties,
pp. 238,
239.

1583.

He records the opposite belief of his opponents that Sunday was ordained " onely to use what kinde of exercises they thinke good themselves." In practice this was the rule of the English people at large. These opposite opinions come into view when Martin Marprelate a few years later berates the Bishop of London for playing at bowls on Sunday.

XVIII.

Dr. Bownd's book on The Sabbath of the Old and the New Testament, which, if we may believe its opponents, was nearly ten years " in the hammering," was the outcome of a sentiment already rising among the Puritans, and not wholly confined to that party. It was preceded by a little work of Richard Greenham which seems to have been circulated for some years in manuscript after a fashion of that time, and to have had at first more influence on practice than Bownd's formal treatise. Greenham was Bownd's stepfather, and his work was the parent of Bownd's, which is distinctly more extreme. But Dr. Bownd's book is none the less memorable as a point of departure, because in it the opinions on this subject which have since prevailed so generally in all English-speaking lands " were for the first time broadly and prominently asserted in Christendom " ; at least, they were here first systematically propounded and defended. Bownd held that the fourth commandment is partly moral, in the phrase of the casuists. He shifted the obligation to the first day of the week by arguments now familiar, and he laid down rules for the observance of the day. Honest recreations and lawful delights he flatly forbids on Sundays, but he rather obsequiously makes some allowance for the "feasts of noblemen and great personages on this day." People of rank do not wholly escape him, however, for he points a moral with the story of a nobleman whose child was born with a face like that of a dog, because the father had hunted on the Lord's Day. He allows the ringing of only one bell to call the people to church on Sunday. Chimes were quite too pleasing to accord with a severe Sabbath.

Note 10.

XIX.

Such rigor fell in with the passion of that age for formal observance and with the exigent temper of the Puritans by whom Bownd's views were rapidly and universally accepted. The stricter divines might well be glad of a new lever for reforming the old English Sunday, which was devoted, out of service time, to outdoor games, to the brutally cruel sports of bull and bear baiting, to merry morris-dances, in which the performers were gayly decked and hung with jingling bells in different keys, as well as to coarse farces called interludes, which were played on stages under booths and sometimes in the churches. As an austere reaction

Spread of Bownd's opinions.

Cartwright's Admonition to Parliament, 1572. Robert's Southern Counties, pp. 37, 38.

10

against frivolity, Puritanism pushed Sabbath-keeping to its extreme, reprobating even the most innocent and domestic recreations, and changing a day of rest and refreshment into one of alternate periods of application to religious devotion and of scrupulous vacuity. Bownd's rather ultra propositions were carried yet further when reproduced by high-strung preachers. It is said that some of these declared that the ringing of more than one bell to call people to church on the Sabbath was as great a sin as murder, adultery, or parricide. The lack of a sense of proportion is the specific distinction of the zealot and the polemic. This lack was not peculiar to the Puritans, however. Joseph Hall, afterward a well-known bishop, could address men so worthy as John Robinson and his colleague in such words as these: "Your souls shall find too late . . . that even whoredoms and murders shall abide an easier answer than separation." Perhaps one may rather say that a lack of the sense of proportion in morals was a trait of that age, an age of zealots and polemics.

XX.

In such a time Dr. Bownd's book easily captivated the religious public, and there arose a passion for a stricter Sabbath. According to Fuller, the Lord's Day, especially in towns, "began to be precisely kept, people becoming a law to themselves, forbearing such sports as yet by statute permitted; yea, many rejoicing at their own restraint herein. On this day the stoutest fencer laid down the buckler; the most skillful archer unbent the bow, counting all shooting beside the mark; May-games and mor-ris-dancers grew out of request; and good reason that bells should be silenced from jingling about men's legs, if their very ringing in steeples were adjudged unlawful." Some learned scholars were impressed by Bownd's argument, and others who did not agree with his conclusions thought it best not to gainsay them, "because they tended to the manifest advance of religion." And indeed the new zeal for Sabbath-keeping must have inciden-tally promoted morals and good order in so licen-tious an age.

Fuller's
Ch. Hist.
of Britain,
book ix,
sect. viii,
20, 21.

But a violent opposition quickly arose. Some opposed the book as "galling men's necks with a Jewish yoke against the liberty of Christians," and many of the clergy of the new high-church type resented the doctrine of a Christian Sab-bath, asserting that it put "an unequal lustre on the Sunday on set purpose to eclipse all other holy days to the derogation of the author-ity of the church." There were those who as-serted that the "brethren," as they styled them, had brought forth Bownd's book, intending by this "attack from an odd corner" to retrieve lost ground. The manifest advantage to Puritan-ism from the shifting of the ground of debate, aroused Archbishop Whitgift. In 1599 he made

Opposi-
tion to
Bownd.

Fuller's
Church
History,
book ix,
sect. viii,
21.

Note 11.

BOOK II.

the tactical mistake of ordering the book called in, and in 1600 Chief-Justice Popham forbade the reprinting of it. The price of the work was doubled at once, and it was everywhere sought for, books being " more called on when called in," as Fuller says. When it could not be had in print, it was transcribed by enthusiastic admirers and circulated " from friend to friend " in manuscript. As soon as Whitgift's " head was laid," a new and enlarged edition was published.

Note 12.

The theory of a Sunday-Sabbath, which from the first was not confined to the Puritans, permeated English and American thought and life. But from that time forward the Puritans made rigid Sabbath-keeping the very mark and password of the faithful. From England the theory spread northward to Scotland, where it found a congenial soil. The strict observance of Sunday

1611.

was embodied in those Laws, Divine, Moral, and Martial, under which Sir Thomas Dale oppressed Virginia, years before the earliest Puritan migration carried it to the coast of New England. On that coast Bownd's Sabbath took on its deepest hue, becoming at last as grievous an

Note 13.

evil, perhaps, as the frivolity it had supplanted.

XXI.

Effect on
Puritan-
ism.

The Puritans protesting against Hebraism in vestments, in priesthood, in liturgy, and in festivals, fell headlong into the Pharisaism of the rigid Sabbath. History records many similar phenomena. To escape from the spirit of one's age is difficult for an individual, impossible perhaps for a sect or party. Nevertheless, the Sabbath agitation had given a new impulse to the Puritan movement—had, indeed, given it a positive party cry, and had furnished it with a visible badge of superior sanctity.

The Calvinistic controversy which broke out almost simultaneously with that about the Sabbath and prevailed throughout the reign of James I, added yet one more issue, by making Puritanism the party of a stern and conservative orthodoxy, as opposed to the newer Arminianism which spread so quickly among the High-Church clergy. From all these fresh developments Puritanism gained in power and compactness, if it lost something of simplicity and spirituality. Standing for ultra-Protestantism, for good morals, for an ascetic Sabbath, for a high dogmatic orthodoxy, Puritanism could not but win the allegiance of the mass of the English people, and especially of the middle class. It was this new, compact, austere, dogmatic, self-confident Puritanism, when it had become a political as well as a religious movement, that obliterated Laud and Charles and set up the Commonwealth. And in studying the evolution of this later Puritanism we have been present at the shaping of New England in Old England.

The new Puritanism.

ELUCIDATIONS.

Evelyn's Diary, pp. 4, 5; date, 1634: "My father was appointed Sheriff for Surrey and Sussex before they were disjoyned. He had 116 servants in liverys, every one livery'd in greene sattin doublets. Divers gentlemen and persons of quality waited on him in the same garbe and habit, which at that time (when 30 or 40 was the usual retinue of a High Sheriff) was esteem'd a great matter. . . . He could not refuse the civility of his friends and relations who voluntarily came themselves, or sent in their servants." Compare Chamberlain's remarks about Sir George Yeardley, whom he styles "a mean fellow," and says that the king had knighted him when he was appointed Governor of Virginia, "which hath set him up so high that he flaunts it up and down the streets in extraordinary bravery with fourteen or fifteen fair liveries after him." Domestic Correspondence, James I, No. 110, Calendar, p. 598. The propriety of keeping so many idle serving men is sharply called in question in a tract entitled Cyuile and Vncyuile Life, 1579, and an effort is made to prove the dignity of a serving man's position, while its decline is confessed in A Health to the Gentlemanly Profession of Servingmen, 1598. Both of these tracts are reprinted in Inedited Tracts, etc., Roxburghe Library, 1868. The serving man was not a menial. He rendered personal services to his master or to guests, he could carve on occasion, and as a successor to the military retainers of an earlier time he was ready to fight in any of his master's quarrels; but his principal use was to lend dignity to the mansion and to amuse the master or his guests with conversation during lonely hours in the country house. Among the first Jamestown emigrants were some of these retainers, as we have seen.

The Anatomie of Abuses, by Philip Stubbes, 1583, Pickering's reprint, pages 16, 17: "It is lawfull for the nobilitie, the gentrie and magisterie to weare riche attire, euery one in their callyng. The nobility and gentrie to innoble, garnish, and set forth birthes, dignities, and estates. The magisterie to dignifie their callynges. . . . But now there is suche a confuse mingle mangle of apparell, and suche preposterous excesse thereof, as euery one is permitted to flaunt it out in what apparell he lusteth himself, or can get by any kinde of meanes. So that it is very hard to know who is noble, who is worshipfull, who is a gentleman, who is not; for you shal haue those which are neither of the nobilitie, gentilitie nor yeomanrie . . . go daiely in silkes, veluettes, satens, damaskes, taffaties and suche like; notwithstanding that they be bothe base by birthe, meane by estate, and seruile by callyng. And this I compte a greate confusion, and a generall disorder in a Christian common wealth."

A Brieff Discourse of the Troubles begun at Frankfort, 1564, is the primary authority. It is almost beyond doubt that Whittingham, Dean of Durham, a participant in the troubles, wrote the book. The Frankfort struggles have been discussed recently in Mr. Hinds's The Making of the England of Elizabeth, but, like all writers on the subject, Hinds is obliged to depend almost solely on Whittingham's account. The several volumes of letters from the archives of Zurich, published by the Parker Society, give a good insight into the forces at work in the English Reformation. See, for example, in the volume entitled Original Letters, 1537–1558, that of Thomas Sampson to Calvin, dated Strasburgh, February 23, 1555, which shows the Puritan movement half fledged at this early date when Calvin's authoritative advice is invoked. " The flame is lighted up with increased vehemence amongst us English. For a strong controversy has arisen, while some desire the book of reformation of the Church of England to be set aside altogether, others only deem some things in it objectionable, such as kneeling at the Lord's Supper, the linen surplice, and other matters of this kind; but the rest of it, namely, the prayers, scripture lessons and the form of the administration of baptism and the Lord's Supper they wish to be retained." Note 3, page 106.

There are many and conflicting accounts of the origin of the name. In the Narragansett Club Publications, ii, 197–199, there is an interesting statement of some of these by the editor of Cotton's Answer to Roger Williams, in a note. Note 4, page 106.

That the Puritans early made common cause with the suffering tenantry is not a matter of conjecture. Philip Stubbes, in 1583, in the Anatomie of Abuses, pp. 126, 127, writes: " They take in and inclose commons, moores, heathes, and other common pastures, where out the poore commonaltie were wont to haue all their forrage and feedyng for their cattell, and (whiche is more) corne for themselves to liue vpon; all which are now in most places taken from them, by these greedie puttockes to the great Note 5, page 111.

impouerishyng and vtter beggeryng of many whole townes and parishes. . . . For these inclosures bee the causes why riche men eate vpp poore men, as beastes dooe eate grasse." One might cite recent economic writers on the effect of inclosures, but the conservative laments of the antiquary Aubrey, in his Introduction to the Survey of Wiltshire, written about 1663, give us a nearer and more picturesque, if less philosophical, view. He says : " Destroying of Manours began Temp. Hen. VIII., but now common ; whereby the mean People live lawless, no body to govern them, they care for no body, having no Dependance on any Body. By this Method, and by the Selling of the Church-Lands, is the Ballance of the Government quite alter'd and put into the Hands of the common People." Writing from what he had heard from his grandfather, he says : " Anciently the Leghs i. e. Pastures were noble large Grounds. . . . So likewise in his Remembrance was all between Kington St. Michael and Dracot-Ferne common Fields. Then were a world of labouring People maintained by the Plough. . . . There were no Rates for the Poor in my Grandfather's Days . . . the Church-ale at Whitsuntide did the Business. . . . Since the Reformation and Inclosures aforesaid these Parts have swarm'd with poor People. The Parish of Caln pays to the Poor 500£ *per annum.* . . . Inclosures are for the private, not for the publick Good. For a Shepherd and his Dog, or a Milk-Maid, can manage Meadow-Land, that upon arable, employ'd the Hands of several Scores of Labourers." Miscellanies on Several Curious Subjects, now first published, etc., 1723, pp. 30–33. It will fall within the province of another volume of this series to treat of the systems of landholding brought from England, and I shall not go further into the subject of inclosures here. A portion of the agricultural population seemed superfluous in consequence of inclosures, and colonization was promoted as a means of ridding the country of the excess of its population.

Note 6, page 112.

In the matter of Church government Puritanism passed through three different periods. In the reign of Elizabeth the Church-Puritan was mainly Presbyterian under Cartwright's lead. But there was even then a current that set toward Independency. Separatism was the outward manifestation of this tendency, and according to Ralegh's estimate, cited in the text, there were about twenty thousand declared Separatists in England in 1593. After the suppression of the presbyteries within the Church in the last years of Elizabeth, and the crushing out of the Separatists by rigorous persecutions, questions of the particular form of Church government fell into abeyance among the Puritans for about forty years. " Indiscriminate anti-prelacy was the prevailing mood of the English people," says Masson, " and the distinction between Presbyterianism and Independency was yet caviare to the general." Life of Milton, ii, 590. Richard Baxter, the Puritan divine (as quoted by Masson), confesses in 1641 that until that year he had never thought what Presbytery or Independency was, or ever spoke with a man who seemed to know it. See also Hanbury's Memorials, ii, 69. Writers on this period do not seem to recognize the fact that the two views were in some rivalry among the early Puritans, and that the theory of the independence of the local church seems to have been at least foreshadowed in the opinions at Frankfort. But there was a long generation in which these differences among the Puritans were forgotten in their life-and-death conflict with the Episcopal party. Then, as Puritanism came into power, the example of other Protestant European countries drew England toward Presbyterianism, while the voice of New England came from over the sea pleading for Congregationalism.

CHAP. I.

A letter of Sandys, afterward Archbishop of York, to Bullinger, quoted by Marsden, Early Puritans, 57, shows that though Puritanism by 1573 had become something other than it was at Frankfort, it was still mainly negative. Sandys writes : " New orators are rising up from among us ; foolish young men who despise authority and admit of no superior. They are seeking the complete overthrow and uprooting of the whole of our ecclesiastical polity; and striving to shape out for us I know not what new platform of a church." He gives a summary under nine heads. The assertion that each parish should have its own " presbytery " and choose its own minister, and that the judicial laws of Moses were binding, are the only positive ones. No authority of the magistrate in ecclesiastical matters, no government of the Church except by ministers, elders, and deacons, the taking away of all titles, dignities, lands, and revenues of bishops, etc., from the Church, the allowing of no ministers but actual pastors, the refusal of baptism to the children of papists, fill the rest of this summary. One misses from this skeleton the insistence on Sabbath-keeping, church-going, " ordinances," and ascetic austerity in morals that afterward became distinctive traits of the party.

Note 7, page 123.

Augustine and other early doctors of the Church held to a Sunday-Sabbath in the fifth century, basing it largely on grounds

Note 8, page 125.

that now seem mystical. Compare Coxe on Sabbath Laws and Sabbath Duties, 284, note, and Cook's Historical and General View of Christianity, ii, 301, cited by Coxe. The question was variously treated during the middle ages, St. Thomas Aquinas and other schoolmen taking the prevalent modern view that the fourth commandment was partly moral and partly ceremonial. There is a curious story, for which I do not know the original authority, of Eustachius, Abbot of Hay, in the thirteenth century, who on his return from the Holy Land preached from city to city against buying and selling on Sundays and saints' days. He had with him a copy of a document dropped from heaven and found on the altar of St. Simon, on Mount Golgotha. This paper threatened that if the command were disobeyed it should rain stones and wood and hot water in the night, and, as if such showers were not enough, wild beasts were to devour the Sabbath-breakers. That there was a difference of opinion in that age is shown by the fact that Roger Bacon, later in the thirteenth century, thought it worth while to assert that Christians should work and hold fairs on Sunday, while Saturday was the proper day for rest. He showed no document from heaven, but, like a true philosopher of that time, the learned friar appealed to arguments drawn from astrology. Hearne's Remains, ii, 177, cites Mirandula. Legislation by Parliament regarding Sunday observance was rare before the Reformation. A statute of 28 Edward III incidentally excepts Sunday from the days on which wool may be shorn, and one of 27 Henry VI forbids the keeping of fairs and markets on Sundays, Good Fridays, and principal festivals except four Sundays in harvest. In 4 Edward IV a statute was passed forbidding the sale of shoes on Sundays and certain festivals.

In the " Injunctions by King Edward VI," 1547, Bishop Sparrow's Collection, edition of 1671, p. 8, there is a remarkable statement of what may be called the Edwardean view of Sunday as distinguished from the opinions and practice that had come down from times preceding the Reformation : " God is more offended than pleased, more dishonoured than honoured upon the holy-day because of idleness, pride, drunkenness," etc. The religious and moral duties to which the " holy-day," as it is called, should be strictly devoted are there specified. But, true to the position of compromise, halfwayness, and one might add paradox, which the English Reformation took from the beginning,

there is added in the same paragraph the following : " Yet notwithstanding all Parsons, Vicars, and Curates, shall teach and
declare unto their Parishioners, that they may with a safe and
quiet conscience, in the time of Harvest, labour upon the holy
and festival days and save that thing which God hath sent. And
if for any scrupulosity, or grudge of conscience, men should su-
perstitiously abstain from working upon those days, that then they
should grievously offend and displease God." See also " Thacte
made for thabrogacion of certayne holy-dayes," in the reign of
Henry VIII, 1536, in the same black-letter collection, p. 167. In
this act " Sabboth-day " occurs, but apparently with reference to
the Jewish Sabbath only. " Sonday " is used for Sunday.

Dr. Bownd's Sabathum Veteris et Novi Testamenti is ex
ceedingly rare. There is a copy in the Prince Collection of the
Boston Public Library. It is the only one in this country, so far
as I can learn. I am under obligations in several matters to Cox's
Literature of the Sabbath Question, to the same author's Sabbath
Laws and Sabbath Duties, and to Hessey's Bampton Lectures
for 1860.

*Note 10,
page 129.*

It is Thomas Rogers, the earliest opponent of the doctrine of
Greenham and Bownd, who sees a deep-laid plot in the publication of their books. " What the brethren wanted in strength
they had in wiliness," he says. " For while these worthies of
our church were employing their engines and forces partly in defending the present government ecclesiastical, partly in assaulting
the presbytery and new discipline, even at that very instant the
brethren . . . abandoned quite the bulwarks which they had
raised and gave out were impregnable : suffering us to beat them
down, without any or very small resistance, and yet not careless
of affairs, left not the wars for all that, but from an odd corner,
and after a new fashion which we little thought of (such was
their cunning), set upon us afresh again by dispersing in printed
books (which for ten years' space before they had been in hammering among themselves to make them complete) their Sabbath
speculations and presbyterian (that is more than kingly or
popely) directions for the observance of the Lord's Day." Preface to Thirty-nine Articles, paragraph 20. He also says, with
some wit, " They set up a new idol, their Saint Sabbath."

*Note 11,
page 131.*

The doctrine of a strict Sabbath appears to have made no
impression in Scotland until the seventeenth century was well

*Note 12,
page 132.*

advanced.　In the printed Burgh Records of Aberdeen from 1570 to 1625 there is no sabbatarian legislation in the proper sense; but there are efforts to compel the people to suspend buying and selling fish and flesh in the market, the playing of outdoor games and ninepins, and the selling of liquors during sermon time only.　Take as an example the following ordinance —as curious for its language as its subject—dated 4th October, 1598, twenty-four years after Knox's death :

"Item, The prouest, bailleis, and counsall ratefeis and approves the statute maid obefoir, bering that na mercatt, nather of fische nor flesche salbe on the Sabboth day in tyme cumming, in tyme of sermone, vnder the pane of confiscatioun of the same; and lykvayes ratefeis the statute maid aganis the playeris in the linkis, and at the kyillis, during the time of the sermones; . . . and that na tavernar sell nor went any wyne nor aill in tyme cumming in tyme of sermone, ather on the Sabboth day or vlk dayes, under the pane of ane vnlaw of fourtie s., to be vpliftit of the contravenar als oft as they be convict."

Note 13,
page 132.
New England Puritanism took a position more ultra even than that of Bownd.　Thomas Shepard, of Cambridge, Mass., developed from some Sermons on the Subject a work with the title, Theses Sabbaticæ, or the Doctrine of the Sabbath.　After a considerable circulation in manuscript among New England students of divinity, it was printed at London in 1650 by request of all the elders of New England.　From the time of Augustine the prevailing theory of advocates of a Sunday-Sabbath has been that the fourth commandment is partly moral, partly ceremonial ; but Shepard, who does not stick at small logical or historical difficulties, will have it wholly moral, by which means he avoids any option regarding the day.　The rest of the Sabbath, according to this authoritative New England treatise, is to be as strict as it ever was under Jewish law, and is to be rigidly enforced on the unwilling by parents and magistrates.　In the spirit of a thorough-paced literalist Shepard argues through fifty pages that the Sabbath begins in the evening.　He admits that only "servile labour" is forbidden, but he reasons that as "sports and pastimes" are ordained "to whet on worldly labour," they therefore partake of its servile character and are not tolerable on the Sabbath.　It appears from his preface that there were Puritans in his time who denied the sabbatical character of Sunday and spiritualized the commandment.

CHAPTER THE SECOND.

SEPARATISM AND THE SCROOBY CHURCH.

I.

To the great brotherhood of Puritans who formed a party within the church there was added a little fringe of Separatists or "Brownists," as they were commonly called, who did not stop with rejecting certain traits of the Anglican service, but spurned the church itself. Upon these ultraists fell the merciless hand of persecution. They were imprisoned, hanged, exiled. They were mostly humble people, and were never numerous; but by their superior boldness in speech and writing, by their attempts to realize actual church organizations on apostolic models, they rendered themselves considerable if not formidable. From this advance guard and forlorn hope of Puritanism, inured to hardship and the battle front, came at length the little band of New England pioneers who made a way into the wilderness over the dead bodies of half their company. The example of these contemned Brownists led to the Puritan settlement of New England. Their type of ecclesiastical organization ultimately dominated the Congregationalism of New England and the nonconformity of the mother country. For these

reasons, if for no other, Brownism, however obscure it may have been, is not a negligible element
in history.

II.

The great body of the Puritans seem to have
agreed with Bishop Hall that it was "better to
swallow a ceremony than to rend a church," and
they agreed with him in regarding Separatism as
criminal. They were, indeed, too intent on reforming the Church of England to think of leaving it.
They made no scruple of defying ecclesiastical
regulations when they could, but in the moral
code of that day schism was the deadliest of sins.

In the early part of Elizabeth's reign, before
the beginning of the rule of Whitgift and the High
Commission Courts, Puritan divines slighted or
omitted the liturgy in many parishes. This became more common after the rise of Cartwright
and the Presbyterian movement, about 1570. For

Scrambler,
Bishop of
Peterbor-
ough, to
Burghley,
13th April,
1573, in
Wright's
Elizabeth
and her
Times.

example, in the town of Overston, in 1573, there
was no divine service according to the Book of
Common Prayer, "but insteade thereof two sermons be preached" by men whom the bishop had
refused to license. The village of Whiston was
also a place of Puritan assemblage, "where it is
their joye," writes the Bishop of Peterborough,
"to have manie owte of divers parishes, principal-
lie owte of Northampton towne and Overston
aforesaid, with other townes thereaboute, there to
receive the sacramentes with preachers and min-

isters to their owne liking, and contrarie to the forme prescribed by the publique order of the realme." Thomas Rogers says, "The brethren (for so did they style them-selves) would neither pray, nor say service, nor baptize, nor celebrate the Lord's Supper, nor marry, nor bury, nor do any other ecclesiastical duty according to law."

Rogers's Preface to Articles. Parker Soc. ed., p. 10.

At this time some of the Puritan divines held high positions in the church. Whittingham, who had been on the Puritan side of the quarrels in Frankfort, and who had received only a Genevan ordination, succeeded in holding his deanery of Durham until his death, in 1579. In 1563 Dr. Turner was sneering at bishops as "white coats" and "tippett gentlemen," while himself Dean of Durham.

But Elizabeth after a while filled the bishoprics with men to her liking, whose heavy hands made the lot of Puritans in the church harder and harder. Many ministers were silenced, but there were many who, by evasion or by straining their consciences, held their benefices. Some Puritan clergymen, when they were to preach, preferred "to walk in the church-yard until sermon time rather than to be present at public prayer." Some Puritan laymen had their own way of conforming to the church. "There is a sort of Semi-Separatist," says Pagitt, as late as 1646, "that will heare our Sermons but not our Common-prayers; and of these you may see every Sunday in our streets sitting and standing about our doores; who, when

The Semi-Separatists.

Bancroft in Barlowe's Svmme and Svbstance.

Heresiography, p. 82.

Prayers are done, rush into our Churches to hear our Sermons."

III.

The growth of Separatist churches was due to two causes. An almost incredible reverence for the letter of the Scriptures had taken the place of older superstitions. There was a strong tendency to revert to the stern spirit of the Old Testament and to adopt the external forms of the New. Religious idealists saw a striking contrast between the discipline of the primitive and almost isolated bands of enthusiastic believers in the apostolic time and the all-inclusive parishes of the hierarchical state church. And in that age of externalism the difference in organic form between the Anglican church and the little synagogues of Christian seceders founded by Paul in the Levant weighed heavily upon the minds of earnest people. It did not occur to them that this primitive organization was probably brought over from the neighboring Jewish congregations from which the converts had withdrawn, and that there might not be any obligation to imitate it under different skies and in a remote age. The Separatist was an idealist. "He

lives by the aire," said an opponent, "and there he builds Castles and Churches; none on earth will please him; . . . he must finde out Sir Thomas More's Utopia, or rather Plato's Community, and bee an Elder there." But Separatism was undoubtedly promoted by persecution. Bradford

says that the sufferings inflicted on them by the
bishops helped some of the Puritans "to see further into things by the light of the word of God.
How not only these base and beggerly ceremonies
were unlawfull, but also that the lordly and tiran-
ous power of the prelats ought not to be submitted unto." Drawn thus by the letter of the
biblical record, while stung by cruel oppression
and galled by the opposition of the constituted
authorities to what they deemed the truth divine,
it is not strange that religious enthusiasts began to
long for societies organized like those of the apostolic age, from which the profane should be excluded by a strict discipline.

Plimoth
Plantation,
p. 8.

IV.

The beginning of Separatism has been commonly attributed to Robert Browne, a contentious
and able advocate of Separatist doctrines. After a
brief and erratic career as an advocate of these
opinions, and after suffering the penalty of his zeal
and proving the sincerity of his belief in thirty-two
different prisons, in some of which he could not see
his hand at noonday, Browne at length began to
waver—now inclined to return to the church, now
recoiling toward dissent. Worn out in nerves by
controversy and persecution, this eccentric man
was so alarmed by a solemn sentence of excommunication from a bishop, that he repented and made
peace with the English church. He accepted a
benefice, but employed a curate to preach for him.

Robert
Browne
and
Brown-
ism.

1581 to
1586.

Browne lingered on to an unhonored age, imperious and contentious, not able to live with his wife, and held in no reverence by churchmen, while he was despised by Separatists. He died at eighty, in Northampton jail, to which he had been carried on a feather bed laid in a cart. The old man had been committed to prison this thirty-third time in his life for striking a constable who sought to collect a rate.

Separatism in some form existed before Browne's zeal made it a thorn in the side of the bishops. Something like a separation existed in 1567. In 1571 there was an independent church of which we know little but the pastor's name. Bradford even dates independency back to the reign of Mary. In truth, the rise of this sect, from which came the earliest New England colony, appears to be lost in obscurity. Significant movements are usually cradled in rustic mangers, to which no learned magi think it worth their while to journey. The beginning of Separatism was probably in the little conventicles held by devout Puritans who, in the words of one of their own writers, " met together to sing a psalm or to talk of God's word." But Browne, so far as we know, was one of the earliest to organize independent churches, with officers named and classified after those of the petty hierarchies of the early Christian congregations, or rather according to such deductions regarding them as he was able to make from the Epistles of Paul. Separatism, though it owed something to

Browne's activity, was not founded by him. Browne's labors began about 1581, and his fiery career as a Brownist had lasted only four or five years when he began to vacillate. A great part of this time was spent in exile, much of it in prison, and very little of it about London. But before 1587 London seems to have been the center of the Separatists, from which they had "sparsed their companies into severall partes of the Realme."

Stephen Breadwell, 1588, in Dexter, 255.

It seems that their rise in London came from the devout meetings of those who had begun to repudiate the Church of England as antichristian. Without any officers or organization apparently, these people, when we first get sight of them, were wont to assemble in the summer time in the fields about London, sitting down upon a bank while the Bible was expounded now by one and now by another of the company. In the winter it was their custom to spend the whole Sunday together from five o'clock in the morning, eating dinner in company and paying for it by a collection. They responded in prayer only by spontaneous groans or sobs, much after the fashion of the early Quakers, Methodists, and other enthusiasts of a later time. If one of their members returned to a parish assembly, they pronounced him an apostate and solemnly delivered him over to Satan until he should repent.

H. M. Dexter's Congregationalism, 255–257.

V.

When they began to organize themselves formally into a church the London Separatists in their
turn resorted to the apostolic epistles. These had
already been treated like the magician's bottle that
is made to yield white wine or red at pleasure.
From them whatsoever form of discipline was desired by Anglican, Presbyterian, or Brownist had
been derived, and now a still different discipline
was deduced, a mean betwixt Presbyterian and
Brownist theories. This is known now as Barrowism. It was the form of church government
brought by the Pilgrims to Plymouth, and substantially that which prevailed in New England
throughout the seventeenth century.

The London Separatists suffered miserably from
persecution. Many of them languished and died
in prison. Barrow and Greenwood, their leaders,
were hanged at Tyburn. A part of them migrated
to Amsterdam, while the rest maintained a furtive
church in London. Those in Amsterdam, having
no lingering abuses of the English church to reform, set every man's conscience to watch his
neighbor's conduct. Having seceded from the
communion of the Church of England on account
of scandals, they were scandalized with the least
variation from their rigorous standard by any of
their own church members, and they were soon
torn asunder with dissensions as the result of this
vicariousness of conscience. The innocent vanity

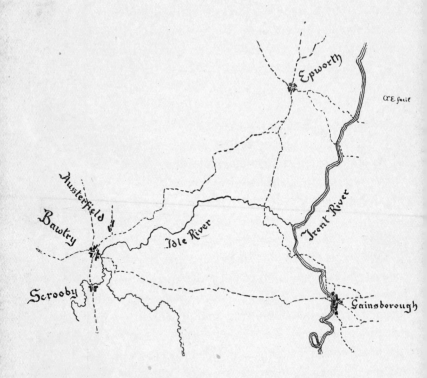

Epworth

Austerfield

Bawtry

Idle River

Trent River

Scrooby

Gainsborough

CrE. facit

of the pastor's wife who could never forego a "toppish" hat and high-heeled shoes was the principal stumbling-block.

Though Separatism had been almost extirpated from England by the close of Elizabeth's reign, there remained even yet one vigorous society in the north which was destined to exert a remarkable influence on the course of history.

VI.

On the southern margin of Yorkshire the traveler alights to-day at the station of Bawtry. It is an uninteresting village, with a rustic inn. More than a mile to the southward, in Nottinghamshire, lies the pleasant but commonplace village of Scrooby. About a mile to the north of Bawtry is Austerfield, a hamlet of brick cottages crowded together along the road. It has a picturesque little church built in the middle ages, the walls of which are three feet thick. This church will seat something more than a hundred people nowadays by the aid of a rather modern extension. In the seventeenth century it was smaller, and there was no ceiling. Then one could see the rafters of the roof while shuddering with cold in the grottolike interior. The country around is level and unpicturesque.

But one is here in the cradle of great religious movements. In Scrooby and in Austerfield were born the Pilgrims who made the first successful settlement in New England. A little to the east lies Gainsborough, from which migrated to Holland in 1606 the saintly Separatist John Smyth, who gave form to a great Baptist movement of modern times. A few miles to the northeast of Bawtry, in Lincolnshire, lies Epworth, the nest from which the Wesleys issued more than a hundred years later to spread Methodism over the world. Religious zeal seems to have characterized the people of this region even before the Reformation, for the country round about Scrooby was occupied at that time by an unusual number of religious houses.

Hunter's Founders of New Plymouth, 24, 25.

The little Austerfield church and the old church at Scrooby are the only picturesque or romantic elements of the environment, and on these churches the Pilgrims turned their backs as though they had been temples of Baal. In the single street of Austerfield the traveler meets the cottagers of to-day, and essays to talk with them. They are heavy and somewhat stolid, like most other rustic people in the north country, and an accent to which their ears are not accustomed amuses and puzzles them. No tradition of the Pilgrims lingers among them. They have never heard that anybody ever went out of Austerfield to do anything historical. They listen with a bovine surprise if you speak to them of this exodus, and they refer you to the old clerk of the parish, who will know about it. The venerable clerk is a striking figure, not unlike that parish clerk painted by Gainsborough. This oracle of the hamlet knows that Americans come here as on a pilgrimage, and he tells you that one of them, a descendant of Governor Bradford, offered a considerable sum for the disused stone font at which Bradford the Pilgrim was baptized. But the traveler turns away at length from the rustic folk of Austerfield and the beer-drinkers over their mugs in the inn at Bawtry, and the villagers at Scrooby, benumbed by that sense of utter commonplaceness which is left on the mind of a stranger by such an agricultural community. The Pilgrims, then, concerning whom poems have been written, and in whose honor orations without number have been made, were just common country folk like these, trudging through wheat fields and along the muddy clay highways of the days of Elizabeth and James. They were just such men as these and they were not. They were such as these would be if they were vivified by enthusiasm. We may laugh at superfluous scruples in rustic minds, but none will smile at brave and stubborn loyalty to an idea when it produces such steadfast courage as that of the Pilgrims.

And yet, when the traveler has resumed his journey, and recalls Scrooby and Bawtry and Austerfield, the stolid men and gossiping women, the narrow pursuits of the plowman and the reaper, and remembers the flat, naked, and depressing landscape, he is beset by the old skepticism about the coming of anything good out of Nazareth. Nor is he helped by remembering that at the time of Bradford's christening at the old stone font the inhabitants of Austerfield are said to have been "a

Book II.

Magnalia,
Book II,
chap. i,
p. 2.

most ignorant and licentious people," and that earlier in that same century John Leland speaks of " the meane townlet of Scrooby."

VIII.

Elder
Brewster.

But Leland's description of the village suggests the influence that caused Scrooby and the wheat fields thereabout to send forth, in the beginning of the seventeenth century and of a new reign, men capable of courage and fortitude sufficient to make them memorable, and to make these three townlets places of pilgrimage in following centuries.

Itinerary,
i, 36, in
Hunter's
Founders,
p. 20.

" In the meane townlet of Scrooby, I marked two things "—it is Leland who writes—" the parish church not big but very well builded ; the second was a great manor-place, standing within a moat, and longing to the Archbishop of York." This large old manor-place he describes with its outer and inner court. In this manor-place, about half a century after Leland saw it, there lived William Brewster. He was a man of education, who had been for a short time in residence at Cambridge ; he had served as one of the under secretaries of state for years ; had been trusted beyond all others by Secretary Davison, his patron ; and, when Elizabeth disgraced Davison, in order to avoid responsibility for the death of Mary of Scotland, Brewster had been the one friend who clung to the fallen secretary as long as there was opportunity to do him service. Making no further effort to establish

himself at court, Brewster went after a while " to
live in the country in good esteeme amongst his
freinds and the good gentle-men of those parts,
espetially the godly and religious." His abode
after his retirement was the old manor-place now
destroyed, but then the most conspicuous building
at Scrooby. It belonged in his time to Sir Samuel
Sandys, the elder brother of Sir Edwin Sandys,
whose work as the master spirit in the later history of the Virginia Company has already been
recounted. At Scrooby Brewster succeeded his
father in the office of " Post," an office that obliged
him to receive and deliver letters for a wide
district of country, to keep relays of horses for
travelers by post on the great route to the north,
and to furnish inn accommodations. In the master
of the post at Scrooby we have the first of those
influences that lifted a group of people from this
rustic region into historic importance. He had
been acquainted with the great world, and had
borne a responsible if not a conspicuous part in
delicate diplomatic affairs in the Netherlands. At
court, as at Scrooby, he was a Puritan, and now in
his retirement his energies were devoted to the
promotion of religion. He secured earnest ministers for many of the neighboring parishes. But
that which he builded the authorities tore down.
Whitgift was archbishop, and the High Commission Courts were proceeding against Puritans with
the energy of the Spanish Inquisition. " The
godly preachers" about him were silenced. The

CHAP. II.

Bradford,
410.

Supra,
Book I,
chap. ii, iii.

people who followed them were proscribed, and all the pains and expense of Brewster and his Puritan friends in establishing religion as they understood it were likely to be rendered futile by the governors of the church. "He and many more of those times begane to looke further into things," says Bradford. Persecution begot Separatism. The theory was the result of conditions, as new theories are wont to be.

IX.

Here, as elsewhere, the secession appears to have begun with meetings for devotion. By this supposition we may reconcile two dates which have been supposed to conflict, conjecturing that in 1602, when Brewster had lived about fifteen years in the old manor-house, his neighbors, who did not care to attend the ministry of ignorant and licentious priests, began to spend whole Sundays together, now in one place and now in another, but most frequently in the old manor-house builded within a moat, and reached by ascending a flight of stone steps. Here, Brewster's hospitality was dispensed to them freely. They may or may not have been members of the Separatist church at Gainsborough, as some have supposed. It was not until 1606 that these people formed the fully organized Separatist church of Scrooby. It was organized after the Barrowist pattern that had originated in London—it was after a divine pattern, according to their belief. Brewster, the nucleus of the church, became their ruling elder.

It was in these all-day meetings at the old manor-house that the Separatist rustics of Scrooby were molded for suffering and endeavor. The humble, modest, and conscientious Brewster was the king-post of the new church—the first and longest enduring of the influences that shaped the character of these people in England, Holland, and America. Brewster could probably have returned to the court under other auspices after Davison's fall, but as master of the post at Scrooby, then as a teacher and as founder of a printing office of prohibited English books in Leyden, and finally as a settler in the wilderness, inuring his soft hands to rude toils, until he died in his cabin an octogenarian, he led a life strangely different from that of a courtier. But no career possible to him at court could have been so useful or so long remembered.

Bradford's Plimoth Plantation, 408–414. Hunter's Founders, *passim.* Winsor's Elder William Brewster, a pamphlet. F. B. Dexter in Narrative and Crit. Hist., iii, 257–282.

X.

But Brewster was not the master spirit. About the time the Separatists of Scrooby completed their church organization, in 1606, there came to it John Robinson. He had been a fellow of Emmanuel College, Cambridge, and a beneficed clergyman of Puritan views. He, too, had been slowly propelled to Separatist opinion by persecution. For fourteen years before the final migration he led the Pilgrims at Scrooby and Leyden. Wise man of affairs, he directed his people even in their

John Robinson.

hard struggle for bread in a foreign country. He was one of the few men, in that age of debate about husks and shells, who penetrated to those teachings concerning character and conduct which are the vital and imperishable elements of religion. Even when assailed most roughly in debate he was magnanimous and forbearing. He avoided the bigotry and bitterness of the early Brownists, and outgrew as years went on the narrowness of rigid Separatism. He lived on the best terms with the Dutch and French churches. He opposed rather the substantial abuses than the ceremonies of the Church of England, and as life advanced he came to extend a hearty fellowship and communion to good men in that church. Had it been his lot to remain in the national church and rise, as did his opponent, Joseph Hall, to the pedestal of a bishopric or to other dignity, he would have been one of the most illustrious divines of the age —wanting something of the statesmanly breadth of Hooker, but quite outspreading and overtopping the Whitgifts, Bancrofts, and perhaps even the Halls. Robert Baillie, who could say many hard things against Separatists, is forced to confess that "Robinson was a man of excellent parts, and the most learned, polished, and modest spirit that ever separated from the Church of England"; and long after his death the Dutch theologian Hornbeeck recalls again and again his integrity, learn-

ing, and modesty.

Shall we say that when subjected to this great

man's influence the rustics of Scrooby and Bawtry and Austerfield were clowns no longer? Perhaps we shall be truer to the probabilities of human nature if we conclude that Robinson was able to mold a few of the best of them to great uses, and that these became the significant digits which gave value to the ciphers.

ELUCIDATIONS.

Note 1, page 146. The eccentricities, moral and mental, of Browne were a constant resource of those who sought to involve all Separatists in his disgrace. Odium has always been a more effective weapon than argument in a theological controversy. Browne's enemies alleged that even while on the gridiron of persecution his conduct had not been free from moral obliquity. I have not been able to see Bernard's charges on this score, but John Robinson, in his Justification, etc. (1610), parries the thrust in these words: " Now as touching Browne, it is true as Mr. B[ernard] affirmeth, that as he forsook the Lord so the Lord forsook him in his way ; . . . as for the wicked things (which Mr. B. affirmeth) *he did in the way* it may well be as he sayeth, . . . as the more like he was to re-turne to his proper centre the Church of England, where he should be sure to find companie ynough in any wickednesse." Edition of 1639, p. 50. One of the most learned accounts of Browne is to be found in H. M. Dexter's Congregationalism, the lecture on Robert Browne. It is always easy to admire Dr. Dexter's erudition, but not so easy to assent to his conclusions. See also Pagitt's Heresiography, p. 56 and *passim* ; Fuller's Church History, ix, vi, 1–7 ; and Hanbury's Memorials, p. 18 and following.

Note 2, page 146. John Robinson, in Justification of Separation from the Church of England, p. 50, edition of 1639, says: " It is true that Boulton was (though not the first in that way) an elder of a Separatist church in the beginning of Queen Elizabeth's dayes, and falling from his holy profession recanted the same at Paul's Crosse and afterwards hung himself as Judas did." Compare Cotton's The Way of the Congregationall Churches Cleared, p. 4, and various intimations in Hanbury's Memorials, which imply the existence of Independent congregations in London and elsewhere in the early years of Elizabeth's reign. But Hanbury's handling of the valuable material he collected with commendable assiduity is sometimes so clumsy that the reader is obliged to grope for facts bearing upon most important questions. One gets from Hanbury's notes and some older publications a vague notion that the Flemish Protestants, recently settled in England in great numbers, exerted an influence in favor of Independency. Robert Browne began his secession in Norwich, a place where the people from the Low Countries were nearly half the population, and Browne was even said to have labored among the Dutch first. Fuller, ix, sec. vi, 2.

Robinson's character may be judged from his works. His good qualities are very apparent in the wise and tender letters addressed to the Pilgrims when they were leaving England and after their arrival at Plymouth, which will be found in Bradford's Plimoth Plantations, 63, 64, 163. See Bradford's character of him, ibid., 17–19. See also Young's Chronicles of the Pilgrims, 473–482. Ainsworth's tribute is in Hanbury's Memorials, 95. See also Winslow's Brief Narration in Young's Chronicles, 379. George Sumner, in 3d Massachusetts Historical Collections, ix, has a paper giving the result of his investigations in Leyden. He quotes Hornbeeck as saying, twenty-eight years after Robinson's death, that he was the best of all the exiles as well as the most upright, learned, and most modest. Hornbeeck's words are: "Optimus inter illos." "Vir supra reliquos probus atque eruditus." "Doctissimi ac modestissimi omnium separatistorum."

CHAPTER THE THIRD.

THE PILGRIM MIGRATIONS.

I.

THE accession of James of Scotland to the English throne in 1603 raised the hopes of the Puritans. James had said, in 1590: "As for our neighbour kirk of England, their service is an ill-said masse in English; they want nothing of the masse but the liftings." Later, when the prospect of his accession to the English throne was imminent, James had spoken with a different voice, but the Puritans remembered his lifelong familiarity with Presbyterian forms, and his strongly expressed satisfaction with the Scottish Kirk. They met him on his way to London with a petition for modifications of the service. This was known as the Millinary Petition, because it was supposed to represent the views of about one thousand English divines.

In January, 1604, the king held a formal conference at Hampton Court between eleven of the Anglican party on one side, nine of them being bishops, and four Puritan divines, representing the petitioners. Assuming at first the air of playing the arbiter, James, who dearly loved a puttering theological debate, could not refrain from taking

CHAP. III.

Accession of James I.

Neal, ii, 28. Compare Burns's Prel. Diss. to Wodrow, lxxiv.

Hampton Court conference.

Book II.

Svmme
and Svb-
stance,
passim.

the cause of the churchmen out of their hands and arguing it himself. The reports of the conference are most interesting as showing the paradoxical qualities of James, who, by his action at this meeting, unwittingly made himself a conspicuous figure in the history of America. The great churchmen were surprised at the display made by the king of dialectic skill. They held Scotch learning in some contempt, and were amazed that one bred among the "Puritans" should know how to handle questions of theology so aptly. James, though he had declared the Church of Scotland "the sincerest kirk in the world" because it did not

Prel. Diss.
to Wod-
row, lxxiv.

keep Easter and Yule as the Genevans did, now had the face to assure the prelates that he had never believed after he was ten years old what he was taught in Scotland. His speeches in the conference are marked by ability, mingled with the folly which vitiated all his qualities. Quick at reply and keen in analysis, he even shows something like breadth of intelligence, or at least intellectual toleration, but without ever for a moment evincing any liberality of feeling. His manifest cleverness is rendered futile by his narrow and ridiculous egotism, his arrogance in the treatment of opponents, and his coarse vulgarity in expres-

Ch. Hist.,
x, vii, 30.

sion. "In common speaking as in his hunting," says Fuller, "he stood not on the cleanest but nearest way." The Puritans were no more able to answer the arguments of the king than was Æsop's lamb to make reply to the wolf. Laying down for his fundamental maxim "No bishop, no king," he drew a picture of the troubles that would beset him when "Jack and Tom and Will and Dick" should meet and censure the king and his council. He would have no such assemblage of the clergy until he should grow fat and pursy and need trouble to keep him in breath, he said. It could not occur to his self-centered mind that so grave a question was not to be settled merely by considering the ease and convenience of the sovereign. "He rather usede upbraidinges than argumente," says Harrington, who was present. He bade the Puritans "awaie with their snivellinge," and, in discussing the surplice, made an allusion that would be deemed a profanation by reverent churchmen of the present time.

With characteristic pedantry he spoke part of the time in Latin, and his clever refutation of the hapless Puritans sounded like the wisdom of God to the anxious bishops. In spite of the downright scolding and vulgar abuse with which the king flavored his orthodoxy, the aged Whitgift declared that undoubtedly his Majesty spoke by the special assistance of God's Spirit; but one of the worldly bystanders ventured, in defiance of the episcopal dictum, to think that whatever spirit inspired the king was "rather foul-mouthed." Bancroft, Bishop of London, theatrically fell on his knees and solemnly protested that his heart melted within him with joy that Almighty God of his singular mercy had given them such a king "as since Christ's

CHAP. III.

Nugæ Antiquæ., i, 181.

The king and the bishops.

12

Book II.

Note 1.

Compare
Nugæ An-
tiquæ, ii,
25, 26.

time the like hath not been seen." The king
in his turn was naturally impressed with the sagacity of a bishop who could so devoutly admire
his Majesty's ability, and, when soon afterward a
fresh access of paralysis carried off Whitgift, it was
not surprising that Bancroft should be translated
from London to Canterbury over the heads of
worthier competitors. From the moment of Bancroft's accession to the primacy the lot of the Puritans and Separatists became harder, for he plumed
himself doubtless on being the originator of the
high-church doctrine, and he was a man whose
harsh energy seems not to have been tempered by
an intimate piety like that of Whitgift.

Results.

Svmme
and Svb-
stance, 35.

When James rose from his chair at the close of
the debate on the second day he said, " I shall make
them conform themselves, or I will harry them out
of this land, or else do worse "; and he wrote to a
friend boasting that he had " peppered the Puritans

Compare
Bacon's
Certain
Considera-
tions
touching
the better
Pacifica-
tion of the
Church of
England.

soundly." But the king had missed, without knowing it, the greatest opportunity of his reign—an
opportunity for conciliating or weakening the Puritan opposition, and consolidating the church and
his kingdom. James could think of nothing but
his own display of cleverness and browbeating
arrogance in a dispute with great divines like Rey-
nolds and Chaderton. The conference had been
for him a recreation not much more serious than
stag-hunting. That it was pregnant with vast and
far-reaching results for good and evil in England
and the New World he, perhaps, did not dream.

By his narrow and selfish course at this critical moment he may be said to have sealed the fate of his son, if not the doom of his dynasty; and his clever folly gave fresh life to the bitter struggle between Anglican and Puritan which resulted in the peopling of New England a quarter of a century afterward.

II.

Every proscription of the Puritans within the church was accompanied by a crusade against the Brownists without, who were counted sinners above all other men. Though Ralegh in 1593 had estimated the Brownists at twenty thousand, they were by this time in consequence of oppression "about worn out," as Bacon said. Upon those who remained the new persecution broke with untempered severity. Badgered on every side by that vexatious harrying which King James and his ecclesiastics kept up according to promise, the little congregation at Scrooby in 1607 resolved to flee into Holland, where they would be strangers to the speech and to the modes of getting a living, but where they might worship God in extemporary prayers under the guidance of elders of their own choice without fear of fines and prisons.

That which is most honorable to the Low Countries, from a historical point of view, namely, that their cities were places of refuge for oppressed consciences, was esteemed odious and highly ridiculous in the seventeenth century. In one of the

CHAP. III.

The storm of persecution.

Bacon's Observation on a Libel.

Toleration in the Low Countries.

plays of that time there is a humorous proposition to hold a consultation about "erecting four new sects of religion in Amsterdam." The Dutch metropolis was called a cage of unclean birds, and a French prelate contemned it as "a common harbor of all opinions and heresies." At a later period Edward Johnson, the rather bloodthirsty Massachusetts Puritan, inveighs against "the great mingle mangle of religion" in Holland, and like a burlesque prophet shrieks, "Ye Dutch, come out of your hodge podge!" Robert Baylie, in a sermon before the House of Lords as late as 1645, says of the toleration by the Dutch, that "for this one thing they have become infamous in the Christian world."

Errours and Induration, p. 27.

Flight of the Pilgrims.

To the asylum offered by the Low Countries the Scrooby Separatists resolved to flee. The pack of harriers let loose by James and Bancroft were in full cry. The members of the Scrooby church found themselves "hunted and persecuted on every side," having their houses watched night and day, so that all their sufferings in times past "were but as flea bitings in comparison." But the tyranny that made England intolerable did its best to render flight impossible. In various essays to escape, the Separatists were arrested and stripped of what valuables they had, while their leaders were cast into prison for months at a time.

The Pilgrims in Amsterdam.

At length by one means or another the members of this battered little community got away and met together in Amsterdam. To plain north country folk this was indeed a strange land, and one can see in the vivid and eloquent language of Bradford of Austerfield, who was a young man when he crossed the German Ocean, the memory of the impressions which these cities of the Low Countries made on their rustic minds. But "it was not longe before they saw the grimme and grisly face of povertie coming upon them like an armed man, with whom they must bukle and incounter."

III.

Robinson discovered that he was not of a piece with those Separatists who had preceded him to Amsterdam. In one division of these, questions of whalebone in bodices, of high-heeled shoes and women's hats, distracted scrupulous minds. In the other, which came from the same part of England as Robinson's church, the agitations were of a theological nature. Questions about the baptism of infants and the inherent righteousness of man and the portion of his nature that Christ derived from his mother, with discussions of the right of a man to be a magistrate and a church member at the same time, were seething in the heated brain of the scrupulous but saintly pastor. Robinson saw that these controversies would involve the Scrooby church if it remained in Amsterdam. In Robinson the centrifugal force of Separatism had already spent itself, and his practical wisdom had set bounds to the course of his

logic. To leave the Dutch metropolis for a smaller place was to reduce the Scrooby exiles to still
deeper poverty, but nevertheless the Pilgrims fled
from discord as they had fled from persecution,
and removed to the university city of Leyden,
called by its admirers "the Athens of the Occi-
dent." After their departure English Separatism
in Amsterdam went on tearing itself to pieces in a
sincere endeavor to find ultimate theological truth,
but Robinson's people in spite of their poverty
were united, and were honored by those among
whom they sojourned. Others, hearing of their
good report, came to them from England, and the
exiled church of Leyden was fairly prosperous.

Bradford's
Plimoth
Plantation.
Winslow's
Relation.

IV.

Danger of
extinc-
tion.

But when ten years of exile had passed the outlook was not a pleasant one. The life in Leyden
was so hard that many chose to return to their
own land, preferring English prisons to liberty at
so dear a rate. The " tender hearts of many a loving father and mother " were wounded to see children growing prematurely decrepit under the
weight of hard and incessant toil; "the vigor of
Nature being consumed in the very bud as it
were." Some of the young people were contami-
nated by the dissoluteness of the city, others joined
the Dutch army or made long voyages at sea, acquiring habits very foreign to the strictness of
their parents. The result of a contest between the
rigid Puritanism of the little church and the laxity

prevalent in Holland was not to be doubted. Human nature can not remain always at concert pitch. Intermarriages with the Dutch had already begun, and all that was peculiar in the English community was about to be swallowed up and lost forever in the great current of Dutch life which flowed about it.

Puritanism was in its very nature aggressive, even meddlesome. It was not possible for a Puritan church, led by such men as Robinson, and Brewster, and Carver, and Bradford, and Winslow, to remain content where national prejudices and a difference in language barred the way to the exertion of influence on the life about them. With destruction by absorption threatening their church, these leaders conceived the project of forming a new state where they "might, with the liberty of a good conscience, enjoy the pure Scripture worship of God without the mixture of human inventions and impositions ; and their children after them might walk in the holy ways of the Lord."

Emigration planned.

Compare Winslow in Young, 387.

V.

What suggested in 1617 the thought of migration to America we do not know. Just twenty years earlier, in 1597, some imprisoned Brownists had petitioned the Privy Council that they might be allowed to settle "in the province of Canada," an indefinite term at that time. Francis Johnson with three others went out in that same year to look at the land. The voyage was an unlucky one, and

Puritans and American settlements.

Waddington's Cong. Hist., ii, 113, 114.

the settlement of Johnson as pastor of the church in Amsterdam was the result. The persecutions which followed the accession of Bancroft to the archbishopric had started as early as 1608 a widespread agitation among the Puritans in favor of emigration to Virginia, but, when only a few had got away, the primate secured a proclamation pre-

Note 2. venting their escape from the means of grace provided for them in Courts of High Commission.

Condition of Virginia. The year 1617, in which the agitation for emigration began among the Pilgrims, was the year after Dale's return with highly colored reports of the condition of the Virginia colony. It is noticeable that among the books owned by Elder Brewster at his death was a copy of Whitaker's Good Newes from Virginia, published in 1613. Whitaker was minister at Henrico in Virginia, and was the son of a Puritan divine of eminence who was master of St. John's College, Cambridge. It is possible that he was known to Brewster, who had been at Cambridge, or to Robinson, who had resigned a fellowship there to become a Separatist. Whitaker himself was Puritan enough to discard the surplice. His Good Newes is an earnest plea for the support of the colony for religious reasons. "This plantation which the divell hath so often troden downe," he says, "is revived and daily groweth to

Note 3. more and hopeful successe." At the very time when the Pilgrims first thought of migrating there was beginning a new and widespread interest in Virginia. This was based partly on religious enthusiasm, such as Whitaker's book was meant to foster, and partly on the hope of new and strange commodities, particularly silk. Even this silk illusion may have had its weight in a secondary way with the Leyden people, for Bradford, afterward governor at Plymouth, was a silk-weaver in Leyden, and there were two books on silkworms in Brewster's library at his death.

CHAP. III.

Inventory of books. Winsor's pamphlet on Elder Brewster.

To European eyes all America was one; even to-day the two Americas are hardly distinguished by most people in Europe. The glowing account of Guiana given by Ralegh helped to feed the new desire for an American home; and it was only after serious debate that North America was chosen, as more remote from the dreaded Spaniard and safer from tropical diseases. One can hardly imagine what American Puritanism would have become under the skies of Guiana. Not only did the Pilgrims hesitate regarding their destination, but there was a choice of nationalities to be made. England had not been a motherly mother to these outcast children, and there was question of settling as English subjects in America, or becoming Dutch colonists there.

Alternatives.

VI.

The Pilgrims preferred to be English, notwithstanding all. But they wished to stipulate with England for religious liberty. In this matter they had recourse to Sir Edwin Sandys, the one man who would probably be both able and willing to

Application to Sandys.

Book II.

Hunter's
Founders
of New
Plymouth,
pp. 22, 23.

help them. Brewster had lived, as we have seen,
in an old episcopal manor at Scrooby. Sandys,
Archbishop of York, had transferred this manor by
a lease to his eldest son, Sir Samuel Sandys, who
was Brewster's landlord and brother of Sir Edwin
Sandys. Of Sir Edwin the great liberal parliamentary statesman, Fuller says, "He was right-
handed to any great employment." In 1617 he
was already the most influential of the progressive
leaders of the Virginia Company, its acting though
not yet its nominal head, and in 1619 he was elected
governor of the Company. Brewster's fellow-sec-
retary under Davison was a chosen friend of Sandys, and, in view of both these connections, we
may consider it almost certain that the two were
not strangers. To Sir Edwin Sandys was due
much of the new interest in Virginia. He and his
group seem to have been already striving to shape
the colony into a liberal state.

To meet the views of the Leyden people,
Sandys endeavored by the intervention of a more
acceptable courtier to gain assurance from the
king, under the broad seal, that their religion
should be tolerated if they migrated to Virginia.
But James's peculiar conscience recoiled from this.
He intimated that he would wink at their practices
but he would not tolerate them by public act.
And, indeed, the Pilgrims reflected afterward that
"a seale as broad as the house flore would not
serve the turne" of holding James to his promise.
At the king's suggestion the archbishops were ap-

plied to, but neither would they formally approve such an arrangement. Nor can one wonder at their unwillingness, since the most profound, liberal, and far-seeing thinker of that age, Lord Bacon himself, was so far subject to the prejudices of his time that he could protest against allowing heretics to settle a colony, and could support his position by a mystical argument fit to be advanced by the most fantastic theologian. "It will make schism and rent in Christ's coat, which must be seamless," he says. He even goes so far as to group Separatists with outlaws and criminals, and to advise that if such should transplant themselves to the colonies they should be "sent for back upon the first notice," for "such persons are not fit to lay the foundation of a new colony." Much more fit than is a speculative philosopher to draw the lines on which practical undertakings are to be carried forward. The transplanting of English speech and institutions to America would have languished as French colonization did, if none but orthodox settlers had been allowed to fell trees and build cabins in the forest. Ever since the age of stone hatchets colony planters have been drawn from the ranks of the uneasy. An early Quaker governor of South Carolina puts the matter less elegantly but more justly than Bacon when he says: "It is stupendious to consider, how passionate and preposterous zeal, not only vails but stupefies oftentimes the Rational Powers: For cannot Dissenters kill Wolves and Bears as well as Churchmen?"

Chap. III.

Bacon's Advice to Villiers.

Archdale's Carolina, 26.

VII.

The liberal and practical mind of <u>Sir Edwin</u>
<u>Sandys</u> harbored none of the scruples of Bacon,
and his more wholesome conscience knew nothing
of the fine distinctions of James and the archbishops between formal toleration and a mere
winking at irregularities. He embraced the cause
of the Pilgrims and became their steadfast friend,
passing through the Virginia Company successively
two charters in their behalf, and the general order
which allowed the leaders of "particular plantations"—that is, of such plantations as the Leyden
people and others at that time proposed to make—

to associate the sober and discreet of the plantation
with them to make laws, orders, and constitutions
not repugnant to the laws of England. This was a
wide door opening toward democratic government.
The patent given to the Pilgrims was also a liberal
one, and it was even proposed to put into their
hands a large sum of money contributed anony-
mously for the education of Indian children, but to
this it was objected that the newcomers would
lack the confidence of the savages. One of the
Virginia Company, possibly Sandys himself, lent

to the Leyden people three hundred pounds without interest for three years. When we consider
that the Pilgrims had to pay in their first year of
settlement thirty and even fifty per cent, interest
on their debts, and that this three hundred pounds,
the use of which they received without interest,

would be equal in purchasing power to five or six thousand dollars of our money, we may readily believe that this loan and the semi-independence offered them under their "large patent" from the company, were the considerations that decided them in favor of emigration after the English Government had refused a guarantee of toleration, and the Dutch Government had declined to assure them of protection against England.

That group of liberal English statesmen who were charged with keeping "a school of sedition" in the courts of the Virginian Company founded the two centers of liberal institutions in America. The Earl of Southampton, the Ferrars, Sir John Danvers, and above all and more than all, Sir Edwin Sandys, were the fathers of representative government in New England by the charter of February 2, 1620, as they had been of representative government in Virginia by the charter of November 18, 1618. When the Pilgrims found themselves, upon landing, too far north to use their patent from the Virginia Company, they reorganized their government on the lines laid down in the general order of the company. The government established by them in their famous Compact was precisely the provisional government which the Virginia Company in the preceding February had given them liberty to found "till a form of government be here settled for them." Under this compact they proceeded to confirm the election of the governor, already chosen under

Authors of the Plymouth Government.

Note 4.

Book II.

the authority derived from the charter, now in-
valid.

Charges
against
Sandys.

The enemies of Sir Edwin Sandys did not fail
to make use of his friendship for the Leyden people
to do him injury. It was afterward charged that

Duke of
Manches-
ter, papers,
Royal
Hist. MSS.
Comm.
viii, II, 45.

he was opposed to monarchical government, and
that he had moved the Archbishop of Canterbury
"to give leave to the Brownists and Separatists to
go to Virginia, and designed to make a free popular state there, and himself and his assured friends
were to be the leaders." That Sandys thought of
emigration is hardly probable, but he succeeded in
establishing two popular governments in America

Note 5.

which propagated themselves beyond all that he
could have hoped to achieve.

VIII.

The fare-
well to
Europe.

"Small things," wrote Dudley to the Countess
of Lincoln in the first months of the Massachusetts
settlement—"small things in the beginning of
natural or politic bodies are as remarkable as
greater in bodies full grown." The obscure events
we have recited above are capital because they had
a deciding influence on the fate of the Pilgrim settlement. It is not within our purpose to tell over
again the pathetic story of that brave departure of
the younger and stronger of the Pilgrims from
Leyden to make the first break into the wilderness,
but courage and devotion to an idea are not common; courage and devotion that bring at last important results are so rare that the student of his-

tory, however little disposed to indulge sentiment, turns in spite of himself to that last all-night meeting in Pastor Robinson's large house in the Belfry Lane at Leyden. "So," says Bradford, as if penning a new holy scripture, "they lefte that goodly and pleasante citie, which had been ther resting place near 12 years; but they knew they were pilgrimes and looked not much on those things, but lift up their eyes to the heavens, their dearest cuntrie and quieted their spirits." Nor is it easy to pass over the solemn parting on the quay at Delft Haven, where, as the time of the tide forced the final tearful separation, while even the Dutch spectators wept in sympathy, the voice of the beloved Robinson in a final prayer was heard and the whole company fell upon their knees together for the last time.

Plimoth Plantation, 59.

These things hardly pertain, perhaps, to a history of life such as this. It is with the influences that are to mold the new life while it is plastic that we are concerned. Chief of these is Robinson himself, a Moses who was never to see, even from a mountain top, the Canaan to which he had now led his people. He must stay behind with the larger half of the church. Rising to the occasion, his last words to this little company are worthy his magnanimous soul. He eloquently charged them "before God and his blessed angels to follow him no further than he followed Christ." . . . He was confident "the Lord had more truth and light to break forth out of his holy word." In whatever sense we

Robinson's influence.

Winslow's Briefe Narration, Young, 397.

take them these were marvelous words in the seventeenth century. Robinson understood the progressive nature of truth as apprehended by the human mind in a way that makes him seem singularly modern. In the same address he declared it " not possible that . . . full perfection of knowledge should break forth at once." He bade them not to affect separation from the Puritans in the

Church of England, but " rather to study union than division."

Admirable man! Free from pettiness and egotism. Fortunate man, who, working in one of the obscurest and dustiest corners of this noisy and self-seeking world, succeeded in training and sending out a company that diffused his spirit and teachings into the institutions and thoughts of a great people!

IX.

On a chain of slender accidents hung the existence of New England. Had the claims of Guiana prevailed, had the tempting offers of the Dutch changed the allegiance of the Robinsonian Independents, had the Mayflower reached her destination in what is now New Jersey, the current of American history would not have flowed as it has. A South American New England, a Dutch New England, or a non-peninsular community of Engglish Puritans west of the Hudson with good wheat fields and no fisheries or foreign trade, would have been different in destiny from what we call

New England, and its influence on events and national character could not have been the same. It will always remain doubtful whether or not Jones, the captain of the Mayflower, was bribed by the Dutch, as the Plymouth people came to believe. Nothing could be more probable in view of the general bad character of the seamen of that time and the eagerness of one political party in Holland to secure a foothold for the Dutch in America; but whether Jones, who seems to have borne a bad reputation, was bribed, or, as he pretended, became entangled in the shoals of Cape Cod and turned back in real despair of finding his way, is of no moment. He turned back and came to anchor in Provincetown Harbor. Here the threats of the brutal seamen, unwilling to go farther, and the clamor of the overcrowded and sea-weary passengers did the rest. To continue longer closely cabined in the little ship was misery and perhaps death. Here was land, and that was enough. And so, after exploration of the whole coast of Cape Cod Bay, the place already named Plymouth on John Smith's map was selected for a settlement. Here the landing was made on the 11th of December, O. S., 1620.

Camden has preserved to us an old English saying accepted in the days of the Pilgrims, to the effect that "a barren country is a great whet to the industry of a people." It was the wedding of an austere creed to an austere soil under an austere sky that gave the people of New England

Morton's Memorial, 6th edition, p. 22, note.

Compare Asher's History of W. I. Company in Bibl. Essay.

Note 7.

Note 8.

Elements of New England.

their marked character, and the severe economic conditions imposed by the soil and climate were even more potent than Puritanism in producing the traits that go to make up the New England of history.

X.

The unwise management that ruined nearly all projects for colonization in that age and that produced such disasters in Virginia, had defeated every earlier attempt to plant English people on the New England coast. Gosnold had taken a colony to Elizabeth Island in Buzzard's Bay in 1602, but the men went back in the ship in order to share the profit of a cargo of sassafras. Captain George Popham was the head of a party that undertook to colonize the coast of Maine in 1607, but having suffered " extreme extremities " during the winter, the colonists returned the following year. In 1615 Captain John Smith himself set out with sixteen men, only to be taken by a French privateer. These and other attempts ending in failure, and many disastrous trading voyages, led to a belief that the Indian conjurers, who were known to be the devil's own, had laid a spell on the northern coast to keep the white people away. This enchanted land might long have lain waste if Captain Jones of the Mayflower, sailing to Hudson River or the region south of it, had not run foul of the shoals of Cape Cod.

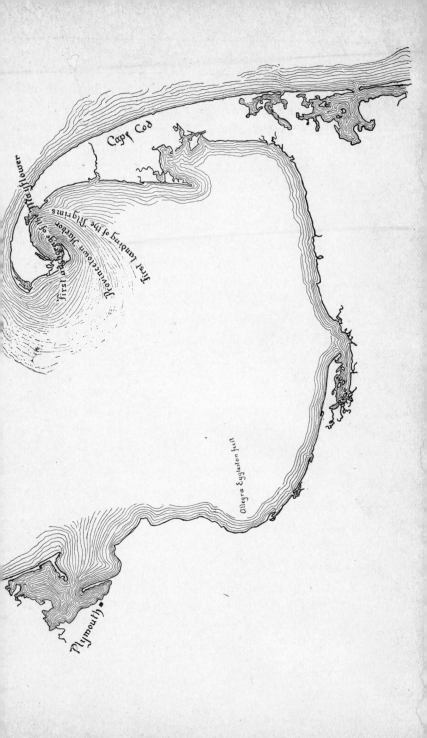

Cape Cod

Mayflower

First landing of the Pilgrims

Provincetown Harbor

First landing of the Pilgrims

Allegra Eggleston fecit

Plymouth

XI.

The Pilgrims suffered, like their predecessors, from the prevailing unskillfulness in colony-planting. They had escaped from the horrors of the Mayflower, but how much better was the wild land than the wild sea; the rude, overcrowded forest cabins than the too populous ship? " All things stared upon them with a weather-beaten face," says Bradford. The horrors of the first winter in Virginia were repeated ; here, as at Jamestown, nearly all were ill at once, and nearly half of the people died before the coming of spring. The same system of partnership with mercenary shareholders or "adventurers" in England that had brought disaster in Virginia was tried with similar results at Plymouth, and a similar attempt at communism in labor and supply was made, this time under the most favorable conditions, among a people conscientious and bound together by strong religious enthusiasm. It resulted, as such sinking of personal interest must ever result, in dissensions and insubordination, in unthrift and famine.

The colony was saved from the prolonged misery that makes the early history of Virginia horrible by the wise head and strong hand of its leader. William Bradford, who had been chosen governor on the death of Carver, a few months after the arrival at Plymouth, had been a youth but eighteen years old when he fled with the rest of the Scrooby church to Holland. He was bred to husbandry and had inherited some property. In Holland he became a silk worker and on attaining his majority set up for himself in that trade. He was still a young man when first chosen governor of the little colony, and he ruled New Plymouth almost continuously till his death—that is, for about thirty-seven years. He was of a magnanimous temper, resolute but patient, devotedly religious, but neither intolerant nor austere. He had a genius for quaintly vivid expression in writing that marked him as a man endowed with the literary gift, which comes as Heaven pleases where one would least look for it.

XII.

After two years of labor in common had brought the colony more than once to the verge of ruin, Bradford had the courage and wisdom to cut the knot he could not untie. During the scarce springtime of 1623, he assigned all the detached persons in the colony to live with families, and then temporarily divided the ancient Indian field on which the settlement had been made among the several families in proportion to their number, leaving every household to shift for itself or suffer want. "Any general want or suffering hath not been among them since to this day," he writes years afterward. The assignment was a revolutionary stroke, in violation of the contract with the shareholders, and contrary to their wishes. But Bradford saw that it was a life-and-death necessity to be rid of the pernicious system, even at the cost of cutting off all support from England. In his history he draws a very clear picture of the evils of communism as he had observed them.

CHAP. III.

Note 9.

XIII.

Why should the historian linger thus over the story of this last surviving remnant of the " Brownists"? Why have we dwelt upon the little settlement that was never very flourishing, that consisted at its best of only a few thousand peaceful and agricultural people, and that after seventy years was merged politically in its more vigorous neighbor the colony of Massachusetts Bay? Historical importance does not depend on population. Plymouth was the second step in the founding of a great nation. When Bradford and the other leaders had at last successfully extricated the little settlement from its economical difficulties, it became the sure forerunner of a greater Puritan migration. This tiny free state on the margin of a wilderness continent, like a distant glimmering pharos, showed the persecuted Puritans in England the fare-way to a harbor.

Signifi-
cance of
Plymouth.

ELUCIDATIONS.

Sir John Harington says: " The bishops came to the Kynge aboute the petition of the puritans; I was by, and heard much dyscourse. The Kynge talked muche Latin, and disputed wyth Dr. Reynoldes, at Hampton, but he rather usede upbraidinges than argumente; and tolde the petitioners that they wanted to strip

Note 1,
page 162.

Christe againe, and bid them awaie with their snivellinge: moreover, he wishede those who woud take away the surplice mighte
want linen for their own breech. ' The bishops seemed much
pleased and said his Majestie spoke by the power of inspiration.
I wist not what they mean; but the spirit was rather foule
mouthede." Nugæ Antiquæ, i, 181, 182. James took pains to
put an example of his bad taste on paper. In a letter on the subject he brags in these words: " We haue kept suche a reuell with
the Puritainis heir these two dayes as was neuer harde the lyke,
quhaire I haue pepperid thaime as soundlie as ye haue done the
papists thaire. . . . I was forcid at the last to saye unto thaime,
that if any of thaim hadde bene in a colledge disputing with their
skollairs, if any of their disciples had ansoured thaim in that sorte
they wolde haue fetched him up in place of a replye, and so
shoulde the rodde haue plyed upon the poore boyes buttokis."
Ellis Letters, Third Series, iv, 162. The principal authorities on
the Hampton Court Conference are, first, " The Svmme and Svbstance of the Conference, which it pleased his excellent Majestie
to have," etc., " Contracted by William Barlovv, . . . Deane of
Chester "; second, Dr. Montague's letter to his mother, in Win-
wood's Memorials, ii, 13–15; third, the letter of Patrick Galloway
to the Presbytery of Edinburgh, in Calderwood, vi, 241, 242; and,
fourth, a letter from Tobie Mathew, Bishop of Durham, to Hutton, Archbishop of York, in Strype's Whitgift appendix, xlv.
Compare Nugæ Antiquæ, 181, 182, and the king's letter to
Blake, in Ellis's Letters, third series, iv, 161, which are both cited
above. Mr. Gardiner has shown (History of England, i, 159)
that this letter is addressed to Northampton. There are several
documents relating to the conference among the state papers
calendared by Mrs. Greene under dates in January, 1604. Of
the vigorous action taken against the Puritans after the conference, some notion may be formed by the letter of protest from the
aged Matthew Hutton, Archbishop of York, to Lord Cranborne,
in Lodge's Illustrations of British History, iii, 115, and Cranborne's reply, ibid., 125.

Stith has not the weight of an original authority, but he is
justly famous for accuracy in following his authorities, and he
had access to many papers relating to the history of Virginia
which are now lost. Under the year 1608 he says: " Doctor
Whitgift, Arch-Bishop of Canterbury, . . . having died four
Years before this, was succeeded to that high Preferment by Dr.

Richard Bancroft. . . . He had very high Notions with Relation to the Government of both Church and State ; and was accordingly a great Stickler for, and Promoter of, the King's absolute Power, and failed not to take all Occasions, to oblige the Puritans to conform to the Church of England. This Prelate's Harshness and Warmth caused many of that People to take the Resolution this Year of settling themselves in Virginia, and some were actually come off for that Purpose. But the Arch-bishop, finding that they were preparing in great Numbers to depart, obtained a Proclamation from the King, forbidding any to go, without his Majesty's express Leave." History of Virginia, 1747, p. 76.

Note 3, page 168.

For Whitaker's filiation, Neill's Virginia Company, 78. Whitaker's Good Newes from Virginia is no doubt intended by the entry in the inventory of Brewster's goods, " Newes from Virginia." I know no other book with such a title. That Alexander Whitaker was himself touched with Puritanism, or at least was not unwilling to have Puritan ministers for colleagues, is rendered pretty certain from passages in his letters. For instance, he writes to Crashaw from Jamestown, August 9, 1611, desiring that young and "godly" ministers should come, and adds, " We have noe need either of ceremonies or bad livers." British Museum, Additional MSS., 21,993. (The letter is printed in Browne's Genesis, 499, 500.) In a letter given in Purchas and in Neill, 95, dated June 18, 1614, he says that neither subscription nor the surplice are spoken of in Virginia. It has escaped the notice of church historians that Whitaker's semi-Puritanism seems to have left traces for many years on the character and usage of the Virginia church. The Rev. Hugh Jones writes as late as 1724 in his Present State of Virginia, p. 68, that surplices were only then " beginning to be brought in Fashion," and that the people in some parishes received the Lord's Supper sitting.

Note 4, page 173.

The late Dr. Neill was the first, I believe, to call attention to this fact, though he did not state it quite so strongly as I have put it in the text. It is worth while transferring Neill's remarks from the New England Genealogical Register, vol. xxx, 412, 413 : " The action of the passengers of the Mayflower in forming a social compact before landing at Plymouth Rock seems to have been in strict accordance with the policy of the London Company, under whose patent the ship sailed. On June 9, 1619, O. S., John Whincop's patent was duly sealed by the Company, but this which had cost the Puritans so much labor and money was not

used. Several months after, the Leyden people became interested in a new project. On February 2, 1619–'20, at a meeting at
the house of Sir Edwin Sandys in Aldersgate, he stated to the
Company that a grant had been made to John Peirce and his associates. At the same quarterly meeting it was expressly ordered
that the leaders of particular plantations, associating unto them
divers of the gravest and discreetest of their companies, shall have
liberty to make orders, ordinances, and constitutions for the better
ordering and directing of their business and servants, provided
they be not repugnant to the laws of England." Bradford, in his
Plimouth Plantation, 90, says they " chose or rather confirmed
Mr. John Carver, . . . their Governour for that year "—that is, for
1620. Mr. Deane, the editor of Bradford, has lost the force of
this by misunderstanding a statement in Mourt's Relation, so
called. See Deane's note, page 99, of Bradford. The statement
in Mourt is under date of March 23d. I quote from the reprint in
Young, 196, 197 : " and did likewise choose our governor for this
present year, which was Master John Carver," etc. Young ap-
plies Bradford's words, " or rather confirmed," to this event, and
Deane also supposes that Bradford confuses two elections. Carver was no doubt chosen in England or Holland under authority
of the charter to serve for the calendar year, and confirmed or
rechosen after the Compact was signed. What took place on the
23d of March was that a governor was elected for the year 1621,
which, according to the calendar of that time, began on the 25th
of March. For the next year they chose Carver, who was already
" governor for this present year," and whose first term was about
to expire. Both Deane and Young failed to perceive the pregnant fact that Carver was governor during the voyage, and so lost
the force of the words " or rather confirmed." Bradford, in that
portion of his History of Plimouth Plantation which relates to this
period, gives several letters illustrating the negotiations of the
Pilgrims with the Virginia Company. The MS. Records of the
Company in the Library of Congress, under dates of May 26 and
June 9, 1619, and February 19, 1620 (1619 O. S.), contain the
transactions relating to the Whincop Charter, which was not
used, on account of Whincop's death, and the Pierce Charter,
which the Pilgrims took with them.

The charge against Sandys is in the Duke of Manchester's
papers, Royal Historical MS. Commission viii, II, 45. It is remarkable that the dominant liberal faction in the Virginia Com-

pany is here accused of seeking to do what the Massachusetts Company afterward did—to wit, to found a popular American government by virtue of powers conferred in a charter. That liberal government in New England had its rise in the arrangements made with the London or Virginia Company before sailing, and not, as poets, painters, and orators have it, in the cabin of the Mayflower, is sufficiently attested in a bit of evidence, conspicuous enough, but usually overlooked. Robinson's farewell letter to the whole company, which reached them in England, is in Bradford, 64–67, and in Mourt's Relation. It has several significant allusions to the form of government already planned. " And lastly, your intended course of civill communitie will minister continuall occasion of offence." The allusion here seems to be to the joint-stock and communistic system of labor and living proposed. In another paragraph the allusion is to the system of government : " Whereas, you are become a body politik, using amongst your selves civill governmente, and are not furnished with any persons of spetiall emencie above the rest, to be chosen by you into office of governmente," etc., " you are at present to have only them for your ordinarie governours, which your selves shall make choyse of for that worke." That the government under the Virginia Company was to be democratic is manifest. The compact was a means of giving it the sanction of consent where the patent and the general order did not avail for that purpose.

Winslow's Briefe Narration appended to his Hypocrisie Vnmasked is the only authority for Robinson's address. Dr. H. M. Dexter has with characteristic wealth of learning and ingenuity sought to diminish the force of these generous words of Robinson in his Congregationalism, 403 and ff. But the note struck in this farewell address was familiar to the later followers of Robinson's form of Independency. Five of the ministers who went to Holland in 1637 and founded churches, published in 1643 a tract called An Apologeticall Narrative Humbly Submitted to the Honourable Houses of Parliament. By Thomas Goodwin, Phillip Nye, Sidrach Simpson, Jer. Borroughs, William Bridge. London, 1643. From the copy in the British Museum I quote : " A second principle we carryed along with us in all our resolutions was, Not to make our present judgment and practice a binding law unto ourselves for the future which we in like manner made continuall profession of upon all occasions." On page

Note 6, page 176.

22 Robinson's words are almost repeated in the phrase "they coming new out of popery . . . might not be perfect the first day." Robinson's early colleague, Smyth, the unpractical, much-defamed, but saintly "Anabaptist," says in a tract published after his death, "I continually search after the truth." Robinson wrote a reply to a portion of this tract. See Barclay's Inner Life, appendix to Chapter V, where the tract is given. This holding of their opinions in a state of flux, this liberal expectancy of a further evolution of opinion, was a trait to be admired in the early Separatists in an age when modesty in dogmatic statement was exceedingly rare.

Note 7,
page 177.

Neill, in the Historical Magazine for January, 1869, and the New England Genealogical Register, 1874, identifies the Mayflower captain with Jones of the Discovery, who was accounted in Virginia "dishonest." But honest seamen were few in that half-piratical age. That he was hired by the Dutch to take the Pilgrims elsewhere than to Hudson River is charged in Morton's Memorial, and is not in itself unlikely. But the embarrassments of Cape Cod shoals were very real ; a trading ship sent out by the Pilgrims after their settlement, failed to find a way round the cape.

Note 8,
page 177.

Early New England writers were not content with giving the Pilgrims the honor due to them. Hutchinson asserts that the Virginia Colony had virtually failed, and that the Pilgrim settlement was the means of reviving it. This has been often repeated on no other authority than that of Hutchinson, who wrote nearly a century and a half after the event. The list of patents for plantations in Virginia as given by Purchas, in which appears that of Master "Wincop," under which the Pilgrims proposed to plant, is a sufficient proof that Virginia was not languishing. "These patentees," says Purchas, "have undertaken to transport to Virginia a great multitude of people and store of cattle." Virginia had reached the greatest prosperity it attained before the dissolution of the company, in precisely the years in which the slender Pilgrim Colony was preparing. It is quite possible to honor the Pilgrims without reversing the order of cause and effect.

Note 9,
page 181.

Bradford's Plimouth Plantation, 135, 136 : "The experience that was had in this commone course and condition, tried sundrie years, and that amongst godly and sober men, may well evince the vanitie of that conceite of Platos and other ancients, applauded by some of later times—that the taking away of propertie, and bringing in communitie into a comone wealth, would make them happy and florishing ; as if they were wiser than God. For this communitie (so fare as it was) was found to breed much confusion and discontent, and retard much imployment that would have been to their benefite and comforte. For the yong-men that were most able and fitte for labour and service did repine that they should spend their time and streingth to worke for other mens wives and children with out any recompence. The strong, or man of parts, had no more in devission of victails and cloaths, then he that was weake and not able to doe a quarter the other could ; this was thought injuestice. The aged and graver men to be ranked and equalised in labours, and victails, cloaths, &c., with the meaner and yonger sorte, thought it some indignite and disrespect unto them. And for mens wives to be commanded to doe servise for other men, as dresing their meate, washing their cloaths, &c., they deemd it a kind of slaverie, neither could many husbands well brooke it. Upon the point all being to have alike, and all to doe alike, they thought them selves in the like condition, and one as good as another ; and so if it did not cut of those relations that God hath set amongest men yet it did much diminish and take of the mutuall respects that should be preserved amongst them. And would have bene worse if they had been men of another condition."

CHAPTER THE FOURTH.

THE GREAT PURITAN EXODUS.

I.

MEN who undertake a great enterprise rarely find their anticipations fulfilled; they are fortunate if their general aim is reached at last in any way. The Pilgrims had migrated, hoping to be "stepping-stones to others," as they phrased it. They thought that many like-minded in matters of religion would come to them out of England, but the Separatist movement had been worn out by persecution. There were few open dissenters left, and the Pilgrims, by their long exile, had lost all close relations with their own country. Among those that came to Plymouth from England were some whose coming tended to dilute the religious life and lower the moral standards of the colony. The fervor of the Pilgrims themselves abated something of its intensity in the preoccupations incident to pioneer life. The hope of expanding their religious organization by the rapid growth of the colony was not fulfilled; discontented Puritans were not eager to settle under the government of Separatists, and ten years after their migration the Plymouth colony contained little more than three hundred people.

None the less the hope of the Pilgrims was realized ; they became stepping-stones to thousands of others. Captain John Smith laughed at the "humorous ignorances" of these "Brownist" settlers, but, humorous or not, ignorant or not, the "Brownists" remained on the coast while other emigrants retreated. In spite of their terrible suffering none of the Pilgrims went back. This is the capital fact in their history. A new force had been introduced into colonization. Henceforth persecuted or discontented religionists, prompted by a motive vastly more strenuous and enduring than cupidity, were to bear the main brunt of breaking a way into the wilderness.

The first effect of the slender success at Plymouth was to stimulate speculative and merely adventurous migration. From 1607 until the arrival of the Pilgrims in 1620 no English colony had landed on the northern coast; but after the Pilgrims came, fish-drying and fur-buying stations began to appear on the banks of the Piscataqua and the coast eastward in 1622 and 1623. These tiny settlements were germs of New Hampshire and Maine, the only New England plantations begun without any admixture of religious motives. A commercial colony was tried in Massachusetts Bay as early as 1622, but it failed. There were other like attempts. In 1624 some men of Dorchester, headed by John White, the "Patriarch" Puritan clergyman, sent out a colony to Cape Ann. The members of this company were to grow maize to

supply fishing ships, and in the season the same
men were to lend a hand on board the ships, which
would thus be saved the necessity for carrying
double crews. But this plausible scheme proved a
case of seeking strawberries in the sea and red her-
rings in the wood. Farmers were but lubbers at
codfishing, and salt-water fishermen were clumsy
enough in the cornfield. Losses of several sorts
forced the Dorchester Company to dissolve. Four
members of their futile colony, encouraged by
a message from White, remained on Cape Ann.
Removing to the present site of Salem, they waited
at the risk of their lives for the coming of a new
colony from England.

John
White's
The Plant-
er's Plea,
in Young's
Chronicles
of Mass.

Individual
settlers.

Solitary adventurers of the sort known on nearly every frontier were presently to be found in several places. The scholarly recluse was represented
by Blackstone, who had selected for his secluded
abode a spot convenient to a spring of good water
where the town of Boston was afterward planted ;
the inevitable Scotch adventurer was on an island
in Boston Harbor ; Samuel Maverick, a pattern of
frontier hospitality and generosity, took up his
abode on Noddle's Island ; while the rollicking and
scoffing libertine was found in Thomas Morton,
who with some rebellious bond servants got possession of a fortified house in what is now Braintree.
Here Morton welcomed renegade servants from
Plymouth and elsewhere. He wrote ribald verses
which he posted on his Maypole, and devised May-
dances in which the saturnine Indian women par-

ticipated. He broke all the commandments with delight, carried on a profitable trade in selling fire-arms to the savages in defiance of royal proclamations, and wrought whatever other deviltry came within his reach, until his neighbors could no longer endure the proximity of so dangerous a firebrand. Little Captain Standish, whom Morton derisively dubbed "Captain Shrimp," descended on this kingdom of misrule at last and broke up the perpetual carnival, sending Morton to England.

The settlement of New England was thus beginning sporadically and slowly. If the Massachusetts Puritans had not come, these feeble and scattered plantations might have grown into colonies after a long time, as such beginnings did in New Hampshire and Maine, and later in North Carolina, but having no strong neighbor to support them, it is likely that they would all have been driven away or annihilated by some inevitable collision with the Indians.

II.

English Puritanism throughout the reign of James I had been the party of strict morals, of austere and Pharisaic scrupulosity, of rigid Sabbath observance, and of Calvinistic dogmatism. During that reign it had passed through its last transformation in becoming a political party—the party of anti-Catholic politics at home and abroad. Because Parliament was on its side, the mere course of events had made the Puritan party favor

the predominance of Parliament, and this brought
it to represent liberalism in politics. By his un-
concealed partisanship, James had contrived to
make the Puritans a permanent opposition suspected of disliking monarchy itself. Charles I was
even more the antagonist of Puritanism than James.

In one other respect the position of Puritanism
had been gradually changed by mere parallax. In
Elizabeth's reign it had been the party of innova-
tion. It was no longer the party of change in religion when Charles came to the throne. The
adoption of the Arminian system of doctrine by
many of the High-churchmen, and the reactionary innovations now proposed by ecclesiastics like
Laud, had left Puritanism to stand for Protestant
conservatism. It was immeasurably the gainer
with the mass of slow-moving people by this
change of relative position. The parliamentary
struggle with James and Charles added to the
religious Puritans a numerous body of political
Puritans who, without much care about religion,
were fain to ally their political discontent with the
discontent of those who resisted ecclesiastical retrogression. This compact party, powerful after
all its defeats, was bound by its position to cherish every aspiration for the improvement of morals,
every indignant movement for the suppression of
abuses, and it became the ally of every popular
resentment against royal absolutism or episcopal
encroachment, and the advocate, almost to fanaticism, of an anti-Spanish foreign policy, and a do-

mestic policy in which repression and persecution of Roman Catholics held first place.

III.

But the king and the High-churchmen were the party in possession. Buckingham, in the first years of Charles, was more than ever dominant at court, and Buckingham's favorite, just rising above the horizon, was Dr. Laud, Bishop of St. Davids at the death of James, and soon afterward translated to Bath and Wells and then to London. It soon came to be understood that he was only waiting for the death of his opponent, Archbishop Abbott, to take the primacy, much of the power of which he had already contrived to grasp. On the death of Buckingham, Laud succeeded him as chief favorite at court. The one great and real service which this able and indefatigable divine rendered the world is the last he would have chosen. He was the main spur to the settlement of Puritan colonies in New England.

Do our best, we moderns shall hardly avoid injustice in our opinion of Laud. The changes of time and the advance of ideas have rendered a sympathetic judgment of him difficult. Ecclesiastic above all, he was not, like Whitgift and Bancroft, a Protestant High-churchman. He sought to make the English church Catholic and mediæval, yet he would on no account attach it to Rome. Like Whitgift, he made the church dependent on royal authority, and in this he was far removed

14

from the earlier churchmen. There was nothing spiritual in his nature; his personal devotion had neither agony nor exaltation. He had none of the mediæval enthusiasm that prompted the vigils of his contemporary, Nicholas Ferrar, for example, and elevated the master of Little Gidding to a saintship, amiable and touching. Notwithstanding the energy of Laud's devotion, his nature was as shallow and objective as it was sincere. It has been remarked that when Laud spoke of the beauty of holiness he meant no more than decorum in public worship, the beauty of a well-ordered church and of proper intonation and genuflexion. He seemed to touch a modern note when he proposed to suppress the futile debate between Calvinists and Arminians because it tended to disturb Christian charity; but Laud's Christian charity, like his holiness, was purely external; it was merely quiet submission to one ritual and one form of discipline. His relentless, vindictive, and even cruel temper toward opponents showed him incapable of conceiving of charity in any spiritual sense. He disliked controversy because it put obstacles in the way of uniformity, and he had no taste for speculative debate because it tended to undermine authority. His intellect was utterly practical and phenomenally acute. It was incredibly energetic, and its energy was intensified by its narrowness. His attachment to the church had no relation to the beneficent utilities of the church. The church was a fetich for which he was ready to die without a murmur. In his zeal he was reckless of personal danger and sometimes unmindful of the moral complexion of his actions. His egotism was so interblended with his zeal that he could not separate one from the other, nor can the student of his character. A disservice to him was an affront to Almighty God. The very honesty of such a man is pernicious; a little duplicity might have softened the outward manifestations of his hard nature. Unhappily, there was not even indolence or self-indulgence to moderate his all but superhuman activity, which pushed his domination to its possibilities, and, with a vigilance aspiring to omniscience, penetrated to the minutest details in the administration of church and state. He even filed papers giving the elements of the debates on good works as an evidence of sanctification carried on between Hooker and Cotton in the cabin meeting-houses of New England. For the rest he presents the paradoxes one expects in so marked a character. While he had no taste for the credulous dogmatism of his time, he showed a certain relish for superstitions in recording dreams and omens, yet he had none of the timidity of superstition. He was, moreover, fearless in peril, and he faced unpopularity without flinching. Stubborn and inflexible with the clergy and the populace, obdurate and pitiless with those who had offended him or his king or his church, he was flexible and insinuating in his relations with those in power. His unworthy yielding to his early patron, the Earl of

Devonshire, in a matter which concerned his eccle-siastical conscience, gave him a bitter and lifelong repentance. His complacence to Buckingham, and his servile devotion to Charles, seem a little des-picable. He was even willing at the last to make terms with Parliament, when it became plain that Parliament was the new master. Though obse-quious, he was the farthest possible from a coward, and he accepted death on the scaffold with the serene composure of a martyr.

Letter to Selden in Chalmers, art. Laud.

IV.

Political conditions promote emigra-tion.

The great migration to New England set in soon after the beginning of Laud's ascendency in the ecclesiastical government of England. It waned as he declined, and ceased forever with his fall. There is a witty justness in the phrase by which a colonial historian dubs Laud "the father of New England." Other archbishops had contented them-selves with crushing the Separatists, but, with char-acteristic boldness and logical thoroughness, Laud struck at the powerful Puritan party which had contrived for more than half a century to remain in the Church of England while protesting against the discipline and service of the church. The arbitrary government of the new king, the dissolu-tion of Parliament, and the imprisonment of liberal leaders cut off hope of securing church reform or a relaxation of oppressive laws. High-church pulpits resounded with arguments in favor of the king's absolute authority and the duty of unques-

Gorges's Briefe Nar-ration.

tioning obedience, while the declared principles of the king and his court left the property, liberty, and life of the subject exposed to the rapacity or the vindictiveness of those in power. In view of these things, some of the Puritans began to think the American wilderness a better place of residence than England.

V.

The state of the church was even more a reason for removal than the oppressions of the government. Persecution had failed to drive Puritan ministers or their followers into what they deemed the capital sin of schism. They hated the domination of the bishops, communion with the ungodly, and the absence of a rigid discipline. But they had been sustained through long years' of waiting by the hope of delivering the church from those who oppressed and defiled her. They proposed, whenever they could gain power, to winnow the chaff from the wheat, and they probably destined the chaff to swift destruction. But the hope of seeing a church without spot or wrinkle, prayer book or bishop, died under the reactionary policy of Buckingham and Laud, and many came to look with favor on a project whose full import was only whispered in the ear, to found in the wilds of America a "particular church," as they phrased it —a new church with a right of priority in a new land and backed by the sanction of the government of the country. It was no modern general-ized love of liberty, civil or religious, but a strenuous desire to find a place where they might make real their ideal of church organization that brought the Puritans out of their comfortable nests in England to dwell in poor cabins in a wilderness. It is a motive for braving dangers by sea and land hard of comprehension in our Sadducean age.

There was one other consideration still more difficult for men of our day to understand. Political and military reverses had apparently well-nigh wrecked Protestantism on the Continent. Many Protestants in the Palatinate and elsewhere were making peace by becoming Roman Catholics. " All other churches of Europe are brought to desolation, & our sinnes, for which the Lord be-ginnes allreaddy to frowne upon us & to cutte us short, doe threatne evill times to be comminge upon us." These words are set down in the Rea-sons for New England as the second consideration. In another part of the same paper it is urged that the "woefull spectacle " of the ruin of "Churches beyound the Seas," "may teach us more wisdome to avoide the Plauge when it is foreseene & not to tarry as they did till it overtake us." The domi-nance of Old Testament ideas is easily seen here. But this fleeing from judgments that were to fall not on the lives or possessions of men, but on the churches themselves—judgments of a spiritual nature, apprehended only by inference—was a re-finement of Hebraism never known to the He-brews. The delusion that Laud meant to hand

over the English church bound hand and foot to
Rome may have made such judgments seem visi-
bly imminent.

VI.

The project for a Puritan colony languished at **Rise of the Massachusetts Company.**
first on account of the failure of the semi-Puritan,
semi-commercial Dorchester farming and fishing
colony on Cape Ann; but White of Dorchester
continued to agitate the planting of a colony. He
had, no doubt, efficient help in the proceedings **Compare The Planter's Plea.**
against the Puritan clergy. From Dorchester the
plan was carried to London, where it soon became,
in the phrase of that time, "vulgar," or, as we
should say, popular. Its countenance to the world,
and especially toward the government, was that of
a commercial venture like the planting of Virginia,
but in its heart it was a religious enterprise. In
March, 1628, the Council for New England gave to
the Massachusetts projectors a patent for lands ex-
tending from the Merrimack to the Charles and
three miles beyond each river. The western
boundary of this tract was the Pacific Ocean, for
holders of grants could afford to be generous in
giving away the interior of an unexplored continent about which nothing was known but that it
abounded in savages.

VII.

In June a small colony was sent to Massachusetts under John Endecott. The next year another

The Puritan Migration.

Leader-
ship and
character
of Ende-
cott.
1628.

company of emigrants was added. Endecott, who was one of the patentees, loved a bold enterprise, and readily consented to take charge of the fore-runners of the colony. He lacked the moderation and saneness needed in a leader, and his long career in connection with Massachusetts was marked from the beginning by mistakes born of a rash temper and impulsive enthusiasm. Two of the gentlemen emigrants who had been named by the company in London as members of the local Council were not willing to go to the unexpected lengths Endecott favored in the organization of the Salem church, though they were probably Puritans of a moderate type. They held a separate service with a small company, using the prayer book. Endecott appears to have made no effort at conciliation; he promptly shipped John and Samuel Browne, pack and prayer book, back to England. This was precisely the course that even Lord Bacon advised in the treatment of schismatics who should contrive to gain access to a colony, and there is no occasion for surprise that a quixotic enthusiast like Endecott did not hold broader views than those of a philosopher of the same period. But Endecott's rash action endangered the whole enterprise, which required at this stage the extreme of prudence. The alarmed managers in England contrived to settle with the Brownes in private, and the affair had no other result than to ruin Endecott's reputation for prudence. Endecott, however, went on fighting the Lord's battles against the Apollyons of his

Bentley's
Descrip-
tion of
Salem.

fancy, regardless of results. Soon after his arrival he marched to the den of Morton, the profligate master of "Merrymount." In the absence of Morton he hewed down the profane Maypole in God's name, and solemnly dubbed the place Mount Dagon, in memory of the Philistine idol that fell down before the ark of the Lord. At a later period he cut one arm of the cross out of the English colors of the Salem trainband, in order to convert the Union Jack to Protestantism. One of the many manifestations of his pragmatical conscience was his Tartuffian protection of modesty by insisting that the women of Salem should keep their faces veiled at church. He was also a leader in the crusade of the magistrates against the crime of wearing wigs. A strange mixture of rashness, pious zeal, genial manners, hot temper, and harsh bigotry, his extravagances supply the condiment of humor to a very serious history—it is perhaps the principal debt posterity owes him. But there was a side to his career too serious to be humorous. Bold against Maypoles and prayer books and women who presented themselves in church immodestly barefaced, and in the forefront against wigs, he was no soldier either in prudent conduct or vigor of attack. When intrusted with the command of an expedition to demand satisfaction of the Pequots, he proved incapable of anything but a campaign of exasperation. When late in life he was governor of Massachusetts, and had become, after the death of Winthrop and Dudley, the domi-

Eliot's Biography, 195.

nant political leader, the putting to death of Quakers left an ineffaceable blot on the history of the colony he had helped to found. When the colony was brought to book in England for this severity, Endecott showed himself capable of writing one of the most cringing official letters on record, as full of cant as it was of creeping servility. In him we may clearly apprehend certain unamiable traits of Puritanism and of the early seventeenth century which appear in his character in exaggerated relief. This hearty and energetic bigot must have been representative of a large, though not of the better, element in Massachusetts Puritanism, for he was chosen to the governorship oftener than any other man during the continuance of the old charter government.

VIII.

It is a pleasure to turn from Endecott to one who was, like him, a seventeenth-century man, and who did not escape the scrupulosity and ridiculosity of Puritanism, but whose amiable personality, magnanimity, and qualities of leadership made him the principal figure in the Puritan migration. Winthrop, like two or three of the conspicuous actors in our later history, owes his distinction to the moral elevation of his character quite as much as to his considerable mental gifts; for character multiplied into sagacity is better than genius for some kinds of work.

He was a late comer in the enterprise. In the

year after Endecott had brought over a colony composed mostly of servants of the company and of the individual patentees, a second company of emigrants had been sent over with a commission to Endecott as governor on the place, assisted by a council. A church had been formed at Salem. Now set in a larger agitation in favor of migration to New England. The course of events in England was so adverse to Puritanism that those who were devoted to that purified church, which was as yet invisible, except to the eye of faith, began to look toward America. Every door for public action in state or church was closed to the Puritans in England, closed and barred by Courts of High Commission, by the Star Chamber, and by the Tower. Into one of the gloomiest rooms of the latter had lately gone, at the arbitrary command of the king, that high-spirited martyr to constitutional liberty, Sir John Eliot. Finding no way by which to come out again except a postern of dishonor, Eliot deliberately chose to languish and die in prison. The almost hopeless outlook at home, the example set by Endecott's emigration to New England in 1628, and by that of Higginson's company in 1629, perhaps also the ever-active propagandism of "Father White" of Dorchester, set agoing among the Puritans a widespread interest in the subject. Some of the leading minds thought it a noble work to organize a reformed church in a new country, since, in their view, the Church of England, under Laud, had taken up its march backward. This purpose of planting a Puritan church in America now began to take the first place ; even the conversion of the Indians,

which had been the chief avowed purpose hitherto, fell into the background.

The manuscript paper entitled Reasons for New England, to which reference has already been made, was widely but secretly circulated, and frequently copied, after a fashion of that time, prevailing especially in the case of tracts or books of a kind to shrink from print. It contained arguments in favor of removing to New England, with answers to the various objections made against emigration. Several copies of these Reasons, or Considerations, have come down to us in various handwritings, and the authorship has been attributed now to one, now to another; to Winthrop, to White of Dorchester, to Sir John Eliot himself. It appears to have been in its earliest form the production of Winthrop. There were horseback journeys, some of them by night, made about this time for the purpose of secret consultation.

Winthrop, a country gentleman of Groton, in Suffolk, and an attorney in the Court of Wards, was a strict Puritan, desiring above all a reformed church and "the ordinances of God in their purity," as the phrase of the time went. Precocious in everything, and inclined to ideal aims, he had been religious from boyhood, had married at a little over seventeen years of age, and had

been made a justice of the peace while still **very**

young. He studied divinity, and only the dissuasion of friends kept him from entering the ministry. Of judicial temper, he came to be often consulted upon points of conscience, which gave much trouble in that age of casuistry and abounding scruples. His kindly visits to those who were in any trouble of spirit were highly prized. He himself makes much of the corruptions of his own nature and of his juvenile aberrancy, but generosity and purity of spirit like his are born and not acquired. His devoutness, accompanied by a habit of self-criticism in the presence of Infinite Justice, doubtless gave additional vigor to his virtues. For the rest, he was a man of independent estate, of prudent and conciliatory carriage, of a clear but not broad mind. What, as much as anything else, fitted him for his function was that all his virtues were cast in Puritan molds and all his prejudices had a Puritan set.

When the question of emigration was under discussion other gentlemen who thought of going turned to Winthrop as the natural leader, declaring that they would remain in England if he should desert them. He was not only the official head, but he was indeed the soul, of the migration of 1630, and he went to America confident of a call divine like that of Moses.

His influence.

Note 6.

IX.

It is a fact worthy of note that the three primary steps toward the establishment of free government

Cradock.

in America were due to Englishmen who did not themselves cross the sea. The Great Charter of 1618 to the Virginia colony, and the "large patent" to the Plymouth Pilgrims, were granted, as we have seen, under the leadership of Sir Edwin Sandys, Governor of the Virginia Company of London. The third of the measures which placed colonial government on a popular basis was due to the governor of another corporation engaged in colony planting.

Cradock's plan.

On the 28th of July, 1629, while Winthrop and his friends were debating their removal to New England, Mathew Cradock, a wealthy and liberal merchant, who held the office of governor, or, as we should say, president, of the Massachusetts Company, read in a "general court" or meeting of the company "certain propositions conceived by himself," as it is carefully recorded. He proposed "that for the advancement of the plantation, the inducing and encouraging persons of worth, quality and rank to transplant themselves and families thither and for other weighty reasons"—reasons which probably it was not thought best to spread upon the records, but which were the core of the whole matter—for these reasons Cradock proposed to "transfer the government of the plantation to those that shall inhabit there," and not to continue it in subordination to a commercial company in London. The sorrows of the Virginia colony under the administration of Sir Thomas Smyth and the disagreements between the Pilgrims and

Mass. Records, July 29, 1629.

their "adventurers" in London had taught a wholesome lesson. Three years earlier Sir Francis Wyatt, the best of all the early governors of Virginia, had set forth in an elaborate report that the principal cause of the "slow proceeding of the growth of the plantation" was that the government had been divided between England and Virginia. Massachusetts escaped from this embarrassment.

CHAP. IV.

Sainsbury's Calendar, May 17, 1626.

X.

The evolution of the Massachusetts government may now be traced through its several stages. A company was formed, partly of Dorchester men, but chiefly of residents of London. This company secured a patent to lands in Massachusetts Bay from the Council for New England. The patentees intended both a commercial enterprise and a Puritan settlement. They sent Endecott, one of their number, as agent or superintendent, with a company of servants and others, to prepare the way for the migration of other patentees. In March, 1628, they secured a liberal charter from the king, which gave them the right to establish in Massachusetts a government subordinate to the company. The plan was to settle a government in the form rendered familiar by that of the Virginia Company. The Massachusetts Company in London sent a commission to Endecott as governor on the place subject to the orders of the company in England. A council of assistants was associated with him,

Evolution of the Mass. government.

Hubbard, chap. xviii.

but there was as yet no provision for giving the people a voice in the government.

Winthrop and his coterie of gentlemen appear to have been dissatisfied with the prospect of living under a government directed from England, and thus subject to English stockholders and liable to interference from the court. Cradock had been a leader and the most liberal investor in the enterprise. He, no doubt, readily foresaw the great advance that the colony would make if Winthrop and his friends should embark their lives and fortunes in it, and he may have intended to emigrate himself. The annulling of the charter of the Virginia Company on frivolous pretexts had shown how easily the Massachusetts charter might meet the same fate in a reign far more devoted to arbitrary government than that of James and entirely hostile to Puritanism. There could hardly be a doubt that the charter would be revoked as soon as its projectors should develop their true purpose before the all-observing eyes of Laud, who was now rising rapidly to dominant influence in the government. It was at this juncture probably that Cradock conceived his ingenious plan. He would resign his place and have the officers of the company chosen from gentlemen about to embark for the plantation. The charter prescribed no place of assembling to the company, which had been left free apparently to make its headquarters at its birthplace in Dorchester or at its new home in London. It was also free to meet in any other

place. The meetings of the company might therefore be held in Massachusetts, where the Puritanism of its proceedings would attract less attention.
The governor and other officers would then be
chosen in the colony; the company and the colony
would thus be merged into one, and the charter
transported to Massachusetts would perhaps be
beyond the reach of writs and judgments.

XI.

No doubt the influential company of friends
who were debating a removal to New England
were informed of Cradock's proposition before it
was mooted in the company on the 28th of July.
The plan was probably thought of in consequence
of their objection to emigration under the Virginia
system. Cradock's proposition was at least the
turning point of their decision. Nearly a month
later, on the 26th of August, the leaders of Winthrop's party assembled to the number of twelve,
at Cambridge, and solemnly pledged themselves,
"in the presence of God who is the searcher of all
hearts," "to pass the Seas (under God's protection)
to inhabit and continue in New England." The
preamble states the object of this migration. It
was not civil liberty, the end that political Puritans had most in view, and certainly there is no
hint of a desire for religious liberty. Even the
conversion of the Indian is not uppermost in this
solemn resolve. "God's glory and the church's
good" are the words used. This has the true ring

The Cam-
bridge
agree-
ment.

1629.

15

of the Puritan churchman. The whole pledge is couched in language befitting men who feel themselves engaged in a religious enterprise of the highest importance.

This pledge contained a notable proviso. The signers agreed to emigrate only on condition that " the whole government together with the patent for said plantation " should be transferred and legally established in the colony by order of the General Court of the Company, and that this should be done before the last of the ensuing month. There was opposition to the removal of the government, and this peremptory condition was necessary. Three days later, after a debate, the company voted that its government should be transferred to Massachusetts Bay.

On the 20th of October Cradock resigned his governorship and Winthrop was chosen in his stead. Puritan ministers were at once elected to the freedom of the company, in order that its proceedings might not want the sanction of prayer. The next year the charter crossed the wide seas,

and in 1630 a court of the company was held in the wilderness at Charlestown. But a subordinate government " for financial affairs only " was maintained in London, with Cradock, the former president, at the head. This seems to have been an effectual blind, and probably the king's government did not know of the flight of the charter until the Privy Council in 1634 summoned Cradock to bring that document to the Council Board.

Thomas Morton, the expelled master of Merry-mount, writes of the wrath of Laud, who had been foiled by this pretty ruse: "My lord of Canterbury and my lord privy seal, having caused all Mr. Cradock's letters to be viewed and his apology for the brethren particularly heard, protested against him and Mr. Humfries that they were a couple of imposturous knaves." Laud had thought to crush the government of Massachusetts by destroying the company, whose office remained in London, with Cradock still apparently its head. The archbishop found too late that he had eagerly pounced upon a dummy. He devised many things afterward to achieve his purpose, but the charter remained over seas.

Chap: IV.

Compare Palfrey, i, 371, and Deane's note in Mass. Hist. Soc. Proc. 1869, p. 185.

Hutchinson's Hist. Mass., p. 31.

XII.

From the point of view of our later age, the removal of the charter government to America is the event of chief importance in this migration of Winthrop's company. The ultimate effect of this brilliant stroke was so to modify a commercial corporation that it became a colonial government as independent as possible of control from England. By the admission of a large number of the colonists to be freemen—that is, to vote as stockholders in the affairs of the company, which was now the colony itself, and a little later by the development of a second chamber—the government became representative.

But we may not for a moment conceive that

the colonists understood the importance of their
act in the light of its consequences. In their
minds the government was merely a setting and
support for the church. The founding of a new
church establishment, after what they deemed the
primitive model, was the heart of the enterprise.
This is shown in many words uttered by the chief
actors, and it appears in strong relief in an incident that occurred soon after the arrival of Winthrop's company. Isaac Johnston, the wealthiest
man of the party, succumbed to disease and hardship, but " he felt much rejoiced at his death that
the Lord had been pleased to keep his eyes open
so long as to see one church of Christ gathered
before his death." Here we have the Puritan passion for a church whose discipline and services
should realize their ideals—a passion that in the
stronger men suffered no abatement in the midst
of the inevitable pestilence and famine that were
wont to beset newly arrived colonists in that time.

XIII.

One salient fact in the history of the Massachusetts Bay colony is the dominant influence of the
example of Plymouth. The Puritans of the Massachusetts colony were not Separatists. No one had
been more severe in controversy with the Separatists than some of the Puritans who remained in the
Church of England. They were eagerly desirous
not to be confounded with these schismatics.
When the great migration of 1630 took place, the

emigrants published a pathetic farewell, protesting with the sincerity of homesick exiles their attachment to the Church of England, "ever acknowledging that such hope and part as we have obtained in the common salvation we have received in her bosom and sucked at her breasts."

It is to be remembered that these Puritans did not agree among themselves. Puritanism was of many shades. There were some, like the Brownes whom Endecott sent out of the colony, that were even unwilling to surrender the prayer book. The greater part of the earlier Puritans had desired to imitate the Presbyterianism of Scotland and Geneva, and in Elizabeth's time they had organized presbyteries. Nothing seemed more probable beforehand than the revival in New England of the presbyteries of the days of Cartwright. But what happened was unexpected even by the Puritans. The churches of Massachusetts were formed on the model of John Robinson's Independency.

Differences among the Puritans.

There must have been a certain exhilarant reaction in the minds of the Puritans when at last they were clear of the English coast and free from the authority that had put so many constraints upon them. There were preachings and expoundings by beloved preachers with no fear of pursuivants. The new religious freedom was delightful to intoxication. "Every day for ten weeks together," writes one passenger, they had preaching and exposition. On one ship the watches were set by the Puritan captain with the accompaniment of psalm-

Effect of emigration.

Roger Clap's Memoirs, 40.

singing. Those who all their lives long had made outward and inward compromises between their ultimate convictions and their obligations to antagonistic authority found themselves at length utterly free. It was not that action was freed from the restraint of fear, so much as that thought itself was freed from the necessity for politic compromises. Every ship thus became a seminary for discussion. Every man now indulged in the unwonted privilege of thinking his bottom thought. The tendency to swing to an extreme is all but irresistible in the minds of men thus suddenly liberated. To such enthusiasts the long-deferred opportunity to actualize ultimate ideals in an ecclesiastical vacuum would be accepted with joy. What deductions such companies would finally make from the hints in the New Testament was uncertain. The only sure thing was that every vestige of that which they deemed objectionable in the English church would be repressed, obliterated, in their new organization.

With the evils and abuses of the English church more and more exaggerated in their thoughts, the sin of separation readily came to seem less heinous than before. There was no longer any necessity for professing loyalty to the church nor any further temptation to think ill of those at Plymouth, who, like themselves, had suffered much to avoid what both Separatists and Puritans deemed unchristian practices. A common creed and common sufferings, flight from the same oppression to find refuge in what was henceforth to be a common country, drew them to sympathy and affection for their forerunners at Plymouth. The Plymouth people were not backward to send friendly help to the newcomers. The influence of the physician sent from Plymouth to Endecott's party in the prevailing sickness soon persuaded the naturally radical Endecott to the Plymouth view of church government. Winthrop's associates, or the greater part of them, drifted in the same direction, to their own surprise, no doubt. There was a lack of uniformity in the early Massachusetts churches and some clashing of opinion. Some ministers left the colony dissatisfied; one or more of the churches long retained Presbyterian forms, and some stanch believers in presbyterial government lamented long afterward that New England ecclesiastical forms were not those of the Calvinistic churches of Europe. But the net result was that Robinsonian independency became the established religion in New England, whence it was transplanted to England during the Commonwealth, and later became the prevailing discipline among English dissenters.

Thus the church discipline and the form of government in Massachusetts borrowed much from Plymouth, but the mildness and semi-toleration— the "toleration of tolerable opinions"—which Robinson had impressed on the Pilgrims was not so easily communicated to their new neighbors who had been trained in another school.

Cotton to Salonstall in Hutch. Papers.

Hubbard's Hist. of New Eng., 117.

Note 10.

ELUCIDATIONS.

Note 1,
page 191.
Morton's settlement has become the subject of a literature of
its own, and of some rather violent and amusing discussion even
in our times.   Morton's New English Canaan has been edited by
Mr. C. F. Adams for the Prince Society.   His defensive account
of himself leaves the impression that the author was just the sort
of clever and reckless rake who is most dangerous to settlements
in contact with savages, and who might be expelled neck and
heels from a frontier community holding no scruples of a Puritan
sort.   The Royal Proclamation in Rymer's Foedera, xvii, 416
(and Hazard's State Papers, i, 151), 1622, sets forth the evil of
the sale of arms to the savages, but it was leveled at earlier
offenders than Morton.   Compare Sainsbury's Calendar, September 29 and November 24, 1630, pp. 120, 122.   There are also
references, more or less extended, to Morton in the Massachusetts Records, Winthrop's Journal, Bradford's Plimouth Plantation, Dudley's Letter to the Countess of Lincoln in Young's
Chronicles of Massachusetts, and in other early accounts.

Note 2,
page 193.
Abbott's account of Laud's rise, Rushworth, i, 440, is traced
with a bitter pen, no doubt, but the student Laud, as Abbott
draws him, is so much like his later self that one can not but
believe that the description of him picking quarrels with the public
readers and carrying information against them to the bishop has
a basis of fact.

Note 3,
page 199.
Rushworth, writing under the later date of 1637, says: "The
severe Censures in Star Chamber, and the greatness of the Fines,
and the rigorous Proceedings to impose Ceremonies, the sus-
pending and silencing Multitudes of Ministers, for not reading in
the Church the Book for Sports to be exercised on the Lord's
day, caused many of the Nation, both Ministers and others, to
sell their Estates, and to set Sail for New England (a late Plantation in America), where they hold a Plantation by Patent from
the King."   Part II, vol. i, p. 410.

Note 4,
page 204.
"We trust you will not be unmindful of the main end of our
Plantation, by endeavouring to bring the Indians to a knowledge
of the Gospel."   Cradock's letter to Endecott, February 16, 1629,
Young's Chronicle, 133; also the official letter, ibid., page 142,
where the "propagation of the Gospel" among whites and

Indians is the "aim." The Royal Charter itself declared that "to win and invite the natives of the country to the knowledge and obedience of the only true God and Saviour of mankind . . . is the principal end of this Plantation." (A similar provision was inserted in the Connecticut Charter in 1662, in imitation of that of Massachusetts.) The common seal of the Massachusetts colony, sent over in 1629, bore an Indian with the inscription, "Come over and help us." Young's Chronicles of Massachusetts, 155, Instructions to Endecott. The paper of "Reasons," attributed to Winthrop, keeps the conversion of the Indians in view, but it is blended with that which was in his mind the main end, the founding of a Puritan church. The first paragraph reads, "It will be a service to the Church of great consequence to carry the Gospell into those parts of the world, to helpe on the comminge of the fullnesse of the Gentiles, & to raise a Bulworke against the kingdome of Ante-Christ which the Jesuites labour to reare up in those parts." Life and Letters of Winthrop, i, 309. The copy of this paper in Sir John Eliot's handwriting has a preamble written in a nervous style that may well be Eliot's own. This preamble goes back to the conversion of the Indians as a main purpose. The Antapologia of T. Edwards, 1644, declares that White of Dorchester and others had the conversion of the Indians in view in promoting emigration to New England. Edwards says, page 41, that the establishing of Congregational churches "was not in the thoughts of them that were the first movers in that or of the ministers that were sent over in the beginning." The statement is quite too strong, but the ecclesiastical purpose seems to have grown rapidly when the number of emigrants revealed the greatness of the opportunity.

Cotton Mather says, Magnalia, Book II, chap. iv, 3, that Winthrop was made a justice at eighteen, but Mather's account of anything marvelous needs support. Winthrop held his first court at Groton Hall several months after he had attained his majority. Life and Letters, i, 62. Compare page 223 of the same volume.

Note 5, page 204.

Of his election to the governorship he wrote to his wife, "The onely thinge that I have comforte of in it is, that heerby I have assurance that my charge is of the Lorde & that he hath called me to this worke." Life and Letters, i, 340.

Note 6, page 205.

The government of the colony under Endecott was substantially that prescribed for "particular plantations" in the general order of the Virginia Company at the time the charter for the

Note 7, page 208.

Pilgrim colony was granted, and like that which was formed at Plymouth under the Compact. The Massachusetts form may have been borrowed from Plymouth. This may be considered the primary form of colony government in the scheme of the Virginia Company. The plan antedates the formation of the Virginia Company by at least twenty years, for it was a form proposed by Ralegh when, in 1587, he organized his colony under the title: "The Governor and Assistants of the city of Ralegh in Virginia." The secondary form of government was that prescribed for Virginia in the charter of 1618, which added a lower house elective by the people. This fully developed government could come only when the population had become large enough to render a representative system possible.

Note 8, page 210.

It has been maintained by several writers that the charter had been worded with a view to removal. See, for example, Palfrey's New England, i, 307. But a paper read before the Massachusetts Historical Society, and printed in the Proceedings for December, 1869, by the late Charles Deane, shows that such a presumption is groundless. In calling the subordinate government of Endecott "London's Plantation in Massachusetts Bay in New England," the company showed that it proposed to keep its headquarters in London. It is open to question, however, whether Deane does not go too far in denying that the charter gave authority for the transfer. In that technical age the letter of the instrument would probably be counted more conclusive than at present, and the evidence of the dockets would have less weight. The removal of the government was not one of the charges made in the *quo warranto* proceedings against the company. On the main question compare also the very significant treatment of the subject by Winthrop in his paper on Arbitrary Government, Life and Letters, ii, 443, where he expressly says that it was intended to have the chief government in England, "and with much difficulty we gott it abscinded." It is to be remembered that the exercise of governmental functions by a commercial corporation was not a novel spectacle in that age. In 1620 the English and Dutch East India Companies, after having been at war while the two nations were allies, concluded a treaty of peace. No doubt the exercise of such powers by trading companies had been made familiar by the mingling of the functions of government with those of commerce by the merchants of the Hanse cities. The East India and the Hudson Bay Companies continued to exercise territorial jurisdiction until a very recent period.

This rebound from their previous attitude of compromise is well exemplified in the church covenant adopted at Dorchester, Mass., in 1636, under the lead of Richard Mather, which contains these words: "We do likewise promise by his Grace assisting us, to endeavour the establishing amongst ourselves all His Holy Ordinances which He hath appointed for His church here on Earth, . . . opposing to the utmost of our power whatsoever is contrary thereto and bewailing from our Hearts our own neglect hereof in former times and our poluting ourselves therein with any Sinful Invention of men." Blake's Annals of Dorchester. Robinson of Leyden, in his Justification of Separation, 1610, declared that the Puritans would soon separate if they might have the magistrates' license ; and Backus, who quotes the passage (i, pp. 2, 3), remarks on the confirmation which the history of Massachusetts gives to Robinson's theory of conformity.

CHAP. IV.

Note 9, page 214.

In his Way of the Churches Cleared, controversial necessity drove Cotton to assert that Plymouth had small share in fixing the ecclesiastical order of Massachusetts, but he is compelled to admit its influence. " And though it bee," he says, " very likely, that some of the first commers might helpe their Theory by hearing and discerning their practice at Plymmouth : yet therein the Scripture is fulfilled, 'The Kingdome of Heaven is like unto leaven,'" etc., pp, 16, 17.

Note 10, page 215.

BOOK III.

BOOK III.

CHAPTER THE FIRST.

THE CATHOLIC MIGRATION.

I.

Centrif-
ugal
forces.

AT every new stage in the history of the American settlement, we are afresh reminded that colonies are planted by the uneasy. The discontent that comes from poverty and financial reverse, that which is born of political unrest, and that which has no other cause than feverish thirst for novelty and hazardous adventure, had each a share in impelling Englishmen to emigrate. But in the seventeenth century religion was the dominant concern —one might almost say the dominant passion—of the English race, and it supplied much the most efficient motive to colonization. Not only did it propel men to America, but it acted as a distributing force on this side of the sea, producing secondary colonies by expelling from a new plantation the discontented and the persecuted to make fresh breaks in the wilderness for new settlements. Connecticut and Rhode Island were secondary plantings of this kind. Religious differences also made twain the Chesapeake region, the first home of the English in America, one of the two rival colonies being intolerantly Protestant, the other a home for Catholic refugees.

II.

George Calvert, the first Baron Baltimore, who projected the Maryland colony and left it to his son to carry forward, belonged to the order of men who are shrewd without being creative—men of sagacity as differentiated from men of ideas. The man in whose mind there is a ferment of original ideas has theories to promulgate or expound. Sagacity has small necessity for speech—its very reticence gives an advantage in the conduct of affairs. The parliamentary antagonist and political rival who confronted Calvert was no other than our old acquaintance Sir Edwin Sandys, of the Virginia Company. Calvert and Sandys were alike men of rare accomplishments, and both were interested in schemes for colonization; otherwise they were antipodal. Sandys was a statesman of advanced ideas, creative, liberal, and original, fitted to be the founder of representative government in the English colonies. In that age of worn and brittle institutions it was not deemed wholly safe to suffer so robust a thinker as Sandys to be always at large, and it was one of Calvert's most difficult duties, as the king's secretary and chosen intermediary, to explain to Parliament why its leader was under restraint. Sandys, as we have already said, was described as " right-handed to

Character of George Calvert.

every great employment"; when Calvert came
upon the scene, he was aptly characterized as "a
forward and knowing person in matters relating to
the state." The phrase denotes, perhaps, clever
adroitness within the limits of that mediocrity which
in those perilous times was a safeguard to the man
who ventured into politics. After having started
well at court, Sandys had fallen into irretrievable
disfavor by his resolute advocacy of the liberties
of his countrymen. The message to the Virginia
Company, already recited, " Choose the devil, but
not Sir Edwin Sandys," expressed the depth of the
king's antipathy. But if Sandys seemed to the
king a devil, Calvert became for him a convenient
angel. Notions about human rights and the liberty
of Parliament did not obstruct Calvert's career.
Not that he was a man to prove unfaithful to his
convictions, as did his bosom friend Wentworth,
or to suppress liberal opinions in order to smooth
an ascending pathway, as did his great contemporary Bacon. Calvert played a far simpler part
and one less dishonorable. It was his fortune to
be a man of facile mind, naturally reverential
toward authority. The principles enunciated by
his sovereign and the measures by which those in
power sought to attain the end in view were pretty
sure to seem laudable or at least excusable to him.
Such a mind can not be called scrupulous, neither
is it consciously dishonest. The quality most
highly esteemed at the court of James was
fidelity, unswerving devotion to the interests of

the king and of one's friends. And this, the
dominant virtue of his time and of his class—this
honor of a courtier—Calvert possessed in a high
degree; it is a standard by which he has a right
to be judged. To a French ambassador he seemed
an honorable, sensible, courteous, well-intentioned
man, devoted to the interests of England, but without consideration or influence.

Whatever his lack of influence in councils of
state, Calvert's fidelity, useful abilities, and many
accomplishments won the friendship of James, and
in that lavish reign when all the fairy stories came
true at a court which was "like a romance of
knight errantry," as the Spanish minister declared,
the favor of the king was sure to result in good
fortune to the favorite. From being secretary to
Burleigh, Calvert rose to be principal Secretary of
State, was knighted, and at last ennobled. Grants
of estates in Ireland and of great unexplored tracts
of territory in the wilderness of America, pensions,
sinecure offices, grants of money out of increased
customs fees, and presents from those who had
ends to serve at court, were the means by which
a successful courtier bettered his estate, and by
some or all of these Secretary Calvert thrived.
That he did thrive is proved by the great sum he
was able to lose in his futile attempt to plant a
colony in Newfoundland. It was believed that he
had accepted a share of the money dispensed lav-
ishly in presents and pensions to English courtiers
by Spain, but this Calvert denied, and one can be-

lieve that a man of his fidelity to king and country would be able to resist a temptation to which others succumbed.

III.

Calvert was very early interested in colonization. He was a member of the Virginia Company in 1609, and later one of the councilors for New England. In 1620 he was one of a commission appointed to settle the affairs of a Scotch company for colonizing Newfoundland, and in the next year he dispatched his first colony to the southeastern peninsula of that island which he had bought from Sir William Vaughan. In this latter year (1621) he secured a grant of the whole vast island, but in 1622 he accepted a re-grant of the peninsula alone, and this became his first proprietary colony. Captain Whitbourne's pamphlet on Newfoundland was just then circulating gratuitously by the aid of collections made in the churches with the sanction of royal authority. It described a Newfoundland of Edenic fruitfulness. Even cool-headed statesmen like Calvert appear to have been captivated by the stories of this veteran seaman and weather-beaten romancer. Calvert called his new province Avalon. The name signifies the land of apples—that is, the fruitful country. In old British mythology it was the paradise of the blessed, the island in the western seas to which King Arthur was translated in the famous legend. This name of promise suited the situation of the new island state, and fitted well the enthusiastic tales of Whitbourne and the groundless hopes of Calvert. The bleak New-foundland coast had already blossomed with fanciful names; there was the Bay of Plesaunce and the Bay of Flowers, Robin Hood's Bay and the River of Bonaventure; there was the Harbor of Formosa and the Harbor of Heartsease. Avalon, the earthly paradise, was but the complement of these.

IV.

Sir George Calvert probably drafted with his own hand—the hand of an expert and accomplished man of the court—the charter of April 7, 1623, that conferred on him an authority little short of sovereignty over his new territory. This masterpiece of dexterous charter-making afforded a model for other proprietary charters, and Calvert himself bettered it but little in the Maryland charter of a later date. The ambiguous passages in the Maryland charter, which have been accounted evidence of a design to make way for the toleration or even the possible dominance of Roman Catholicism, appear already in the charter of Avalon. Was the colony of 1621 or its charter of 1623 intended to supply a refuge, if one should be needed, for Englishmen of the Catholic faith? The question is not easily answered. The primary design of the Avalon colony was, no doubt, to better the fortunes of Sir George Calvert and to lift him and his successors into the authority and dignity of counts-palatine in the New World. But there can hardly be a doubt that, before the charter of 1623 was granted, Secretary Calvert was already a Catholic, secretly or latently, if not overtly. His charter of Avalon naturally left open a door for the toleration of the faith to which he was already attached, or toward which he was tending.

Note 5.

V.

Calvert's conversion.

Calvert's conversion was almost inevitable. He favored the project for the Spanish match, and he was, like some other courtiers, under the influence of Gondomar, a consummate master of intrigue. He was bound by ties of friendship, and later by the marriage of his son, to Lord Arundel of Wardour, a Catholic, and the constitution of his mind and all the habits of a lifetime made him a lover of authority in church and state. Under favoring circumstances such a man becomes a Roman Catholic by gravitation and natural affinity.

There was a Catholic revival in England at this time, especially among the courtiers and upper classes. In 1623 there was a large influx to England of priests and Jesuits. English Romanists flocked to the vicinage of London, and resorted in great numbers to the mass in the houses of foreign ambassadors; and in many English country houses the mass was openly celebrated in defiance of law. The Commons, in alarm, adopted what James fitly called " a stinging petition against the papists."

Petition in Rushworth, Part I, i, 141. Compare Neal, Part II, c. ii.

VI.

Calvert had staked his hopes for himself and
for English Catholicism on the Spanish match.
This otherwise pliant courtier was intractable
where his religious convictions were concerned.
He scrupled to draw back at the bidding of
Charles and Buckingham, when drawing back involved a violation of the treaty oath of the king
and council, the plunging of England into a Spanish war, the sacrifice of the interests of the Catholic church, and a fresh exposure of his co-religionists in England to a harsh persecution. Calvert
was one of that party in the junta for Spanish affairs which was unwilling to break a solemn treaty
in order to gratify the wounded vanity of Buckingham and Charles, and he paid dearly for his
firmness. To bring about his resignation, his antagonists diverted business from his office, thus
reducing his fees and subjecting his pride to morti-
fication. Under this treatment it was noted by a
letter writer of the time that Mr. Secretary Calvert "droops and keeps out of the way." It was
reported that he was ill, and then that he had been
rebuked by the king and the prince, and it was
known that he wished to sell his office to some one
acceptable to Buckingham. Calvert's cleverness
as a courtier did not fail him in his fall. He succeeded at the last in mollifying Buckingham, whose
consent he gained to the sale of the secretaryship.
After nearly a year of the prolonged agony of

holding office in disfavor, he resigned in February, 1625, receiving six thousand pounds for his office, which was worth to the incumbent two thousand a year. He was at the same time raised to the Irish peerage as Baron Baltimore. He made his religious scruples the ostensible reason for his resignation, and he was already known to be " infinitely addicted to the Catholic faith." He made no secret of his proscribed religion ; he exposed to visitors the altar, chalice, and candlesticks in his best room ; and he catechised his children assiduously in the doctrines of the ancient church. At the accession of Charles he retired from the Privy Council rather than take an oath offensive to his conscience.

Note 6.

VII.

During the period of his decline from court favor Calvert's colony of Avalon probably suffered from neglect. He now gave his new leisure to the work of rescuing it. In 1627 he made a voyage to Newfoundland, taking a company of Catholic settlers and two priests. He went again in 1628. From Newfoundland he wrote to one of the Jesuits in England a letter of affection, declaring his readiness to divide with him " the last bit " he had in the world. In Avalon began the long chapter of the troubles of the Baltimores with the Puritan opposition. Besides his contentions with Puritan settlers, who abhorred the mass as a Jewish prophet did idolatry, he found it necessary to fight with French privateers bent on plunder. By the time the almost interminable Newfoundland winter had begun, he discovered that Avalon was not the earthly paradise it appeared in the writings of pamphleteers and in the letters of his own officeholders interested only in the continuance of their salaries. The icy Bay of Plesaunce and the bleak Bay of Flowers mocked him with their names of delight; of little avail was the fast-bound River of Bonaventure to its unlucky lord, or the Harbor of Heartsease to him who had sunk a fortune of thirty thousand pounds in the fruitless attempt to plant a settlement on a coast so cold. Ill himself, and with half his company down with scurvy, some of them dying, Baltimore turned his thoughts toward Virginia, now, after all its trials, prosperous under a genial sun.

He knew the conditions of that colony and the opportunities it afforded. A member of the Virginia Company during nearly all the years of its stormy existence, he had been made one of the fifty-six councilors that took over its effects at its demise, and he was one of the eight who constituted the quorum, and who probably transacted the business of this Council for Virginia. Even under the government of the Company there had been precedents for the establishment of a "precinct" within Virginia independent of the Jamestown government. Such a plantation had been that of Captain Martin and that proposed by Rich and Argall, and a charter for such had been given to the Leyden pilgrims. Baltimore wrote to ask

Chap. I.

Letters of Wynne, Daniel, and Hoskins, in Whitbourne's second ed.

Note 7.

Sails to Virginia.

Rymer's Fœdera, tom. vii, iv, 147.

for a precinct, pleading the king's promise already made that he might choose a part of Virginia. Here he would still be the head of a little independent state—a state in which the mass might be said without molestation. Before another winter set in he abandoned Avalon to fishermen and such hardy folk, and took ship for the James River, where he arrived in October, 1629.

VIII.

Baltimore's reception in Virginia was most inhospitable. He had perhaps counted on his former relation to the colony as a councilor to assure him a welcome. But the Virginians of that time were Sandys and Southampton men. They may have remembered that Calvert had been Sandys's enemy and political rival, and that he belonged to the faction of Sir Thomas Smyth in the company. The members of that faction had been the executioners of the company when they could no longer control it. Calvert was one of the later council, which had tried to take away insidiously the privileges granted to Virginians by their charter from the Virginia Company. This attack on their liberties they had stoutly resisted, even to cutting off a piece of one of the ears of the clerk of their own assembly for abetting it. Now a nobleman of the detested faction, an advocate of absolute government and a close friend of the king, had come among them. Baltimore might easily expect to

secure the governorship of Virginia itself. Perhaps it is hardly necessary to go even so far afield for a motive. The prospect of a settlement of Roman Catholics within the limits of the colony was in itself enough to excite the opposition of the Virginia churchmen. Baltimore's party of Catholics was not the only one repelled from Virginia about this time. Soon after Lord Baltimore's visit, perhaps, or just before, the Virginians refused permission to a company of Irish Catholics to settle within their bounds. These appear to have gone afterward to the island of St. Christopher's, where again Protestant fellow-colonists fell out with them about religion, so that they were finally sent to settle the neighboring island of Montserrat.

Note 9.

The Virginians, after all their sufferings, were now prosperous in a gross way, reaping large profits from tobacco, and living in riotous profusion after the manner of men beginning to emerge from the hardships and perils of a pioneer condition into sudden opulence. Their rude living did not at all prevent the colonists from being fastidious about their religion—it was the seventeenth century. Most of the Virginia clergy at this period were as reckless in life as the people, but the Protestantism of the colony was incorruptible. Some of the rabble even showed their piety by railing at the newly arrived papist nobleman.

Character of the early Virginians.

Leah and Rachel, and De Vries Voyages, *passim.*

A weapon of defense against Baltimore was ready to hand. Three years before his coming instructions had been sent from England to Yeardley

Expulsion of Baltimore.

to proffer the oath of supremacy " to all such as come thither with an intention to plant and reside, which, if any shall refuse, he is to be retorned or shipped from thence home." This order may not have been intended for so great a personage as a nobleman of the Court. It may have been meant only to head off humble Irishmen like those who settled Montserrat, or it may have been merely a fence against Separatists. But it served the turn of the alarmed colonists. Pott and Mathews, Claiborne and Roger Smyth, who led the opposition, offered the oath to Baltimore. Baltimore had sacrificed his place in the Privy Council rather than take this oath so contrary to his conscience, and he now again stood by his religious convictions, and took ship for England as ordered by the Virginia Council. He was disappointed and already shaken in health. The members of the council, appalled at their own boldness, perhaps, wrote to the king in self-defense. There is still extant an old manuscript record book of the seventeenth century which contains the instructions to Yeardley. Immediately following, as if to put it under the shelter of royal authority, is the report of the council, without date or signature, that the oath had been offered to Baltimore and refused.

MS. Book of Instructions, Library of Congress, folio 136.

IX.

Baltimore's zeal.

Baltimore's hardships during two voyages to Newfoundland, and a winter in the rude abodes of pioneers there, his illness during that winter, the constant spectacle of sickness and death about him, and the disappointment caused by his rude reception in Virginia, were enough, one would think, to have broken his resolution. He went back to England "much decayed in his strength," as he confessed; but, strangely enough, this accomplished man of the world, whose career had been that of a courtier, was far from living in ease and quietness as his friends had expected him to do. He was possessed of a passion for peopling the wilderness. He had written to the king from America that he was resolved to spend "the poore remaynder" of his days in colony-planting, his "inclinations carrying him naturally" to such work. To what extent he was prompted by a desire to leave to his heir the semi-sovereignty of a principality, and how far he was carried by a naturally adventurous temper hitherto latent, we have no means of deciding; but one can hardly resist the conclusion that a fervent religious zeal was the underlying spring of a resolution so indomitable. Like many another man of that time, Calvert was lifted from worldliness to high endeavor by religious enthusiasm. The king felt obliged to interpose his authority; he forbade Baltimore's risking his life in another voyage, but he granted him a charter for a new palatinate on the north side of the Potomac.

Lord Baltimore was doomed never to see the desire of his eyes. He died on the 15th of April, 1632, before the charter had passed, leaving the

Death of the first Lord Baltimore.

planting of Maryland to be carried forward by his son and heir, Cecilius. The charter of Maryland passed the seals on the 22d of the following June in favor of Cecilius, the second Lord Baltimore.

X.

The Maryland charter was no doubt the work of George Calvert's own hand. Its main provisions are identical with those of Avalon; but it put the proprietary in a still better position. He held Avalon by knight's service, Maryland in free and common soccage, and the holdings of Maryland settlers would be under the proprietary, not under the crown. In fact, the crown retained practically no rights of value in Maryland beyond the bare allegiance of the settlers. Larger privileges of trade were conceded to Maryland than had been given to Avalon. In one respect the liberties of the future settlers were apparently better guarded in the Maryland charter, for there is a faint promise of a representative government in its phraseology. But even this was not definitely assured. In a single regard the charter of Maryland appears less favorable to the Catholic religion than its predecessors. Historic specialists with a religious bias, doing their small best to render the current of history turbid, have not failed to convince themselves by means of the new clause that Maryland was a Protestant colony. The patronage and advowsons of all churches had been conferred on the proprietary in the Avalon charter, and a like concession is made in the Maryland grant; but to this, in the Maryland charter, is attached a sort of "lean-to"—a qualifying clause that appears to limit the ecclesiastical organization of the colony to Anglican forms. "Together with license and power," runs the charter, "to build and found Churches, Chapels and Oratories in convenient and fit places within the premises, and to cause them to be dedicated and consecrated according to the ecclesiastical laws of our kingdom of England." Note 10. In 1632 the Baltimore family was openly Catholic. The Puritans were raging against every indulgence shown by the court to Romanists. The clamor of the Catholic-baiters did not stop with a demand that Romanists should be expelled from England. The Commons had a few years earlier petitioned the King that they be excluded from "all other Your Highness's dominions." The founding of an English colony that might make a home for English and Irish Romanists was a more difficult project in the reign of Charles than it had been in the time of James when Avalon was granted. The clause which allowed Baltimore to dedicate his churches according to the ecclesiastical laws of England excites admiration. It graciously permitted an Anglican establishment in Maryland; it did Note 11. not oblige Baltimore to do anything at all, nor did it, in fact, put any constraint whatever on his actions in this regard. The impotent clause which seemed to limit, but did not limit, the ecclesiastical organization was breathlessly followed by one far

Rush-
worth,
Part I, vol.
i, 141, 1623.

from impotent—a masterpiece of George Calvert's skill. It gave to the proprietary the legal power exercised from ancient times by the Bishops of Durham as counts-palatine. The regalities of Durham having been pared down by Henry VIII, the charter somewhat furtively reached back after the local absolutism of the middle ages by giving Baltimore all the temporal power ever possessed by any Bishop of Durham. But if alarm should be taken at the giving of powers so vast to a Roman Catholic subject, there might be reassurance for timid souls in a clause in imitation of older charters than Calvert's, which stipulated that no interpretation should be put upon the charter by which God's holy and true Christian religion might be prejudiced. Ambiguity spread from the charter to some of the early Maryland laws, which wore a Protestant or a Catholic face according to the side from which they were approached.

XI.

When George Calvert projected his new southern colony he had every reason to suppose that it would be quickly supplied with settlers from the discontented English and Irish Catholics. The statute enacted in the third year of James, soon after the Gunpowder Plot, put those who adhered to the Roman communion in a precarious and exasperating situation. For the first year that a Catholic wholly neglected the sacraments of the English church he must pay twenty pounds. This was raised to forty the second year, and to sixty for every year of conscientious abstention thereafter. If he did not attend the parish church at all, the luxury of a conscience cost him twenty pounds a month, which, as money then went, was a large sum. If he were a rich landholder, the king might take the use or rentals of two thirds of his land until he should conform. The oath of allegiance by which he was to be tested was made ingeniously offensive to a Catholic conscience. If a Romanist should persuade a Protestant to accept his own faith he was guilty of treason, as was also his convert. The man who harbored a Roman Catholic neglecting to attend the parish church was to be fined ten pounds a month. Marriage by a Romish priest invalidated accruing land tenures. The Catholic was not suffered to send his children beyond seas for an education, nor yet to keep a schoolmaster of his own faith; he could not serve as an executor; he might not have the charge of any child; his house might be searched for Catholic books; he was not allowed to keep weapons; and when at last his vexed and troubled life was over, his dead body might not be buried among the graves of his forefathers in the parish churchyard.

The administration of this law was attended by many aggravations. The pursuivants took the very cattle and household goods of the poor; from the rich they exacted large payments, failing which, they pounced on valuable plate and jewels, which they seized under pretense that these were

CHAP. I.

An act for the better discovering and repressing of popish recusants. Also, An act to prevent, etc., 3 Jac. I, chaps. iv and v.

Administration of the law.

Book III.

Lingard, viii, 189, cites Rymer, xxii, 13; Hardwicke Papers, 1446, and a private letter.

Influence of foreign policy.

1583, reprinted 1688.

1609, sm. 4to, pp. 112.

Ellis Collection, first series, iii, 128.

articles of superstition or the concealed property of Jesuits. It is said that James derived a revenue of thirty-six thousand pounds a year from the fines of lay Catholics. To the several Scotch favorites of the king were assigned certain rich recusants from whom they might squeeze whatever could be got by the leverage of the law.

Very embarrassing to the foreign policy of England was the severity of English laws against Catholics, and Lord Treasurer Burleigh found it needful to publish in Elizabeth's time, for circulation in all the courts of Europe, a treatise on The Execution of Justice in England and the Maintenance of Public Order and Christian Peace; and in the following reign James himself turned pamphleteer and published an Apologie for the Oath of Allegiance. There were periods when pressure from abroad softened the administration of the law. But it was only irregularly and intermittently that the Government could be brought to grant indulgences that roused the pious wrath of Puritans and reduced the revenue of the king and his favorites. If Spain, and afterward France, made it a condition precedent to a marriage treaty that the penal laws against English recusants should be relaxed, Parliament, resenting foreign dictation, demanded of the king a renewal of the severities against papists. Twenty-four Catholics suffered capitally in James's reign, before 1618; and when in 1622 it was necessary to condone Catholicism in order to conciliate Spain, it is said that four hundred Jesuits and priests were set free on bail at one time. The number of Catholics, lay and cleric, released in this year is put at four thousand, but this may be an exaggeration.

CHAP. I.

Neal, ii, ch. ii.

Rapin, 215, 2d ed.

XII.

In 1627, and again in 1628, Lord Baltimore took Catholics with him to Newfoundland and settled priests there. The English court was just then sailing on a Protestant tack, and England had allied itself with the Huguenots of La Rochelle. Another of the good works by which the government of Charles and Buckingham was endeavoring to prove its sanctification was the enforcement of the penal statutes against Roman Catholics. It is notable that Baltimore sailed with the first Catholic emigrants to Avalon about the time of the setting in of the movement toward Massachusetts which swelled at length into the great Puritan exodus. The five years of delay caused by the change from Avalon to Maryland, and also perhaps by the exhaustion of Baltimore's resources and his death, was unfavorable to the project of a Catholic province. The English government by 1634 had grown more lenient toward Romanists, the co-religionists of the queen. The work at which Laud kept all hands busy just then was the suppression of Puritanism, and thousands of Puritans were by this time shaking the dust of England from their feet and seeking a home in the western wilderness, persuaded that the Church of England under Laud

Catholic emigration small.

Harl. Mis-
cell., ii,
492, and
following,
where pas-
sages from
contempo-
rary writers
are quoted.

had all sails set for Rome. This illusion regarding the purposes of the archbishop and his party, which alarmed the Puritans, heartened the Catholics, who naturally preferred to stay at home where a flood tide seemed to be setting toward Catholicism. The small Catholic migration to Maryland was not to be compared with that stream of Puritan emigration that about this time poured into New England twenty thousand people in a decade. The fall of Laud and the rise of the Puritans to power put a complete stop to the New England migration, but it failed to quicken the Catholic movement, for Maryland herself had become sadly involved in the civil commotions of the time.

Cecilius Calvert undoubtedly counted on a large migration of Catholic recusants, and the documents show that the Jesuit order in England took great interest in the movement. The second Lord Baltimore was joined by partners in the financial risks of the venture, and though we meet with more than one allusion to these adventurers whose interest in the colony was apparently still active twenty years after its beginning, they were profoundly silent partners; their names are nowhere recorded, and we are left to conjecture the origin of their interest in Maryland.

XIII.

" The first and most important design of the Most Illustrious Baron, which ought also to be the aim of the rest, who go in the same ship, is, not to

think so much of planting fruits and trees in a land
so fertile, as of sowing the seeds of religion and
piety." This was Lord Baltimore's authoritative
declaration, and because it varies in form from the
stock phrases so common at the time, it bears an
air of some sincerity, though it is diplomatically
ambiguous.

Baltimore's opponents made great exertions
to prevent the departure of the Ark and the
Dove, which were to bear faithful Catholics
across the flood to a new world. A story was
started that these ships were carrying nuns to
Spain, and another tale that found believers was
that they had soldiers on board going to France to
serve against the English. It was told that Calvert's men had abused the customs officers at
Gravesend, and sailed without cockets in contempt
of all authority, the people on board refusing the
oath of allegiance. The Ark was stopped and
brought back by order of the Privy Council, and
the oath of allegiance was given to a hundred and
twenty-eight passengers. But the ships came to
again at the Isle of Wight, and when they got
away at last there were near three hundred passengers on board, including Jesuit priests. Most of
the passengers were "laboring men"; how many
were Catholic and how many Protestant it is impossible now to tell. That the leaders and the
gentry were, most of them, Catholics there is
every reason to believe. The passengers called
Protestants were rather non-Catholics, precisely

17

CHAP. I.

Efforts to
obstruct
the ships.

Letters of
Baltimore
to Went-
worth in
Strafford
papers,
passim.

the kind of emigrants that would give the Jesuits the converts of which they tell exultantly in their letters. There was no Protestant minister on

board, nor was there the slightest provision for Protestant worship, present or future.

XIV.

Toleration was the Baltimore policy from the beginning. It was no doubt in the original plan of George Calvert and his associates, whoever they were. The Provincial of the Society of Jesus pri-

vately furnished Baltimore with arguments in defense of this policy before the first colony sailed. The founders of Maryland were men of affairs shaping plan to opportunity, and the situation was inexorable. Toleration and protection was all that English Roman Catholics could hope to find in traveling thus to the ends of the earth.

Cecilius gave positive instruction that on shipboard acts of the Roman Catholic religion should be performed with as much privacy as possible, so as not to offend the Protestant passengers " whereby any just complaint may hereafter be made by them in Virginia or in England." There is no pretense of theory here; all is based on the exigency of the situation and sound policy. The policy was George Calvert's, whose school was the court of James, and whose whole career shows that he entertained no advanced views of human liberty. Had he held toleration as a theory of government, his doctrine would have been more liberal than

that of Ralegh and Bacon and far in advance of
that of contemporary Puritan leaders. They quite
misunderstand the man who regard him as a progressive thinker; he was a conservative opportunist. Still less was Cecilius a man likely to act
on general principles.

XV.

We have seen how religiously the Puritans
passed their time at sea in long daily expositions of
Scripture and other devotions, and that sometimes
even the watch was set with a psalm. Not less religious were the Catholic pilgrims, and though the
form is strikingly different, the believing and zealous age is the same. To make things safe, the
Jesuit fathers committed the principal parts of
the ship in some detail to the protection of God
in the first place, and then to that "of His Most
Holy Mother and of St. Ignatius and of all the
angels of Maryland." These angels to whom the
safety of Maryland was committed were kept busy
by special spiritual opponents. A dangerous storm
was raised on one occasion by all the "malignant
spirits of the tempest and all the evil genii of
Maryland." But Father White circumvented this
combination of ordinary storm spirits with imps of
Protestant proclivities by setting forth to Christ
and the Blessed Virgin, while the storm was at its
worst, "that the purpose of this journey was to
glorify the Blood of our Redeemer in the salvation of the Barbarians, and also to build up a king-

Religious
observ-
ance at
sea.

Relatio
Itineris,
p. 10.

Note 16.

dom for the Saviour and to consecrate another
gift to the Immaculate Virgin his mother." The
last clause apparently refers to Maryland, as if it
were named in honor of the Virgin. The repre-
sentation was effective; the good father had scarcely ceased speaking when the storm began to abate.

The Puritans when using a geographical name
that began with the word " saint " scrupulously un-
canonized it by leaving off the prefix. But these
devout pilgrims of the Roman faith, when once the
saints and guardian angels of Maryland had piloted
them safe in spite of the malice of storm spirits
and evil genii into landlocked waters and the
bounds of Lord Baltimore's grant, proceeded to
sanctify the whole region by sprinkling it with the
names of saints and angels from Michael the arch-
angel downward. The ancient Indian designations
were marks of a heathenism they purposed to overthrow, and they began by trying to get rid of the
whole " bead roll of unbaptized names." No convenient island, creek, river, bay, or cape escaped
Christian baptism. On Annunciation Day, 1634,
they landed on Heron Island, in the Potomac, which
they named appropriately for St. Clement, who was
martyred by being thrown into the sea attached to
an anchor, and here the sacrifice of the mass was
celebrated, the worshipers reflecting that " never
before had this been done in this part of the world."
After the mass they took upon their shoulders a
great cross hewn out of a tree and advanced in
order to the place appointed, where the governor

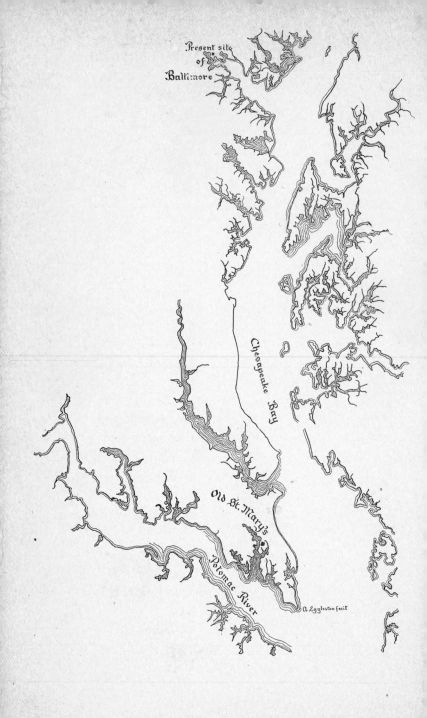

Present site
of
Baltimore

Chesapeake Bay

Old St. Mary's

Potomac River

A. Eggleston fecit

and his assistants took part in its erection. The Catholics of the party, seeing this symbol of the faith erected in a new land, knelt upon the ground and recited the litanies of the cross in a kind of religious ecstasy. Here in another form was that tender attachment to their faith that one finds among the more devout Protestant exiles, and in the nobler natures there was doubtless that element of the heroic and the saintly often evolved in the religious sufferings and activities of that day—a relief to the pettiness of the debates and the irksomeness of the bigotries of the age.

XVI.

The colony had been named Maryland by King Charles in honor of his wife Henrietta Maria; at least there was assigned to the king responsibility for a name that, like nearly everything else about Maryland, was ambiguous. But the phrase *Terra Mariæ* in the charter, though represented there to be the equivalent of Maryland, was significant to a devout Catholic of something better than a compliment to a Catholic queen. The Indian village which with its gardens and cornfields had been bought for the germinal settlement and capital, took the name of St. Mary's, and the whole infant colony is called the Colony of St. Maries, by its own Legislative Assembly in 1638, as though by Maryland were intended the land of Mary. Notwithstanding the manifest care of the second Lord Baltimore to hold the missionaries within the limits

A Catholic colony.

Compare Clarke's Gladstone and Maryland Toleration.

Maryland Archives, i, 23.

of worldly prudence, the zealous fathers lived and labored in a spirit of other-worldliness. They set themselves first of all to convert those sheep without a shepherd, the Protestants of Maryland. Some of these appear to have been men of reckless and immoral lives, who were greatly bettered by an acceptance of religious restraint. Those non-Catholics who were ill, and those who found themselves languishing and dying in the wilderness without the consolations of their own religion, were zealously visited and converted *in extremis* by the Jesuits. The servants and mechanics employed by or apprenticed to the missionaries were brought under their constant influence and were readily won. Nearly all the Protestants who arrived in 1638 were swiftly brought over to the faith of the missionaries, and twelve converts were joyously reckoned as fruits of the Jesuit labors in 1639. There was more than one instance of the miraculous, or at least of the marvelous, to help on this work. One man of noble birth, who had by dissipation brought himself to desperate straits, and then sunk until he became at length a bond servant in Maryland, embraced Catholicism. After the death of this convert a very bright light was sometimes seen burning about his place of burial, and even those who were not Catholics were permitted to see this wonder. The horrible punishments that resulted from the Divine wrath against those who scoffingly rejected the Catholic faith in Maryland remind one of the equal calamities that befell those

Excerpta
de Diversis
Literis,
etc., 56–60.

who were unfaithful to Puritanism in New England. Seventeenth-century Englishmen with sky-wide differences in opinion were one in the traits that belonged to their age. Father White was sure that the destruction of Indians in Maryland was specially ordered by God to provide an opening "for His own everlasting law and light"; but not more sure than were the Puritans that the cruel plague which exterminated whole villages on the Massachusetts coast was sent to open a way for the planting of Calvinistic churches. Each division of Christians in turn reduced the Almighty Creator to the level of a special tutelary divinity, sometimes to that of a rather vindictive genius of the place.

In this work of propagandism the missionaries did not forget the red men. Their labors among the aborigines were fairly successful at first, then interrupted by relapse and by war. Such is the history of Indian missions. Much was made of the solemn profession and baptism of an Indian "king," at which the governor and other distinguished men " honored by their presence the Christian sacraments," the governor marching behind the neophyte in the procession. Maryland was in fact openly a Catholic colony until after 1640.

Note 17.

But as a Catholic colony it was a failure. In fear of the rising Puritan tempest in England, or the violent opposition on several grounds of its stronger neighbor Virginia, and of the mutinous

Failure to make a Catholic state.

bigotry of its own Puritan settlers, who regarded Baltimore's government as a "Babylon" to be overthrown, it was never able to afford to Catholics perfect security, much less was it able to promise them domination. But the Catholics included most of the rich and influential families, and it was a Jesuit boast that they were superior to other American settlers in breeding and urbanity. As they had choice of the best land in the province, the Catholic families remained during the whole

Note 18.

colonial period among the most prominent people of Maryland. There is also evidence that the Catholics were numerically considerable in proportion to the population, though the reports on the subject are vague and conflicting. In 1641 they were about one fourth of the whole. The ranks of the early Catholic settlers, both of the rich and poor, seem to have been recruited from Ireland as well as from England, but the Maryland government in Queen Anne's Protestant time passed acts levying an import tax of twenty pounds on each Irish Catholic servant, in order that the bond

Note 19.

servants and even the transported convicts in Maryland should be orthodox Protestants.

XVII.

Opposition to Maryland.

George Calvert, the first Baron Baltimore, molded the Maryland enterprise until the drafting of the charter, and his spirit was felt in it after his death. Cecilius, his son, was a man of a somewhat different sort, and his traits became more apparent as time went on. He was strongly supported at court by Strafford, his father's most devoted and obliged friend, and no doubt also by the queen, who was godmother to Maryland. The opposition to Maryland was probably embittered by the hatred to Strafford and the jealousy of a Catholic queen.

On his enemies in Virginia the younger Baltimore took ample vengeance. He got one of the queen's household appointed treasurer of the colony, and the Virginians found themselves obliged to pay the quitrents, which had been neglected and apparently forgotten. Other officers of the colony were nominated by Baltimore. Harvey, the governor, hoping to collect money due him from the royal treasury by Baltimore's assistance, was his obsequious tool, to the bitter indignation of the Virginians, who hated Baltimore not only because he was a Romanist, but also because he had divided the first colony and cut off the northern Indian trade from Virginia. In consequence of the quarrel between Harvey and the Virginians over Maryland there ensued a revolution in Virginia; Harvey was shipped to England by the same bold men who had sent the first Lord Baltimore packing. But Harvey was sent back again by the king, and by this counter revolution the colonial constitution of Virginia was modified for the worse. It was altogether an exquisite revenge.

Cecilius meditated even a bolder stroke. He

The second Lord Baltimore and Virginia.

Note 20.

schemed through Windebank to have himself made governor of Virginia, promising to wring out of it eight thousand pounds more of revenue for the king from some neglected sources. To achieve this, he proposed a scheme by which Windebank was to impose on the king's credulity. Secretary Windebank may have recoiled from the part he was to play; it is certain that Charles was not persuaded to hand over Virginia bound hand and foot into the power of the proprietary of the rival colony.

Note 21.

XVIII.

Cautious
policy of
Baltimore.

Intolerance on the part of the authorities of Maryland directed toward Protestants might have brought a swift overthrow of the whole project. The instructions given for the first voyage already cited show throughout the need for extreme caution in the face of extreme peril. It is required of the governor and commissioners that "they be very careful to preserve the peace amongst all the passengers on shipboard, and that they suffer no scandal nor offense to be given to any of the Protestants." The rulers are to instruct the Catholics to be silent "upon all occasions of discourse concerning matter of religion," and those in authority are to "treat the Protestants with as much mildness and favor as justice will permit." These instructions were to hold good after landing, and in one notable case of religious dissension after the arrival in Maryland, justice was meted out against the Catholic offender in a way that showed

Baltimore's
instruc-
tions, 15
Nov., 1633,
Calvert
Papers.

a disposition to observe this policy of conciliation toward Protestants at the expense of some unfairness toward Catholics. Very early a proclamation was issued for the suppression of all religious disputes, and Copley, the business administrator of the Jesuits, thought they ought to be put down for fear the writings should be sent to the governor of Virginia.

The ambiguous charter of Maryland was a necessary hypocrisy. The plan of toleration was also inevitable, and it was carried no further than necessity required, for in that age, when toleration was odious, a liberal policy had also its perils. The Act for Church Liberties of 1639 was a fine example of the studied ambidexterity of the Maryland government. It was enacted " that Holy Church within this province shall have all her rights, liberties, and immunities, safe, whole, and inviolate in all things." Holy Church here is apparently a substitution for " the Church of England " in a similar phrase of Magna Charta. Such an act was worthy of Bunyan's Mr. Facing-bothways. Interpreted by judges holding office at the will of a Catholic proprietary, it could have but one meaning. For the outside world it might bear another sense. It did all that could be done in the circumstances for the Roman Catholic religion and for Catholic ecclesiastics.

CHAP. I.

Necessary ambiguity.

Note 22.

XIX.

In 1643, Parliament, dominated by Puritans, could not let the distant Maryland province rest in peace. It passed an ordinance making the Earl of Warwick Governor in Chief and Lord High Admiral of all the plantations in America. This act contained covert allusions to papists, Spaniards,

and governors recently appointed by the king. Baltimore met the rising tempest in a way characteristic of him. If he could settle a portion of his province with Puritans they might serve to shield him from the storm. Besides, the Catholic emigration had not proved large, and his province needed inhabitants. He wrote to a Captain Gibbons, of Boston, sending him a commission under the Maryland government, and offering "free liberty of religion and all other privileges" to such of the New England people as were willing to remove to Maryland. There were those in New

England in that day who longed for a more genial climate, but to settle under the authority of a papist was to them much like pitching a tent on the confines of perdition.

Though Puritans could not be induced to move from New England, it happened that the Puritans living in Virginia were persecuted in this same

year by that stanch cavalier and retrograde churchman, Sir William Berkeley, who wanted his parsons to read prayers, but did not like preaching ministers of any sort. He was new to his government, and had brought over with him plenty of hostility to the party that had affronted his royal master in England. Virginia Puritans had no choice but to suffer or depart, and Maryland was convenient. They began soon after this to seek a refuge under the protection of a proprietary who was a papist and who practiced toleration—two things almost equally hateful to the Puritans. Mr. James, a Puritan minister, tarried in Maryland a short time, as early as 1643; he was probably the only Protestant minister that set foot on Maryland soil before 1650. But the Puritan was never easy unless he was uneasy, and he was sure to be uneasy within when there was none to molest from without. To take an oath of fidelity to a papist was to him swearing fealty to antichrist; but so desirous was Baltimore of Puritan settlers that even the Maryland oath of fidelity was modified, and a saving clause was inserted for the ease of the Puritan conscience. The coming of Puritans who were in sympathy with the Parliament in England and who abhorred a tolerant papist, contributed something to the multifarious turmoils of the following years.

XX.

What we know of the petty civil wars of Maryland is tedious and perplexing. The broils before 1649 sprang from diverse sources, some of which we know, others we may easily conjecture. There was the old claim of Claiborne to jurisdiction over

Kent Island ; there was a disposition on the part
of some of the Marylanders to relieve the tedium
of existence by taking a hand in the great struggle
against royal authority which was rending England ; there was the tendency common in frontier
communities to carry debates to a violent issue ;
there was perhaps a natural proneness to insurrection on the part of bond servants and men lately
out of service ; and there was an innate hunger for
spoil of any sort in the seamen of that age and in
the rougher class on shore.   But by 1648 the tempest had passed for the time ; order had been re-
established ; the Catholic and the Puritan were living in peace like the lion and the lamb of Hebrew
prophecy ; and the Catholic proprietary, always
promptly bending before the storm, had delegated
his authority to a Protestant governor who took
the Parliament side.

XXI.

Before this epoch Maryland toleration had been
merely a practical fact.   It had not been theoretically stated ; it had not been a matter of legislation
at all ; its extent and limitations were unknown.
But now that this colonial home of Catholics was
to be a land of Protestants, and particularly of
Puritans, it was necessary to formulate the principle of toleration, the more, that Baltimore's own
co-religionists were to be put under a Protestant
governor.   Governor and high officers of state
were required to swear that they would molest on

account of religion no person professing to believe in Jesus Christ, "and in particular no Roman Catholic." By the mere march of events it had come to pass that in the state founded by Catholics as a cradle for the Roman Catholic religion, the Catholic was now compelled to secure as best he could the toleration of his religion at the hands of the heretic. Part of Baltimore's plan for this new settlement of affairs involved the sending over of a code of perpetual laws to be adopted by the Assembly. The proprietary gave orders that the governor should not assent to any of these laws if all were not passed ; but the Assembly of Maryland farmers was too cunning to be entrapped into passing laws which it thought inconvenient and unjust. A humble letter was sent from the members to the lord proprietary complaining that they were "illeterate" and "void of that Understanding and Comprehension" necessary to the discussion of such a code, and that in April they were too busy with their "necessary employment in a Crop" to give attention to it. They selected certain acts out of the code which they passed, among which was the famous Act of Toleration of 1649. That this was part of the code sent from England there can be no doubt ; the "illeterate" colonists were not capable of framing it, and it bears the character-mark of the Baltimore policy throughout. Here is no philosophic theory of toleration, no far-reaching conclusion like that of Roger Williams, that the magistrate may not take cognizance of merely religious offences. Williams was a thinker, a doctrinary, too far in advance of his age to be the successful organizer of a new state. Baltimore, on the other hand, accepted a practical toleration as an expedient—he may even have come to believe in it as a theory by force of his own situation. But he was not primarily a thinker at all. Even here, where Baltimorean toleration reaches high tide, no philosophic congruity is sought. The Jew and the Unitarian who deny the divinity of Christ are to be put to death. Only so much toleration is granted as is needful to the occasion. And even this toleration is not put upon any other ground than public policy; the forcing of conscience in religion "hath frequently fallen out to be of dangerous consequence"; therefore this law is made "to preserve mutual love and amity amongst the inhabitants." The provisions against such offences as blasphemy and Sabbath-breaking and religious disputes precede those for toleration. Very politic is the arrangement by which reviling of God is made a capital offence, while reviling the Virgin Mary is adroitly associated with speeches against the "holy apostles or evangelists" as a sort of second-class blasphemy, a finable offence.

Note 25.

Vicissitudes of toleration.

And yet it was toleration, and the law was all the more influential as an example, perhaps, because it was only practical and quite incongruous. It was eminently prudent and statesmanlike. That it was not perpetually effective was the fault not of Baltimore but of the times. Puritan ideas were rampant. The government of the proprietary was overthrown; the Jesuits fled to the inhospitable Virginia, where they lived concealed in a low hut like a cistern or a tomb, not lamenting their physical privations so much as the lack of wine which deprived them of the consolation of the sacrament. The new government of Maryland, five years after Baltimore's famous "act concerning Religion," passed a new act with the same title — an act brusque and curt, a law with its boots and spurs on. "That none profess and exercise the papist religion" is its rude forbidding. The tables are turned; it is no longer the nonresident Jew and the hypothetical Unitarian who are excepted. But the wheels rolled swiftly once more, and in three years Cecilius, absolute lord and proprietary, was again master of Maryland, and the beneficent act of 1649 resumed its sway. It protected the Catholic element, which, though always rich and influential, came to be in later colonial times but about a twelfth of the population. Toleration also served to make Maryland an early dwelling place for abounding Quakers and others holding religious views not relished in colonies less liberal.

ELUCIDATIONS.

Note 1,
page 223.

"Voto a Dios que la Corte d'Inglatierra es como un libro de cavalleros andantes." Quoted by Chamberlain in Birch, i, 413. In view of the swift mutations of fortune among courtiers, Dudley Carleton the younger wrote on December 18, 1624, "He is happiest who has least to do at court"—a truth which Calvert probably had come to appreciate by that time.

Note 2,
page 224.

"The third man who was thought to gain by the Spaniard was Secretary Calvert; and as he was the only secretary employed in the Spanish match, so undoubtedly he did what good offices he could therein for religion's sake, being infinitely addicted to the Roman Catholic faith, having been converted thereunto by Count Gondomar and Count Arundel. . . . Now this man did protest to a friend of his own that he never got by the Spaniards so much as a pair of pockets; which it should seem is a usual gift among them, being excellently perfumed, and may be valued at twenty nobles or ten pounds price." Goodman's Court of King James, i, 376, 377.

Note 3,
page 225.

Whitbourne gives these names. Those who believe that Calvert was already actuated by religious zeal, remind us that Glastonbury (by a curious legendary confusion of names) was also called Avalon, and that in the Christian legend Joseph of Arimathea began at Glastonbury the planting of the Christian religion in Britain. See Anderson's Church of England in the Colonies, second edition, i, 325, 326. This interpretation of Calvert's intention in naming his colony was early given. British Museum, Sloane MSS. XXG. 3662, folio 24, date 1670. When Calvert's first colony was sent out the Scotch settlement in Newfoundland was of twelve years' standing, while the Bristol colony had been seated there five years. Calvert's enterprise seems to have been pushed with more energy and with a more liberal expenditure than its predecessors. Compare Whitbourne *passim* with the statement of Sir William Alexander in his Encouragement to Colonies, 1624, p. 25.

Note 4,
page 225.

Among the papers at Landsdowne House which I was permitted to examine by the kindness of Lord Edmund Fitzmaurice, there is an unpublished work by James Abercromby, written in 1752. It discusses with acuteness the nature of the several colonial governments. I shall refer to it hereafter under the title of Abercromby's Examination, Landsdowne House, 47. Abercromby was, so far as I know, the first to point out the apparently intentional ambiguity of the passages in the Maryland charter that have to do with religion.

It is interesting that in 1622, the year preceding the division of New England by lot, three shares were laid off and no more. They were at the extreme north of the territory divided the next year, and were assigned respectively to the Duke of Lenox, the Earl of Arundel, and Sir George Calvert. A "grand patent" was then in preparation for a colony on the coast of Maine to be called Nova Albion. Calendar Colonial Documents, July 24, 1622. It seems probable, from the charter of Avalon, that Calvert intended it to be a colony that should harbor Catholics, but on the other hand the first settlers were chiefly Protestants, with a clergyman of their own faith, and there seem to have been few Romanists or none in Avalon until the arrival of a company with the lord proprietary in 1627.

Fuller's oft-quoted account of the circumstances of Calvert's resignation, Worthies, Nuttall's edition, iii, 417, 418, gives probably the commonly received story, and shows that the religious motive was popularly accepted as the reason for his leaving office. Archbishop Abbot was better informed though less impartial. His letter is in the curious work entitled "The Negotiations of Sir Thomas Roe in his Embassy to the Ottoman Porte from the Year 1621 to 1628," etc., published in 1740. Abbot says : "Mr. secretary Calvert hath never looked merily since the prince his coming out of Spaine : it was thought hee was muche interested in the Spanishe affaires : a course was taken to ridde him of all imployments and negotiations. This made him discontented ; and, as the saying is, *Desperatio facit monachum*, so hee apparently did turne papist, whiche hee now professeth, this being the third time that hee hath bene to blame that way. His Majesty to dismisse him, suffered him to resigne his Secretaries place to Sir Albertus Moreton, who payed him three thousand pounds for the same ; and the kinge hath made him baron of Baltimore in Ireland ; so hee is withdrawn from vs, and having bought a ship of 400 tuns, hee is going to New England, or Newfoundlande, where hee hath a colony." Page 372. The letters preserved among the state papers are the main authority, especially those addressed to Sir Dudley Carleton, who desired to buy Calvert's place. See, *passim*, the Calendar of

Domestic Papers for 1624 and 1625 to February 12th. The circumstantial account given in the Salvetti correspondence, though cited as authority by Mr. Gardiner, has never been printed, for which reason it is here given in the original from the British Museum Additional MSS. 27962 C.: "Il Signor Cavalier Calvert primo Segretario et Consigliero di Stato, credendosi, doppo la rottura de' trattati, che si haveva con Spagna, (che per comandamento di sua Maestà haveva lui solo maneggiati,) d'essere eclipsato nell' oppinione del Sig^r. Principe et Signor Duca, et di non essere più impiegato con quella confidenza, che solevano ricorse pochi giorni sono dal Signor Duca di Buchingam per fargli intendere la sua risolutione, la quale era, che vedendo di non potere godere della buona grazia dell' Eccellenza sua nella medesima forma che godeva avanti della sua andata in Spagna era risoluto di rittrarsi dalla Corte, et di mettere in sua mano, come di presente faceva, la sua carica, perchè ne disponasse ovonque le piacesse con molte altre parole tutte piene di valore et magnanimita: soggiugnendoli di più come dicono, che essendo risoluto per l'avvenire di vivere et morire Cattolicamente, conosceva di non poterlo fare nel servizio dove era senza gelosia dello stato et pericolo del Parlamento. Il Signor Duca ancorche non amasse questo Cavaliero, ne nessuno altro che ha hauto le mani nel parentado di Spagna, con tutto ciò vedendo un atto cosi honorato, gli rispose: che non potera negare che non gli fusse stato da non so che tempo in qua nemico; ma che hora vedendo la franchezza et nobiltà d'animo, col rispetto che gli haveva mostrato, l'abracciava per amico, per mostrargliene gli effeti, sempre che ne havesse occasione, con assicuratione de più che operrebbe con sua Maesta gli fusse confermato le suoi pensioni, et di più dato honorevole ricompensa per la sua carica di segretario. Et che quanto alla sua religione egli l'havrebbe protetto quanto fusse mai stato possibile," etc. Salvetti, Correspondence, iii, February 6, 1624–'25.

The letter of the 28th February (O. S.) in the same volume gives an account of the formal resignation to the king, and states that the greater part of the money paid to Calvert was from his successor, and that it was paid *denari contanti*, "cash down," and adds sympathetically that "this good lord will be able to live easily and quietly" hereafter.

Calvert attributes his deception to interested letters. The principal motives to settle in Newfoundland may be seen by the reader who has patience enough to thread his way through the jumble of mythology, allegory, political economy of a certain sort, verse in English and Latin, theology, satire, and an incredible number of what-nots besides " for the generall and perpetuall good of Great Britain," found in Vaughan's Golden Fleece, published in 1626. The nearness of Newfoundland to Ireland and the comparative cheapness of transportation thither, but especially the well-established value of its fisheries and the market they afforded for the produce of the colony, were the most plausible reasons for settling a colony there. Probably there was a lurking purpose to turn the shore fishery into a monopoly such as was contemplated by projectors for the New England coast. The fact was insisted upon that part of Newfoundland was "equal in climate," or at least in latitude, to " Little Britain in France," or Brittany. Then, too, Newfoundland is an island, and Vaughan at least persuaded himself that " Ilanders should dwel in Ilands." As some of the apostles were fishermen, " Newfoundland the grand port of Fishing was alloted to Professors of the Gospell." Golden Fleece, Part Third, pp. 5 and 6 and *passim.*

Note 8, page 230.

Lord Baltimore may have had the governorship of Virginia in view. Cecilius, his son, sought to have himself made governor in 1637. Colonial Papers, ix, 45, Record Office. See an earlier communication on the same subject in Sainsbury, 246, under the date of February 25, 1637. It is almost the only petition of the second Lord Baltimore that was not granted. See also section xvii of the present chapter, and note 21 below.

Note 9, page 231.

I have ventured to conjecture so much on evidence not complete. Father White, who was cordially entertained by the Governor of St. Kitts in 1634, speaks of the people of Montserrat as " pulsos ab anglis Virginiæ ob fidei Catholicæ professionem." White's choice of words does not necessarily imply, I suppose, an actual banishment from Virginia, but at least a refusal of permission to come. Neither Edwards nor Oldmixon mention this fact ; but as White visited St. Kitts only two years after the settlement at Montserrat, which was made immediately from St. Kitts (according to Edwards) and was subject to the same governor, his information was doubtless correct. There seems to have been another project to plant Catholics in Virginia about this time, unless, as is rather probable, we meet the same plan in another form. Sir Pierce Crosby offered to

Воок III.   plant ten companies " of the Irish Regiment into a fruitful part
                 of America not yet inhabited." To make the proposal acceptable,
                 it was stated, somewhat diplomatically perhaps, that the major
                 part of the officers and many of the soldiers were Protestants.
                 Sainsbury's Calendar, p. 95, where the conjectural date is 1628.

Note 10,   The translation quoted is that published by Cecilius Calvert
page 235.   in the Relation of 1635. The original reads : " Unacum licencia
                 et facultate Ecclesias Capellas et Oratoria in locis infra premissa
                 congruis et idoneis Extruendi et fundandi eaque dedicari et sacrari
                 juxta leges Ecclesiasticas regni nostri Anglie facendas." Mary-
                 land Archives.

Note 11,   Sir Edward Northey, Attorney-General of England in the
page 235.   following century, gave this decision : " As to the said clause in
                 the grant of the province of Maryland, I am of opinion the same
                 doth not give him power to do anything contrary to the ecclesi-
                 astical laws of England." This is as ingeniously ambiguous as
                 the clause itself. The attorneys-general and solicitors-general
                 during the eighteenth century set themselves to the task of sub-
                 ordinating colonial government to parliamentary authority by a
                 series of opinions in which they make rather than explain law.
                 In the present instance Northey was more modest than usual, for
                 he reaches a purely negative and impotent conclusion, which
                 Neill turns into a positive one in his text. Founders of Mary-
                 land, 99. There is a collection of opinions on colonial subjects
                 rendered by the attorneys and solicitors-general in the first half
                 of the eighteenth century, in a volume at Landsdowne House
                 which I have examined. This collection was made, or at least
                 furnished, for the use of Lord Shelburne. Before Northey's
                 opinion was given the English Parliament had assumed power to
                 override some provisions of the Maryland charter, as is pointed
                 out in Abercromby's Examination, MS. at Landsdowne House,
                 47. How slowly the Church of England grew in the colony may
                 be inferred from the statement made in 1677, that four clergymen
                 have plantations and settled " beings " of their own—a phrase
                 sufficiently obscure. Others were sustained by voluntary contri-
                 butions. Colonial Papers, No. 49, Record Office, folios 54, 55.
                 This is Baltimore's reply to the paper at folio 56, the order of
                 which is evidently reversed. The population of the province,
                 it is stated, was composed at that time chiefly of dissenters
                 of various sects, Catholics and Anglicans being the smallest
                 bodies.

As early as 1752 it was remarked that the Maryland charter contained " the most extensive power of any charter in British America." Abercromby's Examination, MS., Landsdowne House. In Collier's Ecclesiastical History of Great Britain, vol. ix, is the writ of Edward III, A. D. 1327, by which the regalities of the bishopric of Durham are confirmed after a trial in parliament.

CHAP. I.

Note 12,
page 236.

Cecilius, Lord Baltimore, wrote to Strafford, 10 January, 1633–'34, that he had sent " a hopeful colony into Maryland with a fair and probable Expectation of Success, however without Danger of any great prejudice unto myself, in Respect that many others are joined with me in the Adventure "—that is, in the financial risk. Strafford Papers, i, 179. Twenty years later Cromwell writes to Bennet, Governor of Virginia, " We have therefore at the request of Lord Baltimore and of divers other persons of quality here who are engaged in great adventures in his interest," etc. Thurloe, i, 724. A tradition of this co-operation may have remained in Maryland a century later, for in 1755 or 1756 there was presented to the Lord Baltimore of that day, who was a Protestant, a petition from Roman Catholic residents of Maryland in which this assertion occurs : " The money and persons of this persuasion contributed chiefly to the settling and peopling of this colony." British Museum MS. 15,489.

Note 13,
page 240.

The statement of Father Henry More, in 1642, that " in leading the colony to Maryland by far the greater number were heretics," is not conclusive, though it is relied on by General Bradley T. Johnson and others. More was Provincial of the Jesuits in England, and he is no doubt repeating loosely the information contained in Father White's letter of the year before, which says, " Whereas three parts of the people in four at least are heretics " —a statement true, no doubt, in 1641, when the Kent Islanders and newcomers were counted, but not true, probably, of the company of 1634, as Bancroft seems to say.

Note 14,
page 242.

The original document is in the Stoneyhurst MSS., Anglia, vol. iv. It is reprinted in full in General Bradley T. Johnson's " The Foundation of Maryland." It tends to show that the emigration of many recusants was confidently expected.

Note 15,
page 242.

" Nubes, terrificum in morem excrescentes, terrori erant intuentibus antequam discinderentur : et opinionem faciebant prodiisse adversùm nos in aciem, omnes spiritus tempestatum maleficas, et malos genios omnes Marylandiæ." Relatio Itineris, 15.

Note 16,
page 243.

BOOK III.

Note 17,
page 247.

See *passim*, Letters of Missionaries. A letter of Copley, the Jesuit, to Lord Baltimore, in Calvert Papers, p. 165, implies the possibility of Catholic incumbents of Maryland parishes. He is complaining of the law of the Assembly of 1638 relating to glebe land : " In euery Mannor 100 acres must be laid out for Gleabe lande, if then the intention to bind them to be pastors who enjoy it, we must either by retaining so much euen of our owne land undertake the office of pastors or lesse euen in our owne Mannor maintaine pastors, both which to us would be uery Inconuenient."

Note 18,
page 248.

Letters of Missionaries, p. 77. " The Catholics who live in the colony are not inferior in piety to those who live in other countries ; but in urbanity of manners, according to the judgment of those who have visited the other colonies, are considered far superior to them." More than a hundred years later the Catholics retained a superiority, according to Updike's Appendix to McSparran, 1752 : " The Catholics, having the start in point of time of the after settlers, are also to this day ahead of them in wealth and substance ; by which means the first and best families are for the most part still of the Roman communion," p. 492.

Note 19,
page 248.

The act passed in 1704 was renewed in 1715 and still in force in 1749. I cite from Ogle's Account of Maryland, of the latter date, a manuscript at Landsdowne House, numbered 45, folio 199. In No. 61 at Landsdowne House is a decision of the Attorney-General in England in 1705 that Jesuits may be expelled from Maryland by order of the queen if aliens, but not if they are subjects. The various eighteenth-century enactments against Catholics will be found in Bacon's Laws of Maryland, *passim*. MS. 15,489, British Museum, cites some of these severe laws and the proceedings taken under them. Strong petitions against these measures were signed by Charles Carroll and others.

Note 20,
page 249.

Gabriel Hawley, Robert Evelin, and Jerome Hawley, appointed to places in Virginia, appear to have been Catholics and partisans of Baltimore. Aspinwall Papers, i, page 101, note.

Note 21,
page 250.

Baltimore's letter bears date February 25, 1637, and is in the Record Office, Colonial Papers, xiv, No. 42. The memorial apparently sent with it is No. 49 in the same volume. Baltimore proposes to reward Windebank for his assistance, and he sets down the very manner in which the secretary is to approach the king with a diplomatic falsehood. Both the letter and memorial are printed in Maryland Archives, Council Proceedings, pp. 41, 42.

CHAP. I.

But even in this ambiguous act Baltimore shrewdly puts himself under shelter of a precedent. A statute of Henry IV, 1399, reads : Premierement que seint esglise eit & enjoiez toutes ses droitures libertees & franchises entierement & saunz emblemissement.

Note 22, page 251.

A copy of the ordinance as printed separately at the time is in the Lenox Library. It is reprinted in Churchill's Voyages, viii, 776.

Note 23, page 252.

It is extremely curious that, in the letters of one of the Jesuits reporting the attack upon them in 1645, he should have used an expressive word hitherto supposed to be very modern and American. He says that the assault was made " by a party of ' rowdies ' or marauders." From the way in which the sentence is printed in the Records of the Society of Jesus, iii, 387, I suppose that in the original manuscript the English word "rowdies " is given and explained by a Latin equivalent.

Note 24, page 254.

Charles, the third Lord Baltimore, writes in defense of the Maryland policy of toleration under date of March 26, 1678: " That at the first planteing of this Provynce of my ffather— Albeit he had an absolute Liberty given to him and his heires to carry thither any Persons out of any the Dominions that belonged to the Crown of England that should be found Wylling to goe thither, yett when he comes to make use of this Liberty He found very few who were inclyned to goe and seat themselves in those parts But such as for some Reasons or other could not Lyve with ease in other places, And of these a great parte were such as could not conforme in all particulars to the severall Lawes of England relateing to Religion. Many there were of this sort of people who declared their Wyllingness to goe and Plant themselves In this Provynce soe as they might have a generall toleraĉon settled there by a Lawe by which all of all sorts that professed Christianity in Generall might be at liberty to worship God in such manner as was most agreeable with their respective Judgments and Consciences without being Subject to any Penaltyes whatever for their soe doing." Colonial Papers, vol. xlix, Record Office. Compare Leah and Rachel, p. 23, where the author also implies that the Act of Toleration was a concession to Puritan demands.

Note 25, page 256.

CHAPTER THE SECOND.

THE PROPHET OF RELIGIOUS FREEDOM.

I.

THE centrifugal force of religious differences acted with disastrous results in Maryland, because the Catholic party, which had always a controlling negative there through the proprietary, was in the minority. The Massachusetts people, on the other hand, were fairly homogeneous in religious opinion, and their government was admirably compacted. In Massachusetts religious sentiment was a powerful centripetal force. Magistrates and ministers were nicely poised, and each order relied upon the other to maintain existing conditions. If the magistrates were perplexed or were seriously opposed, the elders were called in to advise or to lend a powerful ecclesiastical sanction to the rulers. When any disturbance of church order was threatened, the magistrates came to the front and supported the clergy with the sharp smiting of the secular arm. In the magistracy and in the ranks of the clergy were men of unusual prudence and ability. If the little Puritan commonwealth seemed a frail canoe at first, it was navigated—considering its smallness one might rather say it was paddled—most expertly. But in Massachusetts, as well as in Maryland, religious opinion was the main source of disturbance. The all-pervading ferment of the time could not be arrested, and more than once it produced explosion. Now one and now another prophet of novelty or prophet of retrogression arose to be dealt with for religious errors; there were divergences from the strait path of Puritanism in the direction of a return to Church of England usage, divergences in the direction of extreme Separatism, in the direction of the everdreaded "Anabaptism," in the direction of Arianism, and of so-called Antinomianism. In the case of the Antinomians, the new movement was able to shelter itself under the authority of the younger Vane, then governor, and for a while under the apparent sanction of the powerful Cotton. But no other religious disturbance was ever allowed to gather head enough to become dangerous to the peace and unity of the little state. Dislike as we may the principles on which uniformity was enforced, we must admire the forehanded statesmanship of the Massachusetts leaders in strangling religious disturbances at birth, as Pharaoh's midwives did infant Hebrews.

II.

One of the most formidable of all those who ventured to assail the compact phalanx presented by the secular and religious authorities of Massachusetts was Roger Williams. Williams was the son of a merchant tailor of London. He mani-

Early life of Roger Williams.

N. Eng. Hist., Gen. Reg., July, 1889.

fested in boyhood that quickness of apprehension which made him successful in acquiring languages later in life. Before he was fifteen the precocious lad was employed in the Star Chamber in taking notes of sermons and addresses in shorthand, and his skill excited the surprise and admiration of Sir Edward Coke. Coke had found time, in the midst of a tempestuous public career and the arduous private studies that brought him permanent renown, to defend the legacy which founded the new Sutton's Hospital, later known as the Charter-House School. Of this school he was one of the governors, and he appointed young Roger Williams to a scholarship there, Williams being the second pupil that ever gained admission to that nursery of famous men. His natural inclination to industry in his studies was quickened by the example and encouragement of Coke, who was wont to say that he who would harrow what Roger Williams had sown must rise early. From the Charter House Williams went to Pembroke College, Cambridge. He early manifested sincere piety and a tendency to go to extremes in his Puritan scruples. Even in his father's house he had begun to taste the bitterness of persecution. His eager temper transformed his convictions into downright passions; his integrity was an aggressive force, and there was a precipitation in his decisions and actions that was trying to his friends. From an early period he showed a conscience intolerant of prudent compromises. Puritanism had contrived to exist and to grow to formidable strength within the church by means of such compromises. Hooker and Cotton, two of the greatest luminaries of that party and afterward the lights that lightened New England, one day urged on the impetuous Williams the propriety of temporarily conforming in the use of the common prayer. By conceding so much to the judgment of his revered elders, Williams would have removed the only obstacle to his advancement, for preferment was offered to the clever and exemplary *protégé* of Coke in the universities, in the city, in the country, and at court. But neither interest nor example could sway the impractical young minister. He took refuge, like other extreme Puritans, in a private chaplaincy, and refused all compromise, in order, as he afterward declared, to keep his "soul undefiled in this point and not to act with a doubting conscience." Most men feel bound to obey conscience only where it clearly commands or forbids; good men may act on the balance of probabilities where there is doubt; but this young man would not do anything concerning which his moral judgment felt the slightest halting. Here is the key to his whole career; his strength lay in his aspiration for a soul undefiled; his weakness, in that he was ever a victim to the pampered conscience of an ultraist. Property of some thousands of pounds, that might have been his had he been willing to make oath in the form required in chancery, he renounced to his scruples. It certainly seemed rash in a young

Note 2.

Note

man just setting out in life, with a young wife to care for, to indulge in such extravagant luxury of scruple.

III.

Laud succeeded in hunting the non-conforming Puritans from their lectureships and chaplaincies. It became with Williams no longer a question of refusing preferments on both hands with lavish self-denial, but of escaping the harsh penalties reserved for such as he by the Courts of High Commission and the Star Chamber. There was nothing left but to betake himself to New England for

safety. He fled hurriedly across country on horseback, feeling it "as bitter as death" that he dared not even say farewell to his great patron Sir Edward Coke, who detested schism.

Here, as in after life, the supreme hardship he suffered was not mere exile, but that exile of the spirit which an affectionate man feels when he is excommnuicate of those he loves. His escape by sea was probably the more difficult because he was unwilling to "swallow down" the oath exacted of those who emigrated. But he succeeded in sailing with his young wife, and in 1631 this undefiled soul, this dauntless and troublesome extremist, landed in

New England. He was invited to become one of the ministers of the Boston church. But Williams was conscientiously a Separatist, and he refused to enter into communion with the Boston congregation

tion because of its position with reference to the church in England.

This protest by withdrawal of communion was a fundamental principle of Separatism. It was not, as it appears on the surface, a manifestation of uncharitableness toward persons, but a solemn protest by act in favor of a principle. Never was any man more forgiving, long-suffering, and charitable toward opponents than Williams, but never was a man less inclined to yield a single jot in the direction of compromise where his convictions were involved, whatever might be the evils sure to result from his refusal.

IV.

Williams repaired first to Salem, the north pole of Puritanism, where the pioneer church of Massachusetts had a more Separatist tone than any other. In the phrase of the time, no other churches in the world were so "pure" as the New England churches, and Salem was accounted the "purest" church in New England. Its surviving minister, Skelton, and its principal layman, Endecott, both tended to extreme Congregationalism; but the General Court of the colony protested against the selection of Williams to be one of the ministers of the Salem church. Skelton's Separatist tendencies, Endecott's impetuous radicalism, and Salem's jealous rivalry with the younger town of Boston, were already sources of anxiety to the rulers. The addition of Williams to these explosive forces was alarming. Williams's ecclesiastical ideals were not those which the leaders of the colony had devoted their lives and fortunes to establish. Had this young radical been less conscientious, less courageous, less engagingly good and admirable, there would not have been so much reason to fear him. A letter was written to Endecott protesting against Williams's ordination, because he had refused communion with the church at Boston, and because he denied the power of the magistrate to enforce duties of the first table—that is, duties of religion. Here at the very outset of his American life we find that Williams had already embraced the broad principle that involved the separation of church and state and the most complete religious freedom, and had characteristically pushed this principle to its logical result some centuries in advance of the practice of his age. The protest of the court prevented his ordination. He yielded to the opposition and soon after removed to Plymouth, where the people were Separatists, modified by the conservative teachings of John Robinson, somewhat modified also by the responsibility of founding a new state, and perhaps by association with Puritans of the neighboring colony.

At Plymouth the young idealist "prophesied" in his turn, but did not take office in the church, which already had a pastor in Ralph Smith, the Separatist, who had been suffered to come over in a Massachusetts ship only on his giving a promise not to preach in that jurisdiction without leave. The congregation at Plymouth was poor, and

Winthrop's Journal, i, 63, 12th April, 1631.

Note 5.

Williams at Plymouth.

Roger Williams mainly supported himself by hard toil "at the hoe and the oar"—that is, perhaps, in farming and fishing. His body seems to have been vigorous, and no physical fatigue abated anything of his mental activity. The Pilgrims had passed more than twelve years in Holland, and almost every adult in Plymouth must have known Dutch. Those of Roger Williams's own age, who were children when they migrated to Leyden and men when they left, probably spoke it as well as they did their mother tongue. The Plymouth people, indeed, were styled "mungrell Dutch" a quarter of a century later. It is probable that Williams, with his usual eagerness to acquire knowledge, now added Dutch to his stock of languages; it is certain that he afterward taught Dutch to John Milton. But he was still more intent on learning the language of the natives, that he might do them good. He resolved not to accept office as pastor or teacher, but to give himself to work among the Indians. Perhaps his tendency to individualism made this prospect pleasing to him. He may have begun already to realize in a half-conscious way that there was scant room in any organization for such as he. The learning of the Indian language was an arduous toil in more ways than one. "God was pleased to give me a painful patient spirit," wrote Williams long after, "to lodge with them in their filthy, smoky holes to gain their tongue." He afterward wrote an excellent treatise on the dialect of the New England Indians.

Maverick's Description of New England, 25.

Williams to Winthrop, 1632.

19

At Plymouth Williams spoke, as he had at
Salem, without restraint from any motive of expe-
diency or even of propriety. Separatist Plymouth,
whose days of advance were over, was a little disturbed by his speech. In his own sweet, reckless
way he sometimes sharply rebuked even the revered Bradford when he thought him at fault.
And in the interest of the aborigines and of justice
Williams laid before Governor Bradford a manuscript treatise which argued that the king had no
right to give away, as he had assumed to do in his
grants and charters, the lands of the Indians merely
because he was a Christian and they heathen.
That it was right to wrong a man because he was
not orthodox in belief could find no place in the
thoughts of one whose conscience was wholly incapable of sophistication. Bradford accepted can-
didly the rebukes of Williams and loved him for

Bradford,
310.

his "many precious parts." But as governor of a
feeble colony he was disturbed by Williams's
course. In spirituality, unselfish fearlessness, and
a bold pushing of Separatist principles to their
ultimate logical results, Roger Williams reminded
the Pilgrims of the amiable pastor of the Separatist
church in Amsterdam whose change step by step
to "Anabaptism," the great bugbear of theology

Knowles's
Life of
Williams,
53.

in that time, had been a tragedy and a scandal to
the Separatists of Leyden. Elder Brewster feared
that Williams would run the same course. Williams wished to return to Salem, where he might
still devote himself to the neighboring Indians, and

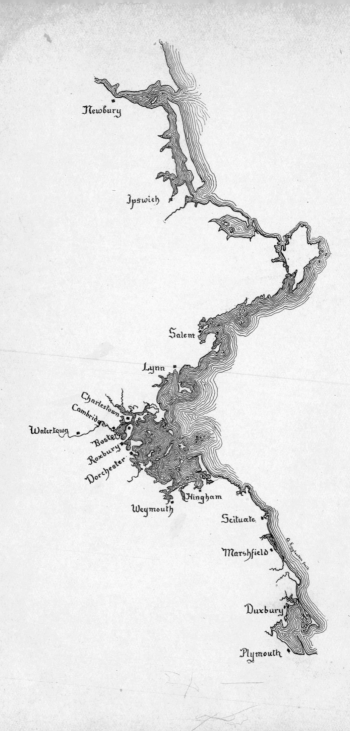

Newbury

Ipswich

Salem

Lynn

Charlestown
Cambridge
Watertown
Boston
Roxbury
Dorchester

Weymouth

Hingham

Scituate

Marshfield

Duxbury

Plymouth

assist Skelton, now declining in health. Brewster persuaded the Plymouth church to give him a letter of dismissal. The leading Pilgrims felt bound to send "some caution" to the Salem church regarding the extreme tendencies of Williams. On the other hand, some of the Plymouth people were so captivated by his teachings and his personal character that they removed with him. This following of an approved minister was common among Puritans; an acceptable preacher was of as much value to a town as good meadows, broad pastures, and pure water.

V.

To understand the brief career of Williams at Salem and its catastrophe, we must recall the character of colonial life in Massachusetts at the time. There were already sixteen settlements or "towns" on the shores of Massachusetts Bay, with an indefinite stretch of gloomy wilderness for background, the dwelling place of countless savages and wild beasts. The population of all the settlements may have summed up five thousand people —enough to have made one prosperous village. The inhabitants of the various towns of the bay were from different parts of England; their dress and dialect were diverse, and their Puritanism was of various complexions. The town system, at first a reproduction on new soil of the township field communes that had subsisted in parts of England from ages beyond the fountain heads of tradition,

gave some play to local peculiarities and prejudices.   There is evidence that the central government relieved itself from strain by means of this
rural borough system.   The ancient town system
in turn appears to have taken on a new youth; it
was perhaps modified and developed by the local
diversity of the people, and it lent to Massachusetts, at first, something of the elasticity of a fed-
eral government.

This community of scattered communes was
cut off from frequent intercourse with the world,
for the sea was far wider and more to be feared in
that day of small ships and imperfect navigation
than it is now.   The noise of the English controversies in which the settlers had once borne a part
reached them at long intervals, like news from another planet.   But most of the time these lonesome
settlements had no interest greater than the petty
news and gossip of little forest hamlets.   The visitor who came afoot along Indian trails, or by
water, paddling in a canoe, to Boston on lecture
day, might bring some news of sickness, accident,
or death.   Sometimes the traveling story was ex-
citing, as that wolves had slaughtered the cattle
at a certain place, while yet cattle were few and
precious.   Or still more distressing intelligence
came that the ruling elder of the church at Watertown had taken the High-church position that
Roman churches were Christian churches, or that
democratic views had been advanced by Eliot of
Roxbury.   A new and far-fetched prophetical ex-

Life in the
Massachu-
setts set-
tlements.

1630 to
1640.

planation of a passage in the Book of Canticles, and a tale of boatmen wrecked in some wintry tempest, might divide the attention of the people. Stories of boats capsized, of boatmen cast on islands where there was neither shelter nor food, of boats driven far to sea and heard of no more, were staples of excitement in these half-aquatic towns; and if the inmates of a doomed boat had been particularly profane, these events were accounted edifying—divine judgments on the ungodly. When the governor wandered once and lost himself in the forest, passing the night in a deserted wigwam, there was a sensation of a half-public character. That a snake and a mouse had engaged in a battle, and that the puny mouse had triumphed at last, was in one budget of traveling news that came to Boston. To this event an ominous significance was given by John Wilson, pastor of the Boston church, maker of anagrams, solemn utterer of rhyming prophecies which were sometimes fulfilled, and general theological putterer. Wilson made the snake represent the devil, according to all sound precedents; the mouse was the feeble church in the wilderness, to which God would give the victory over Satan. Thus enhanced by an instructive interpretation from the prophet and seer of the colony, the story no doubt took up its travels once more, and now with its hopeful exegesis on its back. The Massachusetts mouse was an auspicious creature; it is recorded by the governor, and it was no doubt told along the coast,

that one got into a library and committed depre-
dations on a book of common prayer only, nibbling
every leaf of the liturgy, while it reverently spared
a Greek Testament and a Psalter in the same
covers.

In a petty state with a range of intellectual interests so narrow, the conflict between Williams
and the General Court took place.

VI.

Self-con-
sciousness
of the
Massachu-
setts com-
munity.

It was a community that believed in its own
divine mission. It traced the existence of its settlements to the very hand of God—the God who
led Israel out of Egypt. The New England colonists never forgot that they were a chosen people. Upon other American settlers—the Dutch
in New Netherland, the Virginia churchmen, the
newly landed Marylanders, with their admixture
of papists—they looked with condescension if not
with contempt, accounting them the Egyptians of

the New World. The settlers on the Bay of
Massachusetts were certain that their providen-
tial exodus was one of the capital events in human
history; that it had been predesigned from eternity to plant here, in a virgin world, the only true
form of church government and to cherish a church
that should be a model to the Old World in turn,
and a kind of foreshadowing of the new heaven
and the new earth. Some dreamed that the second coming of Christ would take place among the
rocky woodlands of New England. The theocrat-

ical government was thought to be the one most pleasing to God, and a solemn obligation was felt to import into this new theocracy the harsh Oriental intolerance which had marked that fierce struggle in which the Jewish tribes finally shook off image worship.

The apostle of theocracy who arrived soon after Williams's return to Salem was John Cotton, a Puritan leader in England, in whom devoutness was combined with extreme discretion, a dominant will with a diplomatic prudence and a temper never ruffled. Cotton's ingenious refinements made him a valuable apologist in an age of polemics, but they often served to becloud his vision of truth and right. He was prone to see himself as he posed, in the character of a protagonist of truth. He gave wise advice to the Massachusetts Puritans at their departure from England. When, a few years later, Laud's penetrating vigilance and relentless thoroughness made even Cotton's well-balanced course of mild non-conformity impossible, he fled from his parish of Boston, in Lincolnshire, to London, and escaped in 1633 with difficulty to the new Boston in New England. As John Cotton had been the shining candle of Puritanism in England, his arrival in America was hailed with joy, and from the time of his settlement in the little capital his was the hand that shaped ecclesiastical institutions in New England, and he did much also to mold the yet plastic state. Though he usually avoided the appearance of personal antagonism,

CHAP. II.

John Cotton, 1633.

Note 8.

every formidable rival he had left Massachusetts early. Williams, Hooker, Davenport, and Hugh Peter all found homes beyond the bounds of the colony. There can not be two queen bees in one hive, nor can there well be more than one master mind in the ecclesiastical order of a petty theocratic state. It was the paradox of colonial religious organization that the Episcopal colonies had parishes almost independent of all supervision, while the New England Congregationalists were, from the arrival of Cotton, subject to the dominance of ministers who virtually attained to the authority of bishops.

VII.

Salem refractory.

Salem, the oldest town of the commonwealth, was the most ready to pursue an independent course and it was attached to Williams, whose ability attracted new settlers and who maintained a position of independence toward Cotton and the authorities at Boston. To subdue the refractory Salem was no doubt one of the secondary purposes of the proceedings against Williams. There seems to have been no personal animosity toward Williams himself; his amiable character and his never-doubted sincerity were main obstacles to his punishment.

Collision inevitable.

The return of Roger Williams to such a place as Salem was naturally a matter of alarm to the ministers and magistrates of Massachusetts. Collision was not a matter of choice on either side.

The catastrophe was like one that comes from the irresistible action of physical forces. In a colony planted at great cost to maintain one chosen form of worship and subordinating all the powers of government to this purpose, a preacher who asserted the necessity for a complete separation of religion and government in the interest of soul liberty had no place. His ideal was higher than the prevailing one, but that age could not possibly rise to it.

VIII.

The book against the patent.

Williams was yet only a private member of the church in Salem, but in the illness of the pastor he "exercised by way of prophecy"—that is, preached without holding office. An alarming report was soon in circulation that he had written a book against the king's patent, the foundation of the colonial authority. This treatise, we have said, was written in Plymouth for the benefit of Governor Bradford. Like many of the manuscript books that have come down to us, it appears to have been a small quarto, and, if it resembled other books of the sort, it was neatly stitched and perhaps even bound by its author in the favorite parchment of the time. Williams sent his book promptly to be examined. Some of the "most judicious ministers much condemned Mr. Williams's error and presumption," and an order was made that he "should be convented at the next court." In the charges no fault was found with the main thesis of

Note 9.

the book, that the king could not claim and give away the lands of the Indians; but it was thought that there were disloyal reflections cast upon both James and Charles—at least those eager to condemn construed the obscure and "implicative phrases" of Williams in that sense—and these supposed reflections were the subject of the charges. Williams wrote a submissive letter, and offered his book, or any part of it, to be burned after the manner of that time. A month later, when the governor and council met, the whole aspect of the affair had changed. Cotton and Wilson, the teacher and the pastor of the Boston church, certified, after examination of Williams's quarto, that "they found the matters not so evil as at first they seemed." It was decided to let Williams off easily. There are some things unexplained about the affair; the eagerness of the "judicious ministers" and court to condemn without due examination, the failure even to specify the objectionable passages at last, and the unwonted docility of Williams—all leave one to infer that there was more in this transaction than appears. Laud and his associates were moving to have the Massachusetts charter vacated, and it may have seemed imprudent for the magistrates to found their authority on a base so liable to disappear. If the charter had been successfully called in, Williams's ground of the sufficiency of the Indian title to lands might have proved useful as a last resort. Williams asserted, long afterward, that before his troubles began he had drafted a letter addressed to the king, "not without the approbation of some of the chiefs of New England," whose consciences were also "tender on this point before God." This letter humbly acknowledged "the evil of that part of the patent which relates" to the gift of lands. Had the letter been sent to its destination it would have cut a curious figure among the worldly-minded state papers of the time.

CHAP. II.

Reply to Cotton, 276, 277.

It is probable that most of the land of the colony had been secured from the natives by purchase or by treaty of some sort; at least the Indians were content, and the little quarto had at that time no practical bearing whatever, but that did not matter to Williams. The more abstract a question of right and wrong, the more he relished a discussion of it. It was of a piece with his exquisite Separatism, a mere standing up in the face of heaven and earth for an abstract principle. His purpose was not to right a specific and concrete wrong, for there had been none, but to assert as a broad principle of everlasting application that a Christian king may not dispose of the land owned by heathens merely because of his Christianity. Williams was not a judge or a lawgiver; he was a poet in morals, enamored of perfection, and keeping his conscience purer than Galahad's.

An abstract principle.

IX.

It was in the winter of 1633–'34 that the book about the patent was called in question. Skelton, pastor of Salem, died in the following August,

The alarm.

and the Salem people, in spite of an injunction from the magistrates, made Williams their teacher in his stead. The country was now full of alarm at news from England that the charter was to be revoked, that a general governor of New England was to be appointed, and that a force was to be sent to support his authority. Laud was put at the head of a commission for the government of the colonies in April, 1634. There could be no doubt of the meaning of this measure. For more than a year the alarm in Massachusetts continued. The ministers were consulted regarding the lawfulness of resistance to force. A platform was constructed on the northeast side of Castle Island, and a fortified house was proposed to defend the platform. The trainbands were drilled, muskets, "bandeleroes" or cartridge belts, and rests were distributed to the several towns, and pikemen were required to learn to use the cumbrous musket of the time. Puritans in England, angry that Laud, the new archbishop and old persecutor, should stretch a long arm to America, sent powder and cannon to their co-religionists, the object of whose military vigilance could easily be covered by dangers from the savages, from the French, or from the Spaniards.

Debates not appeased.

But these assiduous preparations, under the supervision of a military commission which had "power of life and limb," did not abate in the least the discussion of questions of doctrine and casuistry. Refinements of theology were quite as real

and substantial to the Puritan mind as trainbands
and fortifications. Sound doctrine and a scrupulous observance of the "ordinances" conciliated God; they were indeed more important elements of public safety than drakes and demi-culverins.

The General Court of September, 1634, undertook to provide for the public safety in both respects. Along with regulations and provisions of a military nature, it set out to remove those flagrant sins that had provoked the divine wrath. The wearing of silver, gold, and rich laces, girdles, and hatbands was forbidden; slashed clothes were also abolished, "other than one slash in each sleeve and another in the back"; ruffs and beaver hats, which last were apparently a mark of dudishness, were not to be allowed. Long hair and other fashions "prejudicial to the general good" were done away with in this hour of penitence. Men and women might wear out the clothes they had, except their "immoderate great sleeves, slashed apparel, immoderate great rayles, long wings," which were to go at once without reprieve or ceremony. The use of tobacco, socially and in public, or before strangers was made an offense. If taken secretly or medicinally, the Court did not take cognizance of it.

Reform in dress.

Mass. Records, 3d September, 1634.

Compare Ward's Simple Cobbler, passim.

X.

Seeing that the millinery sins recounted in this act had cried to Heaven, and that, beside the danger from England, there was the desire of Hook-

The fast-day sermon.

er's party to remove to the Connecticut, and a dissension concerning the power of the Upper House that threatened trouble, the Court appointed the 18th of September a solemn fast day, hoping by repentance, prayer, and the penance of hunger to avert the manifold disasters that threatened them. Roger Williams was sure to speak like a prophet on such an occasion. He did not stop at slashed garments, great sleeves, and headdresses with long wings; he preached on eleven "public sins" that had provoked divine wrath. We have no catalogue left us. The list may have included some of those amusing scruples that he held in common with other Puritans, or some of those equally trivial personal scruples that Williams cherished so fondly. But no sermon of his on public sins could fail to contain a declaration of his far-reaching and cherished principle of religious freedom, including perhaps a round denunciation of the petty inquisition into private opinion which had been set up in Massachusetts. The Sabbath law, the law obliging men to pay a tax to support religious worship, the requirement that all should attend religious worship under penalty, and the enforcement of a religious oath on irreligious and perhaps unwilling residents, the assumption of the magistrate to regulate the orthodoxy of a church under the advice of the ministers, were points of Massachusetts law and administration that he denounced at various times; and some of them, if not all, were no doubt put in pillory in

this fast-day sermon in the early autumn of 1634.
Judged by modern standards, the sermon may
have had absurdities enough, but it was no doubt
a long way in advance of the General Court's
mewling about lace, and slashes, and long hair, and
other customs "prejudicial to the general good."
To this sermon, whatever it was, Williams afterward attributed the beginning of the troubles that
led to his banishment.

XI.

Winthrop, just but gentle, narrow-minded but
ever large-hearted, had been superseded in the
governorship by Dudley, open and zealous advocate of religious intolerance.   Dudley, who was
always hot-tempered, was for proceeding out of
hand with the bold "teacher" of the church in
Salem, but he felt bound to consult with the ministers first, since Williams was an "elder," and even
among Puritans there was a sort of benefit of
clergy.   Cotton had developed a complete system
of church-state organization hammered out of, or
at least supported by, Bible texts linked by ingenious inferences, and from the time of Cotton's
arrival there was a strong effort to secure uniformity.   But Cotton was timid in action, and he
was nothing if not orderly and ecclesiastical.   Williams was an elder, entitled as such to be proceeded with "in a church way" first.   As leader
and spokesman of the clergy Cotton expressed his
charitable conviction that Williams's "violent

course did rather spring from scruple of con-science than from a seditious principle." The clergy proposed to try to convert him by argu-ment, not so much, perhaps, from hope of success as from a conviction that this was the orderly and scriptural rule. Dudley, impatient to snuff out Williams at once, replied that they "were de-ceived in him if they thought he would conde-scend to learn of any of them." But the "elders" now proceeded in the roundabout way prescribed by Cotton's system ingeniously deduced from Scripture. The individual church must deal with its own member; the sister churches might re-monstrate with a church. Cotton and Wilson, for example, could appeal to the Boston church to ap-peal to the Salem church to appeal to Williams, and in this order much of the correspondence went on.

It was, perhaps, when his desire to act promptly against the Salem heretic was thus foiled by Cot-ton's prudent and intricate orderliness in procedure that Dudley relieved his emotions by what is hap-pily the only example of his verse that has sur-vived :

Let men of God in courts and churches watch
O'er such as do a toleration hatch,
Lest that ill egg bring forth a cockatrice
To poison all with heresy and vice.
If men be left and otherwise combine,
My epitaph's I die no libertine.

Marginal notes:

Note 10.

The gov-ernor's verse.

Eliot's New Eng-land Biog-raphy, 156, 157.

XII.

The most substantial grievance of the rulers against Williams was his opposition to "the oath." In order to make sure of the loyalty of the residents in this time of danger a new oath of fidelity to be taken by residents had been promulgated. Practical men are wont to put aside minor scruples in time of danger. David eats the sacred shew-bread when he is famishing; but Williams would rather starve than mumble a crumb of it. He did not believe in enforced oaths; they obliged the wicked man to a religious act, and thus invaded the soul's freedom. Cotton says that Williams's scruples excited such an opposition to the oath that the magistrates were not able to enforce it. He thus unwittingly throws a strong light on the weakness of the age, and extenuates the conduct of Williams as well as that of the rulers. The age was in love with scrupulosity, and Williams on this side was the product of his time. In such an age a scruple-maker of ability and originality like Williams might be a source of danger.

Note 11.

During the year following Williams was several times "convented" before the Court. He was charged with having broken his promise not to speak about the patent, with opposing the residents' oath, with maintaining certain scruples in opposition to the customs of the times, as that a man should not return thanks after a meal, or call on an unregenerate child to give thanks for his

Scruples small and great.

20

Centrifugal Forces in Colony-Planting.

food. These were not more trivial certainly than half a hundred scruples then prevalent, but they chanced to be unfashionable—a damning fault in a scruple. The sense of proportion was feeble in religionists of that day, and neither Williams nor his opponents understood the comparative magnitude of his greater contentions, and the triviality of those petty scruples about which, like the whole Puritan world, he was very busy. Religious freedom and the obligation of grace after meat could then be put into the same category. As years went by, although the mind of Williams was never disentangled from scrupulosity, he came to see clearly what was the real battle of his life. No better fortune can befall a great spirit than such a clarification of vision. The extended works of Williams's later life are written mainly to overthrow the "bloody tenent of persecution." It was this championship of soul liberty as the weightiest matter of the law that lifted him above all others who paid tithes of their little garden herbs.

Williams inflexible.

Savage's Winthrop's Journal, i, 81.

Mass. Rec., i, 135, 136.

Williams was certainly incorrigible. Richard Brown, the ruling elder of the church at Watertown, seems to have submitted to the remonstrance of the magistrates against his too charitable judgment of the Roman churches. Eliot, of Roxbury, afterward the Indian apostle, advanced peculiar opinions also, but he was overborne and convinced. Stoughton, who had denied that the "assistants" of a corporation were scriptural magistrates, was brought to book about this time, and he retracted.

Salem itself was forced to bend its stiff neck at last. The town had been refused its land on Marble Neck because of its ordination of Williams, and having, under Williams's leadership, protested in a letter to the churches against the injustice of spiritual coercion by financial robbery, the deputies of Salem were now summarily turned out of the court. Endecott, with characteristic violence, protested further against the double injustice to Salem. He was promptly put under arrest, and this severity brought swift conviction to his mind, so that he humbly apologized and submitted the same day. The only bond of unity between the rash Salem leader and Williams was a common tendency to go to extremes. In spirit, the heroic, long-suffering Williams, who rested in what he called the "rockie strength" of his opinions in spite of penalties and majorities, was far removed from a leader who bent before the first blast, and who became in later life the harshest persecutor in the commonwealth.

Mass. Rec., i, 156, 157. Winthrop's Journal, i, 194.

XIII.

Williams remained the one resolute, stubborn, incorrigible offender. Eliot, Stoughton, and Endecott, and even Williams's fellow-elder, Sharpe, and the whole church at Salem, might be argued into conformity by the sharp dialectics of the clergy, or bullied out of their convictions by the sharper logic of the magistrates, but Roger Williams could not be overborne. Individualist in his very nature, his

Williams's trial.

self-reliant spirit was able to face isolation or excommunication.   The great Hooker was set to dispute with him.   Hooker's refined arguments were
drawn out by inferences linked to inferences.   He
proved to the satisfaction of everybody but the
culprit that it was not lawful for Williams, with his
opinions, to set food before his unregenerate child,
since he did not allow an irreligious child to go
through the form of giving thanks.   But the wire-
drawn logic of Hooker, though Williams could not
always answer it, had no more influence with him
than the ingenious sophistications of the pious
Cotton; Williams constantly fell back upon the
"rockie strength" of his principles.   On the 9th
of October, 1635, he was sentenced to banishment.
After the manner of that curious age, his banishment was based on charges of great importance
mixed with charges utterly trivial.   His denial of
the authority of the magistrate to regulate the
orthodoxy of the churches and the belief of individuals is, however, made one of the cardinal
offenses in all the trustworthy accounts given at
Note 12.   the time.   With this were joined in the proceedings, but not in the sentence, such things as the
denial of the propriety of grace after meat.   All
the elders but one advised his banishment.

Williams
banished.   The magistrates, though deeply "incensed"
against him, probably felt at the last some reluc-
tance to banish such a man.   Six weeks were ac-
corded him in which to leave.   Winthrop, who
Note 13.   was Williams's friend, and who seems to have been

loath to consent to his banishment, wrote to him to
" steer his course for Narragansett Bay," where
there was territory beyond the bounds of Massachusetts and Plymouth. The forest journeys or
boat voyages to Boston and back, the bitter controversies there, and the uproar of indignation
which was produced in Salem by the news of the
verdict, the desertion of Williams by Endecott, convinced by force, and by Sharpe, the ruling elder,
who had been also dealt with, the natural yielding
of the Salem church after a while to the pressure
from the General Court, and to the desire of the
townsmen to secure the lands at Marble Neck, put
a strain on Williams which, added to his necessary
toil in the field, broke his health and he fell ill.
The General Court probably also felt the recoil of
its act. When six weeks had expired consent
was given that Williams should remain during the
winter provided he would refrain from preaching.
But Williams was in Salem, and in Salem he was
the center of interest—just now he was the center
of explosion. It was impossible for the great Separatist to be silent. A few faithful friends, come-
outers like himself, clave to him and repudiated as
he did communion with the church at Salem, which
could condone the offenses of the magistrates for
the sake of " these children's toys of land, meadows,
cattle, and government." These fellow-Separatists,
some of whom perhaps had removed from Plymouth out of love for this unworldly saint, loved him
none the less for his courage and his sorrows.

Chap. II.

Note 14.

Note 15.

They frequented his house on Sunday as he con-
valesced.   Indeed, the attachment to him was so
great that the "ordinances" which had been appointed by the magistrates and enforced on Salem
as the price of the common land on Marble Neck,

were neglected and almost deserted.   Williams
could not refrain from speech with this concourse
of visitors, and at length word came to Boston that
more than twenty persons had definitely adhered
to the opinions of their former teacher, uncon-
vinced by the argument of the rod of justice applied to Endecott and Sharpe, or by the valuable
land on Marble Neck.   These disciples proposed
to remove in the spring with Williams to the shores
of Narragansett Bay.   This might meet the approval of the sagacious and kindly Winthrop, who
had directed Williams's attention to that promising
place, and who foresaw perhaps the usefulness of
such a man in the dangerous Indian crisis now
threatening the colony.   But to devotees of uniformity, the prospect of a community on the very
border of the land of the saints tolerating all sorts
of opinionists was insufferable.   When once the
civil government weights itself with spiritual considerations, its whole equilibrium is disturbed.
Liberty and justice seem insignificant by the side
of the immensities.   The magistrates, or a part of
them, were alarmed at the prospect of a settlement

of the followers of Williams at Narragansett Bay,
" whence the infection would easily spread into
these churches, the people being, many of them,

much taken with an apprehension of his godliness." It was therefore agreed to send him to England on a ship soon to sail.

XIV.

The hardships of such a voyage in midwinter in his state of health might prove fatal, and his arrival in England would almost certainly deliver him into the hands of Laud. But what is justice or mercy when the welfare of churches and the rescue of imperiled souls is to be considered? A warrant was dispatched ordering him to Boston within a certain time. Probably knowing what was in store for him, he protested that it would be dangerous for him, in view of his health, to make the journey, and some of the Salem people went to Boston in his behalf, and, as was natural in the circumstances, made exaggerated representations regarding his physical condition. But the magistrates had other information. They sent the valiant and notorious Captain Underhill, in whom were mingled about equally devoutness, military courage, and incorrigible lewdness, to bring Williams by sea in a shallop. Williams was probably informed of their purpose, for, while Underhill in his little craft was beating up to Salem in wintry seas on an errand so congenial, expecting perhaps to come upon his quarry unawares, Williams was fleeing from one hamlet of bark wigwams to another. Here among the barbarians he was sure of faithful friends and secure concealment. Underhill found on his arrival that the culprit had disappeared three days before he got there, and nobody in Salem, that could, would tell whither the fugitive had gone.

Meantime Williams was, to use his own figure of speech, "steering his course" "in winter snow" toward Narragansett Bay. "I was sorely tossed for one fourteen weeks in a bitter winter season," he says, in his vivid and hyperbolic fashion of speech, "not knowing what bed or bread did mean." He began one settlement on the eastern bank of the Seekonk River after getting land from the Indians, but his old enemies the royal patents now had their revenge. Winslow, governor of Plymouth, a kind-hearted, politic man, the one born diplomatist of New England, warned him that he was within the bounds of Plymouth, and asked him to remove to the other side of the water, because they "were loath to displease the Bay." It was not enough to drive a heretic from the bounds of Massachusetts; the pragmatic Puritanism of the time would have expelled him from the continent had its arm been long enough. Williams had already begun to build and to plant, but he removed once more to the place which he named Providence. He planted the germinal settlement of the first state in the world that founded religious liberty on the widest possible basis, reserving to the law no cognizance whatever of religious beliefs or conduct where the "civil peace" was not endangered.

Providence

Seakonk River

Narragansett Bay

Portsmouth

Rhode Island

Newport

A. Eggleston fecit

XV.

Local jealousy and sectarian prejudice have done what they could to obscure the facts of the trial and banishment of Williams. It has been argued by more than one writer that it was not a case of religious persecution at all, but the exclusion of a man dangerous to the state. Cotton, with characteristic verbal legerdemain, says that Williams was "enlarged" rather than banished. The case has even been pettifogged in our own time by the assertion that the banishment was only the action of a commercial company excluding an uncongenial person from its territory. But with what swift indignation would the Massachusetts rulers of the days of Dudley and Haynes have repudiated a plea which denied their magistracy! They put so strong a pressure on Stoughton, who said that the assistants were not magistrates, that he made haste to renounce his pride of authorship and to deliver his booklet to be officially burned, nor did even this prevent his punishment. The rulers of "the Bay" were generally frank advocates of religious intolerance; they regarded toleration as a door set open for the devil to enter. Not only did they punish for unorthodox expressions; they even assumed to inquire into private beliefs. Williams was only one of scores bidden to depart on account of opinion.

The real and sufficient extenuation for the conduct of the Massachusetts leaders is found in the

Williams's banishment an act of persecution.

Note 17.

Intolerance as a virtue.

character and standards of the age. A few obscure and contemned sectaries—Brownists, Anabaptists, and despised Familists—in Holland and
England had spoken more or less clearly in favor
of religious liberty before the rise of Roger Williams, but nobody of weight or respectable standing in the whole world had befriended it. All the
great authorities in church and state, Catholic
and Protestant, prelatical and Puritan, agreed in
their detestation of it. Even Robinson, the moderate pastor of the Leyden Pilgrims, ventured to
hold only to the "toleration of tolerable opinions."
This was the toleration found at Amsterdam and
in some other parts of the Low Countries. Even
this religious sufferance which did not amount to
liberty was sufficiently despicable in the eyes of
that intolerant age to bring upon the Dutch the
contempt of Christendom. It was a very qualified
and limited toleration, and one from which Catholics and Arminians were excluded. It seems to
have been that practical amelioration of law which
is produced more effectually by commerce than by
learning or religion. Outside of some parts of the
Low Countries, and oddly enough of the Turkish
Empire, all the world worth counting decried toleration as a great crime. It would have been wonderful indeed if Massachusetts had been superior
to the age. "I dare aver," says Nathaniel Ward,
the New England lawyer-minister, "that God doth
no where in his word tolerate Christian States to
give tolerations to such adversaries of his Truth, if

they have power in their hands to suppress them." To set up toleration was " to build a sconce against the walls of heaven to batter God out of his chair," in Ward's opinion.

CHAP. II.

Simple Cobbler of Agawam, pp. 3 and 6.

XVI.

This doctrine of intolerance was sanctioned by many refinements of logic, such as Cotton's delicious sophistry that if a man refused to be convinced of the truth, he was sinning against conscience, and therefore it was not against the liberty of conscience to coerce him. Cotton's moral intuitions were fairly suffocated by logic. He declared that men should be compelled to attend religious service, because it was " better to be hypocrites than profane persons. Hypocrites give God part of his due, the outward man, but the profane person giveth God neither outward nor inward man." To reason thus is to put subtlety into the *cathedra* of common sense, to bewilder vision by legerdemain. Notwithstanding his natural gift for devoutness and his almost immodest godliness, Cotton was incapable of high sincerity. He would not specifically advise Williams's banishment, but having labored with him round a corner according to his most approved ecclesiastical formula, he said, " We have no more to say in his behalf, but must sit down "; by which expression of passivity he gave the signal to the " secular arm " to do its worst, while he washed his hands in innocent self-complacency. When one scrupulous magistrate

The casuistry of Cotton.

Note 20.

Hutchinson Papers, 406.

consulted him as to his obligation in Williams's case, Cotton answered his hesitation by saying, " You know they are so much incensed against his course that it is not your voice nor the voice of two or three more that can suspend the sentence." By such shifty phrases he shirked responsibility

for the results of his own teaching. Of the temper that stands alone for the right, Nature had given him not a jot. Williams may be a little too severe, but he has some truth when he describes Cotton on this occasion as " swimming with the stream of outward credit and profit," though nothing was further from Cotton's conscious purpose than such worldliness. Cotton's intolerance was not like that of Dudley and Endecott, the offspring of an austere temper; it was rather the outgrowth of his logic and his reverence for authority. He sheltered himself behind the examples of Elizabeth and

James I, and took refuge in the shadow of Calvin, whose burning of Servetus he cites as an example, without any recoil of heart or conscience. But the consideration of the character of the age forbids us to condemn the conscientious men who put Williams out of the Massachusetts theocracy as they would have driven the devil out of the garden of

Eden. When, however, it comes to judging the age itself, and especially to judging the Puritanism of the age, these false and harsh ideals are its sufficient condemnation. Its government and its very religion were barbarous; its Bible, except for mystical and ecclesiastical uses, might as well have closed with the story of the Hebrew judges and the imprecatory Psalms. The Apocalypse of John, grotesquely interpreted, was the one book of the New Testament that received hearty considera-tion, aside from those other New Testament pas-sages supposed to relate to a divinely appointed ecclesiasticism. The humane pity of Jesus was un-known not only to the laws, but to the sermons of the time. About the time of Williams's banish-ment the lenity of John Winthrop was solemnly rebuked by some of the clergy and rulers as a lax imperiling of the safety of the gospel; and Win-throp, overborne by authority, confessed, ex-plained, apologized, and promised amendment. The Puritans substituted an unformulated belief in the infallibility of "godly" elders acting with the magistrates for the ancient doctrine of an in-fallible church.

Note 22.

Savage's Winthrop, i, 211–214.

XVII.

In this less scrupulous but more serious age it is easy to hold Williams up to ridicule. Never was a noble and sweet-spirited man bedeviled by a scrupulosity more trivial. Cotton aptly dubbed him "a haberdasher of small questions." His ex-tant letters are many of them vibrant with latent heroism; there is manifest in them an exquisite charity and a pathetic magnanimity, but in the midst of it all the writer is unable to rid himself of a swarm of scruples as pertinacious as the buzzing mosquitoes in the primitive forest about him. In

Character of Wil-liams. His scruples.

New Eng-land Fire-brand Quenched, 246.

dating his letters, where he ventures to date at all, he never writes the ordinary name of the day of the week or the name of the month, lest he should be guilty of etymological heathenism. He often avoids writing the year, and when he does insert it he commits himself to the last two figures only and adds a saving clause. Thus 1652 appears as " 52 (so called)," and other years are tagged with the same doubting words, or with the Latin "*ut vulgo*." What quarrel the tender conscience had with the Christian era it is hard to guess. So, too, he writes to Winthrop, who had taken part in his banishment, letters full of reverential tenderness and hearty friendship. But his conscience does not allow him even to seem to hold ecclesiastical fellowship with the man he honors as a ruler and loves as a friend. Once at least he guards the point directly by subscribing himself " Your worship's faithful and affectionate in all *civil* bonds." It would be sad to think of a great spirit so enthralled by the scrupulosity of his time and his party if these minute restrictions had been a source of annoyance to him. But the cheerful observance of little scruples seems rather to have taken the place of a recreation in his life; they were to him perhaps what bric-a-brac is to a collector, what a well-arranged altar and candlesticks are to a ritualist.

Two fundamental notions supplied the motive power of every ecclesiastical agitation of that age. The notion of a succession of churchly order and ordinance from the time of the apostles was the mainspring of the High-church movement. Apostolic primitivism was the aim of the Puritan and still more the goal of the Separatist. One party rejoiced in a belief that a mysterious apostolic virtue had trickled down through generations of bishops and priests to its own age; the other rejoiced in the destruction of institutions that had grown up in the ages and in getting back to the primitive nakedness of the early Christian conventicle. True to the law of his nature, Roger Williams pushed this latter principle to its ultimate possibilities. If we may believe the accounts, he and his followers at Providence became Baptists that they might receive the rite of baptism in its most ancient Oriental form. But in an age when the fountains of the great deep were utterly broken up he could find no rest for the soles of his feet. It was not enough that he should be troubled by the Puritan spirit of apostolic primitivism; he had now swung round to where this spirit joined hands with its twin, the aspiration for apostolic succession. He renounced his baptism because it was without apostolic sanction, and announced himself of that sect which was the last reduction of Separatism. He became a Seeker.

Here again is a probable influence from Holland. The Seekers had appeared there long before. Many Baptists had found that their search for primitivism, if persisted in, carried them to this negative result; for it seemed not enough to have apostolic rites in apostolic form unless they were

CHAP. II.

Note 24.

The Seekers.

sanctioned by the "gifts" of the apostolic time. The Seekers appeared in England as early as 1617, and during the religious turmoils of the Commonwealth period the sect afforded a resting place for many a weatherbeaten soul. As the miraculous gifts were lost, the Seekers dared not preach, baptize, or teach; they merely waited, and in their mysticism they believed their waiting to be an "upper room" to which Christ would come. It is interesting to know that Williams, the most romantic figure of the whole Puritan movement, at last found a sort of relief from the austere externalism and ceaseless dogmatism of his age by traveling the road of literalism until he had passed out on the other side into the region of devout and contented uncertainty.

XVIII.

Moral elevation of Williams.

In all this Williams was the child of his age, and sometimes more childish than his age. But there were regions of thought and sentiment in which he was wholly disentangled from the meshes of his time, and that not because of intellectual superiority—for he had no large philosophical views—but by reason of elevation of spirit. Even the authority of Moses could not prevent him from condemning the harsh severity of the New England capital laws. He had no sentimental delusions about the character of the savages—he styles them "wolves endued with men's brains"; but he constantly pleads for a humane treatment of them.

All the bloody precedents of Joshua could not make him look without repulsion on the slaughter of women and children in the Pequot war, nor could he tolerate dismemberment of the dead or the selling of Indian captives into perpetual slavery. From bigotry and resentment he was singularly free. On many occasions he joyfully used his ascendency over the natives to protect those who kept in force against him a sentence of perpetual banishment. And this ultra-Separatist, almost alone of the men of his time, could use such words of catholic charity as those in which he speaks of "the people of God wheresoever scattered about Babel's banks either in Rome or England."

Of his incapacity for organization or administration we shall have to speak hereafter. But his spiritual intuitions, his moral insight, his genius for justice, lent a curious modernness to many of his convictions. In a generation of creed-builders which detested schism he became an individualist. Individualist in thought, altruist in spirit, secularist in governmental theory, he was the herald of a time yet more modern than this laggard age of ours. If ever a soul saw a clear-shining inward light not to be dimmed by prejudices or obscured by the deft logic of a disputatious age, it was the soul of Williams. In all the region of petty scrupulosity the time-spirit had enthralled him ; but in the higher region of moral decision he was utterly emancipated from it. His conclusions belong to ages yet to come.

21

This union of moral aspiration with a certain disengagedness constitutes what we may call the prophetic temperament. Bradford and Winthrop were men of high aspiration, but of another class. The reach of their spirits was restrained by practical wisdom, which compelled them to take into account the limits of the attainable. Not that they consciously refused to follow their logic to its end, but that, like other prudent men of affairs, they were, without their own knowledge or consent, turned aside by the logic of the impossible. Precisely here the prophet departs from the reformer. The prophet recks nothing of impossibility; he is ravished with truth disembodied. From Elijah the Tishbite to Socrates, from Socrates to the latest and perhaps yet unrecognized voice of our own time, the prophetic temperament has ever shown an inability to enter into treaty with its environment. In the seventeenth century there was no place but the wilderness for such a John Baptist of the distant future as Roger Williams. He did not belong among the diplomatic builders of churches, like Cotton, or the politic founders of states, like Winthrop. He was but a babbler to his own time, but the prophetic voice rings clear and far, and ever clearer as the ages go on.

ELUCIDATIONS.

Sir William Martin, an early friend of Williams, describes him as passionate and precipitate, but with integrity and good intentions. Hutchinson Papers, 106. See also, for example, the two letters of Williams to Lady Barrington, in New England Genealogical Register, July, 1889, pp. 316 and following.

Note 1, page 268.

Letter to John Cotton the younger, 25th March, 1671. "He knows what gains and preferments I have refused in universities, city, country and court," etc. Williams's enthusiastic nature gave a flush of color to his statement of ordinary fact, the general correctness of which, however, there is never reason to doubt.

Note 2, page 269.

Letter to John Cotton the younger, Narragansett Club Publications, vi, 356. There is no account of this event elsewhere, but the church records of that early date are imperfect, and there is every reason to accept the circumstantial statement of Williams. That he refused to enter into membership with the church is confirmed by Winthrop's Journal, 12th April, 1631, and such refusal must have had some such occasion.

Note 3, page 270.

"We have often tried your patience, but could never conquer it," were Winthrop's words to Williams, who gave to Massachusetts lifelong service in return for its lifelong severity toward him. The sentence is quoted in Williams's letter to the younger Cotton, cited above, which is itself a fine example of his magnanimity of spirit. Narragansett Club Publications, vi, 351–357.

Note 4, page 271.

There is difference of opinion on this point, but certain words of Williams himself seem to bear on it. After his retirement from Salem to Plymouth he received a letter from Winthrop, which appears to have intimated that no man under twenty-five ought to be ordained. Williams explains in reply that he is "nearer upwards of thirty than twenty-five," but avers, "I am no elder in any church . . . nor ever shall be, if the Lord please to grant my desires that I may intend what I long after, the natives souls." Williams's Letter, Narragansett Club Publications, vi, 2. Of course, these words might have been written if he had resigned the eldership before leaving Salem, but they would have had much less pertinency.

Note 5, page 272.

BOOK III.

Note 6,
page 276.

Mr. Straus, in his Life of Roger Williams, says aptly that Massachusetts was under a government of congregations rather than of towns, since only church members could vote. A fuller discussion of the source and evolution of the town system is deferred to a later volume of this series.

Note 7,
page 278.

David Pieterzen de Vries, in his Voyages, reports this feeling of superiority as freely expressed at Hartford in 1639. There is a quaint humor in what he says of it that is enhanced by the naïve Dutch phrase in which it is set down : " Dit Volck gaven haer uyt det sy Israëliten waren, ende dat wy aen onse colonie Egyptenaren waren, end' Engelsen inde Vergienies waren mede Egyptenaren," p. 151.

Note 8,
page 279.

" And such was the authority . . . Mr. Cotton had in the hearts of the people, that whatever he delivered in the pulpit was soon put into an Order of Court, if of a civil, or set up as a practice in the church, if of an ecclesiastical concernment." Hubbard, History of Massachusetts, 182.

Note 9,
page 281.

Knowles's Life of Williams, 58, note, quotes from a letter of Coddington's appended to Fox's reply to Williams, in which Coddington, who was one of the magistrates that examined the treatise, charges Williams with having " written a quarto against the King's patent and authority."

Note 10,
page 288.

Cotton's Answer to Williams's Examination, 38. I have followed Cotton implicitly here, but without feeling sure that his memory can ever be depended on where his polemical feeling is concerned. On the next page he is guilty of a flagrant but no doubt unconscious suppression of an important fact. "It pleased the Lord to open the hearts of the Church to assist us," etc., he says, putting out of sight the sharp dealing by which the Salem church was brought to ignominious subjection.

Note 11,
page 289.

Cotton's Answer to Williams, 29. Compare also Massachusetts Records of 4th March, 1633, where a mercenary inducement to take the oath is offered by making the regulations for recording the lands of freemen apply also to the lands of " residents " presumably not church members and ineligible to the franchise, but only to the residents " that had taken or shall hereafter take their oathes." Backus supposes that Williams saw some incidental result from the oath that would be prejudicial to religious freedom. This is to suppose that Williams needed a practical consideration to stir him to action—it is to suppose that Williams was not Williams. Practical men were afraid the independence of Massachusetts would be lost; Roger Williams was only afraid that Massachusetts would commit a public sin in trying to escape the impending evil. A conscience undefiled was his objective point in private and public life; safety, public or private, was secondary.

Note 12, page 292.

There has been much ingenious and rather uncandid effort by Cotton first of all, and by other defenders of the General Court since, to prove that Williams's views on toleration were not a cause of his banishment. If those views had been the sole cause, the decree would have been more comprehensible and defensible in view of the opinions of the age. But the question about the validity of the patent, the question of the protest written against the course of the magistrates in blackmailing Salem into a refusal to support him, the question of the freeman's oath, and, what seems to have been deemed of capital importance, the question of grace after meat, are all involved at one time or another. The formal charges in what may be considered the beginning of the banishment proceedings, the trial in July, as given by Winthrop, our most trustworthy authority, are: 1. That the magistrates ought not to punish for a religious offense—"the breach of the first table"—except where it disturbed the civil peace. 2. That the magistrate ought not to tender an oath to an unregenerate man. 3. That a man ought not to pray with an unregenerate person. 4. That thanks were not to be given after the sacrament and after meat. Savage's Winthrop, i, 193, 194. In the final proceedings in October, the letters growing out of the refusal to confirm to Salem its outlying land entered into and embittered the controversy. Winthrop, i, 204. The recorded verdict makes the divulging "of dyvers newe and dangerous opinions against the aucthoritie of the magistrate" the first offense, and the "letter of defamacion" the second. Williams says that a magistrate, who appears to have been Haynes, the governor, summed up his offenses at the conclusion of the trial under four heads: 1. The denial of the authority of the patent. 2. The denial of the lawfulness of requiring a wicked person to take an oath or pray. 3. The denial of the lawfulness of hearing the parish ministers in England. 4. The doctrine "that the Civill Magistrates' power extends only to the Bodies and Goods and outward State of men." Against the evidence of Williams, Winthrop, and the records, I can not attach any importance to the halting accounts given years afterward, for controversial purposes, by Cotton, from what he thought was his memory.

" Whereas Mr. Roger Williams, one of the elders of the church at Salem, hath broached and dyvulged dyvers newe and dangerous opinions, against the aucthoritie of magistrates, as also writt letters of defamacion both of the magistrates & Churches here, & that before any conviccion, & yet maintaineth the same without retraccion, it is therefore ordered that the said Mr. Williams shall departe out of this jurisdiccion within sixe weekes now nexte ensueing, which if hee neglect to performe it shall be lawfull for the Gouernour & two of the magistrates to send him to some place out of this jurisdiccion, not to returne any more without license from the Court." Massachusetts Records, i, 161.

Neal's History of New England, i, 143. " Sentence of banishment being read against Mr. Williams, the whole town of Salem was in an uproar ; for such was the Popularity of the Man and such the Compassion of the People . , . that he would have carried off the greatest part of the Inhabitants of the Town if the Ministers of Boston had not interposed." Neal appears to derive these facts, which wear a countenance of probability, from an authority not now known.

The phrase occurs in Williams's noble letter to Major Mason, 1st Massachusetts Historical Society Collections, i, 275 and following. The magnanimity shown toward those opposed to him in this letter is probably without a parallel in his age ; it has few in any age.

" The increase of the concourse of people to him on the Lord's days in private, to the neglect or deserting of publick Ordinances and to the spreading of the Leaven of his corrupt imaginations, provoked the Magistrates rather than to breed a winters Spirituale plague in the Countrey, to put upon him a winter's journey out of the Countrey." Master John Cotton's Answer to Master Roger Williams, 57.

The main original authorities on the banishment of Williams are Winthrop's Journal and the Massachusetts Records of the period. Some facts can be gathered from the writings of Williams, whose autobiographical passages always have an air of truth while they are sometimes vague and often flushed by his enthusiastic temper. Cotton's memory is less to be trusted ; some of his statements are in conflict with better authorities. He no doubt believed himself to be truthful, but his ingenious mind was unable to be precise without unconscious sophistication. Hubbard was of Presbyterian tendencies and totally opposed to all forms of Separatism. He appears to have recorded every exaggerated rumor cherished by Williams's antagonists to his discredit. Neither in this nor in other matters can we rely much on Hubbard's testimony. No critical student of history puts unquestioning confidence in Cotton Mather. His strange mind could never utter truth unvarnished. In a case like this, where family pride, local feeling, and sectarian prejudice were all on one side, and where he had a chance to embroider upon traditions already two generations old, it is better to disregard the author of the Magnalia entirely. Bentley's Historical Account of Salem, in 1st Massachusetts Historical Society Collections, vi, is a paper that excites admiration for its broadmindedness. It contains information not elsewhere to be found, but it is impossible to tell how far Bentley depended upon sources not now accessible and how far he relied on ingenious inferences drawn from his large knowledge of local history. The publications of the Narragansett Club contain the whole controversy between Cotton and Williams and all the letters of the latter now known to be extant. I have in some cases referred to the originals, in others I have used these careful reprints. Williams has been rather fortunate in his biographers. Mr. Oscar S. Straus, approaching the subject from a fresh standpoint, has produced the latest Life of Williams, written in a judicial temper and evincing a rare sympathy with its subject. The character of Williams has never been better drawn than by Mr. Straus, pp. 231–233. The life by T. D. Knowles is perhaps the best of the older biographies, Arnold's History of Rhode Island contains a sketch of Williams, and Elton's brief biography has a value of its own. Gammell's Life in Sparks's Biography is generally fair. "As to Roger Williams," by the late Dr. Henry Martyn Dexter, is, what it pretends to be, a partisan statement of the case against Williams. It shows characteristic thoroughness of research, it clears up many minor points, and is as erudite as it is one-sided.

Baylie's Sermon before the House of Lords, on Errours and Induration, accuses the Dutch of mere worldly policy in toleration. Williams alludes to the charge, Bloudy Tenent yet more Bloudy,

Note 18, page 298.

p. 8. But the toleration of Holland may rather be traced to that decay of bigotry and that widening of view which are beneficent results of an extended trade. Williams in the Bloudy Tenent yet more Bloudy, p. 10, complains of the exclusion of Catholics and Arminians from toleration in the Netherlands. It would carry us beyond the range of the present work to inquire how far the toleration of Amsterdam was related to that " meridian glory " which Antwerp reached as early as 1550 by making itself a place of refuge for the persecuted of England, France, and Germany. The Articles of Union, adopted at Utrecht in 1579, which have been often called the Magna Charta of the Dutch, go to show that political and commercial considerations counted in favor of toleration, but they also show that some notion of the sacredness of the free conscience had been adopted among the Dutch. Article XIII of the Union provides that the states of Holland and Zealand shall conduct their religious affairs as they think good. More qualified arrangements are made for the other states, as that they may restrict religious liberty as they shall find needful for the repose and welfare of the country. But this significant provision is added, that every man shall have freedom of private belief without arrest or inquisition : " Midts dat een yder particulier in syn Religie vry zal moghen blyven, ende dat men niemandt, ter cause van de Religie, zal moghen achterhalen, ofte ondersoecken." Pieter Paulus Verklaring der Unie van Utrecht, i, 229, 230. Compare Van Meteren, Nederlandsche Historie, etc., iii, 254, 255, and Hooft Nederlandsche Historie, etc., Book IX, where the full text of Article XIII is given.

Barclay, in his Inner Life of the Religious Societies of the Commonwealth, p. 97, cites Peter John Zwisck, a Mennonite of West Frisia, as the author, in 1609, of The Liberty of Religion, in which he maintains that men are not to be converted by force. In 1614 one Leonard Busher petitioned James I in favor of liberty of conscience, and Barclay conjectures that he was a member of that Separatist or General Baptist church returned from Holland, of which Helwyss had been pastor. In 1615 this obscure and proscribed congregation professed a great truth, yet hidden from the wise and prudent, namely, that "earthly authority belonged to earthly kings, but spiritual authority belonged to that one Spiritual king who is king of kings." In more than one matter Roger Williams showed himself attracted to the doctrines of the Mennonites and their offshoot the English General Baptist body.

Chap. II.

Whether directly through his reading of Dutch theological works or indirectly through English followers of Dutch writers, Williams probably derived his broadest principles, in germ at least, from the Mennonites or Anabaptists of the gentler sort, as he did also some of his minor scruples. For the connection between the Mennonites of the Continent and the English cognate sects the reader is referred to Barclay's Inner Life, a valuable work of much research. See also the petition of the Brownists, 1641, cited in Barclay, p. 476, from British Museum, E 34–178, tenth pamphlet.

Note 20, page 299.

Another delightful example of the far-fetchedness of Cotton's logic is his justification of the sentence of banishment against Williams by citing Proverbs xi, 26: "He that withholdeth corn, the people shall curse him." This text, says Cotton, "I alledged to prove that the people had much more cause to separate such from amongst them (whether by Civill or church-censure) as doe withhold or separate them from the Ordinances or the Ordinances from them, which are the bread of life." Reply to Williams's Examination, 40. The reference in the text is to the same work, 37. "Much lesse to persecute him with the Civill Sword till it may appeare, even by just and full conviction, that he sinneth not out of conscience but against the very light of his own conscience." But in Cotton's practice those who labored with the heretic were judges of how much argument constituted "just and full conviction." This logic would have amply sheltered the Spanish Inquisition.

Note 21, page 300.

Cotton's Answer to Williams's Examination, 38, 39. Cotton confesses to having had further conversation of a nature unfavorable to Williams, but he is able to deny that he counseled his banishment. Even Cotton could hardly have prevented it, and he confesses that he approved the sentence. The only interest in the question is the exhibition of Cotton's habitual shrinking from responsibility and his curious sinuosity of conscience.

Note 22, page 301.

In an unpublished work by Mr. Lindsay Swift, of the Boston Public Library, which I have been kindly permitted to read, and which is a treatise on the election sermons mostly existing only in manuscript, the author says: "The early discourses were full of ecclesiasticism, a great deal of theology, some politics; . . . but of humanity, brotherly kindness, and what we understand by Christianity in the human relations, I have been able to discern very little."

Many of Roger Williams's scruples were peculiar, but his scrupulosity was not. Cotton takes pains to call pulpits "scaffolds," to show that they had no sacredness. The scruple about the heathen names of days of the week was felt by many other Puritans. It is evident in Winthrop, and it did not wholly disappear from Puritan use until about the end of the seventeenth century.

Barclay, Inner Life, etc., 410, 411, cites Sebastian Franck's Chronica of 1536, from which it appears that the Seekers in fact if not in name existed about a century before Williams adopted their views. "Some desire to allow Baptism and other ceremonies to remain in abeyance till God gives another command—sends out true laborers into the harvest. . . . Some others agree with those who think the ceremonies since the death of the Apostles, are equally departed, laid waste and fallen—that God no longer heeds them, and also does not desire that they should be longer kept, on which account they will never again be set up but now are to proceed entirely in Spirit and in Truth and not in an outward manner." The relation of Seekerism to Quakerism is manifest. "To be a Seeker is to be of the best Sect next to a finder," wrote Cromwell in 1646.

CHAPTER THE THIRD.

NEW ENGLAND DISPERSIONS.

I.

THE removal of Roger Williams and his friends was the beginning of dispersions from the mother colony on Massachusetts Bay. The company that settled Providence was too small in number at first to be of great importance. The emigration of Williams and his followers to the Narragansett country was an example that may have turned the scale with Hooker and his party in favor of a removal to the Connecticut instead of to some place in the Massachusetts wilderness. Williams certainly prepared a harbor for most of the Hutchinsonians, and pointed the way to Gortonists, Baptists, Quakers, and all others of uneasy conscience. Providence Plantation, and at times all Rhode Island, fell into disorders inevitable in a refuge for scruplers and enthusiasts established by one whose energies were centrifugal and disintegrating. But when at length it emerged from its primordial chaos the community on Narragansett Bay became of capital importance as an example of the secularization of the state, and of the congruity of the largest liberty in religion with civil peace. The system which the more highly organ-

CHAP. III.

Importance of the Rhode Island colony.

315

ized and orderly commonwealths of Massachusetts and Connecticut labored so diligently to establish —a state propping and defending orthodoxy and church uniformity—was early cast into the rubbish heap of the ages. The principle on which the heterogeneous colony of religious outcasts on Narragansett Bay founded itself, was a stone rejected that has become the head of the corner.

II.

The emigration to the Connecticut River was already incubating when Williams sat down with his radical seceders in the Narragansett woods. The Connecticut settlement was impelled by more various and complicated motives than that of Williams, and its origins are not so easy to disentangle. But it, too, has an epic interest; one dominant personality overtops all others in this second of venturesome westward migrations into the wilderness.

We can trace nothing of Hooker to his birthplace, a little hamlet in Leicestershire, except that the imagery of his discourses in after life sometimes reflected the processes of husbandry he had known in childhood. But that he passed through Emmanuel College, Cambridge, while Chaderton was master, is more significant, for Emmanuel was the cradle of Puritan divines, the hatching-place of Puritan crotchets, the college whose chapel stood north and south that it might have no sacred east end, a chapel in which " riming psalms " were sung instead of the hymns, and where lessons different from those appointed in the calendar were read. Hooker was presented to the living of Chelmsford, in Essex. Here his eloquence attracted wide attention, and unhappily attracted at the same time the notice of his diocesan Laud, then Bishop of London, who drove the preacher from his pulpit. Hooker engaged in teaching a school four miles from Chelmsford, where Eliot, afterward the Indian apostle, became his usher and disciple. But Laud had marked him as one to be brought low. He was cited before the Court of High Commission, whose penalties he escaped by fleeing to Holland. Thus early in his career Laud unwittingly put in train events that resulted in the founding of a second Puritan colony in New England.

1630.

III.

The persecution of Hooker made a great commotion in Essex, dividing attention with the political struggle between the king and the people about tonnage and poundage. While Hooker was an exile in Holland a company of people from Braintree and other parts of Essex, near his old parish of Chelmsford, emigrated to New England, chiefly, one may suppose, for the sake of good gospel, since they came hoping to tempt Hooker to become their pastor. This company settled at Newtown, now Cambridge, which had been projected for a fortified capital of the colony, that should be defensible against Indians and out of reach if a sea force should be sent from England to overthrow

Hooker's company.

Walker's First Church in Hartford, 40. Dudley's Letter to Countess of Lincoln, Young's Chron. of Mass., 320. Mass. Records, 14 June, 1631, and 3 February, 1632.

BOOK III.

Holmes's
Hist. Cam-
bridge,
1st Mass.
Hist. Coll.,
vii, 6–8.

the government. Newtown was palisaded and otherwise improved at the expense of the whole colony. Hooker's company were perhaps ordered to settle there because no place was appropriate to the great divine but the new metropolis.

IV.

Failure of
Newtown
as a me-
tropolis.

But a metropolis can not be made at will, as many a new community has discovered. It had been arranged that all the "assistants" or ruling magistrates of Massachusetts should live within

Savage's
Win-
throp,
i, 98, 99.
1632.

the palisades of Newtown, but Winthrop, after the frame of his house was erected, changed his mind and took down the timbers, setting them up again at Boston. This was the beginning of unhappiness at Newtown, and the discontent had to do, no doubt, with the rivalry between that place and Boston. It is probable that there was a rise in the value of Boston home lots about the time of the removal of the governor's house. Trade runs in the direction of the least resistance, and peninsular Boston was destined by its situation to be the metropolis of New England in spite of the forces that worked for Salem and Newtown.

Wonder-
working
Provi-
dence, ch.
xxviii.

Newtown, or Cambridge, to call it by its later name, was a long, narrow strip of land, "in forme like a list cut off from the Broad-cloath" of Watertown and Charlestown. The village was compactly built, as became an incipient metropolis, and

Wood's
N. E. Pros-
pect, 1634.
Young,
402.

the houses were unusually good for a new country. In one regard it was superior to Boston. No wooden chimneys or thatched roofs were allowed in it. To this town came Hooker, and if it had continued to be the capital, Hooker and not Cotton might have become the leading spirit of the colony. But a capital at a place to which only small vessels could come up, was not practical, and the magistrates in the year before Hooker's arrival decided by general consent that Boston was the fittest place in the bay for public meetings.

CHAP. III.

October, 1632.

The hopes of Newtown were perhaps not wholly extinct for some time after. The arrival of Hooker must have been a great encouragement to the people. But Boston was on the alert. That town had neither forest nor meadow land. Hay, timber, and firewood were brought to its wharf in boats. From the absence of wood and marsh came some advantages—it was plagued with neither mosquitoes nor rattlesnakes, and what cattle there were on the bare peninsula were safe from wolves. Not to be behind in evangelical attractions it secured Cotton to balance Newtown's Hooker, when both arrived in the same ship. That Boston was now recognized as the natural metropolis was shown in the abortive movement to pay a part of Cotton's stipend by a levy on the whole colony.

Hooker's arrival, 1633.

Wood's N. E. Prospect. Young, 397, 398.

V.

"Ground, wood, and medowe" were matters of dispute between Newtown and its neighbors as early as 1632, and the frequent references to questions regarding the boundary of Newtown go to

Discontent at Newtown.

BOOK III.

Mass. Rec.,
passim.

Wonder-
working
Provi-
dence, ch.
xxxiii.

Compare
Holmes's
History
of Cam-
bridge,
1 Mass.
Hist. Coll.,
vii, pp. 1, 2.

2d Mass.,
vii, 127.

Cotton and
Hooker.

show dissatisfaction in the discarded metropolis, the number of whose people was out of proportion to its resources. Cattle were scarce in the colony. Each head was worth about twenty-eight pounds, the equivalent of several hundred dollars of money in our time. The Newtown people saw no prospect of foreign trade, and found the plowable plains of Cambridge dry and sandy. They had given up trying to coax fortunes from the stony hill land of the town with hand labor, and turned their attention to the more profitable pursuit of cattle-raising. They took unusual pains to protect their valuable herd from the wolves by impaling a common pasture. Natural meadow was the only resource for hay in the English agriculture of the seventeenth century, and the low grounds of Cambridge yielded a poor grass. Shrewd men in Newtown already saw that as an agricultural colony Massachusetts was destined to failure, and one Pratt, a surgeon there, was called to account for having written to England that the commonwealth was "builded on rocks, sands, and salt marshes."

VI.

There is good authority for believing that a rivalry between Hooker and Cotton had quite as much to do with the discontent as straitened boundaries and wiry marsh grass. Hooker was the greatest debater, perhaps, in the ranks of the Puritans. His theology was somewhat somber, his theory of Christian experience of the most exigent type.

To be saved, according to Hooker, one must become so passive as to be willing to be eternally damned. In other regards he was a Puritan of a rather more primitive type than Cotton. He knew no satisfactory evidence of a man's acceptance with God but his good works. Cotton was less logical but more attractive. His Puritanism grew in a garden of spices. He delighted in allegorical interpretations of the Canticles, his severe doctrines were dulcified with sentiment, and his conception of the inward Christian life was more joyous and mystical and less legal and severe than Hooker's. He was an adept in the windings of non-committal expression, and his intellectual sinuosity was a resource in debate or difficulty. Hooker, on the other hand, had a downrightness not to be mistaken. With an advantage in temperament and the additional advantage of position in the commercial and political center, it is not surprising that Cotton's ideals eloquently and deftly presented soon dominated the colony and that he became the Delphic oracle whose utterances were awaited by the rulers in emergencies.

Theological differences were early apparent in the teachings of the two leaders. Trivial enough to the modern mind are these questions concerning works as an evidence of justification and concerning active and passive faith in justification. Hooker maintained all by himself that there was "a saving preparation in a Christian soule before unyon with Christ." The other ministers pretended

Chap. III.

Compare Walker's First Church of Hartford, 129–132.

Theological differences.

Note 1.

22

to understand what he meant by this, and at first opposed him unanimously. No doubt, too, Hooker and his disciples found some fault with the outer form of the church as shaped by Cotton. Certain it is that Hooker's theories of civil government were more liberal and modern than Cotton's, though like Cotton's they were hung upon texts of Scripture. Hooker lacked Cotton's superfluity of ingenuity; he had less imagination and less poetic sentiment than Cotton, but his intellect was more rugged, practical, and virile. He was not a man to have visions of a political paradise; he did not attempt to limit citizenship to church members when he framed a constitution for the Connecticut towns. Nor did he give so much power and privilege to the magistrate as was given in Massachusetts. He disapproved of Cotton's aristocratic theory of the permanence of the magistrate's office, as

Note 2.

he did apparently of the negative vote of the upper house and of the arbitrary decisions which the Massachusetts magistrates assumed the right to make.

VII.

Attractions of Connecticut.

One other potent motive there was. Stories of the fertility of the "intervale" land on the Connecticut River came by the mouth of every daring adventurer who had sailed or tramped so far. There one might find pasture for the priceless cattle and hay to last the long winter through, and in that valley one might cultivate plains of great fertility.

VIII.

There were dangerous Pequots on the Connecticut, it is true, and the Dutch had already
planted a trading house and laid claim to the territory. The Plymouth people who traded there
were also claimants. And, more than all, leaving
Massachusetts in a time of danger from the machi-
nations of Laud would seem desertion. The government of the Massachusetts Bay colony was
anomalous; it partook of the character of the commercial company from which it sprang, yet it had
traits of a religious or at least a voluntary society.
It was the accepted opinion that those who had
taken the freeman's oath were "knit" together
"in one body," and that none of them ought to
leave the colony without permission. Hooker's
party gained the consent of a majority of the representative members of the General Court, but not
of a majority of the assistants. This precipitated
a debate in the colony on the constitutional question of the right of the assistants, or magistrates, to
form an upper house and veto a decision of the
chosen deputies of the towns.

Savage's Winthrop, i, 167, 168.

IX.

It is no part of our purpose to unravel the tan-
gle of ecclesiastical and civil politics in which the
proposed emigration had now become involved.
The Dorchester church and a part of that of Watertown were ready to follow the lead of Hooker and

Newtown. Days of fasting and prayer were appointed to prevent the removal of these "candle.sticks," as the churches were called, out of their places; but in spite of humiliations and of Cotton's persuasive eloquence, which at one time almost charmed away the discontent, the emigration set in, stragglingly at first.

John Oldham, an adventurous man of a rather lawless temper—one of those half-ruffians that are most serviceable on an Indian frontier—had been expelled from Plymouth. He was now a resident

of Watertown, one of the centers of discontent and next neighbor to Newtown. He had gone with three others on a trading expedition to the westward overland. Walking along trails from one Indian village to another they discovered a large river, which they found to be the Fresh River of the Dutch and the Connecticut of the Plymouth traders. They probably brought back to Watertown accounts that produced a fever for removal. Oldham was not a man to stand on the manner of his emigration. Waiting for nobody's consent, he led out a small company from Watertown the next year. These settled at what is now Wethersfield. From Dorchester, which had no alewife fishery with which to enrich its fields, settlers removed in 1634 to the Connecticut, where the soil did not need to be "fished." In 1635 the number of emigrants was larger, and there was much suffering during the following winter and many of the cattle perished.

X.

But the unit of New England migration was the church. No doubt the cohesiveness of the townships, and of the churches which were the nuclei of the towns, was re-enforced by provincial differences between the several communities. In 1636 Hooker, the real founder of Connecticut, and his congregation of Essex people, sold their houses and meadows and home lots and acre rights in the commonage in Cambridge to a new congregation led by Thomas Shepard. From Newtown and from Dorchester the churches emigrated bodily—pastors, teachers, ruling elders, and deacons—carrying their organization with them through the wilderness like an ark of the covenant. New churches were soon afterward formed in the places they had left. Naturally, town government became the principal feature of civil organization in states thus planted by separate and coherent groups.

XI.

The Connecticut rulers acted at first as a government subordinate to Massachusetts; but the settlements, except that of people from Roxbury at Springfield, were south of the line of the Massachusetts colony, and it was not in the nature of things that Hooker and Haynes should subordinate themselves to Cotton and Winthrop. There was indeed no little exasperation between the two colonies. An independent constitution was adopted

Book III.

in Connecticut, on principles which Hooker thought he found in the first chapter of Deuteronomy, and which were not exactly those that Cotton had managed to deduce from Scripture in his Model of Moses his Judicials. The Massachusetts people, whose government aspired to dominate all New England, seem to have been angered by Hooker's secession and by his refusal to subordinate the new state to their own. Massachusetts asserted its authority over Springfield, which was within its limits, and every effort possible was made to prevent new emigrants who landed at Boston from going to the west. Even in England accounts adverse to Connecticut were circulated. Hooker, the real head of the new state, resented this in a letter of great vigor and some passion.

Conn. Hist. Soc. Coll., i, 20, 21.

Conn. Hist. Soc. Coll., i, 3, and ff.

XII.

Instability of a theocracy.

In its early years Massachusetts had no rest. Three profound disturbances—the expulsion of Williams, the secession of Hooker and his followers, and the Hutchinsonian convulsion—followed one another in breathless succession, and a dangerous Indian war ran its course at the same time. That the early settlements were founded on "rocks and sands and salt marshes" was not the chief misfortune of the Bay colony. Its ecclesiastical politics proved explosive, to the consternation of its pious founders, who like other settlers in Utopia had neglected to reckon with human nature.

XIII.

It has been the habit of modern writers on the subject to dismiss the Hutchinsonian controversy as a debate about meaningless propositions in an incomprehensible jargon. Yet there was in it but the action of well-known tendencies in human nature which might almost have been predicted from the antecedent circumstances. Puritanism had wrapped itself in the haircloth of austerity, it took grim delight in harsh forbiddings, and heaped up whole decalogues of thou-shalt-nots. Nor did it offer, as other intense religious movements have done, the compensation of internal joys for the gayety it repressed. Theoretically Calvinist, it was practically an ascetic system of external duties and abstentions, trampling on the human spirit without ruth.

But the heart will not be perpetually repressed; kept from natural pleasures, it will seek supernatural delights. Men were certain sooner or later to soften the iron rigidity of Puritanism by cultivating those subjective joys for which Calvinism provided abundant materials. While preachers like Hooker were scourging the soul into a self-abasement that could approve its own damnation, and while ingenious scribes were amassing additional burdens of scruple for heavy-laden shoulders, there arose in England a new school of Puritan pietists. These shirked none of the requirements of the legalists, but their spirits sought the sunnier nooks of Calvin-

BOOK III.

Magnalia
B. III, c.
I, 32.

Compare
Cotton's
Fountain
of Life, 35.

Note 4.

Note 5.

Shepard's
Memoirs
in Young,
505.

ism, and they preached the joy of the elect and the delight of a fully assured faith.   Cotton, whose fair complexion, brown hair, and ruddy countenance attested a sanguine temperament, belonged by nature to this new order.   He rejoiced that he had received the " witness of the Spirit " on his wedding day, and he delighted to draw out Scripture imagery to a surprising tenuity in describing the " covenant of marriage " and the intimacy of the " covenant of salt " or of friendship between God and the soul of the believer.   Preachers of the same sort brought relief to multitudes in various towns of England.   The people, tired of churchly routine on the one hand and of legalism on the other, thronged to hear such divines " filling the doores and windows."   It was the evangelicalism of the following century sending up its shoots prematurely into a frosty air.   The old-fashioned Puritan had always conceived of religion as difficult of attainment.   It was a paradoxical system wherein men were saved by the works they theoretically abjured.   Conservative Puritans complained of the preachers who spread a table of " dainties," as though it were meritorious to sustain the soul on a rugged diet of rough doctrine.   In Thomas Shepard's Memoirs of his own Life we may overhear " a godly company " of the time in familiar " discourse about the wrath of God and the terror of it, and how intolerable it was ; which they did present by fire, how intolerable the torment of that was for a time ; what, then, would eternity be ? "

XIV.

Cotton professed that he loved to sweeten his mouth with a piece of Calvin before he went to sleep. His emotional rendering of Calvinistic doctrines wrought strongly on the people of the new Boston, and his advent was followed by widespread religious excitement. More people were admitted to the church in Boston in the earlier months of Cotton's residence than to all the other churches in the colony. Boston seems to have become religious in a pervasive way, and in 1635 measures were taken to prevent persons who were not likely to unite with the church from settling in the town. In this community, which had no intellectual interest but religion, and from which ordinary diversions were banished, there were sermons on Sunday and religious lectures on week days and ever-recurring meetings in private houses. The religious pressure was raised to the danger point, and an explosion of some sort was well-nigh inevitable. Cotton's enthusiasms were modulated by the soft stop of a naturally placid temper, but when communicated to others they were more dangerous.

Cotton's revivalism.

Winthrop's Journal, i, 144.

Report of Record Com. ii, 5. Boston Town Records, 1635. Hutchinson Papers, p. 88.

XV.

Mrs. Anne Hutchinson had been one of Cotton's ardent disciples in old Boston. She crossed the sea with her husband that she might sit under his ministry in New England. She was a woman

Mrs. Hutchinson's character.

BOOK III.

Wonder-
working
Provi-
dence, ch.
lxii.

Note 6.

Short
Story, etc.,
p. 31.

Cotton's
The Way
of the
Churches
Cleared,
Part I,
p. 51.
Short
Story, 31.

Short
Story, 34.

cursed with a natural gift for leadership in an age that had no place for such women. " This Master-piece of Womens wit," the railing Captain Johnson calls her, and certainly her answers before the Massachusetts General Court go to show that she was not inferior in cleverness to any of the magistrates or ministers. Winthrop, whose antipathy to her was a passion, speaks of her " sober and profitable carriage," and says that she was " very helpful in the time of childbirth and other occasions of bodily infirmities, and well furnished with means to those purposes." In the state of medical science at that time such intelligent and voluntary ministration from a " gentlewoman " must have been highly valued. Almost alone of the religionists of her time she translated her devotion into philanthropic exertion. But a woman of her " nimble and active wit " could not pass her life in bodily ministrations. Power seeks expression, and her native eloquence was sure to find opportunity. Mrs. Hutchinson made use of the usual gathering of gossips on the occasion of childbirth to persuade the women to that more intimate religious life of which she was an advocate. It was the custom to hold devotion at concert pitch by meetings at private houses for men only ; women might be edified by their husbands at home. Mrs. Hutchinson ventured to open a little meeting for women. This was highly approved at first, and grew to unexpected dimensions ; fifty, and sometimes eighty, of the principal women of the little town were present at her conferences.

XVI.

In these meetings she emphasized Cotton's favorite doctrine of "a covenant of grace." Her sensitive woman's nature no doubt had beat its wings against the bars of legalism. She was not a philosopher, but nothing could be more truly in accord with the philosophy of character than her desire to give to conduct a greater spontaneity. Cotton himself preached in the same vein. In addition to the Reformation, of which Puritans made so much, he looked for something more which he called, in the phrase of the Apocalypse, "the first resurrection." Mrs. Hutchinson, who was less prudent and more virile than Cotton, did not hesitate to describe most of the ministers in the colony as halting under a "covenant of works." Her doctrine was, at bottom, an insurrection against the vexatious legalism of Puritanism. She carried her rebellion so far that she would not even admit that good works were a necessary evidence of conversion. It was the particular imbecility of the age that thought of almost every sort must spin a cocoon of theological phrases for itself. Spontaneity of religious and moral action represented itself to Mrs. Hutchinson and her followers as an indwelling of the Holy Ghost in the believer and as a personal union with Christ whom they identified with the "new creature" of Paul. Such a hardening of metaphor into dogma is one of the commonest phenomena of religious thought.

Mrs. Hutchinson's doctrines.

Compare Whelewright's Sermon in Proc. Mass. Hist. Soc., 1866, 265. Cotton's Sermon on the Churches Resurrection, 1642.

XVII.

Sir Henry Vane the younger, who had become an ardent Puritan in spite of his father, landed in Boston in October, 1635. He had already shown those gifts which enabled him afterward to play a considerable part in English history. His high connections made him an interesting figure, and though only about twenty-six years of age he was chosen governor in May, 1636. Ardent by nature, and yet in his youth when he " forsook the honors and preferments of the court to enjoy the ordinances of Christ in their purity," nothing was more natural than that he should be captivated by the seraphic Cotton and that he should easily adopt the transcendental views of Mrs. Hutchinson. Winthrop, the natural leader of the colony, having given place in 1635 to Haynes, perhaps in order that Hooker's party might be conciliated and the Connecticut emigration avoided, was a second time thrust aside that a high-born youth might be honored. Winthrop was utterly opposed to Mrs. Hutchinson, in whose teachings his apprehensive spirit saw full-fledged Antinomianism, and, by inference, potential anabaptism, blasphemy, and sedition. The Hutchinsonians were partisans of Vane, who adhered to their doctrine. The ministers other than Cotton and Whelewright, stung by the imputation that they were under "a covenant of works," rallied about Winthrop. Political cleavage and religious division unfortunately coincided.

XVIII.

Supported by the prestige of the young governor and of some conspicuous citizens and inspired by Cotton's metaphorical and mystical preaching, which was interpreted with latitude, the enthusiasm of the Hutchinsonians tended to become fanaticism. We have to depend mainly on the prejudiced account of their enemies, but there is little reason to doubt that the advocates of "a covenant of grace" assumed the airs of superiority usually seen in those who have discovered a short cut to perfection. The human spirit knows few greater consolations than well-disguised self-righteousness. The followers of Mrs. Hutchinson, if we may believe the witnesses, sometimes showed their sanctity by walking out of meeting when a preacher not under "a covenant of grace" entered the pulpit. They even interrupted the services with controversial questions addressed to the minister. Wilson, pastor of the Boston church, was condemned by them as being under "a covenant of works," and also incidentally criticised for his "thick utterance." Nor can one find that Cotton interposed his authority to protect his less gifted colleague. It is quite conceivable that he looked with some satisfaction on the progress of affairs in Boston. The heavenly minded young governor who had chosen to suffer reproach with the people of God was his disciple. The brilliant woman who was easily the leader of the town was the very apostle

Arrogance of the Hutchinson party.

1636.

of his doctrine. The superiority of his opinions on a union with Christ that preceded active faith as compared with those of Hooker and the lesser divines was enthusiastically asserted by the great majority of the Boston church, led by Mrs. Hutchinson. Seeing so much zeal and sound doctrine he may have felt that the first or spiritual resurrection of which he was wont to prophesy from the Apocalypse, had already begun in his own congregation, and that among these enthusiasts were those who had learned to " buy so as though they bought not "—those who had been lifted into a crystalline sphere where they had " the Moone under their feet. And if we have the Moone under our feete, then wee are not eclipsed when the Moone is Eclipsed." Thus did Cotton's imagination revel in cosmical imagery.

Cotton's Churches Resurrection, p. 27.

XIX.

Bitterness of the debate.

The arrogance of the elect is hard to bear, and it is not wonderful that the debate waxed hot. The concentrated religiousness of a town that sought to shut out unbelieving residents made the dispute dangerous. In the rising tempest a ballast of ungodly people might have been serviceable. But in Boston there were few even of the indifferent to be buffers in the religious collision. While the covenant-of-grace people made themselves offensive, their opponents,—Winthrop, the slighted ex-governor, Wilson, the unpopular pastor, and the ministers accused of being under a covenant of works—resorted to the favorite weapons of polemics. They hatched a brood of inferences from the opinions Mrs. Hutchinson held, or was thought to hold, and then made her responsible for the ugly bantlings. They pretended to believe, and no doubt did believe, that Mrs. Hutchinson's esoteric teaching was worse than what she gave out. They borrowed the names of ancient heresies, long damned by common consent, to give odium to her doctrine. That the new party should be called Antinomian was plausible; the road they had chosen for escape from Puritan legalism certainly lay in that direction. But Antinomianism had suffered from an imputation of immorality, and no such tendency was apparent, unless by logical deduction, in the doctrines taught in Boston. The hearers of Mrs. Hutchinson were also accused of having accepted the doctrines of the so-called Family of Love which had of old been accused of many detestable things, and was a common bugaboo of theology at the time. The whole town of Boston and the whole colony of Massachusetts was set in commotion by the rude theological brawl. Such was the state of combustion in Boston that it was thought necessary by the opponents of Vane and Mrs. Hutchinson to hold the court of elections at the former capital, Newtown. The excitement at this court was so great that the church members, who only could vote, were on the point of laying violent hands on one another in a contest growing out of a question relating to the indwelling of the

Holy Ghost. Vane was defeated, and Winthrop again made governor.

XX.

A great synod of elders from all the New England churches was assembled. All the way from Ipswich and Newbury on the east and from the Connecticut on the west the "teaching elders" made their way by water or by land, at public expense, that they might help the magistrates of Massachusetts to decide on what they should compel the churches to believe. For more than three weeks the synod at Cambridge wrestled with the most abstruse points of doctrine. The governor frequently had to interpose to keep the peace; sometimes he adjourned the assembly, to give time for heats to cool. A long list of errors, most of which were not held by anybody in particular, were condemned. A nearly unanimous conclusion on certain fine-spun doctrines was reached at length by means of affirmations couched in language vague or ambiguous. Cotton, who had been forced after debate to recant one opinion and modify others, assented to the inconclusive conclusions, but with characteristic non-committalism he qualified his assent and withheld his signature.

XXI.

The field was now cleared for the orderly persecution of the dissentients. Whelewright, Mrs. Hutchinson's brother-in-law, had been convicted of sedition in the preceding March on account of an imprudent sermon preached on a fast day. But his sentence had been deferred from court to court, apparently until after the synod. At the November court following the synod Whelewright was banished, and those who had signed a rather vigorous petition in his favor many long months before were arraigned and banished or otherwise punished. The banished included some of the most intelligent and conspicuous residents. Not until this November court had her opponents ventured to bring Mrs. Hutchinson to trial. Whelewright, standing by his hot-headed sermon, had just been sentenced; the abler but more timid Cotton had already been overborne and driven into a safe ambiguity by the tremendous pressure of the great synod. Vane had left the colony, and the time was ripe to finish the work of extirpation. The elders were summoned to be present and advise.

Mass. Rec., i, 207.

XXII.

During a two days' trial, conducted inquisitorially, like an English Court of High Commission, Cambridge presented the spectacle of a high-spirited and gifted woman, at the worst but a victim of enthusiasm, badgered by the court and by the ministers, whose dominant order she had attacked. Cotton, with more than his usual courage, stood her defender. The tough-fibered Hugh Peter, who made himself conspicuous in several ways, took it on him to rebuke Cotton for saying a word in de-

Mrs. Hutchinson's trial, 1637.

Hutchinson's Hist. of Mass. Bay, ii, appendix.

23

fense of the accused. Endecott and Hugh Peter, mates well matched, browbeat the witnesses who appeared in Mrs. Hutchinson's behalf, and Dudley, the conscientious advocate of persecution, was rude and overbearing. Winthrop acted as chief inquisitor, the narrow sincerity and superstition of his nature obscuring the nobler qualities of the man.

Mrs. Hutchinson defended herself adroitly at first, refusing to be trapped into self-condemnation. But her natural part was that of an outspoken agitator, and her religious exaltation had been increased, doubtless, by persecution, for combativeness is a stimulant even to zeal. On the second day she threw away "the fear of man," and declared that she had an inward assurance of her deliverance, adding that the General Court would suffer disaster. For this prophesying she was promptly condemned. Cotton had prophesied notably on one occasion, Wilson, his colleague, was given to rhyming prophecies, and Hooker had made a solemn prediction while in Holland. In this very year the plan of the Pequot campaign had been radically changed in compliance with a revelation vouchsafed to the chaplain, Stone. But these were ministers, and never was the ministerial office so reverenced as by the Puritans, who professed to strip it of every outward attribute of priestliness. Above all, for a woman to teach and to have revelations was to stand the world on its head. " We do not mean to discourse with those of your sex," etc., said Winthrop severely to Mrs. Hutchinson during the trial. She was sentenced to banishment, but reprieved, that the church might deal with her. On the persuasion of Cotton and others, Mrs. Hutchinson wrote a recantation apologizing for her assumption to have revelations, and retracting certain opinions of which she had been accused. But she added that she had never intended to teach or to hold these opinions. For this falsehood, as it was deemed, she was summarily excommunicated. Yet nothing seems more probable than that her hyperbolic utterances under excitement had not stood for dogmatic opinions. Under Cotton's fine-spun system of church government a member could not be excommunicated except by unanimous consent. Many of Mrs. Hutchinson's friends were absent from the colony, others had prudently changed sides or stayed away from the meeting. But her sons ventured to speak in her behalf. Cotton at once admonished them. The effect of putting them under admonition was to disfranchise them ; it was one of Cotton's ingenuities of the sanctuary. The sons out of the way, the mother was cast out unanimously—a punishment much dreaded among the Puritans, who believed that what was thus bound on earth was bound in heaven. It was a ban that forbade the faithful even to eat with her. But the melancholy under which Mrs. Hutchinson had suffered vanished at once, and she said as she left the church assembly, " Better to be cast out than to deny Christ."

CHAP. III.

Mrs. Hutchinson is excommunicated.

Note 8.

Rise, Reign, Ruine, etc., and Winthrop's Journal, i, 309, 310.

XXIII.

Mrs. Hutchinson and most of her party settled
on Rhode Island, where they sheltered themselves
at first in caves dug in the ground. Here she
again attracted attention by the charm of her eloquent teaching, and some came from afar to hear
the "she Gamaliel," as her opponents called her.
Such gifts in a woman, and in one who had been
excommunicated by the authority vested in the
church, could be accounted for only by attributing
her power to sorcery. Winthrop sets down the
evidence that she was a witch, which consisted in
her frequent association with Jane Hawkins, the
midwife, who sold oil of mandrakes to cure bar-
renness, and who was known to be familiar with
the devil. At length "God stepped in," and by
his "casting voice" proved which side was right.
Mary Dyer, one of the women who followed Mrs.
Hutchinson, had given birth to a deformed still-
born child. This fact became known when Mrs.
Dyer left the church with the excommunicated
Mrs. Hutchinson. Winthrop had the monstrosity
exhumed after long burial had rendered its traits
difficult to distinguish. He examined it personally with little result, but he published in England
incredible midwife's tales about it. God stepped
in once more, and Mrs. Hutchinson herself, after
she went to Rhode Island, suffered a maternal misfortune of another kind. The wild reports that
were circulated regarding this event are not fit to

Savage's
Win-
throp's
Journal, i,
313, 316;
ii, 11, and
Short
Story of
Rise and
Reign of
Antino-
mianism.

Winthrop,
i, 316.

be printed even in a note ; the first editor of Win-throp's journal felt obliged to render the words into Latin in order that scholars might read them shamefacedly. But Cotton, who was by this time redeeming himself by a belated zeal against the banished sectaries, repeated the impossible tale, which was far worse than pathological, to men and women, callow youths, young maidens, and inno-cent children " in the open assembly at Boston on a lecture day," explaining the divine intent to sig-nalize her error in denying inherent righteousness. The governor, who was more cautious, wrote to the physician and got a correct report, from which the divine purpose was not so evident, and Cotton made a retraction at the next lecture. We are now peering into the abyss of seventeenth-century credulity. Here are a grave ruler and a di-vine once eminent at the university, and now renowned in England and in America, wallowing in a squalid superstition in comparison with which the divination of a Roman haruspex is dignified.

Having suffered the loss of her husband, and hearing of efforts on the part of Massachusetts to annex Rhode Island, Mrs. Hutchinson removed to the Dutch colony of New Netherland with her family. Here she and all her household except one child were massacred by the Indians. This act of Providence was hailed as a final refutation of her errors, the more striking that the place where she suffered was not far removed from a place called Hell Gate.

Savage's
Winthrop,
i, 326.

Death of
Mrs.
Hutchin-
son.

Note 9.

XXIV.

This famous controversy lets in much light up-on the character of the age and the nature of Puri-tanism. It is one of many incidents that reveal the impracticability of the religious Utopia attempted in New England. The concentration of religious people undoubtedly produced a community free from the kind of disorders that are otherwise in-separable from a pioneer state and that were found abundantly in New Netherland, in Maryland, and in Virginia and on the eastward fishing coast. "These English live soberly," said a Dutch visitor to Hart-ford in 1639, "drinking but three times at a meal, and when a man drinks to drunkenness they tie him to a post and whip him as they do thieves in Holland." But while some of the good results to be looked for in an exclusively Puritan community were attained, it was at the cost of exaggerating the tendency to debate and fanaticism and develop-ing the severity, the intolerance, and the meddle-some petty tyranny that inheres in an ecclesiastical system of government. During the lifetime of one generation Massachusetts suffered all these, and it is doubtful whether regularity of morals was not pur-chased at too great a sacrifice of liberty, bodily and spiritual, and of justice. Certainly the student of history views with relief the gradual relaxation that came after the English Restoration and the disappearance from the scene of the latest surviv-ors of the first generation of New England leaders.

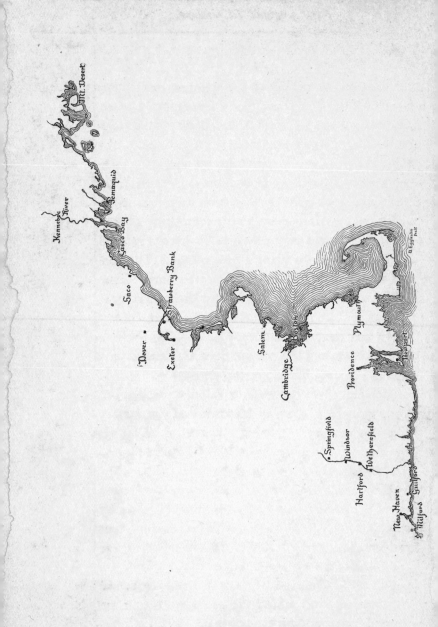

Mt. Desert

Kennebec River

Pemaquid

Casco Bay

Saco

Strawberry Bank

Dover

Exeter

Salem

Cambridge

Plymouth

Providence

Newport

Springfield

Windsor

Wethersfield

Hartford

New Haven

Milford Guilford

G. Eginhart
Scalp

XXV.

During the period of the greatest excitement over the Hutchinson case John Davenport, a noted Puritan minister of London, had been in Massachusetts. Like many other emigrant divines of the time he brought a migrant parish with him seeking a place to settle. Davenport arrived in June, 1637, and took part against the Antinomians in the synod. After examining every place offered them in Massachusetts, he and his friends refused all and resolved to plant a new colony. The people were Londoners and bent on trade, and Massachusetts had no suitable place for their settlement left. The bitterness of the Hutchinson controversy may have had influence in bringing them to this decision, and the preparations of Laud to subject and control Massachusetts perhaps had weight in driving them to seek a remoter settlement. Davenport had ideals of his own, and the earthly paradise he sought to found was not quite Cotton's nor was it Hooker's. He and his followers planted the New Haven colony in 1638. In this little colony church and state were more completely blended than in Massachusetts. The government was by church members only, to the discontent of other residents, and in 1644 New Haven adopted the laws of Moses in all their rigor. The colony was united with Connecticut by royal charter at the Restoration, after which the saints no longer sat upon thrones judging the tribes of Israel.

CONCLUSION.

Later
English
emigra-
tions to
New Eng-
land.

The emigration to New England from the mother country was quickened by the troubles that preceded the civil war. In 1638 it reached its greatest height, having been augmented perhaps by agricultural distress. Fourteen ships bound for New England lay in the Thames at one time in the spring of that year. There was alarm at the great quantity of corn required for the emigrants, lest there should not be enough left in London to last till harvest. "Divers clothiers of great trading" resolved to "go suddenly," in which we may see, perhaps, evidence of bad times in the commercial world. Some parishes it was thought would be impoverished. Laud was asked to put a stop to the migration; but the archbishop was busy trying to compel the Scots to use the prayer book. Most of the lords of the Council were favorable to New England; the customs officers purposely neglected to search for contraband goods, and the ships, twenty in all, got away with or without license, and brought three thousand passengers to Boston. But the tide spent itself about this time, and by 1640 emigration to the New England colonies had entirely ceased. About twenty-one thousand two hundred people had been landed in all.

Lord May-
nard to
Laud,
17 March,
1638, in
Sainsbury.
Savage's
Win-
throp's
Journal, i,
319, 320,
322.
Rushworth,
i, Part II,
409, 718.

Josselyn's
Rarities,
108.

Cavalier
emigra-
tion to
Virginia.

The swing of the political pendulum in England that served to check the Puritan exodus gave impetus to a new emigration to Virginia and Maryland. During the ten years and more before 1640 few had gone to that region but bond servants. There were in that year not quite eight thousand people in Virginia. It is the point of time at which the native Virginians began to rear a second generation born on the soil. The waning fortunes of the king sent to the colony in the following years a large cavalier emigration, and the average character of the colonists was raised. Better ministers held the Virginia parishes and better order was observed in the courts. In 1648 four hundred emigrants lay aboard ships bound for Virginia at one time, and in 1651 sixteen hundred royalist prisoners seem to have been sent in one detachment.

Petition to House of Lords, 15 Aug., 1648. Royal Hist. MS., Com. Rept.. vii, 45.

Sainsbury, 360.

Prospective ascendency of the English colonies.

By the middle, of the seventeenth century the English on the North American continent were in a fair way to predominate all other Europeans. From the rather lawless little fishing villages on the coast of Maine to the rigorous Puritan communes of the New Haven colony that stretched westward to pre-empt, in advance of the Dutch, land on the shores of Long Island Sound, the English held New England. English settlers " seeking larger accommodations" had crossed to Long Island and were even pushing into the Dutch colony. The whole Chesapeake region was securely English. Already there were Virginians about to break into the Carolina country lying wild between Virginia and the Spanish colony in Florida. The French and the Dutch and the Spaniards excelled the English in far-reaching explorations and adventurous fur-trading. But the English had proved their superior aptitude for planting compact agricultural communities. A sedentary and farming population where the supply of land is not limited reaches the highest rate of natural increase. At a later time, Franklin estimated that the population of the colonies doubled every twenty-five years without including immigrants. The compactness of English settlement and the prolific increase of English people decided the fate of North America. The rather thin shell of Dutch occupation was already, by the middle of the seventeenth century, feeling the pressure under stress of which it was soon to give way. A century later collision with the populous and ever-multiplying English settlements brought about the collapse of the expanded bubble of New France.

ELUCIDATIONS.

There is a paper on this debate in the British Record Office indorsed by Archbishop Laud, " Rec : Octob : 7. 1637," " Propositions wch have devided Mr. Hooker & Mr. Cotton in Newe England. 1. That a man may prove his justification by his works of sanctification, as the first, best, and only cheife evidence of his salvation. 2. Whither fayth be active or passive in justification. 3. Whither there be any saving preparation in a Christian soule before his unyon with Christ. This latter is only Hooker's opinion, the rest of the ministers do not concurr with him : Cotton and the rest of the contrary opinion are against him and his party in all." Colonial Papers, ix, 71. In the next paper in the same volume, also indorsed by Laud, the controversy is more fully set forth. Copies of both are in the Bancroft collection of the New York Public Library. Laud indorsed these papers respectively October 7 and 15, 1637. The Cambridge Synod, which met August 30th, had adjourned late in September, and the debates which divided the two divines must have preceded it, and perhaps preceded the migration of Hooker to Connecticut in 1636. When Haynes was Governor of Massachusetts he had pronounced the sentence of banishment against Williams. But some years later, while Governor of Connecticut, he relented a little and wrote to Williams: "I think, Mr. Williams, I must now confesse to you, that the most wise God hath provided and cut out this part of his world for a refuge and receptacle for all sorts of consciences. I am now under a cloud, and my brother Hooker, with the bay, as you have been, we have removed from them thus far, and yet they are not satisfied." Quoted by Williams in a letter to Mason, 1st Massachusetts Historical Collections, i, 280.

Note 2, page 322.

The abstract of Hooker's sermon of May 31, 1638, as deciphered and published by Dr. J. Hammond Trumbull, is in the Collections of the Connecticut Historical Society, i, 20, 21, and the Fundamental Laws of 1639 are in Hinman's Antiquities, 20, and ff., and in Trumbull's Blue Laws, 51. Compare also the remarkable letter of Hooker to Winthrop in Connecticut Historical Society Collections. i, 3–15. Hooker objects strongly to the right of arbitrary decisions by the magistrate: "I must confess, I ever looked at it as a way which leads directly to tyranny, and so to confusion, and must plainly profess, if it was in my liberty, I would choose neither to live nor leave my posterity under such government." This letter exhibits Hooker's intellect to great advantage. One is inclined to rank him above most of his New England contemporaries in clearness and breadth of thought.

Note 3, page 325.

The selling of half-developed homesteads to newcomers by older settlers was of constant occurrence in all the colonies during the colonial period. It was a notable practice on the frontiers of Pennsylvania down to the Revolution, and perhaps later. Hubbard thus describes what went on in every New England settlement: "Thus the first planters in every township, having the advantage of the first discovery of places, removed themselves into new dwellings, thereby making room for others to succeed them in their old." General History of New England, 155.

Note 4, page 328.

The existence in England of a doctrine resembling that of the followers of Cotton and Mrs. Hutchinson is implied in Welde's preface to the Short Story of the Rise, Reign, and Ruine of Antinomianism. "And this is the very reason that this kind of doc-

trine takes so well here in *London* and other parts of the kingdome, and that you see so many dance after this pipe, running
after such and such, crowding the Churches and filling the
doores and windowes."

Giles Firmin's Review of Davis's Vindication, 1693, quotes
from a letter of Shepard of Cambridge, Massachusetts: "Preach
Humiliation, labor to possess Men with a Sence of Misery and
wrath to come. The Gospel Consolations and Grace which
some would have only disht out as the Dainties of the times and
set upon the Ministry's Table may possibly tickle and ravish
some and do some good to some which are Humbled and Converted already. But if Axes and Wedges be not used withal to
hew and break this rough unhewn bold but professing age, I am
Confident the Work and Fruit . . . will be but meer Hypocrisie."

Notwithstanding his early imprudence during the partisan excitement in Boston, Whelewright was a man of sound judgment,
and his testimony regarding his sister-in-law is the most important we have. "She was a woman of good wit and not onely
so, . . . but naturally of a good judgment too, as appeared in her
civill occasions; In spirituals indeed she gave her understanding
over into the power of suggestion and immediate dictates, by
reason of which she had many strange fancies, and erroneous
tenents possest her, especially during her confinement . . . attended by melancholy." Mercurius Americanus, p. 7.

Hugh Peter, after his return to England, adopted the views
in favor of toleration beginning to prevail there. Nine years
after he had obtruded himself so eagerly to testify against Mrs.
Hutchinson, he was writing to New England earnest remon-
strances against persecution. 4 Massachusetts Historical Collections, vi, where the letters are given.

There were those who wished to give time for a second admonition before excommunication, but they were overruled, probably by Wilson. Winthrop, i, 310. It would, perhaps, have
been in better form to take the other and less eager course.
There is a Latin paper in the British Public Record Office, dated
3 March, 1635, which professes to give a brief and orderly digest
of the canons of government constituted and observed in the reformed New England churches. I am unable to trace its authority. From this I quote; "Qui pertinacitur consistorii admonitiones rejecerit a cœna domini suspendatur. Si suspensus, post

iteratus admonitiones nullum pœnitentiæ signum dederit ad ex-
comunicationem procedat Ecclesia."

It would be a waste of time to controvert the ingenious apolo-
gies which have been written to prove that an inexorable necessity
compelled the banishment of the Antinomians. The Massachusetts government was in its very nature and theory opposed to
religious toleration, as we may see by the reference of the case of
Gorton and his companions to the elders, and their verdict that
these men, not residents of the jurisdiction, ought to be put to
death for constructive blasphemy, a decision that the magistrates by a majority vote would have put in execution if the
"deputies" or representative members of the assembly had not
dissented. Savage's Winthrop's Journal, ii, 177. The doctrine
of intolerance is ingeniously set forth in Cotton's "The Powring
Ovt of the Seven Vials, . . . very fit and necessary for this Present Age," published in 1642. Cotton compares Jesuits and heretics to wolves, and says, "Is it not an acceptable service to the
whole Country to cut off the ravening Wolves?" The Puritans
of New England from their very circumstances were slower to
accept the doctrine of religious liberty than their coreligionists in
England.

INDEX.

Abbot, Abp., on Calvert's resignation, 259, n. 6.

Abercromby's Examination, 258, n. 4 ; 262, n. 11 ; 263, n. 12.

Aberdeen Burgh Records, no sabbatarian legislation in, 140, n. 12 ; quaint ordinance from, 140, n. 12.

Accidents, New England hung on a chain of slender, 176.

Act, for Church Liberties, 1639, 251 ; 265, n. 22 ; for discovering popish recusants, 237, m. ; of Toleration, 1649, 255, 256 ; act to prevent, etc., 237, m.

Activity, intellectual, men excited to unwonted, 1.

Adam's needle and thread, garments woven of fiber of, 79 ; efforts to cultivate, 80.

Admonition to the People of England, 115, m.

Advertisements for Planters of New England, 27, m.

Age of romance and adventure, an, 1, 20 ; of colony beginnings, 92 ; dramatic and poetic to its core, 100.

Agrarian and industrial disturbance aids the Puritan movement, 111.

Ainsworth wrote tractate on the Jewish ephod, 108.

Alexander, William, Encouragement to Colonies, 258, n. 3.

Alleghanies deemed almost impassable, 11.

Almond, an, for a Parrat, 116.

America excited the most lively curiosity, 2 ; notion that it was an Asiatic peninsula, 3 ; search for a route through, lasted one hundred and fourteen years, 8 ; a Mediterranean Sea sought in the heart of, 11 ; fact and fable about, 14 ; excepted from the Deluge, 20 ; treasure from flowing into Spanish coffers, 74 ; Hak-luyt spreading sails for, in every breeze, 76 ; all one to European eyes, 169.

Amer. Antiqu. Soc. Trans, 22, n. 4.

Amsterdam, Separatists migrated to, 148 ; called a common harbor of all opinions, 164.

Anabaptism, divergencies in direction of, in Mass., 267.

Anarchy and despotism the inevitable alternatives of communism, 26.

Anderson's Church of England in the Colonies, 258, n. 3.

Anderson's Commerce, 22, n. 5 ; 75, m. ; 76, m. ; 95, n. 3.

Anglican and Puritan party lines not sharply drawn at first, 110.

Anglican Church party, leaders at Zurich and Strasburg, 104 ; held to the antique ritual, 106 ; content with moderate reforms, 109 ; must have a stately liturgy and holy days, 110 ; becomes dogmatic, 113 ; aided by Hooker's Ecclesiastical Polity, 122.

Anglican zeal founded a nation of dissenters, 91.

Animals, notions about American, 18 ; too many kinds for Noah's ark, 20.

Animals for breeding, stock of, 48 ; sold by Argall, 50.

Antinomianism, divergencies in direction of, in Mass., 287 ; found by Winthrop in Mrs. Hutchinson's teachings, 332.

Antinomians sheltered by Vane and Cotton, 267 ; Davenport took part against, in the synod, 343 ; banishment of the, 349, n. 9. See also HUTCHINSON, MRS. ANNE, and HUTCHINSONIAN CONTROVERSY.

Antwerp, a place of refuge for the persecuted, 312, n. 18.

Apocalypse of John, the, received

351

hearty consideration from the New England Puritans, 301.

Apostolic primitivism, aim of the Puritan, 303 ; goal of the Separatist, 303.

Apostolic succession asserted as essential, 113.

Archdale's Carolina, 171, m.

Archer, Gabriel, wounded by the Indians, 28 ; hostile to Smith, 37 ; character of, 64, n. 3 ; a ringleader in disorders, 63, n. 3 ; a paper on Virginia by, 96, n. 7.

Archery on Sunday prohibited, 127.

Arctic continent, an, 2.

Argall, Captain, the first Englishman to see the bison, 24, n. 10, 50 ; sent to the Bermudas, went to the fishing-banks for food, 42 ; to Mt. Desert for plunder, 47 ; bad record and government, 50 ; robbed Company and colonists, 50, 52 ; fitted out a ship for piracy, 51 ; charter procured for a new plantation to protect, 51, 68, n. 13 ; escaped in nick of time, 52.

Argonauts of the New World set sail, 25.

Arianism, divergencies in direction of, in Massachusetts, 267.

Ark, The, and The Dove, efforts to prevent departure of, 241 ; no Protestant minister or worship on board, 242.

Armada, the Spanish, patriotism aroused by the danger from, 121.

Armenian silk-raisers brought to Virginia, 78.

Arminian Nunnery, 93, m.

Arminianism spreads among the High-Church clergy, 133, 192.

Arminians and Calvinists, Laud attempts to suppress debate between, 194.

Arminians excluded from toleration in the Netherlands, 298, 312, n. 18.

Arnold's History of Rhode Island, 311, n. 17.

Articles of Union, the, provided for freedom of private belief, 312, n. 18.

Arundel, Lord, a friend of Sir George Calvert, 226 ; territory assigned to, 259, n. 5.

Asher's History of West India Company, 177, m.

Asia, efforts to reach, 3.

Aspinwall Papers, 56, m. ; 70, n. 15 ; 264, n. 20.

Aubrey's Survey of Wiltshire, 136, n. 5.

Augustine on the Sunday-Sabbath, 137, n. 8 ; 140, n. 13.

Austerfeld, a cradle of the Pilgrims, 149 ; the stolid rustics of, 150 ; the font at which Bradford was baptized, 151 ; inhabitants at Bradford's birth a most ignorant people, 152.

Austerity in morals a Puritan characteristic, 119.

Auxiliary societies formed, 53.

Avalon, Calvert's province in New-foundland called, 224, 258, n. 3 ; charter of, 225, 234 ; primary design of the colony, 225 ; 259, n. 5 ; troubles of Baltimores and Puritans in, 228 ; abandoned by Calvert, 230 ; Catholic emigrants to, 239.

Bacon, Lord, objects to heretics settling a colony, 171.

Bacon's Lord, An Advertisement touching Controversies, 117, m. ; Advice to Villiers, 171, m. ; Certain Considerations, 162, m. ; Essay on Plantations, 27, m. ; Observation on a Libel, 163, m. ; Speech in reply to the Speaker, 25, m.

Bacon's Laws of Maryland, 264, n. 19 ; 265, n. 22.

Bacon, Nathaniel, 60, n. 1.

Bacon, Roger, on the Sunday question, 138, n. 8.

Baillie, Robert, on John Robinson, 156.

Baltimore, first Baron. See CALVERT, GEORGE.

Baltimore, Letters to Wentworth, 241, m.

Baltimore, second Baron. See CALVERT, CECILIUS.

Bancroft, Richard, Bishop of London, theatrical adulation of King James, 161 ; as primate persecutes the Puritans, 162 ; stops emigration to Virginia, 168, 183, n. 2.

Baptist Church, the General, on earthly and spiritual authority, 312, n. 19.

Baptists, Williams and his followers become, 303.

Barclay's Inner Life, 146, m. ; 186, n. 6 ; 312, n. 19 : 314, n. 24.

Barlow's Svmme and Svbstance, 143, m. ; 160, m. ; 162, m. ; 182, n. 1.

Barrow hanged at Tyburn, 148.

Barrowism a mean between Presbyterianism and Brownism, 148 ; the model for the church at Scrooby, 154.

Bawtry, the station near Scrooby, 149, 150, 151.

Baylie, Robert, condemns the toleration of the Dutch, 164, 311, n. 18.

Baylie's Errours and Induration, 164, m. ; 311, n. 18.

Bell, ringing of only one, to call people to church, 129 ; of more than one a sin, 130.

Bentley's Description of Salem, 200, m. ; Historical Account of Salem, 311, n. 17.

Berkeley, Sir William, persecution of Puritans in Virginia by, 252.

Bermudas, Gates and Somers shipwrecked on the, 40 ; birds and wild hogs at the, 41, 65, n. 6 ; marvelous escape from the, 41, 65, n. 6.

Beste, George, 2, m. ; 4 ; on the New World, 21, n. 2.

Biard on Dale's severity to French prisoners, 66, n. 9.

Bible, reading the, as part of the service, reprehended by the extremists, 117.

Birch's Court of James I, 68, n. 10 ; 69, n. 14 ; 72, n. 19 ; 258, n. 1.

Bishoprics filled by Elizabeth, 143.

Bishops, effect of the hostility of the, to the Puritans, 112 ; attacked by the Mar-Prelate tracts, 115 ; reaction in favor of, 121 ; had become Protestant to most people, 123.

Bison found near the Potomac, 50.

Blackstone, William, first settler at Boston, 190.

Blake's Annals of Dorchester, 219, n. 9.

Boston chosen as fittest place for public meetings, 319 ; secured Cotton to balance Newton's Hooker, 319.

Boston church, Roger Williams refused to become a minister of, 270.

Boston Town Records, 329, m.

Boulton, a Separatist, recanted and hung himself, 157, n. 2.

Bowling in the streets the daily work at Jamestown, 44.

Bowls, Calvin playing at, on Sunday,

124 ; Mar-Prelate berates the Bishop of London for playing, 128.

Bownd's, Dr., Sabbath of the Old and the New Testament, 124, 128 ; views rapidly accepted, 129 ; ultrapropositions exceeded, 130 ; captivated the religious public, 130 ; opposition to, 131 ; new edition published, 132, 139, n. 10.

Bozman, 265, n. 22.

Bradford, William, a silk-weaver in Leyden, 169 ; chosen governor at Plymouth, 179 ; abolishes communism, 180 ; of high aspiration restrained by practical wisdom, 306.

Bradford's Dialogue of 1593, 146, m. ; Plimoth Plantation, 145, m. ; 153, m. ; 154, m. ; 155, m. ; 158, n. 3 ; 165, m. ; 166, m. ; 175, m. ; 184, n. 4 ; 186, n 9 ; 274, m.

Brewster, William, at court, 152 ; master of the post at Scrooby, 153 ; secured ministers for neighboring parishes who were silenced, 153 ; the host and ruling elder of the Scrooby church, 154 ; useful career of, 155 ; project of forming a new state, 167 ; books owned by, 168.

Briefe Declaration, MS., 27, m. ; 40, m. ; 43, m. ; 44, m. ; 45, m. ; 46, m. ; 47, m. ; 66, n. 9.

Brieff Discourse of the Troubles begun at Frankfort, 135, n. 3.

Briggs, Henry, on the nearness of the Pacific, 10, 22, n. 6.

Bristol colony in Newfoundland, 258, n. 3.

British Museum, MS., 42, m. ; 44, m.

Broughton wrote a tractate on the Jewish ephod, 108.

Brown, Richard, submitted to remonstrance, 290.

Browne, John and Samuel, sent back to England by Endecott, 200.

Browne, Robert, leader of the Separatists, 145 ; despised for recanting, died in prison, 146 ; career lasted only four or five years, 147 ; John Robinson's justification of, 157, n. 1 ; authorities on, 157, n. 1 ; 158, n. 2.

Brownists. See SEPARATISTS.

Brown's Genesis of the United States, 94, n. 1 ; 183, n. 3.

Bruce's Economic History of Virginia, 95, n. 3.

Buckingham dominant at court, 193 ;

consents to sale of Calvert's secretaryship, 227.

Bull and bear baiting on Sunday, 129.

Bullein's Dialogue against the Fever Pestilence, 23, n. 8 ; 126.

Burgesses, House of, in Virginia, 55.

Burk's History of Virginia, 69, n. 13.

Burleigh, Lord Treasurer, treatise on Execution of Justice in England published by, 238.

Burns's Prel. Diss. to Woodrow, 159, m. ; 160, m.

Busher, Leonard, petitioned James I for liberty of conscience, 312, n. 19.

Cabins at Jamestown, 29.

Cabot, John, discovers America, 3 ; his ships retarded by codfish, 18 ; Deane's voyages of, 21, n. 1 ; Harrisse on, 21, n. 1.

Cabot, Sebastian, not a discoverer, 21, n. 1 ; a doubtful authority, 24, n. 9.

Calendar of Colonial Documents, 70, n. 15 ; 96, n. 5 ; 259, n. 5.

Calendar of Domestic Papers, 259, n. 6.

Calendar of Domestic State Papers James I, 77, m.

Calendar of State Papers America, 224, m.

Caliban suggested by popular interest in savages, 17.

Calvert, Cecilius, second Lord Baltimore, son of George Calvert, 234 ; expected large Catholic migration, 240 ; religious aim of, 240 ; partners in financial risks, 240, 263, n. 13 ; policy of toleration, 242 ; orders the Catholic service to be conducted privately on shipboard, 242 ; a conservative opportunist, 243 ; supported at court by Strafford, 249; schemes against Virginia, 249, 264, n. 21 ; seeks to be governor, 250 ; offer to New England people, 252 ; had Maryland oath of fidelity modified for Puritans, 253 ; yielded office of governor to Protestant, 254 ; again master of Maryland, 257.

Calvert, George, character of, 221 ; his rise in power, 223 ; denied being bribed by Spain, 223, 258, n. 1 ; member of Virginia Company, 1609, 224, 229; councilor for New England, 224 ; establishes colony in Newfoundland, 224, 239 ; his conversion to Catholicism, 226 ; intractable, 225 ; resigned secretaryship and made Baron Baltimore, 228, 259, n. 6 ; in Newfoundland, 228, 229 ; sails to Virginia, 229 ; not received hospitably, 230 ; refuses to take oath of supremacy, and leaves Virginia, 232; religious enthusiasm, 233, 258, n. 3 ; passion for planting colonies, 233 ; death of, 233.

Calvert Papers, 250, m. ; 264, n. 17.

Calvin, John, the dominant influence at Geneva, 104 ; on the Sabbath, 124 ; Cotton a follower of, 329.

Calvinism, materials for subjective joys provided by, 327.

Calvinistic churches, efforts to assimilate the Church of England to the, 112 ; controversy adds another issue, 133 ; doctrines popular, 328, 329, 347, n. 4.

Calvinists and Arminians, Laud's attempt to suppress debates between, 194.

Cambridge settled under the name of Newtown, 317.

Cambridge pledge, the, of Winthrop and others, 209.

Camden's Elements of New England, 177, m.

Canada, Brownists ask leave to settle in, 167.

Cannibalism at Jamestown, 39 ; denied by Gates, 65, n. 5.

Cape Anne, failure of Dorchester Company's colony on, 189, 199.

Cape Cod shoals turn back the Mayflower, 177, 186, n. 7.

Carlisle's treatise, 75, m.

Cartwright, leader of the Presbyterians, 112, 136, n. 6.

Cartwright's Admonition to Parliament, 129, m.

Carver, John, chosen governor, 173, 184, n. 4.

Castle Island, platform constructed on, 284.

Catholic conscience, oath made offensive to the, 237.

Catholic migration, the, 220 ; revival in England, 226 ; settlers in Newfoundland, 228, 239 ; Baltimore family openly, 228, 235 ; migration to Maryland small, 240 ; pilgrims very religious, 243, 244, 245 ; tax on Catholic servants in Maryland,

248 ; colony in Maryland until after 1640, 247; at peace with Puritans in Maryland, 254 ; element protected in Maryland, 257 ; party in minority in Maryland, 266.

Catholicism condoned, to conciliate Spain, 238 ; tide toward, in England, 240.

Catholics, Irish, not allowed to settle in Virginia, 231 ; Baltimore's party of, repelled from Virginia, 231 ; harsh laws in England against, 236, 237, 238 ; enforcement of penal statutes against, 239 ; co-religionists of queen, 239 ; toleration and protection to English Catholics in Maryland, 242; no perfect security for, in Maryland, 248 ; rich and influential families of, in Maryland, 264, n. 18 ; conciliation to Protestants at expense of fairness toward, 251 ; papist religion forbidden, 257 ; excluded from toleration in the Netherlands, 298, 312, n. 18.

Catlet, Colonel, reaches the Alleghanies, 11.

Cattle, scarce in Massachusetts colony, 320 ; perished in Connecticut, 324.

Cavalier emigration to Virginia, 345.

Cedar timber exported, 45.

Ceremonies, observance of pompous, 101 ; bitter debates about, 108 ; ceased to be abhorrent, 123.

Certayne Qvestions concerning the high priest's ephod, 108, m.

Chapman, Jonson and Marston's Eastward, Ho! 23, n. 8.

Charles I, coronation robe of silk for, from Virginia, 78 ; obliterated by Puritanism, 133.

Charles II wore silk raised in Virginia, 78.

Charter, the Great, granted by the Virginia Company, 55, 173, 206 ; only information concerning, 70, n. 15.

Charter for a private plantation obtained by Warwick, 51, 68, n. 13.

Charter of New England, 1620, 173 ; of the Massachusetts Company, 210, 218, n. 7; of Avalon, April 7, 1623, 225 ; for precinct in Virginia granted to Leyden pilgrims, 229 ; for new palatinate on north side of the Potomac granted to Baltimore, 233 ;

of Maryland passed, 234 ; terms of the, 234, 235, 236 ; compared with those of Avalon, 234 ; ambiguous, 251.

Charter-House School founded by legacy as Sutton's Hospital, 268 ; attended by Roger Williams, 268.

Chesapeake Bay mapped by Captain John Smith, 36.

Chesapeake region securely English, 345.

Chimes not in accord with a severe Sabbath, 129.

Church, a "particular," Puritans desire to found, 197 ; the unit of New England migration, 325.

Church at Jamestown enlarged, 42, 65, n. 7.

Church economy, each system of, claimed divine authority, 113.

Church, English, Laud sought to make Catholic, 193.

Church government, three periods of, 112, 136, n. 6 ; questions of, fell into abeyance, 137, n. 6 ; Barrowism, the form of, brought to New England, 148 ; Puritans desire to make real their ideal of, 198 ; Puritan passion for, 212.

Church of England repudiated as antichristian, 147 ; divergencies in direction of, in Massachusetts, 267.

Church of the exiles at Frankfort, the factions in developed into two great parties, 105.

Church quarrels at Strasburg and Frankfort, 105 ; reform, no hope of securing, 196, 197.

Churches of Massachusetts formed on model of Robinson's Independency, 213 ; lack of uniformity in the early, 215 ; borrowed discipline and form of government from Plymouth, 215.

Churchill's Voyages, 265, n. 23.

Churchmen, High, aggressive, 113.

Cities of refuge on the Continent, 104 ; English churches organized in, 104.

Civet cat, Hariot thought, would prove profitable, 19.

Claiborne, claim of, to Kent Island, 253.

Clap's, Roger, Memoirs, 213, m.

Clarendon Papers, 67, n. 9.

Clarke's Gladstone and Maryland Toleration, 245, m.

Clergymen most active writers in favor of colonization, 91 ; some preach sermons but stay away from public prayer, 143 ; supported by magistrates in Massachusetts if church order was disturbed, 266 ; men of unusual prudence in ranks of, 266.

Climate of Great Britain not favorable to raising products of the Mediterranean, 75.

Coddington's Letter, 308, n. 9.

Code of Lawes, Divine, Morall, and Martiall, by Sir Thomas Smyth, 70, n. 16 ; 132.

Codfish, multitude of, on coast of Newfoundland, 18.

Coxe, Sir Edward, defended legacy which founded Charter - House School, 268 ; appointed Roger Williams to a scholarship, 268 ; schism detested by, 270.

College proposed and endowed, 91.

Collier's Ecclesiastical History of Great Britain, 263, n. 12.

Colonial Constitution of Virginia modified for the worse, 249.

Colonial Papers, 68, n. 11 ; 71, n. 18 ; 262, n. 11 ; 264, n. 21 ; 265, n. 25 ; 346, n. 1.

Colonial proprietors, 70, n. 15.

Colonial Records of Virginia, 70, n. 15.

Colonies, secondary, 220.

Colonists, efforts of friends to succor, thwarted, 47 ; loss of life among, in Virginia, 58.

Colonization, English, the fate of, settled by the experiments on the James River, 58 ; promoted, to get rid of excess of population, 136, n. 5 ; unwise management ruined many projects for, 178.

Colony, English, rise of the first, 1 ; motives for founding, 73.

Colony government, primary and secondary forms of, 218, n. 7.

Colony of St. Maries, 245.

Colony-planters drawn from the ranks of the uneasy, 171, 220.

Colony-planting, Hakluyt's tireless advocacy of, 5 ; John Smith on, 37 ; spurred by three motives, 74 ; kept alive by delusions, 74 ; first principles of, not understood, 76 ; an economic problem, 84 ; the religious motive most successful in, 189, 220 ; centrifugal forces in, 220, 266.

Commandment, the fourth, held to be partly moral, partly ceremonial, 138, n. 8 ; 140, n. 13 ; Shepard holds it to be wholly moral, 140, n. 13.

Commerce with the Orient, the hope of, retarded settlement, 4.

Commissions, forged, to "press" maidens, 72, n. 19.

Commodities, sixteen staple, exhibited from Virginia, 49 ; production of, the main hope of wealth for Virginia, 75, 97, n. 9.

Commons inclosed, 111, 135, n. 5.

Commons Journal, 71, n. 18.

Communion, withdrawal of, a fundamental principle of Separatism, 271.

Communism at Jamestown, 26, 42 ; abolished, 56 ; attempted at Plymouth, 169, 185, n. 4 ; abolished by Bradford, 180 ; evils of, 186, n. 9.

Compact, the, of the Pilgrims, 173, 183, n. 4 ; 185, n. 5.

Company's Chief Root of Differences, the, 52, m. ; authors of, 69, n. 13.

Congregationalism, rise of, in New England, 214.

Connecticut, a secondary colony, 220 ; the migration to, has an epic interest, 316 ; independent constitution adopted by, 325 ; accounts adverse to, circulated in England, 326.

Connecticut Historical Society Collections, 326, m ; 347, n. 2.

Connecticut River, stories of the fertility of the intervale land on the, 322 ; dangerous Pequots on the, 323 ; soil did not need to be "fished," 324.

Consciences, oppressed, places of refuge for, in the Low Countries, 163.

Conservative and radical, difference between constitutional, 109; churchman limited his Protestantism, 109.

Constitutional government, starting point of, in the New World, 55.

Continent, an arctic and antarctic, 2 ; crossed by Ingram in a year, 14.

Controversie concerning Liberty of Conscience, 300, m.

Conversion of the Indians, desired for the sake of trade, 16, 90, 216, n. 4 ; orders for the, 42 ; interest in, becomes secondary, 204, 209 ;

authorities on the, 216, n. 4 ; by the Catholics, 247.

Convicts asked for by Dale, 47.

Cook's Historical View of Christianity, 138, n. 8.

Cooper, Dr., Bishop of Winchester, answered first Mar-Prelate tract, 116.

Copley, business administrator of Jesuits, 251, 264, n. 17.

Corn not planted at proper season, 44, 60, n. 2 ; ground for, cleared, 48 ; more raised by private than by public labor, 49.

Cotton, John, apparent sanction of Antinomianism by, 267 ; one of the greatest luminaries of the Puritans and one of the lights of New England, 269 ; apostle of theocracy, shaped ecclesiastical affairs in New England, 279, 308, n. 8 ; his rivals left Massachusetts, 280 ; virtually attained a bishop's authority, 280 ; on Williams's book, 282 ; complete system of church-state organization, 287 ; verbal legerdemain on Williams's banishment, 297 ; casuistry of, 299, 313, n. 20 ; 321 ; attitude toward Williams's banishment, 299, 300, 313, n. 21 ; source of his intolerance, 300 ; belongs among the diplomatic builders of churches, 306 ; uncandid and halting accounts of Williams's trial, 309, 310, n. 12 ; 311, n. 17 ; curious sinuosity of conscience, 313, n. 21 ; secured by Boston to balance Newtown's Hooker, 319 ; rivalry with Hooker, 320 ; Puritanism of, grew in a garden of spices, 321 : of a sanguine temperament, 328 ; his advent followed by widespread religious excitement, 329 ; theological differences between his teachings and those of Hooker, 346, n. 1 ; Model of Moses his Judicials, 326 ; opinions recanted and modified by, 336 ; defends Mrs. Hutchinson, 337 ; persuades her to recant, 339 ; disfranchises her sons, 339 ; belated zeal of, against the sectaries, 341 ; wallows in superstition, 341.

Cotton planted, 29.

Cotton's Answer to Williams's Examination, 308, n. 10, 11 ; 310, n. 16 ; 313, n. 20, 21 ; Fountain of Life, 328, m. ; Sermon on the Church's Resurrection, 331, m. ; 334, m ; Way of Congregational Churches, 157, n. 2 ; 219, n. 10 ; 330, m ; 336, m.

Council for New England grants a patent to the Massachusetts projectors, 199, 207.

Councilors of estate in Virginia, 55.

Counter-Blaste to Tobacco, 84, m.

Country, a barren, a great whet to industry, 177.

Courtier, the honor of a, possessed by Calvert, 223 ; the happiest has least to do at court, 258, n. 1.

Courts of High Commission, penalties of, 270.

Covenant of grace *vs.* covenant of works, 331, 334, 335.

Cox, Richard, followers of, dispute with those of John Knox, 105.

Cox's Literature of the Sabbath Question, 127, m. ; 138, n. 8 ; 139, n. 10.

Cradock, Mathew, Governor of the Massachusetts Company, proposes transfer of the government, 206, 208, 209 ; resigned his governorship, 210 ; denounced by Laud, 211 ; letter to Endecott, 216, n. 4.

Credulity about America, 2, 20 ; abyss of seventeenth century, 341.

Customs, low, advocated by Captain John Smith, 37.

Cyuile and Vncyuile Life, 134, n. 1.

Dainties, preachers who spread a table of, complained of, 328, 348, n. 5.

Dainty, Argall's voyage in the, 50.

Dale, Sir Thomas, sent to Virginia, 43 ; tyranny of, 45–47 ; horrible cruelties of, 46 ; services, 47 ; theatrical return, 48, 68, n. 10 ; glowing reports of the country, 49, 168 ; cruelties of, proved, 66, n. 9 ; his severity, 67, n. 9 ; various authorities on, 67, n. 9.

Danvers, Sir John, interested in the Virginia Company, 54 : in power, 71, n. 17 ; one of the fathers of representative government in America, 173.

Darien, Isthmus of, 6.

Davenport, John, took part in the synod, 343 ; with his followers planted the New Haven colony, 343.

Days of the week, scruples about the heathen names of the, 302, 314, n. 23.

Days of fasting and prayer appointed, 324.

De Costa, in Mag. of Amer. Hist., 23, n. 8.

De la Warr, Lady, plundered by Argall, 50.

De la Warr, Lord, sends expedition for gold, 13 ; arrival of, regretted by the old settlers, 41 ; governor at Jamestown, 41 ; resides at the falls of the James, 43 : flight of, from the colony, 43 ; nominally governor, 44 ; ceremonious landing at Jamestown, 101 ; escorted to church by gentlemen and guards, 102.

Deane, Charles, Voyages of Cabot, 21, n. 1 ; misunderstood a statement by Bradford, 184, n. 4.

Debate, the Puritan, 108 ; bitterness of the, 114 ; new issues, 123 ; advantage of new ground of, to the Puritan, 131.

Debates, theological, concerned with speculative dogmas, 108.

Declaration of Virginia, 95, n. 3.

Delft Haven, the parting at, 175.

Delusions in colony-planting, 74.

Deptford, gold-refining works at, 13.

De Rasieres's letter, 103, m.

Dermer, seeking the Pacific, is driven into Long Island Sound, 9.

Description of the Now-discovered river and Country of Virginia, 96, n. 7.

Desertion, Dale's punishment for, 46.

Devil worship, Indian, belief in, 16.

De Vries's Voyages, m., 231.

Dexter, F. B., in Winsor's Narrative and Critical History, 155, m.

Dexter's H. M., Congregationalism, 147, m. ; 157, n. 1 ; 185, n. 6 ; "As to Roger Williams," as erudite as it is one-sided, 311, n. 17.

Discontent, numerous causes for, 111, 135, n. 5.

Discourse of the Old Virginia Company, 54, m. ; 66, n. 9 ; 68, n. 11 ; 70, n. 16.

Discovery, the pinnace, 25.

Dispersions from the mother colony, 315.

Display, love of, in Elizabeth's time,

98 ; greatness declared itself by, 100, 134, n. 2.

Dissension, outbreak of, among the English Protestant exiles, 104.

Dividends, Dale's aim to make the colony pay, 45.

D'Ogeron supplied buccaneers with wives, 71, n. 18.

Dogs as food, 8.

Domestic Correspondence, James I, 134, n. 1.

Dorchester Company, failure of colony of, on Cape Ann, 189, 199.

Dorchester, Mass., church covenant, 219, n. 9 ; ready to follow the lead of Hooker, 323 ; settlers remove from to Connecticut, 324 ; church emigrated bodily, 325.

Drama, the age of the, 99.

Dress, inordinate display in, 134, n. 2 ; laws to repress, 100 ; excesses in, denounced, 120 ; regulations against, in Massachusetts, 285.

Drunkenness, punishment for, 342.

Dudley, a zealous advocate of religious intolerance, 287 ; impatient to snuff out Williams, 288 ; verse by, 288 ; rude and overbearing, 338.

Dudley to the Countess of Lincoln, 174, 317, m.

Durham, legal power of Bishops of, given to proprietor of Maryland, 236, 263, n. 12.

Dutch Government declined to assure the Pilgrims of protection against England, 173 ; made tempting offers to the Independents, 176 ; despised for showing toleration, 298, 311, n. 18 ; laid claim to the Connecticut, 323 ; occupation giving way, 346.

Duties, heavy, on tobacco, 85, 96, n. 8.

Dyer, Mary, misfortune of, 340.

East India Company's agents, cruelty of, 67, n. 9.

East Indies, desire for a short passage to the, 3, 4, 5, 12, 22, n. 5.

Eastward, Ho ! the play of, 23.

Ecclesiastical Commission, the inquisitorial, 114.

Ecclesiastical extension desired by the English Church, 90 ; organization of the Brownists dominant, 141 ; politics explosive in Massachusetts,

326 ; system of government, petty tyranny that inheres in, 342.

Economic success of the Virginia colony assured, 49 ; adverse conditions more deadly than an ungenial climate, 78 ; problems solved by homely means, 84.

Edwards, T., Antapologia, 217, n. 4.

Eliot, Sir John, confined in the Tower, 203.

Eliot, John, convinced of error, 290, 291 ; usher and disciple of Hooker, 317.

Eliot's Biography, 201, m. ; 288, m.

Elizabeth, Queen, jeweled dresses of, 98 ; gorgeous progresses of, 99 ; could not compel uniformity, 109 ; threatens to unfrock a bishop, 110 ; molded the church to her will, 112 ; her policy of repression resulted in the civil war, 114 ; greatest popularity in last years of her reign, 121.

Elizabethan age, the, 1 ; prodigal of daring adventure, 20.

Ellis Letters, The, 182, n. 1.

Ellis collection, first series, 238, m.

Elton's brief biography of Roger Williams, 311, n. 17.

Emigrants sail for Virginia, 25 ; bad character of the, 27, 59.

Emigration to New England quickened by troubles that preceded the civil war, 344 ; reached greatest height in 1638, 344 ; ceased entirely in 1640, 344 ; to Virginia and Maryland, received impetus from check of Puritan exodus, 344, 345.

Emmanuel College, Cambridge, the cradle of Puritan divines, 316.

Endecott, John, leadership and character of, 200 ; cut arm of cross from English colors, 201 ; put Quakers to death, 202 ; impetuous radicalism of, 271 ; protested against the double injustice to Salem, 291 ; arrested, apologized, and submitted, 291 ; witnesses for Mrs. Hutchinson browbeaten by, 338.

England, danger from, feared in Massachusetts, 284, 285.

English, character of the, at the period of Elizabeth and James, 20 ; sober living of, 342 ; superior aptitude of, for planting agricultural communities, 346 ; compactness of settlement and increase of, decided the fate of North America, 346.

English knowledge and notions of America, 1 ; first protest against oppression, 56 ; jealousy of Spain, 74, 94, n. 1 ; ecclesiastics reproached by Roman Catholics, 90, 97, n. 11 ; Church leaders not content while Spanish priests converted infidels, 90 ; eminent clergy among the exiled, 104 ; churches organized in cities of refuge, 104 ; beginning of two parties in the Church, 107 ; heads of the Church attacked by Mar-Prelate, 115 ; laws against Catholics embarrass the foreign policy, 238 ; rise of the first of the colonies, 1 ; prospective ascendency of the colonies, 345.

English Protestantism. See PROTESTANTISM, ENGLISH.

Ephod of Jewish high priest, discussion of material of, 108.

Epworth, the nest of Methodism, 150.

Esquimaux kidnaped by Frobisher, 17.

Eustachius and his document dropped from heaven, 138, n. 8.

Evans, Owen, accused of "pressing" maidens, 72, n. 19.

Evelyn's Diary, 18, m. ; 134, n. 1.

Excerpta de Diversis Literis, 246, m.

Excommunication dreaded by the Puritans, 339.

Exiles, the English, 104 ; return of, 107 ; results of their squabbles, 107.

Exploration, American, the history of, a story of delusion and mistake, 3 ; retarded settlement, 4.

Extravagance of Indian tales, 8.

Factions at Jamestown, 36, 64, n. 4.

Fairs and markets on Sundays, 138, n. 8.

Faith, devotion to, 245.

Families, the colony a camp of men without, 42 ; a plantation can never flourish without, 57 ; some, sent to Virginia with De la Warr, 65, n. 8.

Family of Love, Anne Hutchinson accused of accepting the doctrines of the, 335.

Famine at Jamestown, 38, 65, n. 5.

Fast day, a, appointed in Massachusetts, 286.

Ferrar, John, election of, 71, n. 17 ; deputy governor, 91.

Ferrar, Nicholas, Jr., deputy governor of Virginia Company, 91 ; established a religious community at Little Gidding, 92 ; austere discipline of, 93 ; mediæval enthusiasm of, 194.

Ferrar, Nicholas, Sr., courts of Virginia Company held at house of, 91 ; gave money for educating infidels in Virginia, 91.

Ferrars, the, among the founders of liberal institutions in America, 173.

Firearms, sale of, to the savages, 191, 216, n. 1.

Firmin's, Giles, Review of Davis's Vindication, 348, n. 5.

Fisheries, American, importance of, foreseen, by Capt. John Smith, 37 ; of Newfoundland, 261, n. 7.

Fishing on Sunday, ordinances against, 127.

Fishing seasons in the James River learned, 49.

Fleet, Henry, only survivor of Spelman's party, 22, n. 7.

Fleet's Journal, 23, n. 7.

Flemish Protestants favored independency, 158, n. 2.

Font, the stone, at which Bradford was baptized, 151.

Food, bad and insufficient, 45, 46.

Force, men not to be converted by, 312, n. 19.

Formalities, proper, never omitted, 41, 101 ; at Plymouth, 102.

Founding of a state a secondary end, 73.

Fox, Luke, sails to the northwest, 10.

Franck's, Sebastian, Chronica, 314, n. 24.

Frankfort, disputes in the church at, produced great results, 105 ; character of debates at, 105 ; rapid changes produced by the, 106, 135, n. 3.

Freemen's oath extended to residents, 289, 308, n. 11 ; opposed by Williams, 289, 309, n. 12.

Fresh River of the Dutch, the Connecticut, 324.

Frobisher's, Sir Martin, voyages, 2, 4, n. 1 ; brilliant failure, 5 ; attempt to plant a colony, 7 ; finds "gold eure," 13 ; Voyages, 21, n. 1.

Fuller, Thomas, judgment of Captain John Smith, 63, n. 3.

Fuller's Church History, 103, m. ; 131, m. ; 157, n. 1 : 160, m. ; Worthies, 259, n. 6.

Gainsborough, the hamlet of, 150.

Gammell's Life of Roger Williams, 311, n. 17.

Gardens, private, apportioned in Virginia, 48, 49, 68, n. 12.

Gates, Sir Thomas, wrecked on the Bermudas, 40 ; abandoned the wreck of Jamestown, 41, 101 ; sent to England for cattle, 41 ; denied that human flesh was eaten, 65, n. 5 ; installed governor in proper form, 101.

General Court of Massachusetts protested against selection of Williams as a minister of the Salem church, 271 ; prevented his ordination, 272, 307, n. 5 ; makes regulations for dress, 285 ; appointed a fast day, 286 ; promulgated a new resident's oath, 289 ; "convented" Williams several times, 289 ; forced Salem into submission, 291, 293 ; tried and banished Williams, 292 ; fearing his settlement at Narragansett Bay, agreed to send him to England, 294 ; banished scores for their opinions, 297 ; the real extenuation for the conduct of the, 297 ; character of the age forbids condemnation of, 300.

Geneva, the city of refuge for the Puritans, 104 ; differences between exiles at, and those at Zurich, 107.

Gibbons, Captain, of Boston, commission sent to, 252.

Gilbert, Sir Humphrey, on a northwest passage, 5 ; attempt to plant a colony, 7.

Glass-blowers ran away to the Indians, 83.

Glass, window, not used in the colony, 65, n. 7.

Glass-works established near Jamestown, 83, 95, n. 5.

Glastonbury, also called Avalon, 258, n. 3.

Glover in Phil. Trans., 11, m.

Godspeed, The, 25.

Gold and silver, exportation of, restrained by law, 75.

Gold, belief in finding, in North America, 12, 14, 22, n. 7 ; 75.

Gold-hunting, 7, 12 ; in Virginia, 13, 23, 42.

Gold mines of the Hudson River, 23.

Gondomar's spies in the Virginia Company, 87 ; influence over Calvert, 226, 258, n. 2.

Goodman's Court of King James, 258, n. 2.

Goodwin, Thomas, and others, Apologetical Narrative, 185, n 6.

Gorges's Briefe Narration, 196, m.

Gowns and litanies, squabbles about, 107.

Gosnold, agitating for a new colony, 33 ; failure of colony in Buzzard's Bay established by, 178.

Government, democratic, established by the Pilgrims before sailing, 185, n. 5 ; three primary steps for, in America, due to Englishmen who did not cross the sea, 205.

Government, representative form of, established, 55, 89 ; faint promise of, in Maryland charter, 234.

Governmental functions exercised by commercial corporations, 218, n. 8.

Grace after meat opposed by Williams, 289, 290, 292, 309, n. 12.

Greenham's, Richard, MS. on the Sabbath, 128.

Greenwood, leader of the Separatists, hanged at Tyburn, 148.

Grenville, Sir Richard, sent to Virginia by Ralegh, 21, n. 3.

Guiana or North America, Pilgrims choose between, 169.

Guicciardini on use of spices, 22, n. 5.

Guilds, dissolution of the, 111.

Haies in Hakluyt's Voyages, 5, m.

Hakluyt, Richard, a forerunner of colonization, 5 ; belief of, in a passage to the Pacific, 6 ; stories of gold, 12 ; of mulberry trees, 76.

Hakluyt's Discourse on Western Planting, 6, m. ; 94, n. 1 ; 97, n. 11 ; Voyages, 2 ; 5, m. ; 8, m. ; 12, m. ; 23, n. 8.

Hamor, Raphe, secretary under Dale, a signer of the Tragicall Relation, 66, n. 9 ; True Discourse, 66, n. 9 ; 68, n. 12 ; 70, n. 16 ; 95, n. 3.

Hampton Court conference, 159 ; authorities on the, 182, n. 1.

Hanbury's Memorials, 157, n. 1, n. 2 ; 158, n. 3.

Hancock, Thomas, the Luther of England, 125.

Hanging clemency, 46 ; preferred to transportation to Virginia, 54 ; and to the old tyranny, 56.

Hardwicke Papers, 238, m.

Hariot's Briefe and True Report, 80, m.

Harleian Miscellany, 240 m.

Harrington's Nugæ Antiquæ, 116, m. ; 161, m. ; 162, m. ; 182, n. 1.

Harrisse's, Henry, John Cabot, the Discoverer of America, 21, n. 1.

Hartlib's Reformed Virginia Silkworm, 79.

Harvey, Sir John, sends expedition for gold, 13 ; Governor of Virginia, 249 ; quarreled with Virginians, 249 ; counter-revolution, 249.

Hawkins, Jane, Mrs. Hutchinson an associate of, 340.

Hawkins, Sir John, lands luckless seamen in Mexico, 14.

Haynes, Governor of Massachusetts, 332 ; pronounced sentence against Williams, 347, n. 1 ; letter to Williams while Governor of Connecticut quoted, 347, n. 1.

Health to the Gentlemanly Profession of Servingmen, 134, n. 1.

Hearne's Langtoft's Chronicle, 93, m.

Hening's Statutes, 78, m. ; 79, m. ; 97, n. 9.

Henrietta Maria, Maryland named for, 245 ; godmother to Maryland, jealous of Calvert, 249.

Henry, Prince, interested in Virginia colony, 43.

Henry, William Wirt, Address, 63, n. 3.

Hessey's Bampton Lectures, 139, n. 10.

Hind's Making of the England of Elizabeth, 135, n. 3.

Hinman's Antiquities, 347, n. 2.

Hogs, brood, of the colony eaten, 38 ; wild, in the Bermudas, 41, 65, n. 6.

Holinshed's Chronicles, 22, n. 5.

Holland, the "mingle mangle of religions" in, 164.

Holmes's History of Cambridge, 318, m. ; 320, m.

Home, Virginia for the first time a, 58.

Home-makers sent to Virginia, 57, 58.

Homesteads at Newtown sold to newcomers, 325, 347, n. 3.

Hooft, Nederlandsche Historie, 312, n. 18.

Hooker, Thomas, one of the greatest

luminaries of the Puritans, 269; desire of his party to move to Connecticut, 285, 315; set to dispute with Williams, 292; early life of, 316; driven from his pulpit by Laud, 317; fled to Holland, 317; a company of his people settled at Newtown, 317; arrival at Newtown, 319; rivalry with Cotton, 320; somber theology of, 320; difference between his teachings and those of Cotton, 321, 346, n. 1; theories of civil government more liberal than Cotton's, 322; limited the power of the magistrate, 322, 347, n. 2; the real founder of Connecticut, 325.

Hornbeck on John Robinson, 158, n. 3.

Horses eaten, 38.

Houses burned for firewood, 40.

Hubbard's History of Massachusetts, 308, n. 8; History of New England, 207, m.; 215, m.; 347, n. 3; testimony of, unreliable, 311, n. 17.

Hudson, Henry, influenced by Captain John Smith, seeks the South Sea, 9.

Hudson River gold, 23, n. 7.

Huguenots of La Rochelle, England allied with, 239.

Humming birds exported, 18.

Hundreds or plantations, 54, 55.

Hunt, Robert, first minister in Virginia, 90.

Hunter, Rev. Joseph, on Shakespeare's Tempest, 65, n. 6.

Hunter's Founders of New Plymouth, 150, m.; 152, m.; 155, m.; 170, m.

Hutchinson, Mrs. Anne, an ardent disciple of Cotton in old Boston, 329: character of, 329, 330; "masterpiece of womens wit," 330; meetings for women opened by, 330; doctrines of, 331; the very apostle of Cotton's doctrine, 333; brought to trial by her opponents, 337; adroit defense, 338; condemned by the General Court, 338; sentenced to banishment, 339; recanted, but was excommunicated, 339, 348, n. 8; her sons disfranchised, 339; settled in Rhode Island with her party, 340; accused of witchcraft by Winthrop, 340; wild reports about, 340, 341;

massacred by Indians at New Netherland, 341.

Hutchinson on the Virginia Colony, 186, n. 8.

Hutchinson Papers, 215, m.; 299, m.; 307, m.; 329, n. 1.

Hutchinson party partisans of Vane, 332; arrogance of the, 333; Pastor Wilson condemned by, 333.

Hutchinson's History of Massachusetts Bay, 211, m.; 337, m.

Hutchinsonian controversy, the, 326, 327; the debate waxed hot, 334.

Hypocrites better than profane persons, 299.

Idolatry, Puritanism a crusade against, 118.

Illusions of discoverers, 3, 75.

Inclosures, effects of, 135, n. 5; for private not the publick good, 136, n. 5.

Independency, tendency toward, 112, 136, n. 6; foreshadowed at Frankfort, 137, n. 6; dated back to reign of Mary, 146; favored by Flemish Protestants, 158, n. 2; Robinsonian, the established religion in New England, 215.

Independents in early years of Elizabeth's reign, 158, n. 2.

Indian children, rewards to colonists for educating, 91.

Indian conjurers laid spell on the coast, 178.

Indian exhumed and eaten at Jamestown, 39.

Indians plot destruction of the colonists, 8; curiosity regarding the, 15; desire to convert, 16, 90; kidnapped and exhibited, 17; attack those first landing in Virginia, 28; constant fear of attack from, 30; supply food to Jamestown, 31, Smith trades with, 34, 36; devilish ingenuity in torturing, 38; outrage the dead, 38, 64, n. 4; slay gold hunters, 43; no danger from, while Dale was in charge, 47; taken to England by Dale, 49, 68, n. 10; unnecessary cruelty to, 64, n. 4; reverence for their sacred house, 64, n. 4; endowed school established for, 83, 91; schemes for educating obliterated, 92; treachery of, emulated by the settlers, 92; destruction of, in Maryland and in Massachusetts divinely ordered, 247 ; right of the king to give away lands of, questioned, 274, 282, 283 ; land secured from, by purchase, 283.

Industrial disturbance aids the Puritan movement, 111.

Infallibility of "godly" elders, 301.

Ingram, Davy, crosses the continent, 14 ; statement, 14, 23, n. 8.

Injunctions by King Edward VI, 138, n. 9.

Interludes sometimes played in churches, 129.

Intolerance sanctioned by logic, 299.

Iron works established at Falling Creek, 83 ; failure of, 96, n. 6.

Isthmus in latitude 40°, belief in an, 10.

James I framed code of laws and orders for the Virginia colony, 26 ; Covnter-Blaste to Tobacco, 84 ; obstinacy of, 87 ; his accession raised the hopes of the Puritans, 159 ; paradoxical qualities of, 160 ; dialectic skill at Hampton Court conference, 160 ; refutes the hapless Puritans, 161 ; boasts that he had peppered the Puritans, 162, 182, n. 1 ; results of his folly, 162 ; would wink at but not publicly tolerate the Pilgrims, 170 ; refused guarantee of toleration, 173 ; friendship with George Calvert, 223 ; revenue from fines of lay Catholics, 238 ; Apologie for the Oath of Allegiance, 238.

James, Puritan minister in Maryland, 253.

James River discovered by the accident of a storm, 27 ; settlement near the falls of the, 37.

James River experiments, the, 25 ; their story the overture to the history of life in the United States, 58.

Jamestown, causes of suffering at, 13 ; founded, 29 ; at first a peninsula, 29 ; abandoned, 41 ; population in 1616, 49 ; in 1889, 59, n. 1 ; some drawings of, 60, n. 1.

Jamestown Company, the. See VIRGINIA COMPANY, THE.

Jamestown emigrants instructed to explore rivers to the northwest, 9.

Jesuits flock to England, 226 ; set

free, 239 ; interested in migration to Maryland, 240 ; the provincial of the Society of Jesus favored toleration, 242 ; religious observances of, at sea, 243 ; conversion of non-Catholics in Maryland by, 246 ; fled to Virginia, 257.

Jesus, the humane pity of, unknown to the laws and sermons of the time, 301, 313, n. 22.

Johnson, Bradley T., Foundation of Maryland, 263, n. 15.

Johnson, Edward, the bloodthirsty Massachusetts Puritan, 164 ; his Wonder-working Providence, 318, m. ; 320, m. ; 330, m.

Johnson, Francis, voyage of, to America, 167 ; pastor at Amsterdam, 168.

Johnston, Isaac, of Winthrop's company, death of, 212.

Jones, captain of The Mayflower, conduct of, 177 ; identified with Jones of The Discovery, 186, n. 7.

Jones's, Rev. Hugh, Present State of Virginia, 183, n. 3.

Josselyn's Rarities, 344, m.

Judgment, present, not a binding law, 185, n. 6.

Judgments, divine, fear of, 198.

Kent Island, Claiborne's claim to, 254.

Knowles's Life of Williams, 274, m. ; 308, n. 9 ; the best of the older biographies, 311, n. 17.

Knox, John, followers of, dispute with the Coxans at Frankfort, 105 ; not more a sabbatarian than Calvin, 124.

Labor, common-stock system of, at Jamestown, 26 ; abolished by distribution of land, 56 ; failure of, at Plymouth, 179 ; evils of, 186, n. 9.

Labor, private, more productive than common-stock system, 49 ; prohibited on Sundays, 127.

Laborers, twelve so-called, in the Virginia colony, 27.

Land, division of, in Virginia, 48, 49, 56, 68, n. 12.

Land grants, various, in Virginia, based on the Grand Charter, 56, 70, n. 15.

Lane, Ralph, governor of Ralegh's

first colony, 7, 21, n. 3 ; seeks gold and the South Sea, 8 ; account in Hakluyt, iii, 8, m. ; hopes for his Roanoke colony, 74 ; to Sydney and Walsingham, 74, m.

Latitude of 40°, belief of a westward passage in, 9, 10.

Laud, Archbishop, obliterated by Puritanism, 133 ; one great service of, to the world, 193 ; character of, 193 ; fearless in peril, 195 ; dubbed "the father of New England," 196 ; Letter to Selden, 196 ; Abbott's account of Laud's rise, 216, n. 2 ; fails to crush the Massachusetts Company, 211 ; suppressing Puritanism, 239 ; fall of, 240 ; non-conforming Puritans hunted from lectureships and chaplaincies by, 270 ; drove John Cotton to New England, 279 ; moving to vacate the Massachusetts charter, 282 ; made head of a commission to govern the colonies, 284; drove Hooker from his pulpit at Chelmsford, 317 ; preparations to control Massachusetts made by, 343 ; asked to stop emigration to New England, 344 ; tries to compel Scots to use prayer book, 344.

Laws, divine, moral, and martial, under which Dale oppressed Virginia, 45, 70, n. 16 ; 132.

Leah and Rachel, 79, m. ; 265, n. 25.

Lederer, voyage of, from Virginia, 11, m.

Legislative body established by the Great Charter, 55.

Leland, John, Itinerary, 152, m.

Lenox, Duke of, territory assigned to, 259, n. 5.

Letters of complaint intercepted, 47.

Letters of Missionaries, 264, n. 17, n. 18.

Leyden, Scrooby exiles remove to, 166 ; Pilgrims set out from, 174.

Liberty in religion congruous with civil peace, 315.

Lingard, 238, m.

Little Gidding, Ferrar's community at, 92 ; devastated by the Puritans, 93.

Liturgy, a, purified of human tradition, 106 ; omitted in many parishes, 142.

London Separatists, 147 ; organize a church, 148 ; miserably persecuted, some flee to Amsterdam, 148.

Long Island Sound, Dermer storm-driven into, 9.

Long Island, English settlers on, 345.

Lord's Prayer, repetition of the, thought dangerously liturgical, 117.

Lotteries of the Virginia Company, 69, n. 14 ; abolished, 53, 70, n. 14.

Low Countries, toleration in the, 163 ; condemned by Baylie, 164.

Luther, Martin, on the Sabbath, 124.

Machyn's Diary, 99, m.

Magellan's Strait, 2, 9.

Magistrates aided by clergy in Massachusetts, 266; men of unusual ability, 266 ; right of, to punish for a religious offense, denied by Williams, 272, 286 ; or to regulate the orthodoxy of churches and the belief of individuals, 292, 309, n. 12 ; 310, n. 13.

Magna Charta, the, of America, 55.

Maids by the shipload sent to Jamestown, 57 ; not coerced into going, 72, n. 19.

Maine, French driven out of, 50 ; first English colony in, 189 ; fishing villages of, 345.

Manchester, Duke of, papers, 71, n. 18 ; 174, m. ; 184, n. 5.

Manuscript Book of Instructions, 71, n. 18 ; 72, n. 19 ; 80, m. ; 96, n. 6 ; 97, n. 9 ; 232, m.

Manuscript Records, Virginia Company, 52, m. ; 61, n. 3 ; 67, n. 9 ; 69, n. 13, 14 ; 70, n. 15 ; 71, n. 18 ; 72, n. 19 ; 81, m.; 82, m. ; 95, n. 3 ; 97, n. 9, 10 ; 172, m. ; 184, n. 4.

Mar-Prelate tracts, the, 114 ; answers to the, 116 ; effects of the reaction against, 121.

Marriage by a Roman priest invalidated accruing land tenures, 237.

Marsden's Early Puritans, 125.

Martial law under Dale, 45 ; Smyth's code of, 70, n. 16 ; 132.

Martin, Sir William, on Roger Williams, 307, n. 1.

Martyr, Peter, Decade III, 24, n. 9.

Maryland, Baltimore's projected colony in, 236 ; change to, from Avalon, 239 ; small migration to, 240 ; policy of toleration in, 242, 250, 265, n. 25 ; committed to guardian angels, 243 ; arrival of the Catholic pilgrims, 244 ; ceremonies of the landing in, 244 ; said to have been named by King Charles, 245 ; called Colony of St. Maries, 245 ; efforts to convert the Protestants in, 246 ; openly a Catholic colony, 247, 264, n. 17 ; import tax on Catholic servants and convicts, 248, 264, n. 19 ; opposition to Maryland, 249 ; Puritan settlers invited, 252 ; civil wars of, 253, 254 ; Act of Toleration passed, 255 ; again a proprietary government under Calvert, 257 ; disastrous results of religious differences in, 266.

Maryland Archives, 245, m.; 262, n. 10 ; 265, n. 21.

Maryland Assembly too cunning to be trapped by Baltimore, 255.

Maryland charter, ambiguity of the, designed, 225, 236, 251, 259, n. 4 ; 262, n. 11 ; compared with charter of Avalon, 234 ; provisions of, 235, 236 ; extensive powers granted by, 236, 263, n. 12.

Mass celebrated in defiance of law, 226 ; abhorred by the Puritans in Avalon, 228.

Massachusetts Bay, failure of commercial settlements on, 189 ; patent to lands in, granted to the Massachusetts Company, 207.

Massachusetts charter, Laud's effort to vacate the, 282, 284.

Massachusetts colony, government under Endecott, 217, n. 7 ; people homogenous in religious affairs, 266 ; religious opinion, main source of disturbance in, 266, 267 ; self-consciousness of the, 278 ; preparations for resistance in, 284 ; failure as an agricultural colony, 320 ; three profound disturbances in, 326 ; in commotion over the Hutchinson controversy, 335.

Massachusetts Company, rise of the, 199, 207 ; first colony of, under John Endecott, 199, 207 ; second company of emigrants, 203 ; fear that the charter might be revoked, 208 ; company and colony to be merged in one, 209 ; transfers its government and charter to Massachusetts Bay, 210 ; the commercial corporation becomes a colonial government, 211 ; the colonists believed they were founding a new church, 212.

Massachusetts government, evolution of the, 207 ; first court of, at Charlestown, 210 ; later became representative, 211 ; relieved from strain by the borough system, 276 ; a government of congregations, 308, n. 6 ; theocratical, 279 ; religious intolerance of the, 297, 349, n. 9 ; anomalous in character, 323 ; angered by Hooker's secession, 326.

Massachusetts Historical Collections, 310, n. 15 ; 318, m. ; 320, m. ; 347, n. 1 ; 348, n. 7.

Massachusetts Records, 206, m. ; 285, m. ; 290, m.; 291, m. ; 308, n. 11 ; 310, n. 13, 17 ; 317, m.; 320, m.; 337, m.

Massacre by the Indians put an end to all projects, 84, 92.

Masson's Life of Milton, 137, n. 6.

Mather's Magnalia, 152, m. ; 154, m. ; 217, n. 5 ; 328, m. ; authority to be disregarded, 311, n. 17.

Maverick, Samuel, on Noddle's Island, 190 ; Description of New England, 273, m.

Maydstown laid off in Virginia, 72, n. 19.

Mayflower, conduct of the captain of the, 177.

Maynard to Laud, 344, m.

May-poles, opposition to, 118 ; pole of St. Andrew Undershaft sawed up, 119 ; law against May-poles, 119 ; the frolics around charged with immorality, 120 ; Morton's, at Merrymount, 190, 201.

Mediterranean Sea, a, looked for in the heart of America, 11.

Meeting, last all-night, in Pastor Robinson's house, 175.

Mennonites, Williams attracted to the doctrines of the, 312, n. 19 ; derived his broadest principles from the, 313, n. 19.

Mercurius Americanus, 348, n. 6.

Merrymount, Morton's dangerous settlement at, 190, 201, 216, n. 1.

Metals, the precious, the only recognized riches, 75.

Mica mistaken for gold, 13, 30, 75.

Migration, the great, to New England, 196, 203.

Millinary Petition, the, 159.

Millinery sins, regulations against, 285.

Mills's British India, 67, n. 9.

Milton, John, learned Dutch from Roger Williams, 273.

Mines, Mexican, reports of wealth of, brought support to Ralegh's undertaking, 74.

Ministerial office never so reverenced as by Puritans, 338.

Ministers, two, over one church, 106 ; might prophesy, but not a woman, 338.

Missionary impulse, first, in the English Church, 89, 94, n. 1.

Monatesseron, the earliest English, 93.

Montserrat, island of, settled by Catholics, 231, 232, 261, n. 9.

Months, scruples about the heathen names of the, 302.

Morals, austerity in, 119 ; advance of, under Puritan influence, 121 ; lack of sense of proportion is a trait of the age, 130 ; regularity of, purchased at a great sacrifice, 342.

More, Father Henry, 263, n. 14.

Morton, Thomas, and his deviltry, 190, 201, 216, n. 1 ; Memorial, 177, m. ; New English Canaan, 216, n. 1.

Motives for founding English colonies, 73 ; commercial and sentimental, 86 ; religious, 89, 189.

Mount Desert, Jesuit settlement at, plundered, 47, 50.

Mourt's Relation, 184, n. 4.

Mouse and snake, battle between, 277 ; interpretation of, by Pastor John Wilson, 277.

Mouse nibbles a Book of Common Prayer, 278.

Movements, significant, usually cradled in rustic mangers, 146.

Mulberries first planted in England, 76 ; law for promoting the raising of, in Virginia, 77 ; repealed, 79.

Muskrat skins valued for their odor, 19.

Names, fanciful, of the Newfoundland coast, 225, 229.

Names, Indian, of places changed, 244.

Nansemond, settlement at, 37 ; settlers driven from, 38.

Narragansett Bay recommended to Williams by Winthrop, 293 ; proposal to remove to, alarmed the magistrates, 294 ; colony on, founded on the true principle, 316.

Narragansett Club Publications, 135, n. 4 ; 268, m.; 307, n. 3, 4, 5; 311, n. 17.

Naval stores, Virginia expected to produce, 82 ; efforts to procure, in Elizabeth's time, 95, n. 4.

Neal's History of New England, 310, n. 14 ; History of the Puritans, 159, m. ; 226, m.; 239, m.

Neill, E. D., on the social compact, 183, n. 4; Founders of Maryland, 262, n. 11 ; Virginia Company, 67, n. 9 ; 183, n. 2.

Netherlands, indirect interest of the, in the Virginia colony, 44.

New England, coast of, explored by Capt. John Smith, 37 ; shaped in Old England by Puritanism, 133 ; pioneers of, came from the Separatists, 141, 146 ; existence of, hung on a chain of accidents, 176 ; elements of, 177 : early attempts to colonize, 178 ; early settlements in, 189; great migration to, 196, 203 ; capital laws of, condemned by Williams, 304.

New England charter of 1620, 173.

New England colonists deemed themselves a chosen people, 278 ; accounted other colonists the Egyptians of the New World, 278, 308, n. 7 ; held to an intolerant theocracy, 279 ; dispersions of the, 315 ; relief at disappearance of the last of the leaders, 342.

New England Firebrand Quenched, 301, m.

New England Historical Gen. Reg., 267 ; 307, n. 1.

New England Puritanism more ultra than Bownd, 132, 140, n. 3.

New England traits due to special causes, 178.

Newfoundland, failure of colony at, 223, 224 ; Capt. Whitbourne's pamphlet on, 224 ; fanciful names in, 225 ; not a paradise in winter, 229, 260, n. 7 ; value of the fisheries, 261, n. 7.

New France bubble ready to collapse, 346.

New Haven, Davenport and his company planted colony at, 343 ; colony united with Connecticut by royal charter at the Restoration, 343; stretching westward, 345.

New Life of Virginea, 63, n. 3.

New Plymouth, Sandys's plans for the foundation of, 88.

Newport, Vice-Admiral, reporter of Virginia affairs, 44; threatened with the gallows by Dale, 44; warned against Archer, 64.

Newtown, Hooker's company settled at, 317; intended for capital and palisaded, 318; superior to Boston in one regard, 318; discontent at, 318, 319, 320; questions regarding boundary, 319; cattle-raising at, 320; the church at, emigrated bodily to Connecticut, 325; court of elections held at, 335.

New World, mirages of the, 2; discovered because it lay between Europe and the East Indies, 3; grotesque and misleading glimpses of the, 20.

New York Colonial Documents, 6, m., 43, m.

New York Hist. Soc. Coll., 23, n. 7; second series, 70, n. 15; 80, m.

Nichols's, Josias, Plea for the Innocent, 146, m.

Nonconformists, severe measures against, 122; in the Church, 142.

North Carolina, coast of, called Wingandacon, 21, n. 3.

Northey, Sir Edward, decision on the Maryland charter, 262, n. 11.

Northwest passage, search for a, 4, 5, 9, 10, 11.

Nova Albion, 259, n. 5.

Nova Brittania, 82, m.

Oath of allegiance, 241; emigration oath refused by Williams, 270; new oath for residents opposed by Williams, 289; magistrates unable to enforce, 289.

Ogle's Account of Maryland, 264, n. 19.

Oil to be distilled from walnuts, 83.

Oldham, John, an adventurous man of lawless temper expelled from Plymouth, 324; led a small company from Watertown, 324.

Opossum, the, described by Purchas, 18.

Opposition, Puritanism the party of, 110.

Original Records of Colony of Virginia, 78, m.

Overston, sermons preached in, by unlicensed men, 142.

Pacific Ocean, discovery of the, 3; belief in a passage to the, 4, 6; nearness to Florida, 6: sought *via* the James River, 8; in latitude 40°, 9, 10; *via* the Delaware, 10; proximity of, to Virginia, 10, 22, n. 6; to North Carolina, 11.

Pagitt's Heresiography, 143, m.; 144, m.; 157, n. 1.

Palfrey's History of New England, 211, m.; 218, n. 8.

Palisades burned for firewood, 40.

Paradox, the, of colonial religious organization, 280.

Parkinson, Marmaduke, explorer, 10.

Parliamentary freedom, struggle for, 87.

Parties, the two great, of Protestantism, rise of, 106; results, 107; lines between, not sharply drawn at once, 110; controversy between, grew more bitter, 114.

Party, a moderate, lamented the excesses of the extremists, 117.

Passage to the Pacific Ocean sought, 3, 4, 9, 10, 22, n. 5; 73, 74. See also NORTHWEST PASSAGE and PACIFIC OCEAN.

Patent, royal, validity of, questioned by Williams, 274, 281, 289, 308, n. 9; 309, n. 12.

Patience, the, pinnace, built wholly of wood, 41.

Paulus, Pieter, Verklaring der Unie van Utrecht, 312, n. 18.

Pearce, Mistress, "near twenty years" in Virginia, 71, n. 18.

Pearl fisheries in Virginia waters, 95, n. 3.

Peckard's Life of Ferrar, 65, n. 5; 87, m.; 93, m.; account of, 97, n. 10; 100, m.

Peirce, John, received a grant from the Virginia Company, 184, n. 4.

Pequot war, Williams denounced slaughter of women and children in, 305; plan of campaign changed through a revelation, 338.

Pequots dangerous on Connecticut River, 323.

Percy, George, on the arrival at Virginia, 28 ; on the sufferings at Jamestown, 30 ; increased the hostility of the Indians, 38, 64, n. 4 ; inefficiency as governor, 44, 60, n. 2 ; succeeded by Gates, 101.

Percy to Northumberland, 46, m. ; Trewe Relacyon, 40, m. ; 60, n. 2 ; 64, n. 4 ; 65, n. 5.

Perfect Description of Virginia, 11, m.

Perfume to be extracted from the muskrat, 95, n. 3.

Persecution in Queen Mary's time, 103 ; spirit of, pervaded every party, 113 ; of the Separatists, 141 ; begot Separatism, 154, 155 ; new storm of, 163, 182, n. 1 ; starts agitation for emigration to Virginia, 168, 183, n. 2.

Peter, Hugh, rebuked Cotton for defending Mrs. Hutchinson, 337 ; browbeat Mrs. Hutchinson's witnesses, 338 ; returned to England and favored toleration, 348, n. 7.

Petition to House of Lords, 345, m.

Pharisaism of the rigid Sabbath, 132.

Philosophical Transactions, 78, m. ; 79, m.

Pilgrims brought Barrowism to New England, 148 ; Scrooby and Austerfeld cradles of the, 149 ; no tradition of, lingers at Scrooby, 150 ; common country folk, 151 ; flee to Amsterdam, 164 ; theological agitations drive them to Leyden, 165 ; danger of extinction, 166 ; intermarriages with the Dutch, 167 ; emigration to Virginia under consideration, 168, 182, n. 2 ; questioned whether to be Dutch or English colonists, 169 ; ask aid of Edwin Sandys, in securing religious liberty, 169 ; receive two charters, a general order, and a liberal patent from the Virginia Company, 172 ; their Compact under the general order, 173 ; departure from Leyden, 174 ; forced to land, select Plymouth, 177 ; suffered for their ignorance of colony-planting, 178 ; honor due, 186, n. 8 ; "stepping stones to others," 188 ; slender success of, stimulated commercial settlements, 189 ; the "large patent" granted to the, through influence of Sandys, 206 ; influence on the Massachusetts colony, 212.

Piscataqua, settlement on the, 189.

Plaine Declaration of Barmudas, 65, n. 6.

Planting, the first, at Jamestown, 29.

Plants of every clime believed to grow in Virginia, 82.

Plays, performance of, on Sundays prohibited, 127.

Pledge signed at Cambridge by Winthrop's party, 209.

Plymouth, ceremony observed at, 103 ; the landing at, 177 ; horrors of Jamestown repeated at, 179 ; the second step in the founding of a great nation, 181 ; Roger Williams "prophesied" at, 272 ; people styled "mungrell Dutch," 273 ; disturbed by Williams, 274 ; gives him a letter of dismissal to Salem, 275.

Pocahontas, 33, 35, 37 ; converted and wedded to Rolfe, 49 ; taken to England, 49, 68, n. 10 ; captured by Argall, 50 ; dies leaving an infant son, 52.

Pocahontas story, the, 63, n. 3.

Pomp and display at the court of Elizabeth, 98 ; imitation of, objected to by the Puritans, 100, 134, n. 2.

Popham, Captain George, attempt of, to colonize in Maine, 178.

Port Royal, map showing strait near, 8, 21, n. 4.

Pory's Report, 70, n. 15 ; 77, m.

Pots and Phettiplace, narrative, 35, 61, n. 2.

Powhatan releases Captain Smith, 33, 34, 35.

Precinct in Virginia asked for by Calvert, 229.

Presbyterianism developed under Cartwright, 112, 136, n. 6 ; swept out by Whitgift, 122 ; hoped for in New England, 213.

Price of commodities, rise of, promoted voyages, 22, n. 5.

Private interest, even a slave's patch of, put life into Virginia, 48.

Proceedings Mass. Hist. Soc., Wheelwright's sermon in, 331, m.

Proceedings of Virginia Assembly, 80, m.

Property, community of. See COMMUNISM ; LABOR.

Prophet, the, and the reformer, 306.

Proportion, lack of sense of, peculiar to zealots and polemics, 130.

Protestant colonists at St. Christopher's oppose Catholic fellow-colonists, 231 ; no Protestant minister or worship on ships coming to Maryland, 242.

Protestant Nunnery, Ferrar's community at Little Gidding called the, 93.

Protestantism, English, rise of the two great parties of, 106, 107 ; controversy grew more bitter, 114 ; incorruptible in Virginia, 231.

Protestantism on the Continent nearly wrecked, 198.

Protestants, English, find refuge on the Continent, 104 ; compromises at home, dissensions in exile, 104 ; the ultra wing tended to democratic church government, 106 ; return after death of Mary, 107 ; their petty squabbles develop into bitter feuds and struggles, 107 ; widespread results, 107 ; Baltimore orders no scandal nor offense to be given to, 250 ; his policy of conciliation toward, in Maryland, 251.

Protestants on the Continent become Roman Catholics, 198.

Providence Plantation founded by Williams, 296 ; fell into inevitable disorders, 315 ; an example of the largest liberty in religion congruous with civil peace, 315.

Provincetown Harbor, the Mayflower in, 177.

Public Records Office Colonial Papers, 54, m.

Pullein's Culture of Silk, 95, n. 2.

Punishments, various, inflicted by Dale, 46.

Purchas his Pilgrimes, 2, 12, m. ; 18, 22, n. 6 ; 24, n. 9, n. 10 ; 28, m. ; 29, m. ; 30, m. ; 64, n. 3 ; 65, n. 6 ; 69, n. 14 ; 80, m. ; 95, n. 3 ; 96, n. 6 ; 97, n. 9 ; 102, m.

Purchas's stories of silver and gold, 12.

Puritan, the, never easy unless he was uneasy, 253.

Puritan community, cost of the good results attained in a, 342.

Puritan conscience, the, let loose against old superstitions, 119.

Puritan divines in high church positions, 143.

Puritan exodus, the great, 188, 239.

Puritan opinions condemned, 103.

Puritan pietists, a new school of, 327.

Puritanism, rise and development of, 98 ; an outgrowth of the time, 103 ; an effort to escape from formalism, 109 ; gathered strength as the leading opposition, 111 ; becomes dogmatic, 112 ; evolutionary, 117 ; importance of secondary development of, 120 ; apparent decline of, 121 ; begun with Elizabeth, seemed doomed to die with her, 122 ; evolves new issues, 123, 137, n. 7 ; opposed to Arminianism, 133 ; set up the Commonwealth, 133 ; threatened destruction of, at Leyden, 167 ; under James I the party of opposition, 191 ; conservative under Charles I, 192 ; unamiable traits of, manifested in Endecott, 202 ; course of events in England adverse to, 203 ; suppression of, by Laud, 239 ; divergencies from, in Massachusetts, 267 ; existed and grew through prudent compromises, 268, 269 ; Salem, north pole of, 271 ; condemned by its false and harsh ideals, 300 ; character of, 300, 301, 342 ; an ascetic system of external duties and abstentions, 327.

Puritans, why so called, 106, 135, n. 4.

Puritans, English, contempt of the, for æsthetic considerations, 94 ; reverence for Bible precepts, 109 ; would have no surplices, no liturgy, 109 ; banished the symbol with the dogma, 111 ; importance of efforts toward the regulation of conduct, 120 ; dubbed Martinists, 121 ; differences forgotten in the conflict with the Episcopal party, 137, n. 6 ; omitted the liturgy, 142 ; present Millinary Petition to James I, 159 ; at the Hampton Court conference, 160, 181, n. 1 ; not eager to join Separatist settlers, 188 ; a powerful party, 192 ; motives for emigration, 197 ; fear of divine judgments, 198 ; barred from all public action, 203 ; plan for a Puritan church in America, 204 ; carried out through the Massachusetts Company, 212 ; differences among the, 213 ; exhilarating effect of freedom from constraints, 213 ; raging against indulgence to Romanists, 235, 238 ; believed the church under Laud would become Roman Catholic, 239 ; dropped "saint" from geographical names, 244 ; rise of, to power, 240 ; dominant in Parliament, 252 ; could not be induced to leave New England for Maryland, 252 ; persecuted in Virginia, leave there for Maryland, 253 ; at peace with Catholics in Maryland, 254 ; their ideas rampant in Maryland, 257 ; send munitions of war to New England, 284 ; conceived of religion as difficult of attainment, 328.

Puritans of the Massachusetts colony not Separatists, 212 ; pathetic farewell to the Church of England, 213; persuaded to the Plymouth view of church government, 215 ; leaving England, 239 ; emigration to New England, 240.

Quakers put to death by Endecott, 202 ; protected in Maryland, 257.

Raccoon, the, called a monkey, 19, 24, n. 10.
Radical and conservative, difference between, constitutional, 109.
Rain, results of Puritan and Indian prayers for, 16.
Ralegh, Sir Walter, sends explorers and colonists, 7 ; History of the World, 21, n. 3 ; distrusts Indian tales, 21, n. 3 ; a lifelong opponent of Spain, 73.
Rapin, 239, m.
Rappahannocks, dress of the chief of the, 28.
Ratcliffe, enemy of Capt. John Smith, 37 ; ambuscaded and tortured to death, 38, 64, n. 4 ; follower of Archer, 64, n. 3 ; cruel to the savages, 64, n. 4.
Ration, a day's, pitiful allowance for, 30, 46.
Records of Virginia Company destroyed, 54, 71, n. 17.
Recreations on Sunday, scruples regarding, 127 ; forbidden by Dr. Bownd, 129.
Reformers, the, of the sixteenth century declared against a priesthood, 123 ; and a Sabbath, 124.

Relatyon of the Discovery of our River, 29, m.
Religion, motive to colonization, 220.
Religious enthusiasts and the Anglican church, 144.
Religious ferments, leavening effects of, 121.
Religious freedom a cherished principle of Roger Williams, 286 ; established at Providence, 296.
Religious liberty befriended by few, detested by Catholic and Protestant, 298.
Religious service, attendance at, should be compulsory, 299.
Report of Record Com., 329 m.
Residents, new oath of fidelity for, 289 ; successfully opposed by Williams, 289, 309, n. 12 ; mercenary inducement offered to, to take the freeman's oath, 308, n. 11.
Retainers, brilliant trains of, 99.
Rhode Island, a secondary colony, 220 ; importance of the, 315.
Rich, Lord. See WARWICK, second Earl.
Rich's, Barnabee, Honestie of this Age, 96, n. 8.
Rites, resistance to, an article of faith, 103.
Ritual, a purified, preferred by the extreme Protestants, 106, 135, n. 3.
Ritual, the antique, desire to change as little as possible, 106, 135, n. 3.
Rivalry with Spain, 73.
Roanoke Island, first colony on, 7 ; Lane's hopes for, 74.
Roanoke River, story of source of, 7.
Robert's Social History of the Southern Counties, 125, m.; 127, m.; 129, m.
Robinson hanged and quartered for extorting money from "pressed" maidens, 72, n. 19.
Robinson, John, joins the Separatists at Scrooby, 155 ; character and influence of, 156, 158, n. 3 ; leads the Scrooby church to Amsterdam, 164 ; to Leyden, 165 ; idea of forming a new state, 167 ; prayer and last words at departure of the Pilgrims, 175, 185, n. 6 ; advised union rather than division, 176 ; farewell letter of, 185, n. 5 ; liberality and breadth of view, 176, 185, n. 6 ; held to "toleration of tolerable opinions," 298.

Robinson's, John, Justification, 157, n. 1, n. 2 ; 219, n. 9.

Rogers, Thomas, opponent of Greenham and Bownd, 139, n. 11.

Rogers's Preface to Thirty-nine Articles, 122, m. ; 139, n. 11 ; 143, m.

Rolfe, John, married Pocahontas, 68, n. 10 ; planted first tobacco at Jamestown, 84.

Rolfe's Relation, 70, n. 16 ; 71, n. 17, n. 18.

Rosier's True Relation, 17, m.

"Rowdies" assault the Jesuits, 265, n. 24.

Royal Hist. MS. Comm., 88, m.

Royal Hist. MS. Com. Rept., 345, m.

Rushworth's Hist. Coll., 216, n. 2, n. 3 ; petition in, 226, m. ; 235, m. ; 344.

Rustics, the, of Scrooby and its neighborhood, 150, 151 ; influence of Brewster on, 153 ; of John Robinson, 157.

Rymer's Fœdera, 229, m. ; 238, m.

Sabbath, the, as a holy day objected to by Luther and Calvin, 124 ; rise of the Puritan, 124 ; Sunday first so called in literature, 126 ; passion for a stricter, 130 ; doctrine of a Christian, resented, 131, 139, n. 11 ; in Scotland, 132, 139, n. 12 ; of deepest hue in New England, 132, 140, n. 13.

Sabbath-breakers, punishments threatened against, 138, n. 8.

Sabbath-keeping, early Puritan ideal of, 127 ; pushed to its extreme, 130 ; new zeal for, promoted morals, 131 ; rigid, a mark of the faithful, 132.

Sadleir, Mrs., indorsement of, on Williams's letter to, 268, m.

Sainsbury's Calendar, 67, n. 9 ; 207, m. ; 262, n. 9 ; 344, m. ; 345, m.

Salem, north pole of Puritanism, 271 ; protest of the General Court against Williams as minister at, 271 ; attached to Williams and refractory toward the authorities at Boston, 280 ; made Williams teacher, 284 ; deputies turned out of court in punishment, 291 ; indignation at Williams's banishment, 293.

Salem church, organization of the, 200.

Salisbury, the Dean of, attacked by Mar-Prelate, 115.

Salvetti, correspondence on Calvert's resignation, 260, n. 6.

Sampson, Thomas, letter to Calvin, 135, n. 3.

Sandy Beach, no trace of, 59.

Sandys, Edwin, Archbishop of York, letter of, 137, n. 7 ; transferred manor place at Scrooby to his son Samuel, 153, 170.

Sandys, Sir Edwin, interested in the Virginia Company, 54 ; approved Dale's course, 67, n. 9 ; arrested, 69, n. 13 ; 89 ; chosen governor of Virginia Company, 71, n. 17 ; 88, 170 ; proposed sending maids to Virginia, 71, n. 18 ; leader of the company, 87, 89, 170 ; established representative government in Virginia, 88 ; plans for foundation of New Plymouth, 88 ; sketch of life of, in Brown's Genesis of the United States, 97, n. 10 ; tried to secure toleration for the Leyden people, 170 ; one of the fathers of representative government in America, 173 ; charges against, 174, 184, n. 5 ; parliamentary antagonist of Calvert, 221 ; in disfavor at court, 222 ; Virginians friendly to, 230.

Sandys, George, would seek the South Sea overland, 10, 11 ; name appended to The Tragicall Relation, 66, n. 9 ; in charge of manufacturing schemes, 83.

Sandys, Sir Samuel, owned manor place at Scrooby, 153, 170.

Sassafras root exported, 45, 68, n. 10 ; 68, n. 11.

Savage life eagerly observed by the English, 29.

Sawmills built in Virginia, 82.

Scharf's History of Maryland, 23, n. 7.

Schism esteemed the deadliest of sins, 142, 197.

Scotch settlement in Newfoundland, 224, 258, n. 3.

Scot's Magazine, 11, m.

Scrambler, Bishop of Peterborough, to Burghley, 142, m.

Scriptures, reverence for the letter of the, 144.

Scrooby, the cradle of the Pilgrims, 149 ; a region noted for religious zeal, 150 ; no tradition of the Pilgrims at, 150 ; called "the meane townlet" by John Leland, 152 ;

owners of manor place at, 153 ; the church at, 154, 155.

Seamen, threats of brutal, 177.

Seekers, the, a sect, the last reduction of Separatism, 303 ; in New England, probably through influence from Holland, 303 ; in England as early as 1617, 304 ; "a Seeker of the best Sect next to a finder," 314, n. 24.

Seekonk River, Williams removes from, to Providence, 296.

Semi-Separatists, the, 143.

Separatism and the Scrooby church, 141 ; promoted by persecution, 144 ; rise of, 146 ; divergencies in direction of, 267 ; protest by withdrawal of communion a fundamental principle of, 271.

Separatist, Roger Williams conscientiously a, 270.

Separatist tendencies of Skelton, 271.

Separatist tone of Pioneer church of Massachusetts at Salem, 271.

Separatists, number of the, 136, n. 6 ; importance of the, 141 ; the advance guard of Puritanism, 141 ; regarded as criminals by the Puritans, 142 ; causes of growth of the, 144 ; idealists, 144 ; rise of the, 146 ; meetings of, in London, 147 ; in Amsterdam, 148 ; one vigorous society of, in the north, 149 ; the Scrooby church of, organized, 154 ; all-day meetings at Brewster's manor house, 155 ; new persecution of the, 163 ; the Scrooby church resolve to flee to Holland, 163, 164 ; petition for leave to settle in Canada, 167 ; classed with criminals by Bacon, 171 ; held their opinions in a state of flux, 186, n. 6.

Servingman, the, not a menial, 134, n. 1.

Servingmen in livery, 99, 134, n. 1.

Settlements, sixteen, in Massachusetts, 275 ; life in the settlements, 276.

Settlers emulate the treachery of the Indians, 92 ; individual, 190.

Shakespeare's good fortune to live in a dramatic age, 99.

Shepard, Thomas, a new congregation led by, 325 ; letter of, quoted, 348, n. 5 ; Theses Sabbaticæ, 140, n. 13 ; Memoirs in Young, 328, m.

Sheriffs had many liveried servants, 99, 134, n. 1.

Ship carpenters sent to the James River, 83.

Silk, craze for, in England, 76, 77, 169 ; wearing of, prohibited in the colony, 78.

Silk culture attempted in England, 76 ; in Virginia, 76, 77 ; causes of failure, 77, 78 ; renewed efforts for, 78, 79, 83 ; authorities on these efforts, 95, n. 3

Silk-grass craze, the, 79.

Silk manufacturing established in England, 77.

Silkworms' eggs, hatching, in one's pocket or bosom, 78, 95, n. 2.

Skelton, minister at Salem, 271 ; extreme Congregationalism and Separatist tendencies of, 271 ; death of, 283.

Sloane manuscripts, British Museum, 22, n. 4.

Smith, Captain John, a trustworthy topographer, 9, 34 ; captured by Indians, 9 ; views of geography of the continent, 22, n. 6 ; becomes leader at Jamestown, 31, 36 ; his character, 31, 32, 33 ; story of his own life, 32, 33 ; the Jonah and Ulysses of his time, 33 ; explorations and narrative, 34, 35, 36 ; overthrown, 36 ; accused of design to wed Pocahontas, 37, 51 ; later years, 37 ; foresight of America's future, 37 ; disabled by an accident, 37, 60, n. 2 ; sent home under charges, 37, 60, n. 2 ; accused of advising Indians to attack settlers at the Falls, 37, 60, n. 2 ; a typical American pioneer, 38 ; account of his writings, 61, n. 3 ; commended by the Virginia Company, 61, n. 3 ; given to romance in narration, 62, n. 3 ; his practical writings and wise speeches, 62, n. 3 ; examples of his exaggeration, 63, n. 3 ; Thomas Fuller's judgment of, 63, n. 3 ; authorities in the debates about, 63, n. 3 ; refusal to share his power, 64, n. 4 ; captured by the French, 178.

——, Generall Historie, 22, n. 6 ; 27, m. ; 34, m. ; 35, 36, m. ; 61, n. 3 ; 66, n. 9 ; 95, n. 3.

——, New Life of Virginia, 27, m.

Smith, Oxford Tract, 34, m.; 35, 36, m.; 42, m.; 61, n. 3; 64, n. 3.

——, True Relation, 61, n. 3.

Smyth, John, the Separatist, migrated from Gainsborough, 150; continually searching for truth, 186, n. 6.

Smyth, Sir Thomas, governor of Virginia Company, 70, n. 16 : resignation, 71, n. 17; aroused the king's opposition to Sandys, 87; resigned, 88; sorrows of the colony under, 206; faction of, 230; defense, 67, n. 9.

Somers, Sir George, wrecked on the Bermudas, 40; builds two vessels and takes provisions to Virginia, 41; returns to the Bermudas, 41; death of, 42; Somers or Summer Islands named from, 65, n. 6.

South Sea delusion, the, 6, 7, 8; an overland route to, 10; behind the mountains, 75. See also PACIFIC OCEAN.

Southampton, Earl of, interested in the Virginia Company, 54; threatened by the Warwick party, 69, n. 13; really in power, 71, n. 17; procures silkworm "seed," 77; elected governor of the company, 89; imprisoned, 89; one of the fathers of representative government in America, 173; Virginians friendly to, 230.

Southwest passage, conjectures of a, 22, n. 5.

Spain, rivalry with, the motive for planting English colonies, 73; England's jealousy toward, 74, 94, n. 1; lavish of gifts to English courtiers, 223; made England relax penal laws against English recusants, 238.

Spanish example, the influence of, on English projects, 73; fishing-boats to be seized at Newfounde lande, 94, n. 1; jealousy of Virginia, 94, n. 1.

Spanish match, the, favored by Calvert, 226, 227, 258, n. 2.

Speed's Prospect, 24, n. 10.

Spelman's Relation, 60, n. 2.

Spices, passion for, in Europe, 22, n. 5.

Spirit of the age, escape from the, difficult, 133.

Squirrels, flying, 18.

Standish, Captain Miles, escorts the

governor to church on Sundays, 103.

Star-Chamber censures, 203, 216, n. 3; Roger Williams as a lad employed by the, 268; harsh penalties for Separatists, 270.

State church, notion of, not easily got rid of, 112.

St. Christopher's Island sought by Catholic refugees, 231.

Stephen, Sir, denounced May-poles as idols, 118; wanted names of days of the week changed, 118.

Stith's History of Virginia, 51, m.; 182, n. 2.

Stoughton retracted, 290, 291; pressure put on, 297.

Strachey's Historie of Travaile into Virginia, 24, n. 10; 36, m.; 59, n. 1; 64, n. 4; 65, n. 7; 95, n. 5; 97, n. 9; 102, m.; True Reportory, 65, n. 6.

Strafford, friend of George Calvert and his son, 249.

Strafford Papers, 241, m.; 263, n. 13.

Strait, a, sought to the South Sea, 4, 6, 8, 9.

Strasburg and Zurich, cities of refuge for conservatives, 104.

Strasburg reformers attempt to reform church at Frankfort, 105.

Straus's Life of Roger Williams, 308, n. 6; 311, n. 17.

Stubbes's Philip, Anatomie of Abuses, 100, m.; 119, 127, 134, n. 2; 135, n. 5.

Succession, apostolic, of churchly order and ordinance the mainspring of high-churchism, 302.

Svmme and Svbstance. See BARLOW.

Sumner, George, on John Robinson, 158, n. 3.

Sumptuary laws, 75.

Sunday had sanctity of a church feast before the Reformation, 125 : English reformers retained the Catholic, 125; first called Sabbath in literature, 126; scruples regarding recreations on, 127; brutally cruel sports on the old English, 129; strict observance of, carried to New England, 132; in the middle ages, 138, n. 8; legislation on, rare before the Reformation, 138, n. 8; in time of Edward VI, 138, n. 9; sabbatical character of, denied, 140, n. 13. See also SABBATH.

Sunday fishing, juries inquire into, 125.

Sunday morning ceremony at Plymouth, 103.

Sunday-Sabbath, theory of a, not confined to the Puritans, 132 ; Augustine on, in the fifth century, 137, n. 8 ; 140, n. 13.

Surplices begin to be used in Virginia, 183, n. 3.

Susan Constant, the ship, 25.

Sutton's Hospital founded by legacy, which Coke defended, later known as Charter-House School, 268.

Swift, Lindsay, on the early election sermons, 313, n. 22.

Symonds, Dr. William, editor of second part of Smith's Oxford Tract, 61, n. 3.

Synod, the, of 1637, 336, 346, n. 1.

Tales, extravagant, of the Indians, 7, 8 ; Ralegh distrusts, 21, n. 3.

Taylor's Observations and Travel from London to Hamburg, 46, m.

Tempest, Shakespeare's, 17 ; suggested by the wreck of Gates and Somers, 65, n. 6.

Tenant, the copy-hold, driven to distress, 111.

Tenantry, the suffering, Puritans make common cause with, 111, 135, n. 5.

Theater, passionate love of the, 99.

Theocracy, instability of a, 326.

Thomas Aquinas, St., on the fourth commandment, 138, n. 8.

Thurloe, 263, n. 13.

Timber sought in Virginia, 82.

Tobacco, profitable cultivation of, in Virginia, 49, 84 ; exported, 68, n. 10, n. 11 ; 96, n. 7 ; more profitable than silk-raising, 78 ; culture of, forbidden, 81 ; King James's Covnter-Blaste to, 84 ; John Rolfe planted the first, at Jamestown, 84 ; heavy duties on, 85, 96, n. 8 ; seven thousand shops in London, 97, n. 8 ; inferiority of Indian, 97, n. 9 ; large profits from, 231 ; public use of, forbidden in Massachusetts, 285.

Toleration, the Baltimore policy, 242, 263, n. 15 ; principle of, formulated, 254 ; Act of, passed in 1649, 255, 256, 257 ; intolerable to the rulers of "the Bay," 297 ; limited and qualified at Amsterdam, 298 ; de-cried as a great crime by all the world, 298 ; a beneficent result of commerce, 298, 312, n. 18.

Tortures, legal, examples of, 46, 67, n. 9.

Town government, the principal feature of civil organization, 325.

Town system, the, 275.

Trade with the Indians by Captain John Smith, 34 ; suspended after Smith's departure, 38 ; renewed by Capt. Argall, 50.

Tragicall Relation, 40, m. ; 56, m. ; 66, n. 9′; 68, n. 12.

Trainbands drilled, 284.

Travel, taste for books of, 2.

Treasure received by Spain from America influenced English colonial projects, 73 ; wrought mischief to England, 94, n. 1.

True Declaration of the Estate of the Colony of Virginia, 40, m. ; 56, m. ; 65, n. 5, n. 8.

Trumbull's Blue Laws, 347, n. 2.

Tucker, Daniel, builds boat at Jamestown, 39.

Underhill, Captain, sent after Williams, 295.

Unicorn, reported find of the, 19, 24, n. 10.

Uniformity not possible, 109.

Upper House, dissension concerning power of the, in Massachusetts, 286.

Utopia, the religious, attempted in New England, 342.

Van der Donck's New Netherland, 23, n. 7.

Van Meteren, Nederlandsche Historie, 312, n. 18.

Vane, Sir Henry, the younger, favored the Antinomians, 267 ; an ardent Puritan, 332 ; arrives in Boston and is elected governor, 332 ; a disciple of Cotton, 333 ; defeat of, 336 ; leaves the colony, 337.

Vaughan's Golden Fleece, 261, n. 7.

Vessel, the first Virginia, built by Captain Argall, 50.

Vestments objected to, in reign of Edward VI, 103 ; bitter debates about, 108 ; ceased to be abhorrent, 123.

Virginia Assembly petitions the king, 56 ; proceedings of the first, 70, n. 15.

Virginia colony, the, 8 ; emigrants set sail, 25 ; code of laws and orders

26 ; character of the emigrants, 27 ; arrival, 27 ; first meetings with the Indians, 28 ; the winter of misery, 29 ; fear of attack from the Indians, 30 ; food bought of the Indians, 31 ; five hundred colonists arrive under Archer and Ratcliffe, 36 ; settlements at Nansemond and the falls of the James River, 37; famine of 1609-'10, 38 ; only sixty survivors in June, 1610, 40 ; arrival of Gates and Somers, 40 ; Jamestown abandoned, 41 ; arrival of De la Warr, 41 ; De la Warr's government, 42 ; flight of De la Warr, 43 ; second lease of life, 43 ; inefficient government of George Percy, 44 ; martial law and slavery under Thomas Dale, 45 ; ten men escape, 47 ; Dale's services, 47 ; private gardens allowed, 48 ; tobacco cultivated, 49 ; Argall's government and treachery, 50–52 ; the Great Charter, 1618, 55, 173 ; joy at its receipt, 56 ; feared re-establishment of the old tyranny, 56, 70, n. 16 ; wives supplied, 57 ; the first homes, 58 ; whole number of colonists, 58 ; four fifths perished, 59 ; petition to the king, 65, n. 5 ; began raising silkworms, 76 ; the silk-grass craze in, 79 ; glass and iron works established and failed in, 83 ; planted tobacco, 84 ; struck root and its life assured, 85 ; gained impetus from the king's opposition, 89 ; government of, passed to the Crown, 92 ; reached its greatest prosperity, 186, n. 8 ; inhospitable to Lord Baltimore, 230 ; opposes Roman Catholics, 231, 261, n. 9 ; reckless living of people and clergy, 231 ; expulsion of Lord Baltimore from, 232 ; new emigration to, 344 ; second generation of native Virginians appears, 345 ; better ministers in the parishes and order in the courts, 345.

Virginia colony, map of, by John White, 1586, 8, 21, 22.

Virginia Company, letter of, to Governor Wyatt quoted, 22, n. 5 ; code of laws and orders for its colonists, 26 ; swindled and robbed, 52 ; fall of the lottery, 53 ; revival of interest, 53 ; records destroyed, 54 ; change in conduct of affairs, 55 ; cruelty

of agents paralleled by those of the East India Company, 67, n. 9 ; overthrow of the company, 70, n. 16 ; dissolved in 1624, 85, 89, 92 ; organized for trading, 86 ; passed out of the control of traders, 87 ; King James interferes with the election, 88 ; grants two charters and a liberal patent to the Pilgrims, 172 ; also leave to establish a provisional government, 173 ; Lord Baltimore a member and councilor of, 224, 229, 230 ; attempt to take away privileges granted to the colonists, 230.

Virginia Company's Manuscript Records. See MANUSCRIPT RECORDS, VIRGINIA COMPANY.

Virginia Richly Valued, 79, m. ; 95, n. 3.

Virginians obliged to pay quitrents in Maryland, 249.

Vries, David P. de, Voyages, 308, n. 7.

Waddington's Congregational History, 167, m.

Walker's First Church in Hartford, 317, m. ; 321, m.

Ward's Simple Cobbler, 285, m.; 299, m.

Warwick, second Earl, intrigues to wreck the Virginia Company, 51, 68, n. 13 ; protects Argall in his plundering, 52 ; has Cavendish and others arrested, 69, n. 13 ; loses influence in the company, 87 ; made Governor in Chief and Lord High Admiral of all plantations in America, 252.

Waterhouse's Declaration of Virginia, 22, n. 6.

Watertown church, part of, ready to follow Hooker, 323 ; one of the centres of discontent, 324.

Welde's Short Story of the Rise, Reign, and Ruine of Antinomianism, 330, m.; 336, m.; 339, m.; 340, m.; 347, n. 4.

Wentworth, friend of Calvert, 222.

West, insubordinate settlers under, 37, 60, n. 2 ; Indians hostile to, 60, n. 2 ; treacherous and cruel, 64, n. 4.

West India plants tried in Virginia, 82.

Weston Documents, 11, m.

Wethersfield, John Oldham and his company settled at, 324.

Weymouth kidnapped Maine Indians, 17.

Whale-fishing in Lake Ontario, 11.

Whelewright, brother-in-law of Mrs. Hutchinson, 336 ; banished at November court following the synod, 337 ; testimony regarding his sister-in-law, 348, n. 6.

Whelewright's sermon, 331, m.

Whincop charter not used, 184, n. 4 ; 186, n. 8.

Whiston a place of Puritan assemblage, 142.

Whitaker, Alexander, praises Dale, 66, n. 9 ; minister at Henrico, 168 ; letters, 183, n. 3.

Whitaker's *Good Newes from Virginia,* 66, n. 9 ; 168.

Whitbourne, Captain, pamphlet on Newfoundland, 224, 258, n. 3 ; letters of Wynne and others in, 229, m.

White, Father, *Relatio Itineris,* 243, m. ; 244, m. ; 263, n. 16 ; on settlement of Montserrat, 261, n. 9 ; 263, n. 14, n. 16.

White, John, of Dorchester, an active colonizer, 189, 199, 203.

White, John, map of Virginia by, 1586, 8 ; in Grenville Collection, 21, n. 4 ; reproduced in the Century Magazine, 22, n. 4 ; copy in Kohl Collection, 22, n. 4

White's, John, *The Planter's Plea,* 190, m. ; 199, m.

Whitgift, Archbishop, efforts of, to suppress nonconformity, 122 ; ordered Bownd's book called in, 132 ; persecuted the Puritans at Scrooby, 153; declared King James inspired, 161.

Whittingham, Dean of Durham, author of *A Brieff Discourse,* 135, n. 3 ; on the Puritan side in Frankfort, 143.

Williams, Roger, in advance of his age, 256 ; opposed the authorities in Massachusetts, 267 ; early career of, 268 ; refused preferments, 269, 307, n. 2 ; flight of, to New England, 270 ; refuses communion with the Boston church, 270, 307, n. 3 ; opposed to compromise, 271, 307, n. 4 ; his selection as minister at Salem opposed by the General Court, 271, 272 ; removed to Plymouth, 272 ; wrote a treatise on the dialect of the New England Indians, 273 ; rebuked Bradford and wrote against

the royal patents, 274, 281, 308, n. 9 ; returned to Salem with some followers, 275 ; his ideal too high for that age, 281 ; preached without holding office, 281 ; " convented at court," 281 ; charges against, based on his book, " not so evil as at first they seemed," 282 ; the broad principle laid down by, 283 ; made teacher at Salem, 284 ; fast-day sermon on eleven " public sins," 286 ; dealt with ecclesiastically, 287 ; scruples against enforced oaths, 289 ; new charges against, 289 ; champion of soul liberty, 290 ; incorrigible, 290, 291 ; trial and banishment, 292, 309, n. 12 ; 310, n. 13, 14, 16 ; authorities, 310, n. 17 ; on account of illness permitted to remain during the winter, 293 ; a few friends faithful to, 293, 294 ; escape to the Indians, 295 ; abandons settlement at Seekonk River and founds ·Providence, 296 ; banishment of, an act of persecution, 297 ; character of, 301, 307, n. 1 ; a collector of scruples, 301, 302, 314, n. 23 ; tenderness and friendship for Winthrop, 302 ; became a Baptist and renounced his baptism, 303 ; a Seeker, 303, 304 ; his moral elevation of spirit, 304 ; ascendency over the Indians, 305 ; an individualist, 291, 305 ; superior to his age and ours, 305 ; his prophetic character, 306 ; a John Baptist of the distant future, 306 ; enthusiastic nature of, 307, n. 2 ; needed no practical consideration to stir him to action, 308, n. 11 ; magnanimity without a parallel, 310, n. 15 ; removal of Williams and his friends the beginning of dispersions from the colony, 315 ; prepared a harbor for all of uneasy conscience, 315.

Williams's letter to Mrs. Sadleir, 268, m. ; 270, m. ; letters to Winthrop, 273, m.; 302, m. ; 307, n. 5 ; Reply to Cotton, 283, m. ; letters to Lady Barrington, 307, n. 1 ; Letter to John Cotton, the younger, 307, n. 2, 3, 4 ; letter to Major Mason, 310, n. 15 ; *Bloudy Tenent,* 311, n. 18.

Wilson, John, interprets battle of mouse and snake, 277 ; on Williams's book, 282 ; condemned by the Hutchinsonians, 333 ; given to rhyming prophecies, 338.

Windebank, schemes of Cecilius Calvert with, 250.

Wine, efforts to produce, in Great Britain, 76 ; in Virginia, 81.

Wingandacon, Indian name of the coast of North Carolina, 21, n. 3.

Wingfield deposed from leadership, 31 ; recognizes Smith's services, 36 ; plot against the life of, 61, n. 2 ; warned Newport against Archer, 64, n. 3.

Wingfield's Discourse, 64, n. 3.

Winslow, of Plymouth, warns Williams from Seekonk River, 296.

Winslow's Briefe Narration, 172, m. ; 175, m. ; 185, n. 6.

Winsor's, Justin, Elder Brewster, 155, m. ; 169, m.

Winsor's Narrative and Critical History of America, 21, n. 1.

Winthrop, John, principal figure in the Puritan migration, 202 ; character and influence of, 204 ; made a justice of the peace, 204, 217, n. 5 ; elected governor, 210, 217, n. 6 ; objected to a government directed from England, 208 ; superseded by Dudley, 287 ; recommended Narragansett Bay to Williams, 293, 294 ; lenity toward Williams rebuked, 301 ; moved house, begun at Newtown, to Boston, 318 ; antipathy to Mrs. Hutchinson, 330 ; ministers rally around, 332 ; again made governor, 336 ; chief inquisitor at the trial of Mrs. Hutchinson, 338 ; evidence to prove Mrs. Hutchinson a witch, 340, 341 ; wallows in superstition, 341.

Winthrop's Journal (Savage's), 252, m ; 272, m. ; 290, m. ; 291, m. ; 294, m. ; 301, m. ; 307, n. 3 ; 309, n. 12 ; 310, n. 17 ; 318, m. ; 323, m. ; 329, m.; 336, m.; 339, m.; 340, m.; 341, m. ; 344, m. ; 348, n. 8 ; 349, n. 9.

Winthrop's Life and Letters, 198, m.; 217, n. 4, 5, 6 ; 218, n. 8.

Winthrop's Reasons for New England, 198, 204, 217, n. 4.

Wives for the Virginia colonists, 57, 71, n. 18 ; supplied to Louisiana and Canada, 72, n. 18.

Women, proposal to send, to Virginia, 71, n. 18 ; in Gates's party, 71, n. 18 ; first two in the colony, 71, n. 18.

Wood, beauty of the, of certain American trees, 65, n. 7.

Woodnoth's Short Collection, 70, n. 16 ; 87, m. ; account of, 97, n. 10.

Wood's New England's Prospect, 18, m. ; 318, m. ; 319, m.

Words had the force of blows, 110.

Wright's Elizabeth and her Times, 142, m.

Wyatt, Sir Francis, name appended to The Tragicall Relation, 66, n. 9 ; opinion of, on a divided government, 207.

Wyckoff, on Silk Manufacture, 95, n. 3.

Yeardley, Sir George, arrival in Virginia, 71, n. 17 ; knighted, 134, n. 1 ; instructed to administer oath of supremacy, 232.

Yong, Thomas, in the Delaware, 10 ; seeks a Mediterranean in America, 11.

Young's Chronicles of Massachusetts, 217, n. 4 ; 317, m.

Young's Chronicles of the Pilgrims, 158, n. 3 ; 167, m. ; 184, n. 4.

Yucatan, meaning of, 21, n. 3.

Yucca, clothing made from the fiber of the, 79, 80 ; a "commoditie of speciall hope and much use," 80.

Zeal, passionate, often stupefies reason, 171.

Zurich and Strasburg cities of refuge for conservatives, 104 ; differences between exiles at, and those of Geneva, 106, 107.

Zurich Letters, 135, n. 3.

Zwisck, Peter John, The Liberty of Religion, 312, n. 19.

CHARLES ALEXANDER NELSON.

THE END.

*W*ITH THE FATHERS. *Studies in the History of the United States.* By JOHN BACH MCMASTER, Professor of American History in the University of Pennsylvania, author of " The History of the People of the United States," etc. 8vo. Cloth, $1.50.

" The book is of great practical value, as many of the essays throw a broad light over living questions of the day. Prof. McMaster has a clear, simple style that is delightful. His facts are gathered with great care, and admirably interwoven to impress the subject under discussion upon the mind of the reader."—*Chicago Inter-Ocean.*

" Prof. McMaster's essays possess in their diversity a breadth which covers most of the topics which are current as well as historical, and each is so scholarly in treatment and profound in judgment that the importance of their place in the library of political history can not be gainsaid."— *Washington Times.*

" Such works as this serve to elucidate history and make more attractive a study which an abstruse writer only makes perplexing. All through the studies there is a note of intense patriotism and a conviction of the sound sense of the American people which directs the government to a bright goal."—*Chicago Record.*

" A wide field is here covered, and is covered in Prof. McMaster's own inimitable and fascinating style. . . . Can not but have a marked value as a work of reference upon several most important subjects."—*Boston Daily Advertiser.*

" There is much that is interesting in this little book, and it is full of solid chunks of political information."—*Buffalo Commercial.*

" Clear, penetrating, dispassionate, convincing. His language is what one should expect from the Professor of American History in the University of Pennsylvania. Prof. McMaster has proved before now that he can write history with the breath of life in it, and the present volume is new proof."—*Chicago Tribune.*

" Of great practical value. . . . Charming and instructive history."—*New Haven Leader.*

" An interesting and most instructive volume."—*Detroit Journal.*

" At once commends itself to the taste and judgment of all historical readers. His style charms the general reader with its open and frank ways, its courageous form of statement, its sparkling, crisp narrative and description, and its close and penetrating analysis of character and events."—*Boston Courier.*

New York : D. APPLETON & CO., 72 Fifth Avenue.

*T*HE RISE AND GROWTH OF THE ENGLISH NATION. With Special Reference to Epochs and Crises. A History of and for the People. By W. H. S. AUBREY, LL. D. In Three Volumes. 12mo. Cloth, $4.50.

"The merit of this work is intrinsic. It rests on the broad intelligence and true philosophy of the method employed, and the coherency and accuracy of the results reached. The scope of the work is marvelous. Never was there more crowded into three small volumes. But the saving of space is not by the sacrifice of substance or of style. The broadest view of the facts and forces embraced by the subject is exhibited with a clearness of arrangement and a definiteness of application that render it perceptible to the simplest apprehension."—*New York Mail and Express.*

"A useful and thorough piece of work. One of the best treatises which the general reader can use."—*London Daily Chronicle.*

"Conceived in a popular spirit, yet with strict regard to the modern standards. The title is fully borne out. No want of color in the descriptions."—*London Daily News.*

"The plan laid down results in an admirable English history."—*London Morning Post.*

"Dr. Aubrey has supplied a want. His method is undoubtedly the right one."—*Pall Mall Gazette.*

"It is a distinct step forward in history writing—as far ahead of Green as he was of Macaulay, though on a different line. Green gives the picture of England at different times ; Aubrey goes deeper, showing the causes which led to the changes."—*New York World.*

"A work that will commend itself to the student of history, and as a comprehensive and convenient reference book."—*The Argonaut.*

"Contains much that the ordinary reader can with difficulty find elsewhere unless he has access to a library of special works."—*Chicago Dial.*

"Up to date in its narration of fact, and in its elucidation of those great principles that underlie all vital and worthy history. . . . The painstaking division, along with the admirably complete index, will make it easy work for any student to get definite views of any era, or any particular feature of it. . . . The work strikes one as being more comprehensive than many that cover far more space."—*The Christian Intelligencer.*

"One of the most elaborate and noteworthy of recent contributions to historical literature."—*New Haven Register.*

"As a popular history it possesses great merits, and in many particulars is excelled by none. It is full, careful as to dates, maintains a generally praiseworthy impartiality, and it is interesting to read."—*Buffalo Express.*

"These volumes are a surprise and in their way a marvel. . . . They constitute an almost encyclopædia of English history, condensing in a marvelous manner the facts and principles developed in the history of the English nation. The work is one of unsurpassed value to the historical student or even the general reader, and when more widely known will no doubt be appreciated as one of the remarkable contributions to English history published in the century."—*Chicago Universalist.*

"In every page Dr. Aubrey writes with the far-reaching relation of contemporary incidents to the whole subject. The amount of matter these three volumes contain is marvelous. The style in which they are written is more than satisfactory. . . . The work is one of unusual importance."—*Hartford Post.*

D. APPLETON & CO.'S PUBLICATIONS.

THE UNITED STATES OF AMERICA. A Study of the American Commonwealth, its Natural Resources, People, Industries, Manufactures, Commerce, and its Work in Literature, Science, Education, and Self-Government. Edited by NATHANIEL S. SHALER, S. D., Professor of Geology in Harvard University. In 2 volumes, royal 8vo. With Maps and 150 full-page Illustrations. Cloth, $10.00.

Every subject in this comprehensive work is timely, because it is of immediate interest to every American. Special attention, however, may be called to the account of "American Productive Industry," by the Hon. Edward Atkinson, with its array of immensely informing diagrams and tables; and also to "Industry and Finance," a succinct and logical presentation of the subject by Professor F. W. Taussig, of Harvard University. Both these eminent authorities deal with questions which are uppermost to-day.

LIST OF CONTRIBUTORS.

HON. WILLIAM L. WILSON, Chairman of the Ways and Means Committee, Fifty-third Congress.
HON. J. R. SOLEY, formerly Assistant Secretary of the Navy.
EDWARD ATKINSON, LL. D., Ph. D.
COL. T. A. DODGE, U. S. A.
COL. GEORGE E. WARING, JR.
J. B. McMASTER, Professor of History in the University of Pennsylvania.
CHARLES DUDLEY WARNER, LL. D.
MAJOR J. W. POWELL, Director of the United States Geological Survey and the Bureau of Ethnology.
WILLIAM T. HARRIS, LL. D., United States Commissioner of Education.
LYMAN ABBOTT, D. D.
H. H. BANCROFT, author of "Native Races of the Pacific Coast."
HARRY PRATT JUDSON, Head Dean of the Colleges, University of Chicago.
JUDGE THOMAS M. COOLEY, formerly Chairman of the Interstate Commerce Commission.
CHARLES FRANCIS ADAMS.
D. A. SARGENT, M. D., Director Hemenway Gymnasium, Harvard University.
CHARLES HORTON COOLEY.
A. E. KENNELLY, Assistant to Thomas A. Edison.
D. C. GILMAN, LL. D., President of Johns Hopkins University.
H. G. PROUT, Editor of the Railroad Gazette.
F. D. MILLET, formerly Vice-President of the National Academy of Design.
F. W. TAUSSIG, Professor of Political Economy in Harvard University.
HENRY VAN BRUNT.
H. P. FAIRFIELD.
SAMUEL W. ABBOTT, M. D., Secretary State Board of Health, Massachusetts.
N. S. SHALER.

Sold only by subscription. Prospectus, giving detailed chapter titles and specimen illustrations mailed free on request.

New York: D. APPLETON & CO., 72 Fifth Avenue.